THE CYPRUS QUESTION AS AN ISSUE OF TURKISH FOREIGN POLICY AND TURKISH-AMERICAN RELATIONS 1959-2003

THE CYPRUS QUESTION AS AN ISSUE OF TURKISH FOREIGN POLICY AND TURKISH-AMERICAN RELATIONS 1959-2003

NASUH USLU

Nova Science Publishers, Inc.
New York

Library of Congress Cataloging-in-Publication Data

The Cyprus question as an issue of Turkish foreign policy and Turkish-American relations, 1959-2003 / Nasuh Uslu.

p. cm.

Includes bibliographical references and index.

ISBN: 1-59033-847-2.

1. Turkey—Foreign relations—United States. 2. United States—Foreign relations—Turkey.
3. Cyprus—History—20th centuty. I. Title.

DR479.U5U845   2003

956.9304—dc22   2003017263

Published by Nova Science Publishers, Inc. ✢*New York*

To my parents, Zeliha and Ahmet Uslu

CONTENTS

Chapter 1

INTRODUCTION

The year 1964, in which Turkey received the famous Johnson letter, is rightly considered by many scholars as a turning point in Turkish foreign policy. Until that time foreign policy discussion among Turkish politicians and public opinion was very rare, if not absent totally, and was far from criticising the official line. In spite of strong disagreements over other matters, Turkish political parties and groups had formed an undeclared consensus on the state's foreign policy decisions and actions, seeing this attitude as a national duty. The new constitution in 1960 prepared the ground for public discussions by providing all political groups with means to voice their ideas. But the subject which brought about the widespread criticism of Turkish foreign policy by the political parties and the public opinion became the Cyprus question. This issue triggered a wide range of events which eventually led to considerable changes not only in Turkish foreign policy but also in Turkish-American relations.

Starting in the last ten days of December 1963, Greek Cypriot atrocities against the Turkish Cypriots attracted the close attention of Turkish people and led them to pressurise their government to intervene in Cyprus militarily. The failure of the Turkish government to intervene in Cyprus apparently because of US pressures, including the Johnson letter with its serious threats, caused widespread criticisms and demonstrations against the United States in Turkey. Subsequently, in the second half of the 1960s, all aspects of US-Turkish relations and Turkish foreign policy became the main subjects of public discussion, overshadowing disputes over internal matters. Turkey's alliance with NATO and its military relations with the USA were particularly questioned by leftist circles and the press and some went so far to suggest withdrawal from NATO. In this atmosphere Turkish rulers, too, felt the need to make some changes in foreign policy by improving relations with the Eastern bloc and the Third World and being more careful in dealings with the United States. As a part of their new approach, they took some actions in the military field, which could displease the Americans.

The Cyprus question was a constant factor in US-Turkish relations in the past and it still conditions the Turkish-American alliance, which is an important element of the present international relations. When the United States and Turkey established alliance relations immediately after the Second World War, foreign policies of both countries were experiencing a radical change. As the most powerful state in the world, the United States had decided to give up its traditional isolationist policy and to undertake global responsibilities. The main aim of US policy after that moment was to confront and contain the Soviet Union and its bloc. The alliance with Turkey was a part of this new US approach. By aligning with the USA, Turkey, too, abandoned her traditional neutralist policy, which had prevented her from establishing alliances, especially with big powers. Her main concern was to be a part of the Western world.

When the cold war ended with the dismemberment of the Soviet Union, the alliance between the United States and Turkey continued to be an important aspect of their foreign policies and to be a significant factor in the world politics. This alliance influences events in important regions such as the Middle East, the eastern Mediterranean, the Balkans, and Central Asia, including Russia and former Soviet republics. The Cyprus question is important in that it influences the operation of this alliance. It is always in the minds of Turkish and American rulers as a potential irritating factor affecting relations and co-operation of the two countries in important areas.

The period of our study (1960-1975) holds a particular importance in Turkish-American relations. After experiencing a perfect honeymoon period in the 1950s, the durability, strength and cohesion of the US-Turkish alliance were tested by severe problems between 1960 and 1975. And at the core of all the problems was there the Cyprus question, affecting the general tendency of the relationship between the two countries and the attitude of policy-makers of both states.

In 1960 the Turkish Republic experienced its first military coup and saw a radical change in its political system. Encouraged by military officers' removing a rightist government and by the more pluralist and pro-freedom constitution of 1960, leftist groups launched an all-out campaign to increase their influence in domestic politics and to this end from 1964 onward they attacked Turkey's relations with the USA and NATO. The bargaining over Turkey's Jupiter missiles by the United States with the Soviet Union during the Cuban crisis of October 1962 occurred without public criticism and damage to the US-Turkish relationship largely because of public ignorance of the incident.

However, when the US response to the Cyprus question, which emerged in December 1963 as a serious matter, was perceived by Turkish rulers and people as anti-Turkish, the domestic politics of Turkey after that time was dominated by criticism of the United States and Turkey's contacts with the Americans. Military relations were particularly targeted to the extent that the Turkish government had to force the US administration to review bilateral agreements signed since 1947 and that Turkey had to take some actions in the military field that would not please the Americans. The Cyprus question still holds the potential to change the whole character of the US-Turkish relationship.

Analysing the Cyprus question between 1960 and 1975 in details will illuminate a period in which the present situation of the Cyprus problem was gradually established. The sides brought different and contrasting explanations to the Cyprus events and tried to prove the rightness of their cause. It is important to analyse the viewpoints of the sides without losing objectivity and thus to put forth the problem with all its aspects. In this regard, it should be stressed that while discussing the present situation of the Cyprus question the period before 1974, in which the roots of the problem are hidden, has been ignored and thus the possibility of its solution has been decreased.

There is no doubt that the Cyprus problem is a continuing problem of both Turkish foreign policy and US-Turkish relations. It is still a national cause for Turkey considerably influenced by public opinion and the United States still tries to find ways to affect Turkey's Cyprus policies. Looking at the roots of the problem and analysing US and Turkish attitudes and interactions on the matter in a historical perspective will certainly help an understanding of the present situation, its future prospects and its impact on the US-Turkish alliance. Any proposed solutions to the problem need to be made in the light of this knowledge.

Turkish-American relations in the 1960-1975 period and the particularly the Cyprus problem present a good case to analyse how an alliance between a relatively small state and a superpower works. The transactions between the United States and Turkey and the features of both states appear to reflect many aspects of the patron-client relationship. The Turkish position during the Cuban missile crisis; US president Johnson's letter to the Turkish prime minister, which included heavy threats to force Turkey not to intervene in Cyprus; considerable US economic and military aid to Turkey; the equipping of the Turkish army with US weapons; US pressures on Turkey to force her to ban opium production; and the US arms embargo against Turkey, aiming to change its Cyprus policy can all lead one to the conclusion that as a small state Turkey fell victim to US influence in this period.

However, one can easily show evidence for the opposite claim: Turkey's improving relations with the Eastern bloc and Third World countries; Turkish support for the Arabs in the Arab-Israeli conflict; some Turkish actions in the military arena such as not allowing U-2 flights from Turkish territory, reviewing bilateral agreements with the USA, not allowing the use of US bases for non-NATO purposes, and changing the duty status formula applied to US personnel in Turkey; not banning opium production and later resuming it after it was banned by a non-party government; and Turkish intervention in Cyprus all point in the other direction.

US President Johnson's letter in 1964 is a good example of a diplomatic mistake which alienated the recipient state considerably and caused changes in its foreign policy. It is still frequently cited by Turkish politicians and scholars in the course of discussing foreign policy and Turkish-American relations. The US arms embargo against Turkey in 1975, which was aimed at forcing Turkish rulers to make concessions in Cyprus, is also fresh in Turkish minds, reminding them how the United States can try to punish their country and how the US Congress can affect relations between the two states.

To analyse the US and Turkish attitudes on the Cyprus problem more correctly, it will be helpful to look at how the both sides perceived the alliance between them and how their special features affected their stance on Cyprus.

The Turks viewed their alliance with the United States in the light of their long-pursued efforts of Westernisation, attributing a great importance to it in the way of becoming an integral part of the Western world. In their opinion, Turkey had to continue its alliance with America because this policy not only helped to fulfil her national interests, but more importantly it represented a relationship between the two states which shared the same ideology and moral principles.[1] In his visit to Washington in June 1964 immediately after receiving President Johnson's disappointing letter, Turkish Prime Minister İsmet İnönü said that "we, the Turks, believe that friendship between states relies not on temporary interests but on common moral principles."[2] Turkish President Cevdet Sunay expressed his belief that close friendship and alliance between Turkey and the United States was a consequence of

---

[1] It is ironic that as late as the spring of 1974, Turkey still had not joined the European bureau of the US State Department but she remained the responsibility of the State's Bureau of Near Eastern and South Asian Affairs. Monteagle Stearns, *Entangled Allies: US Policy Toward Greece, Turkey and Cyprus,* (New York: Council on Foreign Relations Press, 1992), p. 8.

[2] *Cumhuriyet,* 23 June 1964, p. 7.

their shared moral principles and aims such as the love of freedom and democracy.[3] As an example of how far ideological thinking affected the minds of Turkish politicians, the speech of Turkish MP Gökhan Evliyaoğlu may be cited. In an atmosphere of great public criticism directed toward the Western states because of their attitudes on the Cyprus question, Evliyaoğlu claimed that Turkey did not have the right to criticise the West because she failed to become a part of this world and to reach its level of democracy.[4]

This approach of Turkish politicians to the alliance with the United States led them to be anxious to fulfil requirements of this alliance without any hesitation. At almost every opportunity they proudly expressed their loyalty to the alliance.[5] But they felt badly let down when this loyalty did not appear to be reciprocated. In their eyes, Turkey was right in her policy toward the Cyprus question, therefore, she should be supported by the Western states. But the Western states seemed to forget what Turkey did for the Western alliance and simply closed their eyes to the just cause of Turkey on Cyprus. The feeling of not getting enough in return for fulfilling alliance responsibilities really made the Turks angry.

For the Americans, the Turkish-American relationship meant the protection of mutual economic and military interests rather than ideological closeness. In their eyes, both sides had to give something in order to get some gains, meaning that the alliance between Turkey and the United States was a classic alliance relationship whose sides aimed at maximising their gains by establishing an alliance. This also meant restriction of independence of the two states to a reasonable extent. As former US official Harris expressed it, "the virtually complete independence in terms of military and economic self-sufficiency that is often urged by Turkish critics of the United States is clearly impossible."[6] The American perception of the alliance did not include a romantic relationship forcing the two sides to support each other in every event regardless their practical national interests.

In their dealings with the Turks the Americans expressed the importance of having the same ideological principles. President Johnson said in his speech of welcome to Turkish President Sunay on 3 April 1967: "There is a special close friendship between Turkey and the United States, which can be understood only by free people believing in a strong brotherhood relationship."[7] However, it was America's strategic interests in that part of the world that were of prime concern to the Americans.[8] The Americans did not oppose the military regime in Turkey, which came to power on 27 May 1960; they extended recognition to it three days after the military coup and promised more economic and military aid. The most important thing for the Americans was Turkey's continuing membership in NATO and CENTO, helping the protection of Western interests in the Near and Middle East. The Americans tried to protect their interests first in the Cyprus question, too. Turkey should be prevented from intervening in Cyprus not to make the situation harmful for the United States, but this state should not be pressurised to the extent that it would be alienated totally.

---

[3] *Dışişleri Bakanlığı Belleteni,* April 1967, pp. 48, 49.
[4] *Millet Meclisi Tutanak Dergisi,* term 1, sess. 3, vol. 30, p. 295.
[5] Prime Minister İnönü, *Millet Meclisi Tutanak Dergisi,* term 1, sess. 2, vol. 16, pp. 570-571, term 3, sess. 1, vol. 2, p. 290, Foreign Minister F. C. Erkin, *Cumhuriyet Senatosu Tutanak Dergisi,* term 1, sess. 4, vol. 24-3, p. 1017, the Turkish junta's announcement of loyalty to NATO and CENTO, *Cumhuriyet,* 27 May 1960, p. 1.
[6] George S. Harris, *Troubled Alliance: Turkish-American Problems in Historical Perspective 1945-1971,* (Washington: American Enterprise Institute, 1972), pp. 204-205.
[7] *Dışişleri Bakanlığı Belleteni,* April 1967, p. 47, *Amerika'da Onbir Gün,* Ankara: Yarın Yayınları, 1967, pp. 15-16.
[8] M. Stearns, *Entangled Allies,* p. 21.

Military capabilities of the United States were clearly much greater than those of Turkey. Since the USA was the main military and economic aid supplier of Turkey, she had more bargaining power vis-à-vis Turkey on important matters including Cyprus. However, Turkey's strategic importance gave her rulers the capability to affect US decisions to some extent. The US unwillingness to take forceful action against Turkey on the Cyprus question can be cited as an example.

Turkey played quite an important role in the superpower competition with its geographical location controlling vital outlets of the Soviet Union. The United States attributed importance to keeping Turkey in the Western camp. The Western European powers were potential alternatives of patrons for Turkey's security and economy but Turkish rulers believed that they could not get from anywhere else the protection and material support which they obtained from the USA. US officials, too, did not consider leaving Turkey, believing that Turkey's services for the United States were important. This situation determined the limits of the two sides' attitudes on the Cyprus question.

Turkey and the United States were closely tied to each other between 1947 and 1975 though this closeness was more dominant in the 1950s. Especially in the 1950s and in the first half of the 1960s, Turkey closely followed the lead of the United States in the international arena though the USA did not always demand her support. Turkish leaders proudly acted in this way, seeing it as a requirement of the Western alliance. But from 1965 onward, stimulated by the American attitude on Cyprus, Turkish rulers acted more independently, taking some actions against the US stance (supporting the Arabs in the Arab-Israeli conflict is one example). On the other side, the United States did not use direct pressures against Turkish rulers. The Johnson letter in 1964, which forced the Turks not to intervene in Cyprus and the US Congress's decision to impose an arms embargo on Turkey were exceptions in this regard and they caused a deterioration in the two countries' relations. Indirect US pressures forced Turkish rulers to prohibit opium cultivation in 1971 but three years later the Ecevit government reversed the decision in spite of strong US protests. The Ecevit administration also dared to intervene in Cyprus militarily in spite of the high possibility of the American opposition.

US military assistance to Turkey was prominent in the relationship between the two countries. The Turks valued it very highly, but in the détente period they paid more attention to economic development and accepted the aid of the Soviet Union for this purpose. They even risked the loss of US aid with their policies on Cyprus and opium. US Congress tried to influence Turkish policies by using the leverage of military and economic assistance, (the US administration generally opposed the Congress pressures but in some cases such as opium they were privately happy about it) but it was not able to change Turkish attitudes dramatically.

Some propositions of influence can be applied to the matters of the US-Turkish relationship, including the Cyprus problem:[9] A stands for the United States and B for Turkey in the following explanations. Potential influence increases as elites in A perceive a greater need to influence and elites in B perceive a need to accept A's influence. After the World War II the United States came to the position of influencing other states as a result of its global policy. The Cyprus question was not an exception in this regard. US rulers tried to influence

---

[9] Theodore A. Couloumbis, *the United States, Greece and Turkey: The Troubled Triangle*, (New York: Praeger, 1983), pp. 171-195.

Turkish policies on Cyprus in different ways. As proud and obstinate people Turks were frequently resistant to influence. In many occasions they listened to the advice of the Americans on Cyprus but at the end they intervened in Cyprus militarily in spite of the American opposition.

The greater the convergence of ideological orientations and the greater the coincidence of threat perceptions among the elites in A and B, the greater the receptivity of A's influence by B. Ideological closeness with Western powers made Turkish elites more receptive to US influence especially in the 1950s. The Soviet threat gave more leverage to the United States to influence Turkish elites. When the Johnson letter threatened not to come to Turkey's help in case of a Soviet aggression stemming from Turkish actions in Cyprus, Turkish leaders gave up their plan to intervene in Cyprus. With the apparent decrease in the Soviet threat the Turks began to act more independently on Cyprus.

The potential of A's influence in B is modified by A and B leaders' personalities and mentalities. US President Johnson was more interventionist. He did not hesitate in sending his famous letter to prevent the possible Turkish intervention in Cyprus. Turkish Prime Minister Bülent Ecevit seemed less receptive to US influence. In spite of the US opposition he allowed the opium production in Turkey and took the decision to intervene in Cyprus.

The greater the dependency of B upon A for its economic stability and growth, the greater the potential of influence of A upon B. Turkey's economic problems increased its receptivity to US influence. While taking actions in Cyprus, Turkish rulers had to consider the possibility of the termination of the American aid. When the American aid decreased considerably toward the mid-1970s Turkish rulers acted more freely on the Cyprus question. The threats of the US Congress to cut off aid did not deter the Turks in intervening in Cyprus.

The greater the dependency of B upon A for sophisticated weaponry, the greater the potential for A's influence over B. This was very much case for Turkey. The Turkish army was equipped mainly with the American weaponry and its total defence structure was depended on the United States. Therefore, Turkish rulers felt it necessary to accept the American advice on Cyprus. The warning in the Johnson letter that Turkey could not use the US-supplied weapons in Cyprus was particularly shocking for the Turks. The American arms embargo on Turkey led Turkish policy-makers to think about alternative arms sources to break the monopoly of the United States on the Turkish defence structure and thus to decrease her impact on Turkey on the Cyprus question.

The greater the dependency of B on any actors other than A for the importation of vital energy sources, the less the potential for A's influence over B. After 1973 Turkey pursued more pro-Arab policies outside the US influence because of its dependence on oil. She also tried to get the support of the oil-rich countries on the Cyprus problem to decrease the affect of the Western states on the matter.

High-quality diplomatic services maximise capability to transform potential influence into actual influence. The experienced American diplomats managed to prevent the Turkish military intervention in Cyprus in 1964 and 1967. They persuaded Turkish rulers to act moderately during the critical events in Cyprus, especially during the overthrow of the Cypriot regime by the Greek Cypriots. On the other hand, Turkish diplomacy's quality decreased the US influence on the Cyprus question. Turkish diplomats succeeded in getting an influential role for Turkey on the Cyprus question in 1960 and responded to the American pressures on Cyprus successively. İnönü's response to the famous Johnson letter led the American rulers to act more carefully not to alienate Turkey totally.

A's potential of influence in B increases when B is ruled by military regimes. Turkish military regimes were more responsive to US requests. The military-backed Turkish governments between 1971 and 1973 banned opium production in accordance with the American demand and silenced the anti-American leftist opposition. Since the Cyprus question was a delicate matter involving the feelings of the whole Turkish society and since it was a national issue on which there was a public consensus, even the military-backed administrations could not make radical concessions on this problem. The Ecevit government, which came to power just after the end of the military-backed governments period, tried to satisfy public feelings and for this end it allowed opium cultivation and intervened in Cyprus as a demonstration of its independence from the United States.

The potential influence of A over B is proportional to the degree of internal cohesiveness and foreign policy consensus within B. Public consensus on the Cyprus question decreased Turkey's responsiveness to US influence on the matter. Turkish rulers were not free in making concessions on Cyprus even if they wanted to do so. No Turkish governments could dare to do a slightest thing in the opposite direction of the Turkish people's stance on the Cyprus question. The massive support for the Turkish governments during the Cyprus crises restrained the hands of the Americans in forcing Turkey to act in a certain direction.

A's potential influence in B is proportional to benign public attitudes in B regarding the image and reputation of A. Turkish public anger against the United States on the Cyprus question decreased the US leverage to influence Turkey. The widespread anti-Americanism in Turkey led American rulers to act more carefully not to give impression that the Turkish government acted with the advice of the United States. When an American statesman or a political figure came to Turkey during the Cyprus crises the circulation began in the Turkish press that the Americans were pressurising the Turkish government not to take a radical action on Cyprus. This situation decreased the potential American influence on Turkey.

Perception in A with respect to the importance of the strategic location of B relate to the degree of influence A wishes to exert in B. The United States did not put heavy pressure on Turkey after the Turkish intervention in Cyprus partly because of Turkey's strategic importance to her. In spite of heavy pressures from different effective circles, the American administration found itself in a position to defend Turkey against punishing her by cutting arms aid because of her intervention in Cyprus. While defending the continuation of the arms flow to Turkey, American rulers mainly stressed Turkey's strategic importance for the United States and the Western defence.

A's influence over B is proportional to the number of powerful states and the level of tension in the international arena. In the 1950s Turkey was more receptive to US influence than in the détente years. Especially before 1964 Turkish rulers wanted to give the impression that they supported the United States in all international events and they thought in the same way with the American rulers in all matters. During the détente period after 1964 Turkish policy-makers did not hesitate to initiate actions which would be to the dislike of the Americans. On the Cyprus issue they felt themselves more free and tried to get the support of the enemy camp, the Eastern bloc, and the Third World by normalising relations with them. The Ecevit government finally intervened in Cyprus in a period in which it had intensive contacts with the Soviet Union.

A critical approach was adopted in this study. Efforts were spent particularly to find out the American influence on Turkey on the Cyprus question. To analyse the claim that Turkey acted in the Cyprus issue as if it was a satellite of the United States, Turkish newspapers, magazines and parliamentary records were searched and some Turkish statesmen were interviewed. Subsequently a seminar study, titled *Was Turkey a Tool of the US Policy?*, was prepared in the light of the data which the extensive search provided and this paper became the guide of the research in its later stages. Other sources, including the American ones, were obtained and used during the detailed study of each chapter's subjects. In this stage, the problems were reconsidered and the relevance or otherwise of the theories to what had actually happened was examined. Finally, conclusions were drawn and the aspects that deserve future study when documents become available were noted.

Since the period of the study covers very recent events many of the relevant documents, particularly the official records, are still classified by both sides and consequently not available for inspection. Nevertheless, every effort has been made to consult all primary sources that are available, to gain further insights by interviews and correspondence with influential people who were personally involved in the events concerned and to supplement this with recourse to extensive secondary sources and the considered views of scholars and commentators who have reflected at length upon various aspects of this subject.

First of all, almost all published and declassified primary documents concerning US-Turkish relations on the Cyprus issue in the 1960-1975 period were used during the course of the research. These primary sources include public statements of governments, foreign ministries and other interested ministries; agreements between Turkey and the United States; joint communiqués announced at the end of official talks between states; statements of state officials; memoirs of statesmen; parliamentary discussions in Turkey and congressional hearings in the United States; agreements and other official papers on Cyprus; the UN discussions and documents related to the Cyprus question; bulletins of foreign ministries; interviews with former Turkish foreign ministers, etc.

The interviews with former Turkish foreign ministers Osman Olcay and Ü. Haluk Bayülken, former Turkish diplomat and MP Kamran İnan, Turkish academic Seyfi Taşhan and retired Turkish academic and columnist Fahir Armaoğlu were helpful in clarifying some events of Turkish-American relations and understanding characteristics of Turkish foreign policy.

In order to get the whole picture of the Turkish side on US-Turkish relations a great amount of time was spent, going through all issues of major Turkish newspapers and magazines and records of Turkish parliamentary discussions in the period of 1960-1975. Newspapers and magazines had the additional merit of giving the general atmosphere of Turkish domestic politics at that time and providing official statements and news of US-Turkish contacts. Articles by Turkish statesmen, academics, politicians and columnists in these papers reflected the opinion of the Turkish government, opposition and public. Records of parliamentary discussions undoubtedly provide a good contemporary evaluation by the government and opposition of the US-Turkish alliance and its associated events.

The Turkish Foreign Ministry's bulletin, the semi-official Turkish magazine *Foreign Policy*, and official books on the visits of Turkish Presidents and Prime Ministers to the United States provided for the study official documents, records of events, and statements and articles by Turkish officials. The book by Nihat Erim, who was the Turkish representative in the Geneva talks of July-August 1964, provided a first-hand account of Cyprus events. Series of articles and books by Metin Toker, the son-in-law of Turkish Prime Minister İsmet İnönü, too, were useful in conveying information on different topics. Haluk Ulman, who joined the Geneva conferences in July and August 1974 as a member of the Turkish delegation, gave the account of these conferences from the Turkish point of view. Books and articles by other Turkish and Turkish Cypriot officials including Turkish Cypriot leader Rauf Denktash supplied official documents and the viewpoint of the Turkish side on the Cyprus question. A detailed use of books of Turkish political leaders and party and government programs was made in explaining the views of different Turkish political groups on Cyprus.

On the American side, hearings in the US Congress provided a detailed account of views of US congressmen and officials on the arms embargo and the Cyprus problem. Reports prepared by the Library of Congress servicemen for committees of the US Congress clarified the US position and gave detailed information in various subjects including US bases and facilities in Turkey, Turkey's strategic importance for the United States, the Cyprus question, and the arms embargo. Memoirs by some US statesmen supplied first-hand accounts of some events: George Ball's memoirs on the Cyprus question in 1964 and Henry Kissinger's memoirs on the Cyprus crisis in 1974. Books and articles by former US ambassadors, James W. Spain, George McGhee and Monteagle Stearns, too, contributed to the study. Books and articles of former US officials and US experts on Turkey such as George Harris, Ferenc A. Vali, Dankwart A. Rustow, Richard C. Campany, etc., too, were used in analysing US-Turkish relations.

Keesing's Contemporary Archives were helpful in tracking down international incidents concerning US-Turkish relations and the Cyprus problem. *International Organization* was used for the record of UN discussions on the Cyprus question. Memoirs of Greek statesmen, Andreas Papandreou and Dimitri S. Bitsios, cast useful light on the Cyprus question from the point of US-Turkish relations. Finally, numerous secondary sources were also consulted.

During the course of the study, it is explained how the USA was involved in the Cyprus question and worked to station NATO soldiers on Cyprus. In this context, the account of George Ball's visit to Greece, Turkey and Cyprus and US pressures on Turkey to prevent its intervention in Cyprus are given. After mentioning the US attitude during the UN Security Council discussions on the Cyprus question in March 1964, the study explains how President Johnson tried to prevent a Turkish intervention in Cyprus by sending his famous letter to the Turkish prime minister in June 1964 and later tried to mediate between Greece and Turkey on the matter by talking to the Turkish and Greek prime ministers in Washington. The following sections provide information on the Geneva talks between Turkish and Greek delegation in July-August 1964, mediated by Johnson's special envoy Acheson, the August 1964 Cyprus crisis and US and Turkish policies and interests on the Cyprus question.

Before it is focused on the Turkish intervention in Cyprus in July and August 1974 from the point of US-Turkish relations and the subsequent US arms embargo against Turkey, the US role in Greek-Turkish secret talks on the Cyprus question between 1965 and 1974 and in ending the November 1967 Cyprus crisis is explained and then Cyprus policies of the USA and Turkey in the 1967-1974 period are mentioned. Subsequently, the study analyses the Cyprus coup and the Turkish military intervention in Cyprus by focusing on US role in and US attitude toward these events. US reactions to Turkish actions during this critical period are particularly emphasised in this context. Then, the study analyses the arms embargo imposed by the US Congress on Turkey in detail with its causes, consequences and implications. Finally, the period covering from 1974 onward up to the present is generally studied with particular emphasis on Turkish-American relations and a supplementary chapter at the end of the book gives the latest developments from the Turkish point of view.

Chapter 2

THE ESTABLISHMENT AND COLLAPSE OF THE REPUBLIC OF CYPRUS AND THE BEGINNING OF THE AMERICAN INVOLVEMENT IN THE CYPRUS QUESTION (FEBRUARY 1959-FEBRUARY 1964)

The Cyprus question was a constant factor affecting the Western defence structures and especially the character of the Turkish-American relationship. When the Cyprus Republic was established it was thought that the cohesion of the Western defence system was saved. But the undesirable events in Cyprus, which began at end of 1963, not only brought about a potential danger for NATO's strength but also affected the relationship between Turkey and the United States negatively. The Cyprus problem and the American attitude toward it were major influences on Turkish foreign policy and undoubtedly played an important role in shaping Turkish-American relations between 1964 and 1975. Since all the Turkish governments in this period determined their foreign policies in a way to accommodate Turkey's interests in the Cyprus question, it was natural that the general direction of Turkish-American relations would be affected by developments related to the Cyprus problem. In the first place, it will be useful to look at the emergence of the Cyprus question with the breakdown of the 1960 constitutional regime. After examining main developments related to Cyprus between 1960 and April 1964 we can lay down the main aspects of the Cyprus problem more correctly.

THE PERIOD OF UNEASY CALMNESS 1960-1963

Establishment of the Republic of Cyprus

After long-lasting inter-communal clashes and terrorist activities in Cyprus in the 1950s, the foreign ministers of Turkey and Greece, with the encouragement of their NATO allies, especially Great Britain, held bilateral negotiations in Zurich on 5-11 February 1959 to find a solution to the problem of the independence of Cyprus. On 11 February 1959 the two foreign ministers concluded a formal agreement specifying the main features of a future independent state of Cyprus. On 19 February 1959 in London, the agreement was ratified and signed by the prime ministers of Britain, Greece and Turkey, and also by the leader of Greek Cypriots,

Archbishop Makarios, and the leader of Turkish Cypriots, Fazıl Küçük.[1] Based on these agreements a detailed constitution was prepared by a team of Greek, Turkish and Swiss lawyers and it was accepted on 6 July 1960. After matters related to the British bases on the island were solved, on 16 August 1960 the London-Zurich accords were signed by all concerned parties and the independent Republic of Cyprus was proclaimed.[2]

There were three main agreements which were signed in London and constituted the basis of the Cypriot State. The Treaty of Establishment between Britain, the Republic of Cyprus, Greece and Turkey laid down that the island should become an independent sovereign republic and ruled that two base areas totalling 99 square miles be put under the full sovereignty of Britain.[3] The Treaty of Alliance between Greece, Turkey and Cyprus established a tripartite headquarters in Cyprus and allowed the stationing of 950 Greek and 650 Turkish soldiers in Cyprus in order to defend the island against outside aggression and protect the status of Cyprus.[4] Under the Treaty of Guarantee between the Republic of Cyprus, Great Britain, Greece and Turkey; the Republic of Cyprus undertook to maintain its independence, territorial integrity and security and to respect its Constitution and these features of the state were put under the guarantee of Britain, Turkey and Greece. The Treaty also banned union of Cyprus with any other state and partition of the island, which were previous aims of Greece and Turkey.[5] Article IV of the Treaty of Guarantee, which was used by Turkey to justify its intervention threats against the island in the next decades, reads as follows: "In the event of a breach of the provisions of the present Treaty, Greece, Turkey and the United Kingdom undertake to consult together with respect to the representations or measures necessary to ensure observance of those provisions. In so far as common or concerted action may not prove possible, each of the three guaranteeing powers reserves the right to take action with the sole aim of re-establishing the state of affairs created by the present Treaty."[6]

The articles of the constitution of Cyprus set up structures and institutions which would encourage separation of the two ethnic groups. The individual affairs of the each community and the affairs common to all were regulated by the constitution separately.[7] The Cypriot constitution provided for a presidential regime in which the Greek president and the Turkish vice-president were to be elected by their respective communities. Under the regime envisaged by the constitution, the Council of Ministers were to be composed of seven Greek and three Turkish ministers who would be appointed respectively by the president and the vice-president. One of the key posts of defence, foreign affairs or finance minister would be reserved for a Turkish Cypriot. The Council of Ministers would take its decisions by majority

---

[1] For details of the negotiations and agreements see *Keesing's Contemporary Archives*, 1959-1960, vol. 12, pp. 16643-16647, 16657-16661.

[2] Ibid., p. 17730.

[3] Robert Stephens, *Cyprus: A Place of Arms*, (London: Pall Mall Press, 1966), p. 160, Ümit Haluk Bayülken, "The Cyprus Question and the United Nations", Foreign *Policy (Dış Politika)*, vol. 4, Nos. 2-3, February 1975, p. 92, Metin Tamkoç, the *Turkish Cypriot State: the Embodiment of the Right of Self-Determination*, (London: K. Rüstem and Brother, 1988), p. 65.

[4] *Foreign Policy (Dış Politika)*, vol. 4, Nos. 2-3, February 1975, pp. 205-207.

[5] Ibid., p. 203.

[6] Ibid., p. 204.

[7] Zenon Stavrinides, *the Cyprus Conflict: National Identity and Statehood*, (Loris Stavrinides Press, 1976), p. 54, Suat Bilge, "the Cyprus Conflict and Turkey", in Kemal H. Karpat (ed.), *Turkey's Foreign Policy in Transition*, (Leiden: E. J. Brill, 1975), p. 152, John Reddaway, *Burdened With Cyprus: the British Connection*, (London: K. Rüstem and Brother and Weidenfeld and Nicolson Ltd., 1986), p. 129.

vote but the President and the Vice-president would have the right of final veto over its decisions concerning foreign affairs, defence and security. The House of Representatives was to have fifty members, seventy percent of its deputies to be elected by the Greek community and thirty percent to be elected by the Turkish community.

The laws relating to municipalities, duties and taxes required a separate simple majority of both Turkish and Greek deputies. Seventy percent of the public service jobs were to go to Greeks and thirty percent of them to Turks. Seventy percent of police force were to be Greeks and thirty percent of it Turks, whereas the army would be composed of 2000 men in the proportion of 60 percent Greek to 40 percent Turkish. Separate municipalities were to be established in the five largest towns of Nicosia, Limassol, Famagusta, Larnaca and Paphos. Greek and Turkish were to be official languages of the Republic. Under the legal system envisaged by the constitution Greek Cypriots were to be judged by Greek Cypriot judges and Turkish Cypriots by Turkish Cypriot judges.[8] To understand inter-communal relations in Cyprus, it should be stated that according to the census which was carried out in December 1960, the population of Cyprus was composed of eighty percent Greek orthodox, 18.4 percent Turks.[9]

Turkish, US and Cypriot Reactions to the 1959 Settlement

The American reaction to the establishment of the Cypriot state on the basis of the London-Zurich accords can be understood more easily if its policy toward the Cyprus question in the 1950s is mentioned very briefly. In this period the United States pursued a passive policy toward the Cyprus issue and did not openly manifest an interest on the future of Cyprus because American leaders thought that the British control of the island served the Western interests adequately.[10] In the American eyes, Cyprus had great strategic importance and the British control of it left no power vacuum in that region to be filled by enemy powers. The main American concern in the 1950s was that the Cyprus issue should not be allowed to harm relations of the three NATO members, namely Greece, Turkey and the United Kingdom, and thus to weaken the south-eastern flank of NATO and its general cohesion.[11] The United States, therefore, preferred the problem to be solved by trilateral negotiations between the three NATO powers and opposed the internationalisation of the question through its discussion by the United Nations because it feared that the internationalisation would give opportunity to the Soviet Union to harm the cohesion of the Western alliance. In accordance with these concerns American leaders tried to dissuade Greece from taking the problem to international forums.[12]

---

[8] Suha Bölükbaşı, *Superpowers and the Third World; Turkish-American Relations and Cyprus*, (New York: University Press of America, 1988), pp. 33-34, R. Stephens, *Cyprus: A Place of Arms*, p. 161, Theodore A. Couloumbis, *the United States, Greece and Turkey: the Troubled Triangle*, (New York: Praeger, 1983), p. 30, M. Tamkoç, *the Turkish Cypriot State*, p. 62.

[9] Z. Stavrinides, *the Cyprus Conflict*, p. 14.

[10] S. Bölükbaşı, *Turkish-American Relations and Cyprus*, p. 37, Polyvious G. Polyviou, *Cyprus: the Tragedy and the Challenge*, (Washington D. C.: American Hellenic Institute, 1975), p. 45.

[11] S. Bölükbaşı, *Turkish-American Relations and Cyprus*, p. 37, Stephen G. Xydis, "Cyprus: What Kind of Problem?" in Michael A. Attalides (ed.), *Cyprus Reviewed: A Seminar on the Cyprus Problem*, (Nicosia: Jus Cypri Association, 1977), p. 25.

[12] Van Coufoudakis, "United States Foreign Policy and the Cyprus Question" in M. A. Attalides (ed.), *Cyprus Reviewed*, p. 105.

The Zurich-London settlement and the subsequent declaration of independent Republic of Cyprus were welcomed by the United States because they satisfied the American concerns mentioned above. At that time it seemed to American policy-makers that a serious matter which threatened the co-operation of the three NATO powers (Greece, Britain and Turkey) was eliminated and thus the stability of the Western alliance was saved. With the solution of the Cyprus problem through compromises between the three NATO allies, "an embarrassing and potentially dangerous dispute that had undermined NATO's south-eastern flank, American security policies in the Middle East and the Balkans, and had nearly upset the carefully constructed post-civil war Greek political system [had been] peacefully resolved."[13] American President Eisenhower praised the Zurich-London agreements as a "a victory for common sense", an "imaginative and courageous act of statesmanship" and a "splendid achievement".[14] Deputy Under-Secretary of State Murphy endorsed the agreements as a happy solution and the statesmanlike action of America's allies and said: "all Americans wish success to the people of Cyprus in their efforts to create a new state based on the co-operation of different ethnic communities and born out of the understanding and mutual friendship of Greece, Turkey and the United Kingdom."[15] The United States recognised the Republic of Cyprus on 16 August 1960.

After the island achieved its independence, the main goals of the American policy towards Cyprus were as follows: 1- Political stability of Cyprus should be assured and Cyprus should join Britain, Greece and Turkey to form a solid bulwark against communism. 2- Cyprus should be developed economically and it should be encouraged to have free democratic institutions and to pursue pro-Western policies. 3- The United States should enjoy unrestricted use of its existing communication facilities in Cyprus. 4- The British sovereign base areas on the island should be maintained and they should be available for the use of friendly Western nations.[16] To implement these policies, the United States presented its good will and economic assistance to the Republic of Cyprus between 1960 and 1963. From 1960 to 30 June 1963 the United States supplied 20 million-dollar economic and financial aid to Cyprus[17] and also supported cultural and education programs that strengthened conservative political groups in Cyprus, to balance the growing popularity of leftist organisations on the island, which concerned US officials.[18]

Before studying the Cyprus crises in December 1963 and in 1964 it is necessary to look at policies of the Turkish and Greek sides towards the 1960 solution and their concerns on the future of Cyprus. Turkey generally welcomed the London-Zurich agreements though the opposition voiced some concern over their implementation. The MPs of the Turkish opposition party, the Republican People's Party, criticised the agreements on the ground that they ruled out the partition of the island which was the most suitable solution for Turkey. In their opinion, Turkey could not act effectively any more in the event of a Cyprus crisis since Cyprus became an independent state and a member of the United Nations. Opposition MPs also expressed their concerns that Greek Cypriots would not implement the constitutional

---

[13] Ibid., p. 108.

[14] J. Reddaway, *Burdened With Cyprus*, p. 124.

[15] Ellen B. Laipson, "Cyprus: A Quarter Century of US Diplomacy" in John T. A. Koumoulides (ed.), *Cyprus in Transition 1960-1985*, (London: Trigraph, 1986), p. 58.

[16] Thomas W. Adams and Alvin J. Cottrell, *Cyprus Between East and West*, (Baltimore: John Hopkins Press, 1968), p. 56.

[17] Ibid., p. 60.

[18] E. B. Laipson, "Cyprus: A Quarter Century of US Diplomacy", p. 58.

regulations providing for the participation of Turkish community in the administration of the island.[19]

Apart from these views of the opposition which ceased to be voiced after the approval of the agreements by the Turkish Parliament, Turkey was pleased with the settlement of the Cyprus issue since Turkish Cypriots were granted constitutional guarantees which would protect their existence as a separate community and would provide their participation in the administration effectively.[20] Moreover, Turkey's fears that Cyprus could fall into hands of a hostile state and thus her security could be greatly threatened seemed to be eliminated by the Treaty of Guarantee, which authorised Turkey to intervene militarily in the island to protect the present status quo.[21] After Cyprus gained its independence, Turkey's main concern was to ensure the implementation of the London-Zurich accords and the constitution of Cyprus by the Cypriot government and the protection of the rights and privileges of the Turkish Cypriots granted by the international agreements and the Cypriot constitution. In fact, there were strong domestic pressures on the Turkish governments to protect and support Turkish Cypriots.[22]

The Turkish community on the island, too, were pleased with their rights and were not willing to give them up. Since they feared in the light of past experiences that they would be discriminated against by the large majority of Greek Cypriots, Turkish Cypriots believed that the best solution to the problem was the separation of the communities' affairs as regulated by the 1960 constitution. In their opinion, the two ethnic communities in Cyprus, each with its own different national identity, culture, religion and interests were the joint founders and owners of the Republic. The principle of majority rule and self-determination could not be applied in the case of the Cypriot state because the Turks were not a "minority" in Cyprus but equal participants in the affairs of Cyprus under the constitution.[23] Feeling weak against the Greek majority, Turkish Cypriots looked upon mainland Turkey as the protector and defender of their rights.

The Greek Cypriot side was not happy with the solution of the Cyprus problem through the London-Zurich agreements. Their leader Makarios explained to Greek Prime Minister Karamanlis his objections to the agreements before and during the London conference in February 1959. He was mainly opposed to the veto right of the Turkish vice-president, Turkey's right of intervention in Cyprus and stationing of Turkish and Greek armed forces on the island.[24] People who have supported the Greek Cypriot cause generally believe that "Makarios signed all the treaties under conditions of duress and moral blackmail."[25] In the opinion of Greek Cypriots, "the constitution of independent Cyprus under the [London-Zurich] agreements gave such extensive guarantees and privileges to the Turkish minority as to make the day-to-day administration of the island all but impossible."[26] They felt that Turkish Cypriots were granted a disproportionately large share of the cake in relation to their

---

[19] S. Bölükbaşı, *Turkish-American Relations and Cyprus*, pp. 35-36.

[20] *Keesing's Contemporary Archives*, 1959-1960, vol. 12, p. 17069.

[21] S. Bölükbaşı, *Turkish-American Relations and Cyprus*, p. 38. Former Turkish foreign minister Ümit Haluk Bayülken told the author that experienced, high-quality Turkish diplomats obtained successful results on the Cyprus question in the United Nations in the 1950s and succeeded in getting a favourable solution of the problem so that Turkey was able to have a say in the future of Cyprus in the following years.

[22] Thomas Ehlrich, *Cyprus: 1958-1967*, (London: Oxford University Press, 1974), p. 48.

[23] M. Tamkoç, *the Turkish Cypriot State*, p. 49, Z. Stavrinides, *the Cyprus Conflict*, pp. 52-53.

[24] S. Bölükbaşı, *Turkish-American Relations and Cyprus*, p. 33.

[25] P. N. Vanezis, *Cyprus: the Unfinished Agony*, (London: Abelard-Schuman, 1977), p. 9.

numerical strength at the expense of Greek Cypriots.[27] Greek Cypriots saw the London-Zurich agreements as obstacles to the full independence of the Republic of Cyprus because these accords, in their view, allowed outside intervention in affairs of the island and "deprived the Cypriots of any possibility to exercise their right of self-determination and to conduct an independent foreign policy."[28]

Breakdown of the 1959 Regime

Greek Cypriots and their leader Makarios were criticised by many politicians and authors on the ground that they constantly pursued the policy of uniting Cyprus with Greece (Enosis) and eliminating the participation of Turkish Cypriots in the administration of the island. The claims of these critics of Makarios could be summarised as follows: Makarios and the Greek Cypriot leadership regarded the London-Zurich agreements and the independence as a springboard for the ultimate objective of the union of Cyprus with Greece (Enosis) and as the first stage of the Enosis struggle.[29] The main aim of the Greek Cypriots after independence was to abolish the articles of the London-Zurich agreements and the constitution of Cyprus, which granted "excessive" rights to Turkish Cypriots and Turkey. "The Greek strategy was to express their demands for radically revising the Constitution in terms which the international community understood and approved of. So the Turkish privileges would be presented as contravening the principle of self-determination and Turkey's threats to intervene would be denounced on the grounds that the independence and territorial integrity of Cyprus must be respected."[30]

The criticisms went on: "The demand for reasonable amendments would be only the first step of reducing the Turkish community to the status of a mere minority unable to effectively control the will of the Greek majority. Once this achieved, and the Treaty of Guarantee nullified, there would be nothing stopping the Greek leadership from appealing to the principle of self-determination, ...and then proclaim Enosis."[31] In order to achieve these aims, the Greek Cypriot leadership prepared the Akritas plan in 1963. The main purpose of the Akritas plan, which was first published by a local Greek newspaper, *Pataris*, on 21 April 1966, was to dissolve the Republic of Cyprus in pre-determined stages and methods, to eliminate the Turkish Cypriot community and to bring about Enosis.[32]

Those critics of Greek Cypriot leader Makarios cite his statements in different times and occasions as indisputable evidence of his aim of uniting Cyprus with Greece. In a sermon at Paralimini church on 3 November 1963 Makarios said: "What is our desire? We have proclaimed it many times: our union with the Motherland, eternal Greece... The struggle will

---

[26] Andreas Papandreou, *Democracy At Gunpoint: the Greek Front*, (London: Andre Deutsch, 1970), p. 97.

[27] Z. Stavrinides, *the Cyprus Conflict*, p. 45, M. Tamkoç, *the Turkish Cypriot State*, p. 71.

[28] P. N. Vanezis, *Cyprus*, p. 14.

[29] "Speech by Vedat A. Çelik, Representative of Turkish Cypriot Community Before UN Special Committee on October 29, 1974", *Foreign Policy (Dış Politika)*, vol. 4, Nos. 2-3, February 1975, p. 237, S. Bölükbaşı, *Turkish-American Relations and Cyprus*, pp. 49-50, J. Reddaway, *Burdened With Cyprus*, p. 132.

[30] Z. Stavrinides, *the Cyprus Conflict*, p. 52.

[31] Ibid., p. 61.

[32] Rauf R. Denktash, *the Cyprus Triangle*, (London: K. Rüstem and Brother, 1988), p. 231, J. Reddaway, *Burdened With Cyprus*, pp. 83, 133-134, Pierre Oberling, *The Road to Bellapais: the Turkish Cypriot Exodus to Northern Cyprus*, (New York: Columbia University Press, 1982), p. 81.

continue until complete fulfilment."[33] In his interview with a correspondent of the Stockholm newspaper *Ulusi Suomi*, Makarios said: "it is true that the goal of our struggle is to annex Cyprus to Greece."[34] On the occasion of a visit to Cyprus by the Greek Minister of Defence on 27 September 1964 Makarios stated: "Greece has come to Cyprus and Cyprus is Greece. I firmly believe that the Pan Hellenic struggle for the union of Cyprus with the motherland Greece will shortly be crowned with success."[35] In his interview with *Ethniki* newspaper on 1 October 1967, Makarios said: "The real victory will be achieved when Cyprus will be annexed to Greece without any concession whatever... I am for Enosis, but it must be genuine Enosis without curbs or strings."[36] In an interview on 19 August 1970, Makarios told *Elefheros Kosmos* and *Ta Simerina* of Athens: "I shall never violate my oath and I shall never deviate from my goal. I have always desired Enosis and I have never struggled for anything other than its achievement."[37]

While the Turks were suspicious of the "evil" aims of Greeks and Greek Cypriots, the latter, too, believed that the real purposes of the Turkish side were to partition the island into Greek and Turkish parts, and then to annex the latter part to mainland Turkey. In the opinion of people who have supported the Greek cause, Turkish Cypriots tried to mutilate the Cypriot administration between 1960 and 1963 in order to create excuses for Turkish intervention to achieve partition. Supporters of the Greek cause also claimed that especially after the December 1963 crisis Turkish Cypriots concentrated in the northern parts of the island to make a Turkish intervention and partition of the island feasible. Under the mutual mistrust between the Turkish and Greek communities, some important articles of the establishment agreements and the constitution were not implemented in the period of 1960-1963 and with the outbreak of the December 1963 crisis, the 1960 constitutional arrangements virtually broke down.

Reddaway summarises different opinions, explaining the causes of the breakdown as follows: "1- The constitution itself was inherently unworkable... 2- It could not be made to work because it depended on a degree of goodwill from the leaders of both communities and because that necessary goodwill was lacking. 3- It was deliberately wrecked either by the Greek Cypriots in the continuing pursuit of Enosis or by the Turkish Cypriots in the continuing pursuit of partition."[38] Crawshaw briefly comments on the subject that "the Greeks discriminated from time to time against the Turks... The Turks, for their part, made excessive use of their constitutional powers."[39]

The major points of disagreement between the Turkish and Greek communities on the island in implementing the constitutional regime were as follows: 1- The establishment of separate municipalities in the five districts. 2- The 70/30 communal ratio in the public service. 3- The income tax legislation. 4- The establishment of the Cypriot army with the participation of Greek and Turkish Cypriot soldiers. 5- The separate majority right in the House of

---

[33] Z. Stavrinides, *the Cyprus Conflict*, p. 64, Andrew Faulds (ed.), *Excerpta Cypria for Today: a Source Book on the Cyprus Problem*, (London: K. Rüstem and Brother, 1988), p. 28.

[34] R. R. Denktash, *the Cyprus Triangle*, p. 26.

[35] A. Faulds (ed.), *Excerpta Cypria for Today*, p. 28.

[36] Z. Stavrinides, *the Cyprus Conflict*, p. 64.

[37] "Speech by Vedat A. Çelik", p. 239.

[38] J. Reddaway, *Burdened With Cyprus*, p. 127.

[39] Nancy Crawshaw, *the Cyprus Revolt: an Account of the Struggle for Union With Greece*, (London, Boston: G. Allen and Unwin, 1978), p. 365.

Representatives. 6- The veto power of the vice-president.[40] It should be noted that the Greek majority had the upper hand in choosing its own way and the Turkish Cypriots could not do anything more than trying to protect their constitutional rights. The Turks could gain nothing from blockading the implementation of the laws determining the character of the Cyprus Republic. The present condition suited the interests of the Turkish community but irritated the Greeks since they were extremely unhappy on not governing the island as they wished in spite of their majority position.

Turkish and US Reactions to the Disagreements of the Cypriots

Turkey's reaction to the violation of the Cypriot constitution was to send warning notes to President Makarios. As Turkish Prime Minister İsmet İnönü stated, "between 1960-1964, Turkey has [also] drawn the attention of Greece and Britain to every single violation of the Zurich and London agreements by the Greek administrators."[41] During his visit to Ankara between 22 and 24 November 1962, Makarios implied that he wanted to change the constitution. The reaction of Prime Minister İnönü was as follows; "It was felt from one of his statements in the course of our talks with Archbishop Makarios that he wished to amend the constitution. I clearly explained to the Archbishop that we had treaty rights over the constitution and that there cannot be any deviation therefrom without our consent."[42] While warning the Greek Cypriots on their attitude harming the constitutional regime created by the 1960 arrangements[43] Turkish officials carefully avoided creating a crisis. Their reactions, therefore, were not strong enough to dissuade the Greek Cypriots from trying to alter the constitution. İnönü explained Turkey's attitude as follows: "As a peace-loving nation with no wish for aggression, we have responded to every move with the importance and seriousness it deserved, but in all of these we have said that we are not going to accept a fait-accompli and have clearly emphasised what the outcome would be."[44]

Inter-communal disagreements in Cyprus between 1960-1963 and the growing strength of the Cypriot communist party, AKEL, greatly worried the American leadership. American officials feared that inter-communal relations would deteriorate to such an extent that the Cyprus issue would be a problem again between the NATO powers, threatening the strength of the alliance. They were also concerned that growing influence of communist elements in Cyprus would harm Western interests in the eastern Mediterranean and would attract Soviet power to the region. As early as the summer of 1961, American President Kennedy had worried that the system of guarantees assuring the stability of Cyprus would break down soon and that unrest in Cyprus would bring about the further strengthening of the communist movement on the island. In August 1961, Kennedy said: "It seems to me if the situation is as desperate as we hear it is, we cannot continue to rely upon our policy of hoping that the

---

[40] Halil İbrahim Salih, *Cyprus: the Impact of Diverse Nationalism in a State*, (Alabama: University of Alabama Press, 1978), pp. 18-19, S. Bölükbaşı, *Turkish-American Relations and Cyprus*, pp. 50-53.

[41] İnönü's Address in the Turkish National Assembly on 5 May 1964 as quoted by Suat Bilge et al., (eds.), *Cyprus: Past, Present, Future*, (Ankara, 1964), p. 97.

[42] Ibid., p. 98.

[43] Foreign Minister Feridun Cemal Erkin's speech in Parliament on 9 January 1963 in *Keesing's Contemporary Archives*, 1963-1964, vol. 14, p. 19257.

[44] Suat Bilge et al., (eds.), *Cyprus*, p. 99.

guarantor powers will shoulder the principal share of the Western burden."[45] During the visit of Makarios to Washington in June 1962, Kennedy urged Makarios to calm the situation in Cyprus and expressed his worries that the strength of communism in Cyprus was growing.[46]

A White House memorandum dealing with Makarios' visit advised "President Kennedy to pressure Makarios to establish his own party and lessen his reliance on AKEL."[47] Later in 1962 Vice-President Johnson visited Cyprus. Expressing the concern of the American administration over the growing communist influence in the island, "Johnson warned Cypriot leaders to take into account the threat presented by a strong communist movement and urged them to act to deter its further growth."[48] In February 1963, the State Department was fearful that the inter-communal dispute on the municipalities issue would bring about serious clashes between the Turkish and Greek communities.[49] Finally, in November 1963, on the eve of the widespread fighting of December 1963 in Cyprus, President Johnson's aide Harold Saunders reported to National Security Adviser McGeorge Bundy: "the Cyprus situation is going from bad to worse... Both Greek and Turkish Cypriots have readied their paramilitary forces and Athens is talking about military intervention if trouble flares."[50]

In spite of all these American worries, the United States was extremely reluctant to intervene directly in the Cyprus issue. American officials thought that to intervene in the matter would bring about troubles for the United States because Turkey and Greece were on the opposite sides of this issue and therefore at least one ally would be alienated by an American action.[51] When inter-communal disputes in Cyprus worried the State Department officials in February 1963, they wanted Britain to intervene in the matter to warn the Greek and Turkish sides. Secretary of State Rusk sent a cable to the American Ambassador in London, stating,: "We want Britain to emphasise to Greeks and Turks similarities [in] their present positions and guide them to a common stance and co-ordinated three-power pressure on Cypriot communities."[52]

THE CYPRUS CRISIS OF DECEMBER 1963

The Cyprus crises of 1964 began at the end of 1963 with serious outbreak of fighting between the Greek and Turkish communities in the island. Largely the Turkish community was targeted by the Greek terrorist organisations that wanted unification of the island with the mainland Greece. At the beginning the United States was not involved in the dispute in any way. But when it seemed that the two NATO allies, Greece and Turkey, could fight against each other on Cyprus, the United States decided to act as mediator between the disputing sides to solve problem, thus to prevent its allies from fighting each other. During the crisis, the Turkish government threatened several times to intervene in the island in order to stop massacres by using its right of intervention given by the Guarantee Treaty of 1960. Each time

---

[45] H. W. Brands, Jr., "America Enters the Cyprus Tangle, 1964", *Middle Eastern Studies,* vol. 23, No. 3, July 1987, p. 350.
[46] Ibid., p. 350.
[47] S. Bölükbaşı, *Turkish-American Relations and Cyprus,* p. 54.
[48] T. W. Adams and A. J. Cottrell, *Cyprus Between East and West,* pp. 59-60.
[49] S. Bölükbaşı, *Turkish-American Relations and Cyprus,* p. 55.
[50] H. W. Brands, Jr., "America Enters the Cyprus Tangle, 1964", p. 351.
[51] Ibid., pp. 349, 350-351.
[52] S. Bölükbaşı, *Turkish-American Relations and Cyprus,* p. 55.

the United States prevented a Turkish intervention in Cyprus by putting pressure on Turkish authorities.

The Thirteen Amendment Proposal of Makarios

On 30 November 1963 Cypriot President Makarios submitted to Turkish Vice-President Fazıl Küçük a memorandum proposing thirteen substantive amendments to the Cypriot constitution. Makarios' main proposals were as follows: 1- The elimination of veto rights of the president and the vice-president. 2- The abolition of constitutional provisions requiring separate majorities for enactment of certain laws by the House of Representatives. 3- The establishment of unified municipalities. 4- The unification of the administration of justice and security forces. 5- The election of president and vice-president of the House of Representative by the House as a whole, not separately. 6- The modification of the proportion of Greek and Turkish Cypriots in the public service and the police forces of the Republic in proportion to the ratio of the population of Greek and Turkish Cypriots.[53]

As Stephens stated, "the effect of the Archbishop's thirteen points would have been to abolish many of the provisions for separate communal institutions and rights and to create an integrated unitary state with [majority rule and] some limited guarantees for the Turkish community."[54] In practical terms, if adopted, Makarios' proposals would have abolished all provisions of the constitution, which were regarded by Turkish Cypriots as essential guarantees for their survival as participants in the Cypriot administration. Makarios' initiative was, therefore, seen by supporters of the Turkish cause as an evil action aimed "to destroy the communal structure of the state of Cyprus and abolish or make ineffective the Treaty of Guarantee."[55] In their view, Makarios' proposals would have shifted the constitutional balance of power so as to favour the Greek majority and hence would have assured the Greek Cypriot rule and this facts were later confirmed by published accounts of the Akritas plan.[56] In the opinion of many Turkish and independent observers, with his amendment proposals Makarios wanted to oust Turkish Cypriots from the state apparatus because he "calculated if he were able to make Turkey accept a Cypriot state dominated by Greek Cypriots, he would have less trouble achieving Enosis in the long run, especially if Turkey were preoccupied with another security problem."[57]

In the eyes of supporters of the Greek Cypriot cause, Makarios' proposals "were intended to remove some of the obstacles that had developed in the functioning of the state machinery since independence" and to create "a unified Cypriot state"[58] based on the principles of majority rule and self-determination, which were widely accepted by world states. With this thinking the Greeks were ignoring the unique situation of Cyprus and were seeing Cyprus as

---

[53] Ibid., pp. 55-56, *Keesing's Contemporary Archives,* 1963-1964, vol. 14, p. 20113, M. Tamkoç, *the Turkish Cypriot State,* p. 73, Z. Stavrinides, *the Cyprus Conflict,* p. 12.

[54] R. Stephens, *Cyprus,* p. 179.

[55] "Speech by Vedat A. Çelik", p. 238.

[56] M. Leigh, "the Legal Status in International Law of the Turkish Cypriot and the Greek Cypriot Communities" in Necati Minür Ertegün (ed.), *the Status of the Two Peoples in Cyprus,* (Lefkoşa: The Public Information Office of the Turkish Republic of Northern Cyprus, 1990), p. 48.

[57] S. Bölükbaşı, *Turkish-American Relations and Cyprus,* pp. 56-57.

[58] Van Coufoudakis, "the Dynamics of Political Partition and Division in Multiethnic and Multireligious Societies-the Cyprus Case" in Van Coufoudakis (ed.), *Essays on the Cyprus Conflict,* (New York: Pella Publishing Company, 1976), p. 39.

an ordinary state not different from the others. In this point the sincere goals of the Greeks in uniting the island with Greece, too, should not be forgotten.

On 16 December 1963, the Turkish government rejected the entire memorandum submitted by Makarios as totally unacceptable and insisted that no change whatsoever could be made in the constitution.[59] Turkish Vice-President Küçük rejected Makarios' proposals "on the grounds that they attacked very roots which gave life to the Republic and that their ulterior intention was to leave the Turks at the mercy of the Greeks."[60]

Inter-Communal Clashes in Cyprus in December 1963

Within few days of the Turkish rejection of Makarios' proposals, widespread shootings and killings began in Cyprus. On 21 December 1963 a Greek Cypriot police patrol stopped a Turkish car on the fringe of the Turkish quarter of Nicosia to search the Turks inside the car. When the Turks refused to be searched, Greek police forced them out at gunpoint and handled them roughly. A hostile Turkish crowd gathered to protest against the incident, Greek police opened fire on the crowd and as a result two Turks were killed.[61] This incident triggered widespread inter-communal violence. Greek police, members of ex-terrorist organisation EOKA and Greek irregulars launched an all-out attack against a number of Turkish quarters, but the main Greek aim was "the subjugation of the Nicosia Turks by a swift knockout blow and, in consequence, the automatic surrender of the smaller Turkish communities in the rest of the island."[62] After the fighting began, the Turks in mixed villages moved to the Nicosia region and concentrated there.[63] On 24 December 1963 Greek police and armed irregulars launched a massive attack on the Turkish position in the Nicosia region.[64] "Former EOKA members and other irregulars in groups of a hundred, usually led by the police, took part."[65] According to one book prepared by Turkish Cypriot officials, "during these attacks, 103 Turkish villages were destroyed, and about 25,000 Turkish Cypriots were forced to flee... In Lefkoşa [Nicosia] alone 92 Turkish Cypriots were murdered."[66]

In the opinion of Professor Ernst Fortshoff, the first neutral supreme judge heading the Supreme Constitutional Court of Cyprus between 1960 and 1963, the December 1963 clashes were products of the policy of Greek Cypriots. He said: "The Greek Cypriots do not want the participation of Turks in the administration and deem the status of an ordinary minority fitting for the Turks. The Greek Cypriot diplomacy, while determining its own destiny on the one hand, was trying to free itself from the obligations imposed by the Constitution and the treaties of 1959 and 1960 on the other... The December 1963 events are products of Makarios' anti-Turkish policy."[67] On 30 December 1963, Fortshoff told a UPI correspondent: "All these happened because Makarios wanted to remove all constitutional rights from the

---

[59] R. Stephens, *Cyprus*, p. 180, Dimitri S. Bitsios, *Cyprus: the Vulnerable Republic*, (Thessaloniki, Greece: Institute for Balkan Studies, 1975), p. 125, *Keesing's Contemporary Archives*, 1963-1964, vol. 14, p. 20113.
[60] J. Reddaway, *Burdened With Cyprus*, p. 137.
[61] Ibid., pp. 137-138.
[62] N. Crawshaw, *the Cyprus Revolt*, p. 366.
[63] R. Stephens, *Cyprus*, p. 182.
[64] Ibid., p. 184, *Keesing's Contemporary Archives*, 1963-1964, vol. 14, pp. 20113-20114.
[65] N. Crawshaw, *the Cyprus Revolt*, p. 367.
[66] *The Historical Background of Cyprus and the Turkish Republic of Northern Cyprus*, (Ankara: The Cyprus-Turkish Cultural Association), pp. 31-32.
[67] Ibid., pp. 23-24.

Turkish Cypriots. From the moment Makarios started openly to deprive the Turkish Cypriots of their rights, the present events were inevitable."[68]

Turkey's Attitude During the December 1963 Events

The Turkish side's perception of the December 1963 events was that after the Turkish government rejected his amendment proposals President Makarios tried to achieve these changes by force under a pre-planned programme.[69] In the opinion of the Turkish side, Makarios prepared himself before December 1963 to achieve the constitutional changes and the abrogation of the London-Zurich accords at any cost. "To this end he authorised the formation of underground armies to carry out a planned programme of action known as the Akritas plan."[70] Under the Akritas plan the Zurich-London agreements would be revised in order to prepare the way for Enosis. If Turkish Cypriots resisted the revision, it would be necessary "... to suppress this forcefully in the shortest possible time, since if we manage to become the masters of the situation within a day or two, outside intervention [by Turkey] would not be possible, probable or justifiable."[71] Makarios chose December 1963 as the date to implement his plan because at that time Turkey was experiencing a government crisis, and therefore was preoccupied with domestic problems.[72] The Makarios initiative was tantamount to the destruction of the Republic of Cyprus and a coup d'état which would eliminate participation of Turkish leaders in the government and civil and military services.[73]

Turkey's reaction to the December 1963 fighting in Cyprus was one of threatening to intervene in the island to protect lives and rights of Turkish Cypriots. On 23 December 1963, the Turkish government informed the governments of Greece, Britain and the United States that it took the events in Cyprus very seriously and wanted them to take every kind of initiative to stop attacks and atrocities of Greek Cypriots.[74] While the fighting continued, on 25 December 1963 Turkish President Cemal Gürsel sent a message to the premiers of the United States, France, the German Federal Republic and Greece, stating that "I ask you most earnestly to do all in your power in order that this bloodshed be stopped forthwith."[75] On the same day Turkey issued a warning that it would intervene in the island unilaterally if the fighting did not stop[76] and Turkish jets flew over Cyprus to warn Greek Cypriots. In his message to leaders of the world states on 4 January 1964 Turkish Prime Minister İnönü explained Turkey's action as follows: "All means of concerted action having been tried, as the bloodshed went on and the Turkish casualties increased every passing hour Turkey decided to use her right of unilateral intervention on the basis of Article IV of the Treaty of Guarantee. But she confined her intervention to a single warning flight of five jet fighters of

---

[68] J. Reddaway, *Burdened With Cyprus*, p. 137.

[69] Nihat Erim, *Bildiğim ve Gördüğüm Ölçüler İçinde Kıbrıs*, (Ankara: Ajans-Türk, 1975), p. 207.

[70] R. R. Denktash, *the Cyprus Triangle*, p. 26. See also Yuluğ Tekin Kurat, *Elli Yıllık Cumhuriyetin Dış Politikası 1923-1973*, (Ankara: Türk Tarih Kurumu, 1975), pp. 294-295. Independent observers and even Greek Cypriots confirmed the existence of the plan. Clement H. Dodd, *The Cyprus Issue: A Current Perspective*, Huntingdon: the Eothen Press, 1994, p. 4.

[71] S. Bölükbaşı, *Turkish-American Relations and Cyprus*, p. 57.

[72] N. Erim, "Reminiscences on Cyprus", *Foreign Policy (Dış Politika)*, vol. 4, Nos. 2-3, February 1975, p. 158.

[73] R. R. Denktash, *the Cyprus Triangle*, p. 27, M. Tamkoç, the *Turkish Cypriot State*, p. 74.

[74] N. Erim, *Bildiğim ve Gördüğüm Ölçüler İçinde Kıbrıs*, p. 208.

[75] S. Bilge et al., (eds.), *Cyprus*, p. 5.

[76] R. Stephens, *Cyprus*, p. 184, *Keesing's Contemporary Archives*, 1963-1964, vol. 14, p. 20114.

the Turkish air force at 2 p.m. on 25 December 1963 over the terror striken city of Nicosia... No other flights were ever made over the island nor has any naval action been undertaken in the island's territorial waters."[77]

The warning flight of Turkish jet fighters had its effect on the following day. On 26 December 1963 Greece and Britain joined Turkey for a joint action and the three states proposed to the Cypriot government to help her in restoring peace and order on the island by means of a joint peace-making force under British commander Major-General Young and composed of British, Turkish and Greek contingents already present in Cyprus under the Treaties of Establishment and Alliance.[78] The Cypriot leadership who initially did not expect a strong reaction from Turkey feared after the flight of Turkish jets that Turkey might invade the island, therefore they accepted the joint peace operation if reluctantly.[79] The establishment of the joint peace force eased tension in Cyprus though violence continued at a lower scale. On 27 December 1963 the UN Security Council held an emergency session to examine complaints of the Cyprus government on the Turkish actions against Cyprus. The issue was debated in the session, but no formal conclusion was reached.[80] On 1 January 1964, Cypriot President Makarios announced that the Cyprus government abrogated its treaties with Britain, Greece and Turkey but when the British Secretary for Commonwealth Affairs, Duncan Sandys objected to his decision, Makarios had to say that he did not abrogate the treaties but abrogation of the treaties were their intention.[81]

During the December 1963 Cyprus crisis and in its aftermath, the Turkish government chose not to intervene in the incident militarily though it claimed that it had the right of intervention under the Treaty of Guarantee and could use it at any time if necessary. On 3 January 1964 Turkish Prime Minister İnönü explained to the Turkish Senate that Turkey could not intervene in the events in Cyprus immediately because she had to have consultations with Greece and Britain under the Treaty of Guarantee and that when these two states offered the establishment of a joint peacekeeping force, the Turkish government had no option but to accept it.[82] Three reasons could be cited for Turkey's decision of not intervening in Cyprus during the December 1963 crisis: "[Prime Minister] İnönü's personality, Soviet support for Makarios and the lack of readiness of the Turkish armed forces to undertake an intervention in Cyprus."[83] Firstly, as a result of his cautiousness İnönü was extremely reluctant for a military intervention, he thought that it was too early for a military operation since the world opinion did not understand the justness of Turkey's cause. Secondly, since the Soviet Union had complained about Turkey's actions and expressed its support for Makarios, Turkish Prime Minister İnönü feared that a military intervention by Turkey could cause an unwanted Soviet reaction. Finally, the Turkish armed forces were not ready for an amphibious landing in Cyprus. In January 1964, İnönü told the opposition leaders that Turkey

[77] S. Bilge et al., (eds.), *Cyprus,* p. 7.
[78] T. Ehlrich, *Cyprus: 1958-1967,* p. 58, R. Stephens, *Cyprus,* p. 185, *Keesing's Contemporary Archives,* 1963-1964, vol. 14, p. 20114.
[79] N. Crawshaw, *the Cyprus Revolt,* p. 367.
[80] A. J. Jacovides, "the Cyprus Problem and the United Nations" in M. A. Attalides (ed.), *Cyprus Reviewed,* p. 186.
[81] Murat Sarıca et. al., *Kıbrıs Sorunu,* (İstanbul: İstanbul Üniversitesi Yayınları, No. 2071, 1975), p. 56, R. Stephens, *Cyprus,* p. 185.
[82] S. Bölükbaşı, *Turkish-American Relations and Cyprus,* p. 60.
[83] Ibid., pp. 65-69.

had no military plan for invading Cyprus.[84] He also said to Republican MP Nihat Erim that Turkey had no enough military preparations and military equipment for a military landing.[85]

American Attitude During the December 1963 Crisis

As the hostilities began and spread over Cyprus in December 1963, the immediate American concern was to bring about a cease-fire or at least contain the fighting and thus to prevent a military clash between Turkey and Greece and to save the south-eastern flank of NATO.[86] From the American point of view, this was necessary to avoid the breakdown of the political system of the Cyprus Republic and to eliminate conditions that could be exploited by AKEL and the Russians.[87] During the crisis the United States also continued to oppose the internationalisation of the Cyprus question through the discussion of the problem in the United Nations and to prefer solution of the problem "within a Western setting securing Western strategic interests."[88]

Thomas W. Adams and Alvin J. Cottrell summarise the American policy towards Cyprus during and after the December 1963 crisis as follows: "... in the legalistic US view, both communities should adhere to the terms of the Zurich-London agreements. But the first step is to maintain law and order..., so as to allow Greek and Turkish negotiators the opportunity to discuss the matter diplomatically. The United States wished to aid the three guarantor powers and the leaders of the two ethnic communities... to establish a permanent political settlement in Cyprus, but it also sought to avoid an excessive national commitment in any search for a solution."[89]

Immediately after the clashes broke out in Cyprus, the United States tried to contain the fighting. On 23 December 1963, American Secretary of State Dean Rusk asked the US ambassadors in Ankara, Nicosia and Athens to "urge maximum restraint on the three governments and on both communities in Cyprus."[90] On the same day, when the 650 Turkish troops on the island took positions in the northern Cyprus against Greek Cypriots to protect Turkish Cypriots, the American ambassadors in Athens and Ankara went so far to warn the Turkish and Greek governments that the "use of MAP [Military Assistance Program] equipment by either [Greek or Turkish] contingent[s] on Cyprus... without clear prior consent of [the] US [is considered] a violation of the letter and intent [of] MAP agreements."[91]

The action of Turkish jet fighters on 25 December 1963 was not criticised and condemned by the United States though "for their sorties, the Turks used aircraft provided under NATO auspices and assigned to the NATO command."[92] However, as Dean Rusk

---

[84] Ibid., p. 68.
[85] N. Erim, *Bildiğim ve Gördüğüm Ölçüler İçinde Kıbrıs*, p. 218.
[86] Van Coufoudakis, "United States Foreign Policy and the Cyprus Question" in M. A. Attalides (ed.), *Cyprus Reviewed*, p. 110, Joseph S. Joseph, *Cyprus: Ethnic Conflict and International Concern*, (New York: Peter Lang, 1985), p. 127, T. W. Adams and A. J. Cottrell, *Cyprus Between East and West*, p. 56.
[87] V. Coufoudakis, "United States Foreign Policy and the Cyprus Question", p. 110.
[88] J. S. Joseph, *Cyprus*, p. 127.
[89] T. W. Adams and A. J. Cottrell, *Cyprus Between East and West*, p. 56.
[90] S. Bölükbaşı, *Turkish-American Relations and Cyprus*, p. 58.
[91] Ibid., p. 58.
[92] George S. Harris, *Troubled Alliance: Turkish-American Problems in Historical Perspective 1945-1971*, (Washington D. C.: American Enterprise Institute, 1972), p. 108.

stated in one of his cables on 25 December 1963, the United States urged "Turks in both Washington and Ankara [to] avoid unilateral intervention."[93]

On 24 December, American President Johnson sent a joint personal message to the leaders of Greek and Turkish Cypriots, Makarios and Küçük, to urge them to stop the fighting. He stated in his message: "I will not presume to judge the root causes or rights and wrongs as between Cypriots of the two communities. This is inappropriate when innocent human lives are at stake. I hope that tomorrow will find all Cypriots living at peace with one another and with the three nations which have special treaty responsibility for the security of Cyprus. I cannot believe that you and your fellow Cypriots will spare any efforts, any sacrifice, to end this terrible fraternal strife."[94] To tone down the Turkish threats of invading Cyprus unilaterally, President Johnson sent a letter on 26 December 1963 to Turkish President Cemal Gürsel, stating that the United States was ready "to support any and all actions proposed by the three guarantor powers which offer any reasonable hope of assisting in a peaceful solution."[95]

The State Department's policy directive on 27 December 1963 advised the US representatives in the United Nations to pursue a policy as follows: "The UK, Greece and Turkey have treaty responsibilities. We look to [the] UK to take [the] lead to keep debate in constructive channels... The US should take a back seat during debate but should discreetly seek [to] keep discussion in [a] moderate key, particularly when chair... We assume, however, it will be necessary for the US to speak. Our statement should not discuss [the] merits of Cypriot complaint against Turkey or of background issues which brought on recent communal violence, but should stress [the] need for those concerned to work out their differences... We would hope [that] the Security Council by consensus and without formal resolution would take note of consultation machinery in [their] efforts [to] resolve [the] Cyprus problem." Mentioning that the Greek Cypriots were trying to abrogate the 1959 treaties by involving the United Nations in the Cyprus question and by involving the right of self-determination, the State Department cable stated that the United States did not want to "do anything to abet [the] Greek Cypriots in their efforts [to] bypass [the] treaties."[96]

W. Averell Harriman, the American under-secretary of state for political affairs, summarised his impressions and worries after the UN Security Council meeting on 27 December 1963 in a cable to various American embassies: "The results of this meeting were to weaken current efforts to re-establish law and order on Cyprus, to strengthen the hands of extremists in both communities on Cyprus and in Greece and Turkey and to provide an opportunity for Soviet and other anti-Western propaganda initiatives."[97] To summarise, the United States was concerned about the fighting in Cyprus, but did not want to become involved in the matter, but rather preferred the question to be solved by the three NATO powers through trilateral negotiations.

---

[93] S. Bölükbaşı, *Turkish-American Relations and Cyprus*, p. 60.
[94] H. I. Salih, *Cyprus: the Impact of Diverse Nationalism in a State*, p. 35, H. W. Brands, Jr., "America Enters the Cyprus Tangle, 1964", p. 351.
[95] H. I. Salih, *Cyprus*, p. 35.
[96] S. Bölükbaşı, *Turkish-American Relations and Cyprus*, p. 61.
[97] H. W. Brands, Jr., "America Enters the Cyprus Tangle, 1964", p. 351.

THE NATO PLAN OF JANUARY-FEBRUARY 1964

The London Conference

While violence continued in Cyprus, the British government called a conference in London apparently to find a way out of the Cyprus question, which would bring the peacekeeping operation to an end.[98] The London Conference, which was convened on 15 January 1964, was attended by the foreign ministers of Turkey and Greece, Costopoulos and Erkin, British Secretary of State for Commonwealth Affairs Duncan Sandys and the representatives of the Greek and Turkish Cypriots, Klerides and Denktaş. During the conference three different plans were proposed by Greek and Turkish Cypriots and Britain.

The Greek Cypriot side demanded an independent unitary state, the termination of the Treaties of Alliance and Guarantee and the withdrawal of Turkish and Greek regiments from Cyprus and they offered a minority status to Turkish Cypriots with minority rights.[99] The Turkish side, too, suggested revision of the 1959 treaties and demanded additional guarantees by explaining that the 1959 agreements were not sufficient to protect the lives and property of the Turkish Cypriot community.[100] Turkish Cypriot representative Denktaş proposed "the establishment of one or two Turkish cantons and the transfer of the Turkish population to these areas" and "added that if federation were not accepted, partition would be the only alternative left."[101] The plans of the Turkish and Greek Cypriots were not compatible with each other's interests. A British plan, which was proposed by Duncan Sandys on 20 January 1964, too, satisfied neither the Turkish nor the Greek side.[102]

After consultations with the United States, on 31 January 1964 Britain proposed the immediate stationing in Cyprus of a 10,000-men peacekeeping force composed of contingents from NATO countries under British command.[103] By proposing the NATO plan, British officials thought that the present peacekeeping operation could be extended rapidly to NATO as a whole and thus Britain could be relieved of its own responsibilities. The British government also might have believed that if it had threatened to withdraw its own troops from Cyprus, it could have forced the opposing parties to agree on a compromise very quickly.[104] The British Secretary of State for Commonwealth Affairs, Duncan Sandys, explained Britain's intention in proposing the NATO plan in the House of Commons a short time later: "The British government and the governments of Greece and Turkey considered that it would be best to invite certain other members of the NATO alliance to provide the necessary troops, though not of course as a NATO operation or under NATO control. There were two reasons why we took this view. The first was that these countries had forces close at hand and immediately available. The second was that all NATO members had a direct interest in stopping an inter-communal conflict in Cyprus which, if allowed to develop, could also too easily lead to a clash between two NATO allies. Our first approach was made to the

---

[98] Philip Windsor, *NATO and the Cyprus Crisis*, Adelphi Papers No. 14, (London: the Institute for Strategic Studies, 1964), p. 11.
[99] *The Historical Background of Cyprus*, p. 35, N. Crawshaw, *the Cyprus Revolt*, p. 367.
[100] *The Historical Background of Cyprus*, p. 35.
[101] S. Bölükbaşı, *Turkish-American Relations and Cyprus*, p. 62.
[102] Ibid., pp. 62-63.
[103] R. Stephens, *Cyprus*, p. 188, D. S. Bitsios, *Cyprus: the Vulnerable Republic*, p. 130.
[104] P. Windsor, *NATO and the Cyprus Crisis*, p. 12.

government of the United States, and together we worked out a plan for international force in these lines. This was approved by the governments of Greece and Turkey."[105]

As Sandys stated, the United States accepted the NATO plan and joined Britain to draw up its main features and on 1 February 1964 Turkey and Greece gave their approval to the plan but on 4 February 1964 Cyprus President Makarios denounced the London conference and rejected the NATO plan, believing that it would provide for take-over of the island by NATO and deny the Republic of Cyprus full independence and non-alignment policy on which independence rested.[106] Thus the London Conference brought about no solution for the Cyprus question.

The American Involvement in the NATO Plan

On 25 January 1964, the British Ambassador to Washington, Sir David Ormsby-Gore, called American Under-Secretary of State George Ball to present the official notice of Britain's intention to seek a broader peacekeeping for Cyprus through NATO. Ormsby-Gore informed Ball that Britain could no longer undertake primary responsibility alone for keeping peace in Cyprus[107] and said that "Her Majesty's government has concluded that it is best to establish an international force on Cyprus, and early rather than later."[108] Such a force could be broadly based but should include detachments only from NATO countries. Britain needed American diplomatic support and a US contingent with supplies and airlift for the international force.[109] When George Ball responded that the United Stated did not want to get involved because it "had far too much on [its] plate", the ambassador insisted on the British proposal and said that Britain could no longer bear the Cyprus burden alone.[110] He even expressed the British intention that if such a NATO force could not be summoned, Britain would turn the Cyprus question over to the United Nations.[111]

On the same day George Ball reported his meeting with Ormsby-Gore to Secretary of Defence Robert McNamara and General Maxwell Taylor. Ball told them, "we must tell the British that we have other responsibilities which we will continue to bear. They must bear theirs." America could offer support to the British but should avoid any commitment of American troops.[112] Like George Ball, McNamara, too, was reluctant to broaden American responsibilities by taking commitments in the Cyprus question but "he was fully aware that an exploding Cyprus could not only endanger... Mediterranean position [of America] but undermine the whole southern flank of NATO."[113]

In the evening of 25 January 1964 Ball discussed the matter with President Johnson. The President was reluctant to accept the British proposal but since he understood the seriousness

---

[105] Ibid., p. 13.

[106] S. G. Xydis, "Cyprus: What Kind of Problem" in M. A. Attalides (ed.), *Cyprus Reviewed*, p. 26.

[107] George Ball, *The Past Has Another Pattern: Memoirs*, (New York, London: W. W. Norton, 1982), p.340, H. W. Brands, Jr., "America Enters the Cyprus Tangle, 1964", p. 349.

[108] Edward Weintall and Charles Bartlett, *Facing the Brink: A Study of Crisis Diplomacy*, (London: Hutchinson, 1967), p. 18.

[109] G. Ball, *The Past Has Another Pattern*, p. 340.

[110] Ibid., p. 340, E. Weintall and C. Bartlett, *Facing the Brink*, p. 18.

[111] H. W. Brands, Jr., "America Enters the Cyprus Tangle, 1964", p. 349, E. Weintall and C. Bartlett, *Facing the Brink*, p. 18.

[112] H. W. Brands, Jr., "America Enters the Cyprus Tangle, 1964", p. 352.

[113] G. Ball, *The Past Has Another Pattern*, p. 341.

of the Cyprus question he directed Ball to draw up an acceptable solution.[114] Half an hour later George Ball conveyed the message of the American administration to British ambassador Ormsby-Gore, stating that the United States would support a NATO force diplomatically and logistically, but that no American troops would be committed.[115] He said, "[we] did not wish [to] move into another political problem with no end in sight... We are prepared to do what we could with Greeks and Turks but [we are] not sure what could be said that [is] new... [The] UK should understand that we viewed getting involved with greatest reluctance."[116]

As the situation in Cyprus deteriorated, the American administration decided to revise its decision on the British proposal within a few days and to take more active role in the Cyprus question. On 25 January 1964, the Turkish ambassador to Washington, Numan Menemencioğlu, discussed the Cyprus question with American Assistant Secretary of State Phillips Talbot, telling him that Turkish Prime Minister İnönü "needs something to help calm potentially serious public reaction to new Cyprus incidents."[117] On the same day İnönü told a Turkish journalist that he wanted the United States to know all the facts about the Cyprus question and then undertake its responsibilities.[118]

In order to appease the Turkish commanders who were in favour of a military intervention in Cyprus and to show that the United States was not ignoring the Cyprus question, President Johnson dispatched General Lyman Lemnitzer, the American commander of NATO, to Ankara and Athens on 28 January 1964. The mission of Lemnitzer was to remind Greece and Turkey of their responsibilities to the alliance and to warn them of the fatal consequences of a unilateral military intervention in Cyprus and an armed clash between the two states for the NATO alliance.[119] The same day Turkish Prime Minister İnönü told American ambassador to Ankara, Raymond Hare, that Turkey was going to invade Cyprus unless the United States gave Turkish officials some kind of answer by the next morning.[120] Under these circumstances, by 29 January 1964 President Johnson had decided to approve a plan for American participation in a peace force.[121]

The conditions of the American administration for participation in the NATO plan were summarised by George Ball to Defence Secretary McNamara: "We should insist... 1- that the duration of the force be limited to three months, 2- that the Greeks and Turks agree not to use their unilateral intervention rights for three months, and 3-that they agree on a mediator who was not representative of any of the three guarantor powers but from another NATO European country."[122] As mentioned above, the NATO plan which included the above American conditions was disclosed by the British on 31 January 1964. According to the plan, apart from the American conditions the peacekeeping force would be composed of no less than 10,000 service men to be provided by volunteering NATO members. The force would be put under the command of the British unit and would be joined by the Greek and Turkish

---

[114] Ibid., p. 341.
[115] H. W. Brands, Jr., "America Enters the Cyprus Tangle, 1964", p. 352.
[116] S. Bölükbaşı, *Turkish-American Relations and Cyprus*, p. 63.
[117] Ibid., p. 63.
[118] Ibid., p. 64.
[119] H. I. Salih, *Cyprus*, p. 34, H. W. Brands, Jr., "America Enters the Cyprus Tangle, 1964", p. 352.
[120] G. Ball, *The Past Has Another Pattern*, p. 341.
[121] H. W. Brands, Jr., "America Enters the Cyprus Tangle, 1964", p. 352.
[122] G. Ball, *The Past Has Another Pattern*, p. 341. For the full text of the Anglo-American proposal for a NATO force see *Keesing's Contemporary Archives*, 1963-1964, vol. 14, p. 20116.

contingents on the island. The force would receive political guidance from an inter-governmental committee including representatives of the participating countries.[123] It seems that the announcement of the NATO plan by the British on 31 January 1964 and the approval of the plan by the United States was a result of the warning of the Turkish Prime Minister on 28 January 1964 that Turkey was about to intervene in Cyprus.[124]

The Ball Mission

Even after the Greek Cypriot side rejected the NATO plan on 4 February 1964,[125] the United States tried to achieve the implementation of the plan. On 7 February 1964 American Secretary of State Dean Rusk stated in a press conference that the United States was willing to participate in a peacekeeping operation in Cyprus with other NATO partners.[126] Under-Secretary of State George Ball was dispatched by President Johnson from 9 February 1964 to Athens, Ankara and Nicosia to sell the plan. In the first stage of his visit Ball stopped in London on 9 February 1964 to talk to the British officials. In London Ball also talked to the Cypriot foreign minister, Sypros Kyprianou. Kyprianou was so adamant in rejecting the NATO plan that, in the view of Brands, "Ball came convinced that the idea was futile... He began to fear that even if such a force made it to the island, the American contingent would be singled out for attack by Cypriot terrorists - an opinion seconded by the CIA. However, because the United States had made a commitment to the NATO force, Ball did not want the Johnson administration to be seen as backing out... As he described to Johnson, his plan was to place on Makarios' shoulders the primary onus for... [America's] non-participation."[127]

On 10 February 1964 George Ball talked to Turkish Prime Minister İsmet İnönü in Ankara and persuaded him to accept the NATO plan.[128] Ball cited in his memoir that İnönü insisted that the United States must "move swiftly; Turkish patience was running out. Given the excited state of public opinion, any overnight flare up of killing on the island might force the Turkish military to intervene... So long as nothing was done to impair Turkey's right of intervention to protect the Turkish Cypriot population, the Turkish government was prepared to go along with the Anglo-American proposal for a NATO force."[129] Meanwhile, on 10 February 1964, the American State Department clarified that the United States had no intention of imposing any solution on any side on the Cyprus question and that it "has no preconceptions or preference as to the shape or form of final solutions that might be developed for the Cyprus problem... The United States must emphasise that it does have a major interest in the maintenance of peace in the eastern Mediterranean... It will do whatever it can to assure that objectives."[130]

George Ball knew that his pre-arranged meeting with Cypriot President Makarios would be very difficult. The American ambassador to the United Nations, Adlai Stevenson, had told

---

[123] J. S. Joseph, *Cyprus*, p. 173, *The Historical Background of Cyprus*, p. 36.

[124] S. Bölükbaşı, *Turkish-American Relations and Cyprus*, p. 64.

[125] For Makarios's note to Britain and the USA see *Keesing's Contemporary Archives*, 1963-1964, vol. 14, p. 20116.

[126] H. I. Salih, *Cyprus*, p. 33.

[127] H. W. Brands, Jr., "America Enters the Cyprus Tangle, 1964", p. 353.

[128] Metin Toker, "İsmet Paşa ile 4 Buhranlı Yıl", *Milliyet*, 7 February 1969, p. 5.

[129] G. Ball, *The Past Has Another Pattern*, p. 343.

[130] H. I. Salih, *Cyprus*, p. 33, *Cumhuriyet*, 11 February 1964, p. 7.

Ball that the Archbishop was "a wicked, unreliable conniver who concealed his venality under the sanctimonious vestments of a religious leader; the only way to deal with Makarios... was by giving the old bastard absolute hell."[131] During their meeting on 12 February 1964, Makarios rejected Ball's proposal for a NATO force to keep peace in Cyprus and suggested that·the whole matter of peacekeeping force must be submitted to the United Nations. The Security Council and the United Nations must guarantee the political independence and territorial integrity of Cyprus. That meant, in George Ball's view, that "Makarios's central interest was to block off Turkish intervention so that he and his Greek Cypriots could go on happily massacring Turkish Cypriots. Obviously we would never permit that."[132] As he planned before, Ball warned Makarios that if he continued to block a solution that would eliminate Turkey's reason for intervening, "the Turks... would inevitably invade, and neither the United States nor any other Western power would raise a finger to stop them."[133] In the evening of the same day, Ball communicated with President Johnson and Secretary of State Rusk, telling them that "overwhelming pressure must be brought on Makarios to frighten him sufficiently to consider some move to halt the killing."[134]

Meanwhile, on 12 February 1964, while George Ball was still in Cyprus, Greek Cypriots broke a cease-fire agreement and launched a massive attack against the Turkish positions in Limassol. While Turkish Cypriots in Limassol suffered heavy losses in terms of human life and property, Turkey declared that Turkish Cypriots were not protected adequately. There were rumours that the Turkish ships were sailing for Cyprus. American diplomatic efforts and the deliberate obstruction of the American Sixth Fleet succeeded in preventing the Turks from a military intervention.[135] Secretary of State Rusk directed George Ball to return to Turkey "to keep [the Turks] at home."[136] and to tell them the United Stated had not given up to solve the Cyprus problem. In his meeting with Turkish Prime Minister İnönü, Ball wanted İnönü not to intervene in Cyprus until the UN Security Council discussed the issue and assured him that the United Nations would take no action nullifying Turkey's intervention right and that Makarios would get at the United Nations a severe lesson.[137] In Ball's words, "İnönü reluctantly agreed but emphasised that if there were further serious violence on the island, Turkey would no longer stand still."[138]

When he left Ankara, Ball was convinced that Turkey was seriously thinking of intervening in Cyprus. He cabled to President Johnson from London on 16 February: "we can count only a few days. Even that time could be foreshortened by a major incident in Cyprus. The Turks are not bluffing."[139] "Both the governments and people of Turkey and Greece want peace but... they cannot, by their own unaided efforts, avoid catastrophe. They can be pushed off a collision course only by some outside agency... The Greek Cypriots do not want a

---

[131] G. Ball, *The Past Has Another Pattern,* pp. 340-341.
[132] Ibid., pp. 344-345.
[133] Ibid., pp. 342, 345.
[134] Ibid., p. 345.
[135] R. Stephens, *Cyprus,* p. 189.
[136] S. Bölükbaşı, *Turkish-American Relations and Cyprus,* p. 71.
[137] G. Ball, *The Past Has Another Pattern,* p. 347, "Prime Minister İnönü's letter to President Johnson, 13 June 1964", *Middle East Journal,* vol. 20, summer 1966, pp. 368-369, Metin Toker, "İsmet Paşa ile 4 Buhranlı Yıl", *Milliyet,* 7 February 1969, p. 5.
[138] G. Ball, *The Past Has Another Pattern,* p. 347.
[139] S. Bölükbaşı, *Turkish-American Relations and Cyprus,* p. 71.

peacemaking force; they just want to be left alone to kill Turkish Cypriots."[140] As a last minute attempt, Ball proposed to bypass Makarios entirely and organise a joint peace force composed of Greek, Turkish and British units. It would be an action of the three guarantor powers to exercise their rights of intervention under Article 4 of the Treaty of Guarantee.[141] President Johnson accepted the proposal and asked the British Prime Minister, Sir Alec Douglas-Home, to convene a summit conference to implement the plan,[142] but the British refused to go along with the plan.[143] When Ball reported this development to President Johnson, "Johnson agreed that the United States had gone as far as we should try to deflect a tribal conflict. Now our only available course was to work through the United Nations."[144]

The Americans certainly would have liked the discussion of the Cyprus problem within the NATO framework. In this way, they could have asserted their influence more easily and the involvement of the Eastern bloc and non-aligned countries in a matter which mainly concerned NATO powers could have been prevented. However, since Makarios was adamant in rejecting it and he was supported by Greek rulers the Americans saw no way other than allowing the discussion of the matter in the United Nations.

Turkey's Attitude Toward the NATO Plan

As mentioned above, Turkey accepted the joint Anglo-American proposal of a NATO force for Cyprus without voicing any objections to it because it provided for American participation. In fact, the Anglo-American proposal suited Turkey's interests at that time. The Turkish leadership had wished that the United States would have interest in the Cyprus question and help solving the matter, preferably by putting pressure on the Greek side. They hoped that the American intervention at least would deter Greek Cypriots from continuing their atrocities against the Turks. Since the NATO plan provided for the American participation, Turkish leaders welcomed the proposal. On 29 January 1964 Turkish Deputy Prime Minister Kemal Satır expressed his satisfaction with the American decision to send troops to Cyprus and said: "It has been our thesis from the outset that the forces of our friends and allies should intervene in Cyprus to help the two sides in establishing security on the island."[145] In his statement to the press on 29 January 1964, the spokesman of the Turkish government, Ali İhsan Göğüş, praised the NATO plan and said: "The members of NATO and our great ally America have recognised the importance of the Cyprus question and, therefore, have decided to work for the restoration of peace and security in Cyprus."[146]

It could be said that Turkish Prime Minister İnönü accepted the NATO plan mainly because it provided for the American participation. "US involvement in the crisis would make it easier for him to call for US mediation and resist the pressures of pro-intervention circles,

---

[140] H. W. Brands, Jr., "America Enters the Cyprus Tangle, 1964", p. 354, G. Ball, *The Past Has Another Pattern,* p. 347.

[141] H. W. Brands, Jr., "America Enters the Cyprus Tangle, 1964", p. 354, S. Bölükbaşı, *Turkish-American Relations and Cyprus,* p. 71.

[142] S. Bölükbaşı, *Turkish-American Relations and Cyprus,* p. 71, E. Weintall and C. Bartlett, *Facing the Brink,* p. 21.

[143] H. W. Brands, Jr., "America Enters the Cyprus Tangle, 1964", p. 354, E. Weintall and C. Bartlett, *Facing the Brink,* p. 21.

[144] G. Ball, *The Past Has Another Pattern,* p. 348.

[145] *Cumhuriyet,* 30 January 1964, p. 7.

[146] *Cumhuriyet,* 30 January 1964, p. 7.

including the military."[147] By accepting the plan, Turkey would not be seen as the main troublemaker on the Cyprus question. Moreover, the plan would provide for a temporary solution in the absence of Turkish military intervention which stemmed from Turkey's technical unpreparedness.[148] One reason for Turkish acceptance of the NATO plan was that Turkish leaders wanted NATO to intervene in the Cyprus question as a matter between its two members and to stop violations of human rights and international laws, which were against the spirit of the alliance. In his speech to the Turkish National Assembly on 5 May 1964 Turkish Prime Minister İnönü said: "Under NATO obligations and provisions NATO is obliged to examine and consider the dangers which are likely to bring the relations of its two allies to a standstill. We have insisted to the Secretary-General on this point and told him we were obliged to apply to NATO. As a matter of fact we have done so."[149] The insistence of the Greek Cypriot side on the involvement of the United Nations instead of NATO in the Cyprus question and the unsuitableness of the UN involvement for Turkey's interests made Turkish leaders more anxious to accept the Anglo-American NATO plan and to attempt achieving the NATO involvement in the following months.[150]

The Soviet Reaction to the NATO Plan

It is necessary to mention the Soviet reaction to the NATO plan because it affected the American perception of the Cyprus question and the future American moves on the matter. From the outset of the crisis, the Soviet Union supported the independence and non-alignment policy of the Cyprus Republic. It strongly objected to any Western and NATO involvement in the Cyprus question and gave support for Cypriot President Makarios' attempts to involve the United Nations in the issue. Makarios' views of non-intervention in Cyprus, and the establishment of a unitary state structure with unfettered independence received full support from the Soviets. An official Soviet statement which was published by TASS on 30 January 1964 condemned the London conference on Cyprus. The statement also noted that safeguarding the independence of Cyprus was the responsibility of the UN Security Council rather than NATO.[151]

After the NATO plan was disclosed, on 7 February 1964 Soviet Premier Nikita Khrushchev sent almost identical notes to the permanent members of the UN Security Council, Turkey, Greece and the Republic of Cyprus. In his note, Khrushchev stated that "certain powers... are attempting to impose on the people and government of Cyprus a solution of those powers' own choosing to problems which affect only the Cypriot people... The purpose of all these plans is basically the same; the *de facto* occupation by NATO armed forces of the Republic of Cyprus which is pursuing a policy of non-alignment with military blocs."[152] Khrushchev's note warned the Western powers that any move against the island would be "the source of international complications fraught with grave consequences."[153] In

---

[147] S. Bölükbaşı, *Turkish-American Relations and Cyprus*, p. 65.
[148] M. Toker, "İsmet Paşa ile 4 Buhranlı Yıl", *Milliyet*, 7 February 1969, p. 5.
[149] S. Bilge et al., (eds.), *Cyprus,* p. 101.
[150] P. Windsor, *NATO and the Cyprus Crisis*, pp. 10-11.
[151] T. W. Adams and A. J. Cottrell, *Cyprus Between East and West,* p. 35, Michael A. Attalides, *Cyprus: Nationalism and International Politics*, (Edinburgh: Q Press Ltd., 1979), p. 141.
[152] H. I. Salih, *Cyprus*, p. 38.
[153] E. Weintall and C. Bartlett, *Facing the Brink,* p. 19.

his note, Khrushchev also wanted the Western powers to respect the sovereignty of the Republic of Cyprus and to leave the Cypriots on their own to solve the problem and he also proposed the discussion of the matter in the United Nations.[154]

As a response to these Soviet moves, American President Johnson sent a letter to Khrushchev on 4 March 1964, stating that American policy was formulated through co-operation with the Cypriot officials and aimed at only helping the Cypriots to restore peace and security on the island. Johnson's letter urged the Soviets to avoid any kind of action which would aggravate the situation in the eastern Mediterranean and assured Khrushchev that the United States would pursue the same kind of policy.[155]

---

[154] M. Sarıca et. al., *Kıbrıs Sorunu,* p. 61.

[155] T. W. Adams and A. J. Cottrell, *Cyprus Between East and West,* p. 35, *Cumhuriyet,* 7 March 1964, p. 1, E. B. Laipson, "Cyprus: A Quarter Century of US Diplomacy", p. 60.

Chapter 3

HEAVY AMERICAN INVOLVEMENT IN THE CYPRUS PROBLEM AND RIFT IN TURKISH-AMERICAN RELATIONS (MARCH 1964-JUNE 1964)

The Americans had been drawn reluctantly to the Cyprus question because of the serious developments concerning the Western security structures. As the events in Cyprus got complicated, the Americans found themselves in a hopeless situation which would force them to alienate at least one NATO ally (Greece or Turkey). Since the oppressed side were the Turkish Cypriots and since the American leaders prevented the Turks from intervening in Cyprus not to make the situation more dangerous, the alienated side, too, became the Turks. The disappointing American attitude on the Cyprus question really shocked the Turkish leaders who always expected the American help in Turkey's national interests. In that period the Turkish-American alliance went through a serious test.

THE UN SECURITY COUNCIL MEETING ON CYPRUS

American Actions Before the Meeting

Before the UN Security Council met to discuss the Cyprus problem, the United States tried to dissuade Greek Cypriots from taking the matter to the United Nations and working for a resolution which would support mainly the Greek cause and alienate Turkey. However, American officials knew that they had no choice other than going to the UN and trying to do their best to pass a neutral resolution which would make both sides happy. Allegedly, US officials threatened the Greek delegation in the United Nations with not preventing Turkish intervention in Cyprus and proposed to them a draft resolution which seemed to support the Turkish viewpoint. The Greek representative to the United Nations in 1964, Dimitri S. Bitsios, cited in his book that about two weeks before the Security Council meeting the American representatives in the UN told him that "if Archbishop Makarios rejected the London Conference proposals and appealed to the Security Council, [the American] delegation would challenge the legal basis of his appeal, by claiming that Cyprus was not threatened by a Turkish military invasion and that the problem was merely an inter-communal conflict. Furthermore, they would insist that the cause of the crisis was to be found in the proposals submitted by Makarios for the amendment of the constitution. Finally, the American delegation would propose that the Security Council should hear representatives of both communities and would declare that the United States would not finance a UN peace force should the council decide to send one to Cyprus." According to Bitsios' accounts, the American delegation also informed him that the United States still recognised the Treaty of Guarantee as valid, and therefore, if the peace efforts of the NATO allies failed and Turkey intervened, the United States would consider the Turkish action legitimate.[1]

Bitsios further states his contacts before the UN Security Council meeting: he met with American Ambassador to the UN Adlai Stevenson on 17 February 1964 to ask an explanation for rumours that the United States had supported the Turkish cause and opposed to Makarios' views. After the meeting on the same day, Stevenson sent a statement to Bitsios explaining the American position: "Press reports from London that the United States is seeking to isolate Archbishop Makarios, and favours settlement of the communal conflict in Cyprus by partition, are untrue. The only interest of the United States is the re-establishment of law and order in the island to permit the conflict to be settled between the parties peacefully. This is urgent business. We hope the Security Council will be able to exert a calming influence on the situation and make possible concrete measures to restore law and order promptly. We have no other objectives in the Security Council and the United States has no position on the terms of any settlement."[2]

On the same day, on 17 February 1964, George Ball, Adlai Stevenson and Phillips Talbot and Harlan Cleveland, the under-secretaries at the State Department, visited the Greek mission in the United Nations. According to Bitsios' account, the American delegation gave him a draft resolution for the UN Security Council which they requested him to convince the Greek Cypriots to accept. The draft resolution "called upon all the states and authorities concerned to respect the independence, territorial integrity and security of the Republic of Cyprus in accordance with the Treaty of Guarantee and as established and regulated by the basic articles of the constitution." If approved by the Security Council, the American draft, in the opinion of Bitsios, "would have made the independence of Cyprus dependent upon the 1960 Treaties", which reflected Turkey's point of view. When Bitsios rejected the suggestion of the American delegation, George Ball said: "The Greek Cypriots must understand that they cannot obtain from the Security Council a resolution to their entire liking. We shall not allow that."[3] Bitsios cites that Ball finally suggested that the Greek delegation should continue their effort with Adlai Stevenson to work for the re-establishment of peace and security in Cyprus within the framework of the United Nations.[4]

The Security Council Debate on Cyprus

While the NATO plan went nowhere and disorder continued in Cyprus, the British appealed to the United Nations on 15 February 1964 for the discussion of the Cyprus question. Angered with being beaten by the British in appealing to the UN, the Greek Cypriot

---

[1] Dimitri S. Bitsios, *Cyprus: the Vulnerable Republic*, (Thessaloniki, Greece: Institute for Balkan Studies, 1975), p. 141.
[2] Ibid., pp. 142-143.
[3] Ibid., pp. 144-145.
[4] Ibid., p. 146.

delegation to the UN made a similar request an hour later.[5] The Security Council was convened on 18 February 1964 to debate the Cyprus issue and its sessions on the matter continued until 4 March 1964.

Speaking at the 1096th meeting of the Security Council,[6] the American ambassador to the UN, Adlai Stevenson, supported the validity of the London-Zurich agreements, he said: "I think we all know that the Treaty of Guarantee forms an integral part of the organic arrangements that created the Republic of Cyprus. In fact, it is so-called a basic article of the Constitution of Cyprus... This treaty or any international treaty cannot be abrogated, cannot be nullified, cannot be modified either in fact or in effect by the Security Council of the UN"[7] In his speech Stevenson also made following points: "The major business before the Council and the prime responsibility of Cyprus was the restoration of communal peace and order. His government had no position as to the shape of a final settlement of the Cyprus problem. The leaders of the two communities had to work out their differences together but in the present climate this was patently impossible. The Security Council had therefore to make an effective contribution to the re-establishment of conditions in which a long-term political solution could be sought with due regard to the interests, the rights and the responsibilities of all parties concerned... [The United States] was [not] even proposing that the international force be comprised only of NATO military units [but] recommended that the Council, in consultation with the Secretary General, appeal to the parties concerned to move ahead quickly in working out peace-keeping arrangements to which other states could make a contribution."[8] As the first part of Stevenson's speech supported mainly the Turkish theory of the validity of the London-Zurich agreements, the second part of it sought a more balancing attitude which aimed to accommodate the views of both sides.

During the Security Council debate, the Soviet delegation held an anti-Western stance, accusing the West because of its actions on the Cyprus question. The main points which were voiced by the Soviet representative to the UN, Fedorenko, were as follows: "The Security Council was faced with a clear attempt by certain powers of NATO to force their will upon the people and government of Cyprus. The real cause of tension in Cyprus was that the discord between the two communities which had been fomented from outside was being used as an excuse for unmasked interference by certain specific powers in the internal affairs of Cyprus... The primary source of the present complications lay in the agreements which were not based on a foundation of equality and which were forced upon a small country... The Security Council had to ensure the maintenance of peace in Cyprus which was impossible to do without ending outside interference. The Council should therefore take immediate steps to protect Cyprus from aggression and to end foreign intervention in the domestic affairs of that small state."[9]

---

[5] Edward Weintall and Charles Bartlett, *Facing the Brink: A Study of Crisis Diplomacy*, (London: Hutchinson, 1967), p. 20.

[6] *Keesing's Contemporary Archives 1963-1964*, vol. 14, pp. 20118-20119.

[7] Halil İbrahim Salih, *Cyprus: the Impact of Diverse Nationalism in a State*, (Alabama: University of Alabama Press, 1978), p. 37.

[8] "Cypriot Complaint of Turkish Aggression and Interference in its Internal Affairs", *International Organization*, vol. 18, 1964, p. 482.

[9] Ibid., p. 482.

The UN Security Council Resolution of 4 March 1964

As mentioned above, the United States and Britain had prepared a draft resolution which regarded the London-Zurich agreements as the basis of the independence of Cyprus and which mentioned the rights of the guarantor powers to intervene in Cyprus separately. Believing that the Anglo-American resolution would undermine the legality of Makarios' government, the Greek and Greek Cypriot delegation struggled to block it.[10] On 4 March 1964 the UN Security Council accepted a different resolution from the Anglo-American proposal, which regarded the London-Zurich agreements as the basis of the independence of Cyprus and which mentioned the rights of the guarantor powers to intervene in Cyprus.[11] Yet the American officials did not consider it a defeat for the United States. According to George Ball, the main American aim in the Security Council meeting was "to install a UN force as quickly as possible, while assuring that the resolution did not nullify the intervention rights of the guarantor powers, since the Turks would not stand still for that. We sought also to keep the Soviet Union as far as possible out of the action." In Ball's view, the masterful policy of the American mission in the United Nations brought about the Security Council resolution of 4 March 1964. It was in fact a success for the United States because both sides were happy; "Makarios regarded it as foreclosing the Turkish right to intervene, the Turks saw it as preserving their intervention rights."[12]

The United States endorsed the Security Council resolution which provided for an international peacekeeping force and the appointment of a mediator to solve the Cyprus problem and even pledged financial support for the force and help with the airlift of its troops.[13] In the eyes of American officials, the creation of the United Nations Force in Cyprus (UNFICYP) served practical American interest which was the restoration of calm and stability in Cyprus. It "was a satisfactory substitute for a direct NATO presence on the island, since the participating countries did not include any eastern bloc nations."[14] In March 1965, American ambassador to the United Nations Stevenson told the Security Council that "the continued presence of UNFICYP is still essential to the creation of the conditions necessary to the working out of an agreed solution."[15] The other aspect of the Security Council resolution, the appointment of a mediator, did not satisfy American officials entirely, therefore they sought alternative peace mediation ways in the following months.[16]

The Security Council resolution 186 on 4 March 1964 called "upon all member states, in conformity with their obligations under the Charter of the United Nations, to refrain from any action or threat of action likely to worsen the situation in the sovereign Republic of Cyprus, or to endanger international peace." It asked the government of Cyprus "to take all additional

---

[10] John Reddaway, *Burdened With Cyprus: the British Connection*, (London: K. Rüstem and Brother and Weidenfield and Nicolson Ltd., 1986), p. 159.

[11] For the text see *Keesing's Contemporary Archives 1963-1964*, vol. 14, p. 20119.

[12] George Ball, *The Past Has Another Pattern: Memoirs*, (New York, London: W. W. Norton, 1982), p. 348.

[13] Ellen B. Laipson, "Cyprus: A Quarter Century of US Diplomacy" in John T. A. Koumoulides (ed.), *Cyprus in Transition 1960-1985*, (London: Trigraph, 1986), p. 60.

[14] Ibid., p. 61. On the UNFICYP see also Thomas W. Adams and Alvin J. Cottrell, "American Foreign Policy and the UN Peace-Keeping Force in Cyprus", *ORBIS*, vol. 12, No. 2, Summer 1968, pp. 490-503, James M. Boyd, "Cyprus: Episode in Peacekeeping", *International Organization*, vol. 20, 1966, pp. 1-17, Rosalyn Higgins, "Basic Facts on the UN Force in Cyprus", *The World Today*, vol. 20, January-December 1964, pp. 347-350.

[15] "Cypriot Complaint of Turkish Aggression and Interference in its Internal Affairs", *International Organization*, vol. 19, 1965, pp. 983-984.

[16] E. B. Laipson, "Cyprus: A Quarter Century of US Diplomacy", p. 61.

measures necessary to stop violence and bloodshed in Cyprus" and called upon "the communities in Cyprus and their leaders to act with the utmost restraint." The resolution recommended "the creation, with the consent of the government of Cyprus, of a United Nations peacekeeping force in Cyprus. The composition and size of the force shall be established by the Secretary General, in consultation with the governments of Cyprus, Greece, Turkey and the United Kingdom..." The resolution of the Security Council also recommended that "the Secretary General designate, in agreement with the government[s] of Cyprus,... Greece, Turkey and the United Kingdom, a mediator... for the purpose of promoting... an agreed settlement of the problem confronting Cyprus..."[17] On 24 March 1964, UN Secretary General U Thant appointed a Finnish diplomat, Sakari Tuomioja, as the UN mediator for Cyprus. UNFICYP became operational on 27 March 1964 and reached its planned level of 7,000 men in May 1964.[18]

The Security Council resolution was interpreted differently by the parties to the Cyprus question. Greek Cypriots welcomed it because it prevented Turkish intervention for that moment at least. In their view, the resolution "formally recognised the legality of the government of Cyprus"[19] and "indirectly vindicated the Cyprus government's claim that the Treaty [of Guarantee] conferred no right to use military force against Cyprus" by calling all states for the respect of the UN Charter.[20] For Greek Cypriots the fact that the resolution did not mention the Zurich-London treaties was a great success.[21] The Turkish side, too, seemed happy with the acceptance of the Security Council resolution. In their opinion, the resolution did not abrogate Turkey's right of intervention under the article 4 of the Treaty of Guarantee, Turkey could still intervene in Cyprus if necessary. Turkish politicians welcomed the resolution in their public statements, believing that it would help the restoration of peace and stability in Cyprus. On 5 March 1964 Turkish Foreign Minister F. Cemal Erkin stated that he was happy with the resolution because it aimed at the re-establishment of peace and security in the island, which had been Turkey's primary purpose for weeks.[22]

EVENTS FOLLOWING THE UN SECURITY COUNCIL RESOLUTION

Fightings in Cyprus (March 1964)

After the UN Security Council meeting ended on 4 March 1964, violence and fighting in Cyprus increased again. On 8 March 1964 Greek Cypriots attacked Turkish positions in Paphos, Nicosia and Kyrenia.[23] The Turkish side saw the attacks as a last minute attempt of Makarios before the United Nations force arrived in the island to solve the Cyprus problem permanently in the favour of Greek Cypriots by creating a *fait accompli*.[24] On 12 March 1964

---

[17] *Foreign Policy (Dış Politika)*, vol. 4, Nos. 2-3, February 1975, pp. 214-215.

[18] Robert Stephens, *Cyprus: A Place of Arms*, (London: Pall Mall Press, 1966), p. 191, Thomas Ehlrich, *Cyprus: 1958-1967*, (London: Oxford University Press, 1974), p. 61.

[19] D. S. Bitsios, *Cyprus*, p. 155.

[20] A. J. Jacovides, "the Cyprus Problem and the United Nations" in Michael A. Attalides (ed.), *Cyprus Reviewed: A Seminar on the Cyprus Problem*, (Nicosia: Jus Cypri Association, 1977), pp. 186-187.

[21] D. S. Bitsios, *Cyprus*, p. 156.

[22] Mehmet Gönlübol et al., *Olaylarla Türk Dış Politikası*, (Ankara: A.Ü., S.B.F. Yayınları, No. 407, 1977), p. 396.

[23] Suha Bölükbaşı, *Superpowers and the Third World: Turkish-American Relations and Cyprus*, (New York: University Press of America, 1988), p. 72.

[24] Nihat Erim, *Bildiğim ve Gördüğüm Ölçüler İçinde Kıbrıs*, (Ankara: Ajans-Türk, 1975), pp. 256-257.

the National Security Council of Turkey, which included the prime minister, the ministers of defence, domestic affairs and foreign affairs and the top commanders of the armed forces, met and decided to send a strong ultimatum to Makarios, urging him to put an end to the attacks against the Turkish Cypriots and to set free the Turkish Cypriots taken as hostages by the Greek Cypriot irregular bands. The ultimatum threatened that if attacks did not stop, Turkey would be obliged to intervene unilaterally in Cyprus in accordance with the Treaty of Guarantee.[25] On the same day, Turkish Foreign Minister Erkin saw American Ambassador Raymond Hare and showed him a copy of the note before it was sent to Makarios. Hare asked for twenty-four hour delay of Turkish action[26] and told Erkin that the United States appreciated Turkey's worry about the situation in Cyprus and therefore it would work for the landing of UN Force as soon as possible.[27]

The next day, on 13 March 1964, the Turkish ultimatum was sent to Makarios. American Secretary of State Dean Rusk made telephone calls to government officials of Canada, Sweden, Finland and Ireland regarding the immediate stationing of the UN Force in Cyprus and then informed Raymond Hare that the departure of the force for Cyprus would be possible in a short time.[28] At the night of the same day, the Turkish government summoned the British and American ambassadors in Ankara, telling them that Turkish troops at İskenderun would invade Cyprus within thirty six hours unless Greek Cypriots stopped their attacks.[29] At 6 p.m. the UN Security Council met to discuss the crisis and passed a resolution which reaffirmed its resolution 186 of 4 March 1964 and called upon "all member states... to refrain from any action or threat of action likely to worsen the situation in the sovereign Republic of Cyprus..."[30] With the arrival of the first UN contingent to Cyprus on 14 March 1964 the situation in Cyprus eased. This was seen by Turkish officials as a big diplomatic success. To demonstrate its seriousness, the Turkish government asked special authorisation from the Turkish parliament to land troops in Cyprus if it was necessary and this authorisation was granted on 16 March 1964.[31]

According to accounts of Turkish Republican MP Nihat Erim, Turkish Prime Minister İnönü chose not to use the option of military intervention because he thought that Turkey could achieve its aim through diplomatic means and he did not want to alienate the Soviet Union and the United States.[32] In his letter to President Johnson on 13 June 1964, İnönü stated that Turkey postponed its intervention in March 1964 because the United States assured Turkish officials that the UN Force would be set up very shortly and insisted that Turkey refrain from intervening.[33]

---

[25] S. Bölükbaşı, *Turkish-American Relations and Cyprus*, p. 73, D. S. Bitsios, *Cyprus*, p. 159, N. Erim, *Bildiğim ve Gördüğüm Ölçüler İçinde Kıbrıs*, p. 257, *Keesing's Contemporary Archives 1963-1964*, vol. 14, p. 20120.

[26] S. Bölükbaşı, *Turkish-American Relations and Cyprus*, p. 73.

[27] *Cumhuriyet*, 13 March 1964, p. 7.

[28] S. Bölükbaşı, *Turkish-American Relations and Cyprus*, p. 73.

[29] R. Stephens, *Cyprus*, p. 191.

[30] *Foreign Policy (Dış Politika)*, vol. 4, Nos. 2-3, February 1975, p. 216.

[31] Metin Tamkoç, *The Warrior Diplomats: Guardians of National Security and Modernization of Turkey*, (Salt Lake City: University of Utah Press, 1976), pp. 266-267.

[32] N. Erim, *Bildiğim ve Gördüğüm Ölçüler İçinde Kıbrıs*, p. 264.

[33] "Prime Minister İnönü's Response to President Johnson, 13 June 1964", *Middle East Journal*, vol. 20, summer 1966, p. 389.

Other Developments Concerning the Cyprus Problem

At the beginning of April 1964, just after the arrival of UN mediator Tuomioja to Cyprus, the Cyprus government sent a note to the Turkish government announcing the abrogation of the Treaty of Alliance.[34] The Turkish government rejected the note, Foreign Minister Erkin said: "Turkey refuses to accept such an illegal abrogation. There is no provision in the Treaty for its unilateral cancellation or abrogation."[35] In early April 1964, Cyprus President Makarios visited Athens and held talks with Greek Prime Minister George Papandreou. According to accounts of Papandreou's son Andreas Papandreou, the two premiers agreed on four principles: "1- They would seek a solution of the problem through the United Nations. 2- The ultimate target, the basic orientation, was Enosis (the unification of Cyprus with Greece). 3- Every effort should be made not to provoke the Turks... 4- Greece would come to the aid of Makarios' government if Turkey attacked."[36] In their talks, the Greek prime minister also proposed to Makarios to send Greek troops and arms to Cyprus. "If Greece, by shipping troops and arms to Cyprus in a clandestine way, could raise the cost of a Turkish landing, it might well be in a position to prevent it." Makarios accepted the proposal and then, in Andreas Papandreou's words, "a clandestine operation began on a huge scale of nightly shipments of arms and troops of volunteers who arrived in Cyprus in civilian clothes and then joined their Cypriot units." In the opinion of Andreas Papandreou, these forces "provided a decisive defensive force that prevented the Turks from being able to promenade to Cyprus. And they strengthened the Greek government's bargaining position in Washington and New York."[37]

In early May 1964, American President Johnson sent Senator J. William Fulbright, the chairman of the Senate Foreign Relations Committee, to London, Athens and Ankara on a mission to find the views of the parties to the Cyprus problem. In a White House statement issued on 3 May 1964, it was stated that Senator Fulbright would convey the concern of the American president and the Congress over the continuing disorder in Cyprus to the governments of Greece and Turkey.[38] The White House was very careful in emphasising that the mission of Fulbright was not a mediation effort nor would he submit any proposal on behalf of the American administration for a settlement of the Cyprus problem.[39] During his visit to Turkey on 7 May 1964, Fulbright himself told journalists: "We do not propose any solution for the problem. We do not want to interfere in internal affairs of other states. We only try to prevent the outbreak of another war."[40] However, Salih cites that during his visit Fulbright suggested that Turkish Cypriots be transferred from Cyprus to Asia Minor, but Turkey rejected the proposal.[41]

---

[34] Murat Sarıca et. al., *Kıbrıs Sorunu*, (İstanbul: İstanbul Üniversitesi Yayınları, No. 2071, 1975), p. 64, N. Erim, *Bildiğim ve Gördüğüm Ölçüler İçinde Kıbrıs*, p. 265, Nancy Crawshaw, *The Cyprus Revolt: an Account of the Struggle for Union With Greece*, (London, Boston: G. Allen and Unwin, 1978), p. 369.

[35] H. I. Salih, *Cyprus*, p. 41.

[36] Andreas Papandreou, *Democracy At Gunpoint: the Greek Front*, (London: Andre Deutsch, 1970), p. 100.

[37] Ibid., p. 100.

[38] *Cumhuriyet*, 4 May 1964, p. 7.

[39] Thomas W. Adams and Alvin J. Cottrell, *Cyprus Between East and West*, (Baltimore: John Hopkins Press, 1968), pp. 62-63.

[40] *Cumhuriyet*, 8 May 1964, p. 1.

[41] H. I. Salih, *Cyprus*, p. 46.

TURKISH PERCEPTION OF US POLICY TOWARDS CYPRUS

Turkish leaders wanted the United States to intervene in the Cyprus question to solve it in a short time; they did not want the United States to stand aside. They were of the opinion that the United States, as the leader of the Western camp, should not ignore a problem which concerned two NATO allies. Turkish leader believed that Turkey was right in its policy towards Cyprus, therefore should be supported by its allies within NATO, especially by the United States. They expected that America would intervene in the Cyprus problem in favour of the Turkish Cypriots and stop the killings in the island. On 25 January 1964, Turkish Prime Minister İnönü told the correspondent of the Associated Press Agency in Istanbul that the United States should understand the events in Cyprus and should show its concern over the matter.[42] On 8 June 1964 the Turkish radios broadcast that "the United States, who is the spokesman of the peace cause all over the world, should have warned their ally Greece that her illegal actions could not be tolerated."[43] During the parliamentary debate on the Cyprus question on 3 September 1964, Prime Minister İsmet İnönü said that they informed the United States about developments in Cyprus since the issue concerned her two allies, Greece and Turkey. He stated that "we wanted the United States to play a very active role in solving the problem, rather than staying indifferent to it."[44] Many Turks believed that the United States had to intervene in the Cyprus dispute because she was the leader of democratic, freedom-loving Western camp. Turkish intellectual Cahit Talas wrote in the *Forum* magazine that if America wanted to continue being the leader of the West, she should pay the closest attention to the Cyprus problem and should fulfil her responsibility on the matter.[45]

In the opinion of Turkish leaders, the Cyprus events were products of unjust actions of Greek Cypriots and they should be stopped by the West, which was the champion of legality and peace. They believed that the United States had the power to influence Greek Cypriots and to force them to stop atrocities in Cyprus, therefore they expected that the United States would intervene decisively in the matter and solve it once for all. This kind of action of the United States would be an inevitable result of the alliance between Turkey and America as well. As the fighting and violence in Cyprus continued in the months of 1964 and all Western initiatives to solve the problem brought no positive result, Turkish leaders grew impatient and began to criticise the West, especially the United States, because of its lack of interest in finding a solution to the problem. Metin Toker, the son-in-law of Turkish Prime Minister İnönü, summarised these feelings of Turkish policy-makers in his article on 4 April 1964: "We determined our Cyprus policy in co-operation with the Americans. As a loyal ally of the United States, we informed Washington about our every action and intention... We seriously listened to advice of the Americans. When the Anglo-American plan of a NATO peacekeeping force was submitted to us, we accepted it though it had some points contrary to our policy. We patiently waited for attempts of George Ball in February 1964 although we were sure that his proposals would not be accepted by Makarios. Finally, we gave consent to taking the Cyprus problem to the United Nations after the United States promised that a good

---

[42] *Cumhuriyet*, 26 January 1964, p. 1.
[43] *Cumhuriyet*, 9 June 1964, p. 7.
[44] *Cumhuriyet*, 4 September 1964, p. 7.
[45] Cahit Talas, "Kıbrıs, Avrupa, NATO, Amerika", *Forum*, 15 September 1964, p. 9.

result would be achieved in the UN. Although we had the right to intervene in Cyprus under the Cyprus treaties, we heeded warnings of Washington and did not intervene."[46]

Thus, Turkish leaders thought that they had made extremely generous concessions on the Cyprus question and therefore expected that after the stationing of the UN force in Cyprus the United States would take a more pro-Turkish stance and pressurise Makarios and the Greek side to make concessions for a settlement of the problem. In Turkish eyes, this expected American attitude never materialised and on the contrary, American officials demanded more concessions from Turkey each time Makarios rejected a new American proposal.[47] It was under these circumstances that Turkish Prime Minister İnönü made some statements severely criticising the West and hinting change in Turkey's traditional pro-Western foreign policy. In his interview with *Time* magazine in mid-April 1964, İnönü stated that while Turkey had done her best to preserve its alliance with the West, her allies had been competing with the enemies of the Western camp in destroying the Western alliance and warned that "if our allies do not change their attitude, the Western alliance will break up and then a new kind of world order will be established under new conditions, and in this world Turkey will find itself a place." Criticising lack of American pressure on the Greek side, which violated the Cyprus constitution and international agreements, İnönü said that "I had trusted in the leadership of America, who had responsibility within the Western alliance, I am suffering now as a result of this attitude."[48]

Turkish President Cemal Gürsel expressed his dissatisfaction with the attitude of the Western powers on the Cyprus question in his statement on 16 April 1964. He said that if the NATO powers did not support Turkey in her national and just cause, i.e. her Cyprus policy, he would see it as an unfriendly action.[49] The next day Turkish Defence Minister İlhami Sancar criticised the NATO alliance on the ground that it did not take serious and effective actions to protect peace in Cyprus and in the eastern Mediterranean, and it did not offer support for Turkey, which was a requirement for co-operation within NATO.[50] On 21 April 1964 the semi-official Turkish radios broadcast a comment which criticised the American inactivity on the Cyprus question, stating that the United States had to warn and pressurise Greece on its actions on Cyprus, otherwise the NATO alliance would lose its meaning.[51] During the parliamentary debate on 5 May 1964, Nihat Erim, an influential MP of the Republican People's Party which was in power, accused the United States and other NATO members of not condemning the Greek Cypriots and Greece, which violated the international agreements on Cyprus openly. He asked: "If our allies show this hesitation in a small matter how can we trust them in more important matters such as national security and defence."[52]

It seemed from these criticisms that the Turks were acting in an emotional base. They ignored the fact that the United States was a separate country caring about her own interests as a first priority. Some Turkish politicians were aware of this fact but they still wanted an American intervention in favour of their side. The United States chose to intervene in the Cyprus disagreement not to please Turkey or Greece but to stop a fighting which could

---

[46] Metin Toker, "Türkiye Yol Ağzında", *Akis*, 4 April 1964, p. 7.
[47] Metin Toker, "İsmet Paşa ile 4 Buhranlı Yıl", *Milliyet*, 19 February 1969, p. 5.
[48] *Cumhuriyet*, 17 April 1964, pp. 1, 7, M. Sarıca et. al., *Kıbrıs Sorunu*, p. 67.
[49] *Cumhuriyet*, 17 April 1964, p. 1.
[50] *Cumhuriyet*, 18 April 1964, p. 7.
[51] *Cumhuriyet*, 22 April 1964, pp. 1, 7.
[52] N. Erim, *Bildiğim ve Gördüğüm Ölçüler İçinde Kıbrıs*, pp. 286-287.

eventually harm American interests. As Turkish Prime Minister İnönü told the correspondent of United Press International News Agency and the Turkish Parliament, the main concern of the United States about the Cyprus issue was to prevent fighting between two members of NATO,[53] which could damage the cohesion of the alliance. Justice Party MP Saadettin Bilgiç expressed the same fact in his speech to Turkish Parliament on 7 September 1964 by saying that the real intention of America was to prevent a war between the two NATO members and thus to avoid harming the NATO alliance.[54]

In fact, the United States carefully tried not to take sides to maintain good relations with its both allies, Greece and Turkey. American Senator J. William Fulbright, who came to Ankara during the crisis, told journalists that the United States did not propose any solution for the problem and did not intend to interfere in internal affairs of Greece and Turkey to pressurise them for any solution.[55] The Turkish-American joint communiqué on 11 June 1964 issued after the visit of American mediator George Ball stated: "the American government believed that any solution for the Cyprus problem should not violate interests of both Turkey and Greece."[56]

The criticism of the Western powers by Turkish policy-makers on the Cyprus question did not go so far as to make important changes in Turkey's foreign policy orientation. Thinking that his statements criticising the Western states could be interpreted wrongly, Turkish Prime Minister İnönü clarified the policy of the Turkish administration in his speech to the Turkish Parliament on 5 May 1964. He said: "In their dealings in connection with the Cyprus question our allies have from time to time created the impression that they are not interested in the problem or have no influence on it. In complaining about these actions of our allies we have been obliged from time to time to use such expressions as would indicate the psychological mood of a sincere and sorrowful friend. Beyond this, the interpretation to the effect that we are to depart from the main course of our foreign policy which we have followed and that we are to abrogate our treaties are untrue. We see that the United States and Great Britain have lately evaluated the dangers which the Cyprus crisis has brought about in a better way and that they are making better efforts. We sincerely hope that our allies will take a stance which distinguishes the guilty from the innocent and show their loyalty to the [Western] alliance, legal principles and justice."[57] During his visit to the United States in June 1964, in a press conference the Turkish Prime Minister stated that "our allies in NATO have neither left nor betrayed us. They only insist that Turkey and Greece should agree with each other. We want our allies help us. Any change in Turkey's foreign policy is out of the question.[58]

The Turkish opposition party, too, declared that there could be no change in Turkey's foreign policy because of the Cyprus events. At the 5 May 1964 session of the Turkish National Assembly, opposition MPs Faruk Sükan and Gökhan Evliyaoğlu criticised Prime Minister İnönü's statement to *Time*, which complained about the attitude of the Western states towards the Cyprus question. Sükan stated that any change in Turkey's policy toward the United States and NATO would be a reckless act which would bring about fatal results for

[53] *Cumhuriyet*, 30 January 1964, p. 7, 4 September 1964, p. 7.
[54] *Millet Meclisi Tutanak Dergisi*, vol. 32, term 1, sess. 3, p. 322.
[55] *Cumhuriyet*, 8 May 1964, p. 1.
[56] *Cumhuriyet*, 12 June 1964.
[57] *Millet Meclisi Tutanak Dergisi*, vol. 30, term 1, sess. 3, 5 May 1964, p. 210.
[58] N. Erim, *Bildiğim ve Gördüğüm Ölçüler İçinde Kıbrıs*, pp. 335-336, *Cumhuriyet*, 26 June 1964, p. 7.

Turkey, and therefore Turkey could not afford it. Arguing that İnönü's complaint about the American attitude was a mistake in terms of its reasons and results, Sükan inserted that Turkey's interest was to have very close ties with the Western world.[59] Gökhan Evliyaoğlu's argument was that the West could not be won over through blackmail and that first Turkey had to westernise itself to deserve the support of the West in any matter. Evliyaoğlu also stated that Turkey would get nothing from the destruction of the Western camp, and therefore the Turkish nation would never allow the Western bloc, which was the most important guarantee of the Turkish regime, to break down.[60]

In spite of these pro-Western statements, Turkish policy-makers continued from time to time to express their disappointment with the attitude of the Western states on the Cyprus question. On 8 June 1964, the semi-official Turkish radios broadcast that the United States, which was the spokesman of the peace cause, should have warned its ally Greece about its illegal actions on Cyprus and should have announced that it would not be indifferent to the actions of Greece.[61] During his visit to the United States, Turkish Prime Minister İnönü told the directors of *Time* magazine on 24 June 1964 that the American attitude toward the Cyprus question worried the Turkish rulers and that if the trust of Turkey in America was destroyed because of this American attitude, it would be very difficult for the United States to gain the friendship of Turkey again.[62]

THE JOHNSON LETTER OF JUNE 1964

The Cyprus Crisis

In April and May 1964 violence in Cyprus continued and some Turkish positions were attacked by Greek Cypriots. In the last two weeks of May 1964 many Turks were abducted and some of them were killed. The rapid militarisation of the Greek side worsened the situation on the island. On 18 May 1964 the Makarios government announced its decision to buy heavy weapons and warplanes.[63] On 27 May 1964 the Turkish government protested against this decision and the attempt of the Greek side of the Cypriot House of Representatives to enact a law introducing military conscription.[64] In spite of Turkish protests, on 1 June 1964 Greek Cypriot MPs passed the conscription law which authorised the Cyprus government to establish an army which would later be called the Cypriot National Guard.[65]

The Turkish government took the Greek Cypriot initiatives very seriously. It felt that the position of the Turks in Cyprus were weakening rapidly because of intensive militarisation efforts of the Greek side. On 2 June 1964, the Turkish National Security Council (NSC) held a meeting and decided to intervene in Cyprus militarily. The intervention would be performed

---

[59] *Millet Meclisi Tutanak Dergisi*, vol. 30, term 1, sess. 3, 5 May 1964, pp. 231-232.

[60] *Millet Meclisi Tutanak Dergisi*, vol. 30, term 1, sess. 3, 6 May 1964, pp. 295-297.

[61] *Cumhuriyet*, 9 June 1964, p. 7.

[62] N. Erim, *Bildiğim ve Gördüğüm Ölçüler İçinde Kıbrıs*, pp. 330-331.

[63] *Keesing's Contemporary Archives 1963-1964*, vol. 14, p. 20125, Erol Mütercimler, *Kıbrıs Barış Harekatının Bilinmeyen Yönleri*, (İstanbul: Yaprak Yayınevi, 1990), p. 97.

[64] N. Erim, *Bildiğim ve Gördüğüm Ölçüler İçinde Kıbrıs*, p. 298.

[65] Theodore A. Couloumbis, *The United States, Greece and Turkey: the Troubled Triangle*, (New York: Praeger, 1983), p. 62.

by the Turkish armed forces which were deployed in the İskenderun area on Turkey's southern Mediterranean coast. As stated by Weintall and Bartlett, the mission of these Turkish forces "was to establish a political and military beachhead on the island in the hope of gaining for Turkey an advantage over the Greek and Cypriot governments in the negotiations that were expected to get under way immediately after the landing." The decision of the Turkish NSC was reported to Washington by American Ambassador Raymond Hare in the evening of 2 June 1964.[66] President Johnson was determined to prevent any Turkish invasion of Cyprus, he cabled to Hare, ordering him "to meet at once with Turkish Prime Minister İnönü, calling him out of a cabinet meeting if necessary, to express the administration's gravest concern and to urge restraint."[67]

The Turkish government apparently was determined to invade Cyprus. According to accounts of Republican MP Nihat Erim, he was called from Erzurum, where he was campaigning for the Senate election, to help the Turkish delegation in the United Nations in facing the criticism against a possible Turkish invasion of Cyprus.[68] Nevertheless, Turkish Prime Minister İnönü decided to consult with American officials before starting military operations. Foreign Minister Feridun Cemal Erkin opposed İnönü's decision, arguing that if the United States were informed of the Turkish action it would certainly stop it.[69] But İnönü insisted on his decision and on 4 June 1964 he saw American Ambassador Hare to inform him of the Turkish decision to intervene in Cyprus. İnönü told Hare that in spite of all American assurances and the presence of the UN force in Cyprus attacks against Turkish Cypriots had not stopped and the situation in the island had worsened. İnönü finally said that: "all GOT [Government of Turkey] has in mind is [to] occupy part of [the] island and stop there. Greeks could [also] occupy part [of it] and [the UN] force could remain between them. From that position one could get down to meaningful discussion."[70] American Ambassador Hare asked for a twenty-four hour delay of Turkish action to consult the American administration and İnönü accepted it.[71]

Meanwhile, the United States moved to prevent a Turkish military operation against Cyprus. The American commander of NATO, General Lemnitzer, was directed by President Johnson to warn Turkish military leaders about possible harmful results of a Turkish military intervention in Cyprus for NATO interests. The American administration ordered a Carrier Task Force of the American Sixth Fleet consisting of one carrier, one cruiser and four destroyers to position itself between Cyprus and Turkey[72] and used electronic means to block Turkish communications so that Turks could not carry out the military operations successfully. Rodger Davies, US Deputy Assistant Secretary of State, denied these allegations in his testimony before a Senate committee in 1970: He promised to senators to supply the information where the Sixth Fleet was at that time but later it was recorded in the Senate

[66] E. Weintall and C. Bartlett, *Facing the Brink*, pp. 21-22.
[67] H. W. Brands, Jr., "America Enters the Cyprus Tangle, 1964", *Middle Eastern Studies*, vol. 23, No. 3, July 1987, p. 354.
[68] N. Erim, *Bildiğim ve Gördüğüm Ölçüler İçinde Kıbrıs*, pp. 300, 309.
[69] Cüneyt Arcayürek, *Yeni Demokrasi, Yeni Arayışlar*, (Ankara: Bilgi Yayınevi, 1984), p. 274, Mehmet Ali Birand, Can Dündar, Bülent Çaplı, *12 Mart: İhtilalin Pençesinde Demokrasi*, Ankara: İmge Kitabevi, 1994, pp. 104-105.
[70] S. Bölükbaşı, *Turkish-American Relations and Cyprus*, p. 75.
[71] Ibid., p. 75.
[72] Ibid., p. 76.

papers that this information was classified.[73] This American action was later criticised by Turkish public opinion as an anti-Turkish act which aimed at stopping Turkish warships sailing to Cyprus.[74]

The Johnson Letter

In Washington, American Secretary of State Dean Rusk, aided by Assistant Secretary of State Harlan Cleveland and his deputy Joseph Sisco, prepared a letter to be sent by the American president to the Turkish prime minister in order to stop a Turkish invasion of Cyprus. In the view of Under-Secretary of State George Ball, who saw the letter before it was submitted to Johnson, the letter was "the most brutal diplomatic note" which he had ever seen and "the diplomatic equivalent of an atomic bomb."[75] In Ball's words, he said to Rusk: "I think that may stop İnönü from invading but I don't know how we'll ever get him down off the ceiling after that. The Secretary looked at me with a sweet smile. "That'll be your problem' he said."[76] On 5 June 1964, the letter was signed by President Johnson and sent to Turkish Prime Minister İnönü.

In his letter to İnönü,[77] President Johnson expressed his grave concern on the Turkish decision to intervene by military force to occupy a portion of Cyprus and stated that "such a course of action by Turkey, fraught with such far-reaching consequences, is [not] consistent with the commitment of your government to consult fully in advance with us... I must... first urge you to accept the responsibility for complete consultation with the United States before any such action is taken." Johnson claimed that Turkey's action was inconsistent with the Treaty of Guarantee because it did not consult with other guarantor powers and its action would result in partition of the island which was excluded by the Treaty. Calling İnönü's attention to the possibility of a war between Turkey and Greece as a result of Turkish action, Johnson reminded him that a war between the two countries was unthinkable. He stated that "adhesion to NATO... means that NATO countries will not wage war on each other" and that therefore a war between Turkey and Greece was unthinkable. This was interpreted as meaning that only the United States could determine who could be Turkey's enemy and that Turkey could have no enemy other than the Soviet Union. If a NATO country violated Turkey's rights NATO's interests would prevent her from taking any action.

Pointing to the threat of Soviet involvement in the matter Johnson warned İnönü: "I hope you will understand that your allies have not had a chance to consider whether they have an obligation to protect Turkey against the Soviet Union if Turkey takes a step which results in Soviet intervention without full consent and understanding of its NATO allies." The Turks were really shocked because they had based all their security on the guarantee provided by

---

[73] *United States Security Agreements and Commitments Abroad: Greece and Turkey,* Hearings Before the Subcommittee on United States Security Agreements and Commitments Abroad of the Committee on Foreign Relations, US Senate, 91st Congress, 2nd Session, Part 7, June 9 and 11, 1970, Washington: US Government Printing Office, 1970, p. 1831.

[74] İlhan Selçuk, "Pencere", *Cumhuriyet,* 9 April 1965, p. 2.

[75] G. Ball, *The Past Has Another Pattern,* p. 350. Former US ambassador Stearns calls the letter, "a startling specimen of diplomatic overkill." Monteagle Stearns, *Entangled Alliance: US Policy Toward Greece, Turkey and Cyprus,* New York: Council on Foreign Relations Press, 1992, p. 36.

[76] G. Ball, *The Past Has Another Pattern,* p. 350.

[77] "President Johnson's Letter to Prime Minister İnönü", June 5, 1964, *Middle East Journal,* vol. 20, Summer 1966, pp. 386-388.

NATO and now doubts began to emerge about the credibility of the NATO umbrella in case of a Soviet attack. It seemed that the US-Turkish alliance was favouring one side; the Turks had taken risks to support the United States (in Cuba and Korea) but the United States even did not agree to the working of the NATO commitment for Turkey's survival. It seemed that Johnson "reserved to himself the right to define when and under what conditions the Soviet Union could be a threat to the security of Turkey."[78]

Reminding İnönü that "under Article IV of the Agreement with Turkey of July 1947, your government is required to obtain United States consent for the use of military assistance for purposes other than those for which such assistance was furnished", Johnson clarified that "the United States cannot agree to the use of any United States supplied military equipment for a Turkish intervention in Cyprus under present circumstances." Finally, Johnson assured İnönü that the United States had "no intention of lending any support to any solution of Cyprus which endangers the Turkish Cypriot community" and would remain "deeply concerned about the interests of Turkey and of the Turkish Cypriots and will remain so." Johnson also invited İnönü to Washington to discuss the Cyprus question.

In the opinion of American officials harshness of Johnson's letter was necessary to deter the Turks effectively from invading Cyprus and thus to prevent likely fatal results. Secretary of State Rusk and Under-Secretary Ball believed that only a though US warning could have an effect on the Turks. If a mild warning were sent so as not to alienate Turkey, and a Turkish invasion took place, it would be more disastrous for the United States.[79] Although the Johnson letter aroused bitter resentment in Turkey, American leaders did not regret it and believed that the letter had its desired effect since no Turkish military action was taken. They believed that they had chosen the lesser evil, i.e. alienating the Turks, rather than having a war between Greece and Turkey.[80]

Interpretation of the Johnson Letter by the Turks

Turkish policy-makers interpreted the Johnson letter as abandonment of Turkey by the United States in favour of Greece. In their opinion, the letter was clear indication of America's anti-Turkish and pro-Greek stance on the Cyprus issue. They were greatly disappointed because the United States, which was seen as the closest ally and the most important guarantor of Turkey's security, in a sense, left them alone in facing enemy powers. Prime Minister İnönü was reported to have said to his cabinet: "Our friends and our enemies have joined hands against us."[81] In the eyes of the Turks, the Johnson letter was also a clear American intervention in Turkey's sovereign affairs. It was an ultimatum dictated by the United States, ordering Turkey to act in a certain way which would be acceptable to American interests.[82] The letter demonstrated such an American pressure on Turkey that, in

---

[78] Duygu Sezer, "Turkey's Security Policies" in Jonathan Alford (ed.), *Greece and Turkey: Adversity in Alliance*, (Aldershot: Gower, International Institute for Strategic Studies, 1984), pp. 65-66.

[79] E. Weintall and C. Bartlett, *Facing the Brink*, p. 24, Haluk Şahin, *Gece Gelen Mektup: Türk-Amerikan İlişkilerinde Bir Dönüm Noktası*, (İstanbul: Cep Kitapları, 1987), pp. 48-50, George S. Harris, *Troubled Alliance: Turkish-American Problems in Historical Perspective 1945-1971*, (Washington D. C.: American Enterprise Institute, 1972), p. 115.

[80] Rodger Davies' statement in *United States Security Agreements and Commitments Abroad*, pp. 1834-1835.

[81] Ferenc A. Vali, *Bridge Across the Bosporus: The Foreign Policy of Turkey*, (Baltimore: the John Hopkins Press, 1971), p. 132.

[82] "Amerikan Elçisinin Siyasi Komiser Edası", *Forum*, 15 January 1966, p. 6.

Nihat Erim's words, it included every kind of threat except only one sentence, that was that if Turkey did not comply with the letter's content within six hours, the American Sixth Fleet would have bombed the Turkish ports.[83] In Republican MP Bülent Ecevit's opinion, the Johnson letter represented a violation of Turkey's sovereignty by the United States because it showed that the American administration wanted Turkey to consult fully in advance with America before taking any action even in matters which did not concern Washington directly and legally and it also demonstrated that American officials considered it their right to dictate to Turkey how to use its armed forces and military equipment.[84]

According to former Turkish foreign and defence minister Bayülken, high-level Foreign Ministry officials saw Johnson's threat as bluff because they believed that the United States could not let the Soviet Union attack Turkey since it would harm US interests first.[85] This explanation does not reflect the general political atmosphere in Turkey and the tone of Turkish rulers' statements at that time and it does not eliminate the fact that the Turks really feared that they could be abandoned by the West. But the explanation coincides with İnönü's real intention which will be mentioned later in this section.

The Johnson letter eliminated from the thinking of Turkish policy-makers that interests of the United States and Turkey would always be identical and would never clash with each other. The letter made it clear that the American policy toward the Cyprus issue was different from Turkey's point of view and that the United Stated was opposed to the Turkish stance on the problem. This caused a great shock for Turkish leaders and led them to think that America cared about only its own interests. On the Cyprus issue, the American interest was to prevent a war between Greece and Turkey; apart from this concern, Turkey's interests on the Cyprus question meant nothing for American policy-makers. The violation of these interests could not justify a Turkish action against Cyprus, it could not be tolerated by Washington.[86]

For the Turks, the most worrying fact which was manifested by the Johnson letter was that NATO did not protect Turkey's security adequately and that it did not necessarily serve Turkey's national interests. They began to think that Turkey needed extra arrangements to preserve its national security. Prime Minister İnönü explained this Turkish worry in his letter to President Johnson on 13 June 1964: "The part of your message expressing doubts as to the obligation of the NATO allies to protect Turkey in case she becomes directly involved with the USSR as a result of an action initiated in Cyprus, gives me the impression that there are as between us wide divergences of view as to the nature and basic principles of the North Atlantic Alliance. I must confess that this has been to us the source of great sorrow and grave concern. Any aggression against a member of NATO will naturally call from the aggressor an effort of justification. If NATO's structure is so weak as to give credit to the aggressor's allegations, then it means that this defect of NATO needs really to be remedied."[87]

The Johnson letter made Turkish leaders feel that Turkey was isolated in the international arena. Since the end of the Second World War they had based almost all their policies on Turkey's alliance with the West and had taken a stance against the Eastern bloc and the Third World. The Johnson letter and the Western attitude toward the Cyprus question demonstrated

---

[83] *Millet Meclisi Tutanak Dergisi*, vol. 2, term 2, sess. 1, 29 December 1965, p. 164.

[84] Bülent Ecevit, "Mektuplar", *Akis*, 22 January 1966, pp. 8-9.

[85] The author's interview with Bayülken.

[86] M. Gönlübol et al., *Olaylarla Türk Dış Politikası*, pp. 516-517.

[87] "Prime Minister İnönü's Response to President Johnson, 13 June 1964", *Middle East Journal*, vol. 20, summer 1966, p. 391.

to Turkish policy-makers that the alliance with the West alone would not be enough to protect Turkey's interests and Turkey needed to improve its relations with the Eastern bloc and the Third World countries as well. The letter became a turning point for Turkish rulers in re-evaluating Turkey's foreign policy and making changes in its orientation. They knew that they could not afford to sever ties with the West and that having a close relationship with the West was still in the interest of Turkey. However, they came to the conclusion that there was nothing wrong in improving relations with other countries as well. As some Western countries had done, Turkey could have a more flexible attitude in her dealings with non-western countries and this new approach could help her to gain support of these states in international matters which concerned her, including the Cyprus problem. With this new thinking, from 1964 onward the Turks intensified their efforts to mend their fences with the Soviet Union, other eastern bloc states and the Third World countries.

The prevention of Turkish military intervention in Cyprus through the Johnson letter also had a great effect on general Turkish public opinion. For the first time, Turkey's foreign policy became the subject of public discussion, and anti-Americanism gained popularity among ordinary Turkish people. It was clear to the Turkish public that the United States had prevented Turkey from intervening in Cyprus but she found no solution to the problem, thus she permitted the continuation of Turkish Cypriots' suffering. Especially leftist circles, university students, intellectuals and the Turkish press began to loudly criticise and condemn the American policy toward Cyprus. Students arranged mass demonstrations against the United States, American public buildings in Turkey were attacked and the shouting of "Yankee, go home!" was heard in the Turkish streets for the first time. Ordinary Turkish people also felt resentment against America and saw her as the main cause of the events in Cyprus. The Johnson letter was kept secret from the public but Turkish people knew that it had prevented Turkish military intervention in Cyprus. When the text of the letter was released by the White House in January 1966,[88] the anti-Americanism was already popular among Turkish people. Leftist circles saw it as confirmation of the fact that Turkey was merely a satellite state of the United States.[89] Other people thought that the United States went too far in pressurising Turkey while not preventing the Greek side from violating rights of Turkish Cypriots.

The question of why Turkey complied with the Johnson letter and did not intervene in Cyprus in June 1964 should be dealt with here very briefly. One reason might be the fear of Turkish leaders that US military assistance could be suspended. Ehlrich suggests that Johnson's warning to Turkish leaders not to use US-supplied weapons for intervention in Cyprus and the possibility of suspension of American military assistance could have an effect on the decision of Turkish policy-makers. A suspension of American assistance would have seriously weakened Turkey's military strength. Even American "refusal to furnish repair and replacement parts might have been almost as effective within a short period as the removal of equipment already provided" and might have mutilated Turkish military forces.[90] Secondly, Turkish leaders could not act against the will of the two super-powers. In the opinion of Nihat

---

[88] On the occasion of the release of Johnson's and İnönü's letters, the US ambassador to Turkey, Parker T. Hart, stated that US-Turkish relations continued to be friendly even after the exchange of these letters. He showed İnönü's visit to Washington in June 1964 and the joint communiqué at the end of this visit as the proofs of this fact. *Dışişleri Bakanlığı Belleteni*, January 1966, p. 60.

[89] İlhan Selçuk, "Pencere", *Cumhuriyet*, 14 January 1966, p. 2.

[90] T. Ehlrich, *Cyprus: 1958-1967*, p. 84.

Erim, Turkey could not intervene in Cyprus in June 1964 because both the United States and the Soviet Union were opposed to it. In his speech to the Turkish Parliament in October 1964, Erim stated that in the closed session of the Turkish National Assembly discussing the Johnson letter no Turkish MP suggested ignoring the American warning and invading Cyprus and that this was the right attitude because Turkey could not afford to act in a way that would displease both superpowers.[91] The Turks could not afford to have a major rupture at least in their relations with the United States.[92]

However, the most important reason lies in Turkish P.M. İnönü's reluctance to intervene in Cyprus militarily. According to accounts of some scholars and people close to the Turkish government, Turkish Prime Minister İnönü was reluctant to intervene in Cyprus militarily because he was worried that a Turkish operation against the island might not bring good results for Turkey's interests as expected.[93] First of all, he was not sure that the Turkish armed forces would achieve a decisive military victory in Cyprus because they were neither trained, equipped nor positioned to undertake a landing on Cyprus.[94] Secondly, İnönü feared that a Turkish military intervention in Cyprus might endanger Turkey's security by involving the Soviet Union in the matter. Soviet leaders had already warned Turkey not to invade Cyprus and had announced their support for Makarios in case of an outside aggression. If Turkey initiated a military operation against Cyprus, the Soviet Union could join in the fighting on the side of Makarios, this could result in the failure of the Turkish operation and the outbreak of hostilities between Turkey and the USSR.[95] The best option for İnönü was to consult with American rulers and to seek their approval for a military intervention in Cyprus. This could eliminate at least the alienation of the United States. American leaders could give their consent to a limited Turkish military operation and they could prevent an outbreak of war between Turkey and Greece as a result of Turkish intervention in Cyprus.[96] Even if American rulers announced their opposition to a Turkish action against Cyprus, it would not be a bad point for the Turkish government.

Some suggest that İsmet İnönü deliberately informed American leaders of the decision of the Turkish government to intervene in Cyprus and he deliberately leaked preparations of Turkish armed forces to the public. He was sure that the United States would step in and warn Turkish rulers not to resort to military action.[97] Then, İnönü would cancel the military operation and blame the United States for his own inactivity.[98] Thus, he would be able to appease pro-intervention public opinion and military leaders at home. İsmet İnönü also might have assumed that apparent Turkish insistence on military intervention would lead American leaders to put more pressure on the Greek and Greek Cypriot side[99] and would deter Greek Cypriots from attacking the Turkish community in Cyprus.[100] Other instances of İnönü's political acumen lend plausibility to this interpretation. Metin Toker, the son-in-law of İsmet

[91] *Millet Meclisi Tutanak Dergisi*, vol. 32, term 1, sess. 3, 7 October 1964, p. 327.

[92] *United States Security Agreements and Commitments Abroad*, pp. 1834-1835.

[93] Metin Toker, "İsmet Paşa ile 4 Buhranlı Yıl", *Milliyet*, 7 February 1969, p. 5.

[94] G. S. Harris, *Troubled Alliance*, p. 107, H. Şahin, *Gece Gelen Mektup*, pp. 104-105.

[95] S. Bölükbaşı, *Turkish-American Relations and Cyprus*, p. 76.

[96] Ibid., p. 76.

[97] Metin Toker's statement in M. A. Birand et al., *12 Mart*, p. 105.

[98] G. S. Harris, *Troubled Alliance*, p. 114, H. Şahin, *Gece Gelen Mektup*, p. 105, M. A. Birand et al., *12 Mart*, p. 104. In their interviews with the author former Turkish foreign ministers Osman Olcay and Ü. H. Bayülken confirmed this point.

[99] G. S. Harris, *Troubled Alliance*, p. 114.

[100] M. Tamkoç, *The Warrior Diplomats*, pp. 266-267.

İnönü, wrote in his article: "in those days İsmet İnönü was reluctant to enter a war on Cyprus since he thought that joining the fighting in Cyprus would be like inserting a stick in a beehive... Beyond political disagreements, it became apparent that we were not ready technically for a military operation against the island.[101] Haluk Şahin claimed in his book on the Johnson letter that a high-ranking Turkish diplomat told him about the real intention of Turkey at that time. According to this diplomat, Turkey was not ready militarily for an intervention in Cyprus. In spite of all preparations and threats of intervention, Turkey would not land on the island. But Prime Minister İnönü was trying to deter the Greek forces by using the threat of military intervention, therefore some Turkish jets flew above the island. Eventually the American rejection of intervention was gained, thus the United States was held responsible for non-intervention.[102]

Before closing the section on the Johnson letter, it should be mentioned that J. M. Landau's article, "Johnson's Letter to İnönü and Greek Lobbying at the White House", suggests that the campaigning of Greek-Americans on the Cyprus question influenced the timing of the Johnson letter and its undiplomatic, brutal tone.[103] According to Landau's research, Greek-American individuals, various associations of Greek people including the Orthodox Church, bombarded President Johnson with letters and cables urging him to pressurise Turkey not to invade Cyprus. It appeared from the texts of messages that this Greek campaign was conducted under some sort of over-all organisation. Many messages referred to Johnson's candidacy for presidency, thus reminding him of the Greek-American power to raise voter support for the Democratic Party. President Johnson was aware of the importance of Greek-American votes for the presidential election in November 1964. Greek-Americans were far more numerous than Turkish ones and were located in some of the big urban centres that controlled large numbers of electors. Some Democrats, including Johnson, were concerned that American policy toward the Cyprus issue would affect the votes of Greek-Americans and that Republican candidate Goldwater would gain their votes by trading on the Cyprus question. Landau concludes in his study that "these factors [White House lobbying, the number of Greek-Americans, the approaching presidential elections] evidently combined to influence the timing of the [Johnson] letter and probably account for its no-nonsense tone."[104]

İnönü's Response to Johnson

Turkish Prime Minister İnönü sent a letter to American President Johnson on 13 June 1964 to respond to Johnson's arguments against a Turkish intervention in Cyprus.[105] Firstly, İnönü stated that the Turkish government, at Johnson's request, had postponed its decision to exercise its right of unilateral action in Cyprus, which was granted by the Treaty of Guarantee. Secondly, he expressed the disappointment of Turkish rulers with the American warning: "Your message, both in wording and content, has been disappointing for any ally

---

[101] Metin Toker, "İsmet Paşa ile 4 Buhranlı Yıl", *Milliyet,* 7 February 1969, p. 5.

[102] H. Şahin, *Gece Gelen Mektup,* pp. 104-105.

[103] Jacob M. Landau, *Johnson's 1964 Letter to İnönü and Greek Lobbying at the White House*, (Jerusalem: The Hebrew University Press, 1979).

[104] Ibid., p. 18.

[105] "Prime Minister İnönü's Response to President Johnson, 13 June 1964", *Middle East Journal*, vol. 20, summer 1966, pp. 388-393.

like Turkey who has always been giving the most serious attention to its relations of alliance with the United States and has brought to the fore substantial divergences of opinion in various fundamental matters pertaining to these relations." Thirdly, as a response to Johnson's claim that Turkey did not consult with the United States before taking any action in Cyprus, İnönü explained that on several occasions Turkey informed American leaders of its decision to intervene in Cyprus, and that when the United States opposed its decisions Turkey complied with American demands though no positive development was achieved in the Cyprus question.

Fourthly, İnönü clarified that, contrary to Johnson's claim, Turkey did consult with the other guarantor powers before deciding to take action against Cyprus. Fifthly, the Turkish prime minister reiterated that Turkey's compliance with American warnings did not mean that it gave up its right to intervene in Cyprus under international agreements. Sixthly, İnönü described how Turkish rulers were disappointed with Johnson's warning that if the Soviet Union attacked Turkey because of its action in Cyprus the NATO countries would not come to the aid of Turkey. Finally, the Turkish premier stated: "As a member of the [NATO] alliance our nation is fully conscious of her duties and rights. We do not pursue any other aim than the settlement of the Cyprus problem in compliance with the provisions of the existing treaties. Such a settlement is likely to be reached if you lend your support and give effect with your supreme authority to the sense of justice inherent in the character of the American nation." At the end of his letter İnönü accepted Johnson's invitation to Washington to discuss the Cyprus problem.

The Johnson letter constitutes the most important event of US-Turkish contacts on the Cyprus question, which affected the subsequent situation of relations between the two countries. It is clear that the Americans heavily pressured Turkish authorities to prevent their intervention in Cyprus. The Turks had expected US opposition to their planned action but the severe tone of the US warning certainly disappointed them to the extent they began to have doubts on the value of their alliance with the United States. Up to that point they had not faced a US action which appeared to treat Turkey as a satellite. As proud people, the Turks could not stomach Johnson's threats which put Turkey in a position of puppet state which was expected to listen to advice from its big partner. The most unacceptable thing for Turkish rulers was the use of the US-Turkish alliance (which was supposed to serve Turkish interests) by the Americans as a threat to prevent their action in a vital national interest. The Americans probably made a mistake by ignoring realities of Turkish politics and interests and by concentrating only on prevention of Turkish intervention which was expected to bring grave dangers for NATO and US interests.[106]

AMERICAN MEDIATION EFFORTS ON THE CYPRUS PROBLEM

George Ball's Visit to Greece and Turkey

From the outset of the Cyprus crisis the United States tried to pursue a policy which would not alienate both Greece and Turkey. After a Turkish military operation against Cyprus was prevented through the harsh warning of the Johnson letter, American President Johnson

---

[106] M. Stearns, *Entangled Alliance*, p. 24.

felt that an equally severe presentation should be made to Greek rulers, warning them not to provoke the Turks on the Cyprus question. Johnson also thought that neither the NATO machinery nor the United Nations mediation efforts would provide a solution to the Cyprus issue, and that therefore the United States should intervene in the matter directly, offering its mediation between the concerned parties. He considered it necessary to encourage Turkey and Greece to find a solution to the problem through bilateral talks. In order to achieve these aims, Under-Secretary of State George Ball was dispatched to Greece and Turkey in mid-June 1964.

When George Ball was about to return to the United States after attending the United Nations conference on trade and development at Geneva, Secretary of State Rusk called him from Washington, telling him that President Johnson was worried about Cyprus and wanted him to go to Greece and Turkey. On 10 June 1964 Ball arrived in Athens and held talks with Prime Minister Papandreou. He told Papandreou that the Cyprus problem was a threat to world peace, it worried the NATO members and therefore "it is imperative that the matter be settled definitively."[107] Summarising Johnson's letter to İnönü, Ball said that "disaster was avoided only by President Johnson's forceful intervention and his adamant insistence that there could be no war between NATO allies"[108] and he added that if Greece did not show greater co-operation, the United States would not take such a hard line again.[109]

According to accounts by Andreas Papandreou, Prime Minister Papandreou was disappointed with Ball's warning. "Would the United States sit back and let a NATO member, armed and financed by NATO, attack a NATO ally? If this were the case, what was the nature of the Western alliance?"[110] Papandreou complained that all the trouble in Cyprus stemmed from Turkey's invasion threats. As he later reported to the State Department, Ball's response was as follows: "I told him I knew that one; then I said I believed he was too well grounded in philosophy to overlook the complexity of any inter-theory of causation. I told him nobody could determine how the threat of intervention contributed to the turbulence over Cyprus, nor how the turbulence gave reality to the intervention threat. I said he should know that the explanation he offered was oversimplification."[111]

George Ball also told Papandreou that the United States had no formula for a Cyprus settlement, was committed to no side in the matter and only insisted that some solution should be found very quickly. He had known that both Greece and Turkey wanted the United States to offer at least some outline for a settlement but the USA would not do so because any proposal from America would be rejected by one or another side of the crisis.[112] Then Ball pressed Papandreou to undertake talks with Turkish Prime Minister İnönü.[113] He said that the Cyprus crisis was so tangled and so complicated that it required concessions from both Greece and Turkey. President Johnson's opinion was that only the prime ministers of the two countries could work out a satisfactory formula for a settlement. Ball stated: "If you, Mr Prime Minister, and the Turkish government, take no immediate and effective action, the Cyprus crisis can expand into war, or open the way to communism in the eastern

---

[107] E. Weintall and C. Bartlett, *Facing the Brink*, p. 25.
[108] Ibid., pp. 25-26.
[109] G. Ball, *The Past Has Another Pattern*, p. 353.
[110] A. Papandreou, *Democracy At Gunpoint*, p. 101.
[111] E. Weintall and C. Bartlett, *Facing the Brink*, p. 26.
[112] Ibid., p. 26.
[113] G. Ball, *The Past Has Another Pattern*, p. 353, A. Papandreou, *Democracy At Gunpoint*, p. 101.

Mediterranean."[114] Papandreou seemed unmoved, he did not accept Ball's proposal. In Ball's words, "against all the evidence, he [Papandreou] still seemed to assume that Greece could pursue its goal of Enosis without danger of the Turks invading Cyprus, since he apparently took it for granted that the United States would always stand ready to thwart the Turks."[115]

Nevertheless, George Ball persuaded Papandreou to visit the United States to have talks with President Johnson. Papandreou's condition was that "his visit to Washington [would] not be interpreted as meaning that he would be willing either to meet with İnönü or to bypass the United Nations [mediation on the Cyprus question]."[116] In Ball's opinion, Papandreou's realistic attitude toward Makarios was another good result of his meeting with Papandreou. In Ball's words, "the Archbishop had... alarmed responsible Greek opinion by his flirtations with Moscow and Khrushchev... Papandreou implied that the Archbishop might be excluded from negotiations aimed at settling it [the Cyprus issue], which... was exactly what I had in mind."[117]

George Ball arrived in Ankara on 11 June 1964 and told journalists that he came to Turkey only to learn views of Turkish officials on the situation in Cyprus and that he brought neither any formula of settlement for the Cyprus crisis nor any proposal to be given to the parties to the problem.[118] In his meeting with Prime Minister İnönü, in his words, Ball "reassured him regarding the warmth of America's friendship for Turkey and our desire to co-operate closely with the Turks in resolving a festering quarrel... America, I told him, was not partial to the Greek side; indeed, we recognised that the Greek Cypriot majority had largely created the problem by terrorising the Turkish Cypriots. I made clear that we totally mistrusted Makarios."[119] To show his confidence in the Turks, Ball revealed to İnönü his meeting with Papandreou, and the latter's insistence on Enosis as a solution of the Cyprus problem.[120]

As Ball stated in his memoirs, "İnönü was deeply troubled and personally hurt by the scolding he had received from President [Johnson]." After Ball gave reassurances, İnönü told him that the American "attempt to promote a settlement based on strong principles is an encouraging development, but experience had shown that principles are sometimes abandoned when the time comes to translate them into concrete measures."[121] However, İnönü welcomed the change in the attitude of the Greek government toward Makarios, saying that it was one of "the first rays of light in the dark situation." At the end of the meeting İnönü privately told Ball that Johnson's letter included "all the juridical thunderbolts that could be assembled. And, of course, as a result, you have committed some errors and some unjust things. Our foreign office will answer the thunderbolts."[122] On the same day, after he talked to George Ball, Turkish Foreign Minister Erkin told journalists that America was involved in the Cyprus question very actively and that she wanted the problem to be solved decisively and very quickly."[123] The joint communiqué which was issued at the end of George Ball's talks

---

[114] E. Weintall and C. Bartlett, *Facing the Brink*, p. 26.
[115] G. Ball, *The Past Has Another Pattern*, p. 353.
[116] A. Papandreou, *Democracy At Gunpoint*, p. 101.
[117] G. Ball, *The Past Has Another Pattern*, p. 353.
[118] *Cumhuriyet*, 12 June 1964.
[119] G. Ball, *The Past Has Another Pattern*, p. 354.
[120] E. Weintall and C. Bartlett, *Facing the Brink*, p. 27.
[121] G. Ball, *The Past Has Another Pattern*, p. 354.
[122] E. Weintall and C. Bartlett, *Facing the Brink*, p. 28.
[123] M. Gönlübol et al., *Olaylarla Türk Dış Politikası*, p. 397.

with Turkish officials stated that America believed that any solution of the Cyprus problem should be compatible with the interests of both Turkey and Greece.[124]

In the opinion of Windsor, George Ball was unsuccessful in his mission which was "to revive the tripartite machinery of the original guarantees [as regulated by the Treaty of Guarantee] -but this time with the United States as an independent arbitrator, helping the other three [Greece, Turkey and Britain] to work out the conditions for a settlement." The reasons which were cited by Windsor for the failure of Ball's mission could be summarised as follows: "The United Nations had taken over the most important function of the tripartite machinery: the maintenance of peace in Cyprus. The three powers had no responsibility toward Cyprus as they had had in the early days of the crisis." Only Turkey continued to threaten to intervene in Cyprus and if she could not be restrained by the United Nations and NATO, she also could not be prevented by the tripartite machinery. Another condition for the success of Ball's mission was that Greece should disassociate itself from the Cyprus administration and this seemed unlikely at that time. Under these circumstances "Greece and Turkey could not be brought to concert their interests in Cyprus by appeals to their solidarity as members of NATO."[125] Windsor's explanations also give clues for the failure of the American mediation efforts in July and August 1964.

İnönü's Visit to the United States

Before going to the United States, Turkish Prime Minister İsmet İnönü decided to get a vote of confidence of the Turkish Parliament on the government's Cyprus policy because there was a great deal of public criticism in Turkey on the developments in Cyprus in the aftermath of the prevention of Turkish military action by the Johnson letter. On 19 June 1964 the İnönü government won the vote of confidence but only with a six-vote margin (200 to 194).[126] İnönü's visit to the United States took place between 22 and 26 June 1964. The joint Turkish-American communiqué which was issued on 23 June 1964 at the end of the talks between Johnson and İnönü, reaffirmed the validity of the existing treaties on Cyprus as a starting point for a new solution mentioning "the binding affects of treaties."[127] This was a great success for Turkish rulers because they based their struggle on Cyprus on the validity of the Cyprus treaties which gave Turkey the right of unilateral intervention in Cyprus. In his press conference in New York on 25 June 1964, the Turkish Prime Minister explained his government's Cyprus policy: "We believe in the present regime in Cyprus, which based on the Cypriot constitution and the international agreements on Cyprus. But we even accept Enosis on the condition that it should be implemented with its original form, i.e. one part of the island is left to Turkey, another to Greece."[128]

According to accounts by Nihat Erim, who was in İnönü's official delegation, officials from the State Department inquired the opinion of the Turkish delegation on the proposal of

---

[124] *Cumhuriyet*, 12 June 1964.

[125] Philip Windsor, *NATO and the Cyprus Crisis*, Adelphi Papers No. 14, (London: the Institute for Strategic Studies, 1964), p. 15.

[126] M. Gönlübol et al., *Olaylarla Türk Dış Politikası*, p. 397, M. Sarıca et. al., *Kıbrıs Sorunu*, p. 76.

[127] N. Erim, *Bildiğim ve Gördüğüm Ölçüler İçinde Kıbrıs*, p. 329, *Dışişleri Bakanlığı Belleteni*, July 1964, pp. 16-17, *Keesing's Contemporary Archives 1963-1964*, vol. 14, p. 20268.

[128] N. Erim, *Bildiğim ve Gördüğüm Ölçüler İçinde Kıbrıs*, p. 330, M. Sarıca et. al., *Kıbrıs Sorunu*, p. 76.

leaving Cyprus to Greece in return for a Greek island on the Aegean Sea.[129] Erim also cites in his book that while they were in New York they received the news that General Grivas (the Greek general who fought for Cyprus's independence and was famous with his pro-Enosis ideas) had landed on Cyprus. When it was mentioned to American officials at a dinner, George Ball told the Turks that this should not be considered a bad development since General Grivas had gone there to fight communists not the Turks.[130] It seems that Enosis in return for some concessions to Turks was on the agenda even at that time.

After returning to Turkey from his visits to the United States, Britain and France, Turkish Prime Minister İnönü told journalists on 2 July 1964 that main disagreement points on the Cyprus question between Turkey and its allies had disappeared and that therefore he was happy with his visits. However, he stated that during his visits they did not talk about a certain formula of settlement for the problem.[131]

Papandreou's Visit to the United States

On 24 June 1964, two days after the Turkish Prime saw Johnson, the Greek Prime Minister, George Papandreou, and President Johnson held talks in Washington. During Papandreou's visit, President Johnson and other high-level US officials allegedly pressured him to have direct talks with Turkish Prime Minister İnönü on the Cyprus problem by threatening that otherwise they would not prevent a Turkish military intervention in the island. Andreas Papandreou, who was present during the talks, reported this meeting as follows: "President Johnson talked: The United States was faced by a possibility of a confrontation between two allies. It could not take either side, and it could not afford to stop Turkey once more from intervening by military force. It had done so already on a number of occasions. He did not have a formula for the solution of the problem. Such a formula could be found by direct talks between the two interested parties, Greece and Turkey. İnönü was still in Washington. Would George Papandreou be ready to meet with him? İnönü was willing. He, Johnson, had selected Camp David, a well-suited retreat for just that purpose. An American, Dean Acheson, would be on hand to offer his advice, his guidance. The Western alliance could not afford an outbreak of war between Turkey and Greece. Those two countries had the responsibility to find a solution. If they did, he was prepared to come to Greece for a visit and announce that the United States would generously support an economic development program... George Papandreou said: A summit meeting between Greece and Turkey contained serious dangers if a basis of agreement had not been established beforehand. If İnönü and Papandreou met and reached no agreement the next step would be war. Did President Johnson have some formula in mind? Johnson retorted that he had no particular plan in mind. He reiterated that he believed in negotiation... Papandreou should meet with İnönü, that summit-level negotiations should take place."[132]

According to accounts by Andreas Papandreou, the next day, on 25 June 1964, Secretary of State Dean Rusk visited the Greek delegation and warned them again that if Greece did not follow Johnson's proposal, Turkey would attack Cyprus and the United States would not lift a

---

[129] N. Erim, *Bildiğim ve Gördüğüm Ölçüler İçinde Kıbrıs*, p. 328.
[130] Ibid., p. 334.
[131] M. Gönlübol et al., *Olaylarla Türk Dış Politikası*, pp. 398-399.
[132] A. Papandreou, *Democracy At Gunpoint*, p. 102.

finger to stop it. During the dinner at the Greek ambassador's house, Secretary of Defence McNamara implicitly threatened the Greek Prime Minister, telling him that Turkey had a powerful air force and if a war took place between Turkey and Greece, the Turkish planes would literally burn up the Greek countryside.[133]

George Ball writes in his book that President Johnson "liked Prime Minister İnönü, with whom he could talk straight forwardly. If the Greek leader had shown anything like the same understanding, serious progress could have been made."[134] Johnson, Rusk and Ball had pushed Papandreou hard but he remained unmoved. In an open press conference Papandreou announced that the London-Zurich agreements had lost their validity and that the Greek government supported independence for Cyprus and its right of self-determination. He rejected direct bilateral negotiation with the Turks on the Cyprus problem because "no one is more competent to do that than the United Nations mediator."[135]

In Andreas Papandreou' account, on 26 June 1964 the Greek delegation met with President Johnson and other American officials in the White House. "George Ball proposed that a Greek representative meet, separately from the Turkish representative, with Dean Acheson in Geneva. In this fashion, there would be no direct talks between the Greeks and the Turks, and George Papandreou's objection would be met. George Papandreou pointed out that this arrangement bypassed the United Nations. If the United Nations were willing to supervise this pattern of negotiations in Geneva, he would have no objection."[136] On the same day, George Ball flew to New York and talked to the UN Secretary General, U Thant, to sell the American plan to him. He suggested to the Secretary General that Greek and Turkish representatives meet with Acheson, "who was almost a legendary force figure in Greece and Turkey" because of his substantial role in formulating the Truman doctrine in 1947. Ball had suggested Camp David as meeting place. U Thant strongly opposed the American proposal because it might imply that the United States was taking the diplomatic initiative away from the United Nations. U Thant's suggestion was that such a meeting should take place in Geneva not in America and that UN mediator Sakari Tuomioja should meet with Greek and Turkish representatives separately. Otherwise, Papandreou would not accept it. As a compromise, Ball and U Thant agreed that Acheson should go to Geneva and set himself up in the next room so as to be available for consultation.[137] The next day George Ball met with the Greek delegation in New York and warned them again that if a solution were not found in a short time, Turkey would attack Cyprus and that the United States would not intervene.[138] When U Thant officially informed Papandreou of the American proposal which was agreed between him and Ball, Papandreou reluctantly accepted it.

---

[133] Ibid., pp. 102-103.
[134] G. Ball, *The Past Has Another Pattern*, p. 355, *Keesing's Contemporary Archives 1963-1964*, vol. 14, p. 20268.
[135] G. Ball, *The Past Has Another Pattern*, p. 355.
[136] A. Papandreou, *Democracy At Gunpoint*, p. 103.
[137] G. Ball, *The Past Has Another Pattern*, pp. 355-356, E. Weintall and C. Bartlett, *Facing the Brink*, pp. 28-29.
[138] A. Papandreou, *Democracy At Gunpoint*, pp. 103-104.

Chapter 4

THE AMERICAN MEDIATION ON THE CYPRUS QUESTION (JULY 1964-SEPTEMBER 1964) AND AMERICAN AND TURKISH INTERESTS ON THE PROBLEM

In spite of their acceptance of the UN mediation on the Cyprus question, the Americans privately did not trust it in solving the problem and therefore they wanted to go their own way. The United States was the leader of the Western security establishment and could pressurise its two allies to solve a potentially dangerous problem for the whole Western defence system. But to alienate at least one of these allies and thus to weaken the cohesion of the Western security arrangements was another danger. The biggest and the most serious American mediation effort on the Cyprus question came to existence under these circumstances and coincided with the end of the first phase of the Cyprus crisis. Analyses of American and Turkish interests on the Cyprus question, given toward the end of the chapter, comprehends all periods and even concerns the present situation.

THE AMERICAN MEDIATION EFFORTS ON THE CYPRUS PROBLEM

US Efforts to Promote Talks Between Turkey and Greece

After a Turkish military intervention was forestalled at the beginning of June 1964 by the Johnson letter, American officials had concentrated their efforts on bringing Turkish and Greek representatives together for bilateral talks. In their opinion, only through direct talks between the two countries could Turkey give up its intervention in Cyprus and Greece could pressurise Greek Cypriots to end their attacks against the Turkish community. Since Turkey seemed more willing for bilateral talks, and had already been scolded by Johnson, American officials put more pressure on the Greek side.

On 6 June 1964, Secretary of State Rusk instructed the American ambassador to Greece to warn the Greek leaders about the close possibility of outbreak of a war because of Cyprus. He wrote: "it is important that Greeks in Athens (and Nicosia) understand fully that the sword of Damocles is still hanging by a thread, now one fiber weaker."[1] On 11 June 1964, President Johnson summoned the Greek ambassador to the United States, Alexander Matssos, to the White House to tell him that Greece should negotiate with Turkey to reach a settlement on Cyprus. The United States had saved Greece from war once, but in the future America might not be influential in stopping Turkey. Johnson said, "if I can't get you to talk, I can't keep the Turks from moving."[2]

Johnson's talks with the Turkish and Greek prime ministers on 22-25 June 1964 seemed influential in persuading both sides for bilateral talks. However, in order to ensure that talks would be held George Ball advised Johnson to send "further letters to Papandreou and İnönü, appealing to them to try to find a solution through negotiations."[3] But Johnson's letter to Papandreou, dated as 2 July 1964, caused great resentment on the Greek side. The letter urged Papandreou to send delegates to Geneva, reiterating the American warning that if Turkey intervened in Cyprus the United States would stand aside.[4] In the view of American officials Johnson's letter was a message of conciliation, but in George Ball's words, "Papandreou responded with a childish tirade against the United States, asserting that Johnson's letter was an ultimatum of the same kind Greece had received from the Nazis in 1940."[5] Papandreou's talk to the American embassy official who brought the letter was cited by Weintall and Bartlett as follows: "The Johnson letter was an ultimatum... and Greece was no more prepared to accept such a fiat than it had been willing to accept commands from the Nazis in 1940. The United States professed to lead the free world.... but where was its plan for a Cyprus settlement? The United State professed devotion to the principle of self-determination,... but why would it not support that principle on Cyprus?... The United States seemed to imply it would stand aside if Greece and Turkey went to war over Cyprus... Why did the United States not forbid Turkey as well as Greece to use their American-supplied weapons except in self-defence?" Nevertheless, at the end of the meeting, Papandreou told the American official that he would send delegates to Geneva.[6]

While encouraging Turks and Greeks to have direct talks under the auspices of American mediation, American officials emphasised that their efforts were not intended to forestall the UN mediation. When the news that the United States would mediate directly between Greece and Turkey began to circulate and when the American administration was criticised in the United Nations because of its attempt, the White House issued a statement claiming that the American initiative was not incompatible with the UN mediation efforts. The statement said that the peace-keeping and peace-making role belonged entirely to the United Nations and the only aim of the American efforts was to prevent an armed combat in the eastern Mediterranean.[7]

---

[1] H. W. Brands, Jr., "America Enters the Cyprus Tangle, 1964", *Middle Eastern Studies*, vol. 23, No. 3, July 1987, p. 355.

[2] Ibid., p. 355.

[3] George Ball, *The Past Has Another Pattern: Memoirs*, (New York, London: W. W. Norton, 1982), p. 356.

[4] Van Coufoudakis, "United States Foreign Policy and the Cyprus Question" in Michael A. Attalides (ed.), *Cyprus Reviewed: A Seminar on the Cyprus Problem*, (Nicosia: Jus Cypri Association, 1977), p. 113, Halil İbrahim Salih, *Cyprus; the Impact of Diverse Nationalism in a State*, (Alabama: University of Alabama Press, 1978), p. 47.

[5] G. Ball, *The Past Has Another*, p. 356.

[6] Edward Weintall and Charles Bartlett, *Facing the Brink: A Study of Crisis Diplomacy*, (London: Hutchinson, 1967), p. 30.

[7] Dimitri S. Bitsios, *Cyprus: the Vulnerable Republic*, (Thessaloniki, Greece: Institute for Balkan Studies, 1975), p. 166.

The Acheson Mission

Before former American Secretary of State Dean Acheson left for Geneva to mediate between Turkish and Greek representatives, George Ball and Phillips Talbot defined the American position on the Cyprus problem to him on 2 July 1964. Allegedly, American officials regarded an independent state of Cyprus as a threat to American interests because the current situation led Turkish rulers to threaten to intervene militarily and hence it created the danger of a Greco-Turkish war. It was weakening the Greek and Turkish ties with the United States, undermining the cohesion of NATO, creating a serious problem for the United Nations and strengthening the position of the Cyprus communist party, AKEL, and the USSR on Cyprus. The most suitable solution for the Cyprus problem could be achieved through Enosis (the unification of the island with Greece) with some concessions to Turkey such as the return of a Greek island to Turkish hands; a Turkish military presence on Cyprus; resettlement of Turkish Cypriots that desired to leave and pledges by Greece to apply the Lausanne Treaty minority provisions on Turkish Cypriots, disarm all irregulars, eliminate AKEL's influence and neutralise Makarios' political capability.[8]

In George Ball's account, before leaving he and Dean Acheson considered every possible solution for the Cyprus question, including partition and resettlement, federal, confederal schemes and a cantonal plan and double Enosis (unification of Cyprus with Greece in return for a Turkish presence on the island).[9]

As agreed between the UN Secretary General and American officials, the Geneva talks between Turkish and Greek representatives began on 8 July 1964 under the chairmanship of UN mediator Sakari Tuomioja. No Cypriot representative had been called to the talks. Dean Acheson was present at Geneva as the special envoy of President Johnson but he undertook the actual mediation responsibility. On 14 July 1964 Acheson submitted American proposals to the Turkish and Greek delegations headed by Nihat Erim and Nicolareisis. Acheson's proposals which were known as the Acheson plan included the following points: 1- Cyprus was to be free in choosing to unify itself with Greece (Enosis). 2- On the Carpas peninsula in the north-east of Cyprus a territory was to be given to Turkey. This territory was to become an indivisible part of Turkey and Turkey was to have full sovereignty over it and to have the right of stationing as large a military force as it wished on the territory. Thus, Turkey would be able to safeguard the lives of Turkish Cypriots and its own security. The territory would also provide for a refuge for Turkish Cypriots who were under Greek control. 3- In one, two or three small areas in which Turkish Cypriots were in majority, the Turkish community were to have the right of local self-administration. 4- Turkish Cypriots living under Greek control in other parts of the island were to enjoy all human and minority rights granted by the Treaty of Lausanne to Turks remaining in Greece. 5- An international commissioner was to be appointed either by the United Nations or by the International Court of Justice to observe whether or not the Turkish Cypriots' communal and individual rights were being respected. 6- The Greek island of Kastellorizion (Meis) was to be ceded to Turkey.[10]

In Acheson's opinion, the time was ripe for his proposals because "the Greek interest seemed to pass through the formal stage of unconditional independence to Enosis, with

---

[8] Van Coufoudakis, "United States Foreign Policy and the Cyprus Question", p. 114.
[9] G. Ball, *The Past Has Another*, p. 356.
[10] Nihat Erim, *Bildiğim ve Gördüğüm Ölçüler İçinde Kıbrıs*, (Ankara: Ajans-Türk, 1975), pp. 351-359, H. İ. Salih, *Cyprus*, pp. 47-48.

guarantees of rights of the Turkish minority, vaguely described as adequate. The Turks were prepared to accept Enosis for some part of the island with Greece, provided there was a compensating Enosis of another part with Turkey, a solution called double Enosis."[11] In Acheson's own words, his plan was to bring the union of Cyprus with Greece but also provide for Turkey "a military presence unhampered by the need for tripartite consent at every turn. A sequestered base for ground, air and sea forces not only could be a defence for Cyprus but prevent its being used hostilely against Turkey, could defend the sea approaches to the south Turkish seaports, and be a constant reminder on the island of Turkish presence and interests."[12]

Some American officials thought that the Acheson plan would solve the Cyprus problem permanently to the advantage of the United States and the West. If it were implemented, Cyprus would be removed from the non-alignment camp and would be placed in the NATO sphere. The power of Makarios and AKEL which were thought to be harmful to Western interests would be neutralised. Friction between two NATO allies would be eliminated and the alienation of Turkey and Greece from the Western alliance would be prevented. Both Greece and Turkey would be kept happy since each would think that its viewpoint was accepted. The extension of Soviet influence to the region would be blocked.[13] For other American officials, the Acheson plan was just a trial balloon, a suggestion for the Cyprus problem not a formula to which American rulers were firmly tied.[14]

For Turkish rulers, the Acheson plan seemed to satisfy Turkey's interests, therefore they generally accepted the plan as a basis for further negotiation. Their main concern was that the sovereign base area which would be left to Turkey should be large enough to meet Turkey's security interests. On 18 July 1964 the head of Turkish delegation, Nihat Erim, received instructions from Prime Minister İnönü to continue negotiations on the basis of the Acheson plan and to try to achieve the enlargement of Turkish sovereign base area. The Turkish cabinet also authorised Erim to negotiate Acheson's proposals.[15] During the talks, while Erim emphasised Turkey's security interests on Cyprus and the necessity for Turkish control over a portion of the island, Turkish commander Turgut Sunalp claimed that the base area offered to Turkey was too small to provide for enough space for Turkey's military activities.[16]

On July 12, Acheson brought the Greek counter-proposals to the Turkish delegation. The Greeks accepted the cession of Meis to Turkey but rejected having a Turkish sovereign base area in Cyprus. They could give consent to the stationing of a Turkish military force in the British bases. The Turkish delegation totally rejected the Greek proposal stating that the British bases would not meet Turkey's security interests and that some territory had to be left under Turkey's sovereignty if the island was to be unified with Greece.[17] Meanwhile, on 30 July 1964, Greek Cypriot leader Makarios publicised Acheson's proposals in Athens and

---

[11] Dimitri S. Bitsios, *Cyprus,* p. 195.

[12] Polyvious G. Polyviou, *Cyprus: the Tragedy and the Challenge,* (Washington D. C.: American Hellenic Institute, 1975), p. 47, Thomas W. Adams and Alvin J. Cottrell, *Cyprus Between East and West,* (Baltimore: John Hopkins Press, 1968), p. 66.

[13] Theodore A. Couloumbis, *the United States, Greece and Turkey: the Troubled Triangle,* (New York: Praeger, 1983), p. 47, Michael A. Attalides, *Cyprus: Nationalism and International Politics,* (Edinburgh: Q Press Ltd., 1979), p. 19, P. N. Vanezis, *Makarios: Pragmatism v. Idealism,* (London: Abelard-Schuman, 1974), p. 133.

[14] Ellen B. Laipson, "Cyprus: A Quarter Century of US Diplomacy" in John T. A. Koumoulides (ed.), *Cyprus in Transition 1960-1985,* (London: Trigraph, 1986), p. 63.

[15] N. Erim, *Bildiğim ve Gördüğüm Ölçüler İçinde Kıbrıs,* pp. 360, 372.

[16] Ibid., pp. 347-350, 359-362.

[17] Ibid., pp. 363-366, 372-373.

announced that they would not accept the Acheson plan at all.[18] He was of the opinion that Acheson's solution would have resulted in the end of the existence of Cyprus as an independent sate and the partition of the island in a masked way.[19] On 6 August 1964, the Greek delegation's official proposal was presented to the Turkish representatives by Dean Acheson. The Greeks were totally opposed to the idea of cession of Cypriot territory to Turkey, instead they offered to lease a small base on the Carpas peninsula to Turkey for twenty-five years. The Turkish delegation rejected the Greek proposal.[20] Meanwhile, the Geneva talks were interrupted by the outbreak of new violence in Cyprus.

Before studying the August 1964 fighting in Cyprus, another American initiative on the Cyprus question, which was conducted by George Ball secretly, should be mentioned. American officials thought that exploiting the hostility between Makarios and Greek General Grivas could be useful in solving the Cyprus problem. Through the course of the summer 1964, the American intelligence reported that the antipathy between the two persons still existed and was growing. "Though Grivas was... a passionate advocate of Enosis", George Ball thought that "he might be easier to work with than Makarios" and established an underground contact with Grivas through Socrates Iliades, chief lieutenant to Grivas who was director of the defence of Cyprus.[21] After exile in Greece, Grivas had secretly returned to Cyprus in June 1964 to take charge of the Cypriot armed forces.[22] During their contact in the July-August 1964 period, Ball and Grivas agreed on a plan for Cyprus. According to the plan, Cyprus would be united with Greece and as compensation some bases would be turned over to Turkey. The plan provided protection for Turkish Cypriots remaining on the island and compensation for those wishing to leave. Makarios, who was the chief obstacle to such designs, would be ousted.[23] When clashes broke out in Cyprus in August, all these schemes were upset. In the opinion of Grivas, Makarios organised attacks against the Turks to break up the Geneva negotiations which discussed the double Enosis plan.[24]

The August 1964 Fighting in Cyprus

On 6 August 1964, the Greek Cypriot forces, equipped with heavy weaponry, launched a major attack from land and sea against the Turkish positions in the Kokkina-Mansoura area in the north-western part of the island. Their main aim was to neutralise the Kokkina beachhead which was allegedly used by Turkey as a landing spot to supply military equipment and men to Turkish Cypriots.[25] The United Nations Forces in the area were unable to stop the fighting, they made unsuccessful attempts to achieve cease-fire and to evacuate women and children.

---

[18] Ibid., p. 375.

[19] T. A. Couloumbis, *the United States, Greece and Turkey*, p. 47.

[20] N. Erim, *Bildiğim ve Gördüğüm Ölçüler İçinde Kıbrıs*, pp. 376-378.

[21] G. Ball, *The Past Has Another*, p. 357.

[22] *Keesing's Contemporary Archives, 1963-1964*, vol. 14, p. 20270.

[23] G. Ball, *The Past Has Another*, p. 357, V. Coufoudakis, "United States Foreign Policy and the Cyprus Question", p. 116, M. A. Attalides, *Cyprus: Nationalism and International Politics*, p. 70, H. W. Brands, Jr., "America Enters the Cyprus Tangle, 1964", p. 357, E. Weintall and C. Bartlett, *Facing the Brink*, p. 32.

[24] M. A. Attalides, *Cyprus: Nationalism and International Politics*, p. 70.

[25] Thomas Ehlrich, *Cyprus: 1958-1967*, (London: Oxford University Press, 1974), pp. 62-63, Robert Stephens, *Cyprus: A Place of Arms*, (London: Pall Mall Press, 1966), p. 196, Nancy Crawshaw, *the Cyprus Revolt: an Account of the Struggle for Union With Greece*, (London, Boston: G. Allen and Unwin, 1978), p. 371, H. I. Salih, *Cyprus*, p. 50, *Keesing's Contemporary Archives, 1963-1964*, vol. 14, p. 20265.

When Greek Cypriot forces rejected their calls, the UN forces withdrew.[26] In Turkey, the government was under substantial pressure from public opinion and military leaders to resort to military force to stop the Greek Cypriot attacks. The deterrent value of Turkey's intervention threats seemed to lessen because Turkey did not carry out its threats. Turkish politicians and leaders feared that, encouraged by Turkey's inactivity, Greek Cypriots would try to resolve the Cyprus question by force and remove the major pockets of Turkish Cypriot resistance. On 7 August 1964 the Turkish National Security Council met. Although almost all ministers and military commanders favoured aerial bombing to stop the fighting, Prime Minister İnönü rejected the idea since he was assured by American Ambassador Hare that Makarios was ready to stop the attacks.[27] As a result, the NSC decided to wait one more day before military operations. On the same day, the head of the Turkish delegation in the Geneva talks, Nihat Erim, told İnönü that he had the impression from his talks with American mediator Acheson that the Americans would not oppose a limited military action to give a lesson to Archbishop Makarios.[28]

When the Greek Cypriot attacks continued on 8 August 1964, the Turkish National Security Council decided to launch a limited air action on access roads being used by Greek Cypriots to save the Kokkina area and its inhabitants. Turkish Foreign Minister Erkin informed American Ambassador Hare of Turkey's decision to launch a limited military action against Cyprus and requested that the United States use all its influence with the Greek and Greek Cypriot governments to prevent the spread of violence in Cyprus and a possible war with Greece.[29] In the afternoon of the same day, Turkish jet fighters originally supplied by the United States bombed the positions of Greek forces around Kokkina.[30] In its statement to the public, the Turkish government announced that since the UN peace-keeping force could not stop the atrocities of Greek Cypriots, Turkey bombed the Kokkina-Mansoura area under the Treaty of Guarantee in order to protect the rights and security of Turkish Cypriots.[31] In New York, the Turkish representative to the United Nations called the Security Council to hold an emergency meeting and declared that the Turkish bombing was a limited action aimed at putting an end to the annihilation of the Turkish Cypriots. The Security Council met and listened also the complaint of the Greek Cypriot representative that Turkish invasion of Cyprus was very near. The Council did not adopt any resolution that day.[32] Meanwhile, the Greek government warned Turkey and notified the United States that unless the Turkish bombings were not stopped it would intervene to assist Greek Cypriots.[33]

American officials moved to contain the fighting in Cyprus and prevent a possible Greco-Turkish war. On the night of 8 August 1964, President Johnson sent identical letters to Makarios, Papandreou and İnönü, urging the greatest possible restraint. Johnson's letters stated that no statesman would wish to bear the responsibility for death and bloodshed, which

---

[26] T. Ehlrich, *Cyprus: 1958-1967*, p. 63, R. Stephens, *Cyprus*, p. 196.
[27] Suha Bölükbaşı, *Superpowers and the Third World: Turkish-American Relations and Cyprus*, (New York: University Press of America, 1988), p. 82.
[28] N. Erim, *Bildiğim ve Gördüğüm Ölçüler İçinde Kıbrıs*, p. 381.
[29] S. Bölükbaşı, *Turkish-American Relations and Cyprus*, pp. 82-83.
[30] *Keesing's Contemporary Archives, 1963-1964*, vol. 14, p. 20270.
[31] Murat Sarıca et. al., *Kıbrıs Sorunu*, (İstanbul: İstanbul Üniversitesi Yayınları, No. 2071, 1975), p. 81.
[32] D. S. Bitsios, *Cyprus*, p. 170.
[33] H. I. Salih, *Cyprus*, p. 51, E. Weintall and C. Bartlett, *Facing the Brink*, pp. 32-33.

were bound to accompany military operations.[34] In a companion message to Papandreou, Secretary of State Rusk urged the Greek prime minister to co-operate with General Grivas in neutralising Makarios, who was threatening a general massacre in Cyprus unless the Turkish air raids were not stopped. The next day, on August 9, Rusk sent a cable to the American ambassador to Greece, Henry Labouisse, instructing him to persuade Papandreou to prevent further attacks by Makarios against the Turkish Cypriots. Rusk's cable stated; the United States was urging the Turks to halt their air raids, Papandreou must abandon "horsetrading or equivocation or passionate oratory and act decisively to restore peace in Cyprus". If Makarios continued its attacks he would be publicly branded as a murderer. Pointing to the fact that Makarios had told the United States and Britain that it was seeking military intervention from the Soviet Union, Rusk advised Labouisse that it was essential to exclude Russian, United Arab Republic or other foreign troops from Cyprus.[35]

While the Turkish air raids against the Greek Cypriot positions continued, on the same day, August 9, in New York the British and American representatives to the United Nations tabled a draft resolution in the Security Council meeting.[36] The draft requested the interested parties to call for an immediate cease-fire, invited all parties to co-operate fully with the commander of the UN force in the re-establishment of peace and security and called all the UN members to refrain from any action liable to aggravate the situation or to contribute to spreading the hostilities. In presenting the draft to the Council, American Ambassador Adlai Stevenson emphasised that all hostilities should stop, because as long as any of them continued all would continue and it would mount up to a dangerous international war.[37] In the account of Bitsios, the Greek ambassador to the United Nations, Stevenson sought a balancing resolution because he was convinced that if the resolution were directed only to Turkey the Greek Cypriots would resume the hostilities.[38] The Security Council accepted the Anglo-American draft resolution and called on the Turks to stop their air attacks and on the Greek Cypriots to halt the fighting on the island. On the same day, abandoning his firm stance, Soviet Premier Khrushchev told Makarios that he was sympathised with his cause but believed a cease-fire would be a very important act to restore peace.[39]

On the same day, August 9, Khrushchev also sent a message to Turkish Prime Minister İnönü, calling on Turkey to end air raids against Cyprus. Khrushchev warned İnönü that Turkey should be aware of its responsibility stemmed from its military operation.[40] Since the Soviets were reluctant to help him, Makarios accepted the UN's cease-fire call. On 10 August 1964, the Turkish National Security Council met to discuss the latest situation. Some minister and military commanders strongly suggested to continue the air raids against Cyprus, land Turkish forces on the island and invade it.[41] Especially the commander of the Turkish Air Forces, İrfan Tansel, was in favour of bombing all Greek Cypriot positions in Cyprus.[42] However, Prime Minister İnönü ignored all objections and ordered cessation of air raids of

---

[34] E. Weintall and C. Bartlett, *Facing the Brink*, p. 33, H. W. Brands, Jr., "America Enters the Cyprus Tangle, 1964", p. 357, *Keesing's Contemporary Archives, 1963-1964,* vol. 14, p. 20266.

[35] E. Weintall and C. Bartlett, *Facing the Brink*, pp. 33-34.

[36] *Keesing's Contemporary Archives, 1963-1964,* vol. 14, p. 20265.

[37] D. S. Bitsios, *Cyprus*, pp. 173-174.

[38] Ibid., p. 174.

[39] E. Weintall and C. Bartlett, *Facing the Brink*, p. 34.

[40] S. Bölükbaşı, *Turkish-American Relations and Cyprus*, p. 83, N. Erim, *Bildiğim ve Gördüğüm Ölçüler İçinde Kıbrıs*, p. 385.

[41] N. Erim, *Bildiğim ve Gördüğüm Ölçüler İçinde Kıbrıs*, p. 393.

Turkish jet fighters. He informed the UN Security Council that in order to reconfirm Turkey's respect for the United Nations, his government decided to stop the actions of the Turkish air force.[43]

The Second Acheson Plan

On 15 August 1964 the Greek and Turkish representatives met again with the UN mediator and Dean Acheson in Geneva to resume the talks for a political settlement of the Cyprus question. On 20 August 1964, Dean Acheson put forward his so-called Second Acheson Plan whose main aim was to overcome the objections of the Greek side. In the account of Turkish representative Nihat Erim, Acheson told him that the new proposal was not his own but that of the State Department and of President Johnson. Acheson also stated that the American administration was worried about a Soviet intervention and therefore put forward the new plan to be agreed on by both Greece and Turkey and wanted him to work kindly and forcefully to persuade both sides to accept the plan.[44] The Second Acheson plan included the following points: 1- Cyprus was to be free in choosing independence or Enosis. 2- A military base on the Carpas peninsula was to be leased to Turkey for fifty years. 3- The Greek government was to give strong guarantees to the Turkish Cypriot community regarding human and minority rights. 4- With the consent of the Greek and Turkish governments, a high commissioner from the United Nations or any other organisations was to be appointed for Cyprus.[45]

Turkish officials rejected the second plan because it did not give Turkey a territory over which she would have full sovereignty, to be an integral part of the Turkish mainland. The renting of a base for a certain time was not acceptable to the Turks. On 21 August 1964, the Turkish delegation informed Acheson that the Turkish government decided to reject the plan because the renting of a small territory in return for Enosis did not meet Turkey's long-term security interests.[46]

Acheson told the Turkish representatives that he was not going to press the Greeks to make more concessions. The plan was the last opportunity to find a peaceful solution to the problem with the help of the American administration. If the Turks rejected it, no NATO countries would appreciate Turkey's position.[47] In Ankara, American Ambassador Hare presented the American proposal to Prime Minister İnönü on August 23, İnönü rejected the plan, saying that they could continue the Geneva talks only on the basis of the first Acheson plan.[48]

The second Acheson plan seemed a favourable proposal to the Greeks. They accepted it as a basis of discussion. Greek Prime Minister Papandreou was reported to have told his associates; "listen, we are being offered an apartment building and subletting only one

---

[42] Cüneyt Arcayürek, *Yeni Demokrasi, Yeni Arayışlar*, (Ankara: Bilgi Yayınevi, 1984), p. 283.
[43] Metin Tamkoç, *The Warrior Diplomats: Guardians of National Security and Modernization of Turkey*, (Salt Lake City: University of Utah Press, 1976), p. 275, *Keesing's Contemporary Archives, 1963-1964*, vol. 14, p. 20266.
[44] N. Erim, *Bildiğim ve Gördüğüm Ölçüler İçinde Kıbrıs*, p. 399.
[45] Ibid., pp. 399-400, M. Sarıca et. al., *Kıbrıs Sorunu*, pp. 82-83, H. I. Salih, *Cyprus*, p. 49.
[46] N. Erim, *Bildiğim ve Gördüğüm Ölçüler İçinde Kıbrıs*, p. 401.
[47] Ibid., p. 402.
[48] Ibid., pp. 403-404, Metin Toker, "İsmet Paşa ile 4 Buhranlı Yıl", *Milliyet*, 11 February 1969, p. 5.

penthouse to our neighbours, the Turks."[49] Nevertheless, when the Makarios administration strongly opposed the new Acheson proposals, the Greek government had no option but to reject them.[50] In fact, Dean Acheson was convinced from the beginning of the second round of talks that the Turkish and Greek representatives would not agree on a settlement. As early as 18 August 1964 he sent a message to George Ball, advising the American administration "liquidate" its Geneva effort and call him back to Washington. Acheson suggested that the United States should continue its close contact with Greece and Turkey to prevent Cyprus from becoming a satellite of the USSR. Ball flatly rejected Acheson's proposal of liquidating the American effort, stating that it would encourage Makarios to drive the island into another crisis. Ball expressed his fear that if the talks were ended without a solution, the Turks could resort to military action and suggested that pressures must be maintained on both the Greeks and the Turks. In his reply to Ball, Acheson stated that the United States should stop irritating the Turks and Greeks by trying to pressure them into a Cyprus agreement. If the United States walked away, both sides would realise that they alone were responsible for finding a way out. Finally Acheson said that if an American retreat from Cyprus brought on a showdown with Makarios, "then let it come."[51]

After the rejection of the second Acheson plan by both sides, the American administration adjourned its Geneva efforts on 31 August 1964 by calling Acheson to Washington and thus the Geneva talks collapsed without producing any settlement.

The Aftermath of the Geneva Talks

After he returned to Washington, Dean Acheson met with President Johnson and other top administration officials in September 1964 in order to discuss a way out of the Cyprus deadlock. According to the article by Brands, Acheson stated that a stalemate was reached in the Cyprus question. The main reasons were Papandreou's weakness and Makarios' strength. Each passing day Makarios was becoming stronger while the Turks were becoming more impatient. If the situation were allowed to continue in this direction, a violent and uncontrolled Turkish invasion of the island would be inevitable. Acheson and Ball argued that the only solution to the problem was the fait accompli of a controlled Turkish invasion of the island. In their plan, the Turks would seize the part of Cyprus which they would have received under the first Acheson plan and then the Greek and Greek Cypriots would instantly proclaim the unification of the rest of Cyprus with Greece.[52]

In fact, Acheson had raised the issue with the Turks during the Geneva talks and had received a positive response. On 4 August 1964 Acheson told the Turkish delegation that he did not advise them to resort to military force but if they did so, America would not oppose them.[53] After the Turks rejected the second Acheson plan, Acheson told the Turkish representatives at Geneva: "I am privately and friendly telling you: Can you invade the part of Cyprus which was reserved for you without causing too much bloodshed? If you can do so, you can invade it. The American Sixth Fleet does not obstruct your way, on the contrary it

[49] H. W. Brands, Jr., "America Enters the Cyprus Tangle, 1964", p. 357.
[50] *Keesing's Contemporary Archives, 1963-1964,* vol. 14, p. 20269.
[51] E Weintall and C. Bartlett, *Facing the Brink,* pp. 34-35.
[52] H. W. Brands, Jr., "America Enters the Cyprus Tangle, 1964", pp. 358-359.
[53] N. Erim, *Bildiğim ve Gördüğüm Ölçüler İçinde Kıbrıs,* p. 369.

protects you." Turkish commander General Turgut Sunalp took Acheson's proposal to İnönü the next day. İnönü rejected it by saying that he could not initiate such an adventure without the official approval of the American administration.[54]

In the meeting of American officials in September 1964, Acheson and Ball told Johnson that the Turks liked their scheme and all that was required to put the plan into motion was a signal from Washington. In order to be sure that he understood the plan of Ball and Acheson correctly, President Johnson summarised the scheme and said that they believed that a resort to force was inevitable and that the only question was "whether it should be messy and destructive or controlled and eventually productive, in accordance with a plan." Acheson agreed that this was a fair summary. Initially Johnson seemed interested in Acheson's proposal but in the end he rejected it. A war (the Vietnam War) was already a major trouble for him, he could not consent to the outbreak of another one. He thought that Turkish invasion might not be as clean as Acheson and Ball expected and that it might escalate to a major war. At least the next few months would not be a good season for a war because of the approaching presidential election.[55]

American officials were of the opinion that the Greek side was primarily responsible for the failure of the Geneva talks. A few months later Dean Acheson wrote to the American ambassador to Egypt: "We came to close an understanding which might have cropped the Archbishop's whiskers and solved the idiotic problem of Cyprus to your Mr Nasser's disappointment and chagrin. Our weakness was Papandreou's weakness, a garrulous, senile wind bag without power of decision or resolution. He gave away our plans at critical moments to Makarios, who undermined him with the Greek press and political left. A little money, which we had, the Greek 7th Division in Cyprus, which the Greeks had, and some sense of purpose in Athens, which did not exist, might have permitted a different result. The Turks could not have been more willing to co-operate."[56]

In his speech before the Chicago Bar Association on 24 March 1965, Dean Acheson said: "The primary concern of the US government was over the effect of the Cyprus dispute upon the relations between Greece and Turkey... There was little doubt that from a legal point of view the treaties were binding upon the parties... Merely to restrain the Turks from intervention would be, in fact, to intervene against them... Time was running strongly against the Turks, due to the military build up on the island and the Archbishop's increasing pressure to crush Turkish Cypriot resistance to his imposed regime... The Turks were quite willing to pick up discussions at the point where the Kokkina fighting interrupted them. But they saw that in making any further concession to unresponding Greeks, they would merely be negotiating with themselves."[57] Acheson stated: "we had come very close to an agreement but Archbishop Makarios did not go out of his way to be helpful. He threw a monkey wrench into the machinery."[58] In his speech, Acheson claimed that the United States had a grave responsibility by preventing Turkish intervention in Cyprus because its action encouraged Makarios to impose his own regime on the Turkish community in the island.[59] Acheson also

---

[54] Ibid., p. 406.
[55] H. W. Brands, Jr., "America Enters the Cyprus Tangle, 1964", pp. 359-360.
[56] Ibid., p. 358.
[57] Seyfi Taşhan, "Turkish-US Relations and Cyprus", *Foreign Policy (Dış Politika)*, vol. 4, Nos. 2-3, February 1975, p. 169.
[58] H. I. Salih, *Cyprus*, p. 50, M. A. Attalides, *Cyprus: Nationalism and International Politics*, p. 20.
[59] Abdi İpekçi, "Durum", *Milliyet*, 16 January 1966, p. 1.

said: "The losers are plainly the NATO nations whose alliance has been gravely weakened, and especially Greece and Turkey whose confidence both in one another and in the United States and Britain has been strained. The gainers are the Archbishop..., the Russians who have weakened NATO and perhaps, gained another toehold in the eastern Mediterranean and Colonel Nasser who has added to the fire under his old enemies, the British."[60]

The reaction of President Johnson to the stubbornness of the Greek side was harsher. When the Greek ambassador to America told Johnson that even if Papandreou had approved the first Acheson plan, the Greek constitution would have not allowed it since the parliament in Athens would have never accepted it, the president exploded: "F... your parliament and your constitution. America is an elephant. Cyprus is a flea. Greece is a flea. If those two fellows continue itching the elephant, they may just get whacked by the elephant's tail... If your Prime Minister gives me talk about democracy, parliament and constitution, he, his government and his constitution may not last very long."[61]

The Cyprus question was discussed by the UN Security Council again in September 1964. The American ambassador to the UN, Stevenson, stated that the United States disapproved any air attacks on Cyprus launched from outside the island, hinting Turkish air attacks against Cyprus. He also clarified that the United States had never agreed to the use of arms furnished under its military assistance for any purpose not specified in assistance agreements. Soviet representative Morozov claimed that the differences between the two Cypriot communities were being used by some members of NATO to transform Cyprus into a military fortress. He argued that the Turkish Air Force could not have carried out its attack on Cyprus without the approval of the NATO military bloc. Morozov also said that the essential condition of ending the tense situation in Cyprus was the cessation of all pressures from outside Cyprus, of all interference in its internal affairs, and of these imperialist games played with the fate of the Cypriot people.[62]

The Turkish representative mainly complained about troops and arms shipments to Cyprus from Greece and the economic embargo imposed on Turkish Cypriots, who were deprived of even basic commodities they needed to survive.[63] The UN Security Council resolution which was adopted on 25 September 1964 reaffirmed the previously adopted resolutions on Cyprus, calling all members to refrain from actions violating Cyprus' independence, security and integrity, extended service period of the UN force in Cyprus for another three months, and approved the appointment by the Secretary General of Galo Plaza as a mediator.[64]

AMERICAN INTERESTS IN THE CYPRUS QUESTION

The main American concern on the Cyprus question was to contain the conflict and to prevent it from escalating to a greater war between two NATO allies, Greece and Turkey, which could also involve enemy powers such as the Soviet Union. In the opinion of American

---

[60] T. W. Adams and A. J. Cottrell, *Cyprus Between East and West*, pp. 74-75.
[61] H. W. Brands, Jr., "America Enters the Cyprus Tangle, 1964", p. 358.
[62] *International Organization*, vol. 19, 1965, p. 87.
[63] *The Historical Background of Cyprus and the Turkish Republic of Northern Cyprus*, (Ankara: The Cyprus-Turkish Cultural Association), p. 38.
[64] Ibid., p. 38, D. S. Bitsios, *Cyprus*, p. 194.

officials, the American administration had to prevent a Greco-Turkish war because as the leader of NATO, the United States had responsibility to keep peace among its allies and because such a war would bring grave dangers for American interests. From the American point of view, Greece and Turkey were important countries for Western and American interests, and therefore it was vital to restore their relations through installing peace in Cyprus or at least containing the Cyprus conflict. Greece and Turkey were strategically located, guarding the vital gates of warm-water entry and exit into the Black Sea and the soft underbelly of the Soviet Union. Turkey provided the direct control over the Straits, air corridors to the eastern Mediterranean and shared with Iran a land bridge from the Caucasus to Iraq and the Persian Gulf. She also shared the Black Sea with the Soviet Union and other eastern bloc countries and had common frontiers with the USSR and Bulgaria. Greece provided control over the southern approaches to the Turkish Straits, air corridors to the eastern and central Mediterranean regions and shared with Italy the control of Adriatic. She had common frontiers with two non-Warsaw pact communist states, Yugoslavia and Albania.[65]

The American interest was to maintain and to have full use of American and NATO bases in this strategic region and to deny similar opportunities to the eastern bloc countries.[66] If a war broke out between Greece and Turkey or one of these two countries left the Western alliance because of the Cyprus problem, the security of the eastern Mediterranean would have been greatly compromised and Western and American interests would have been severely damaged. The deterioration of Greco-Turkish relations and the possibility of an outbreak of an armed combat between the two countries contained the following dangers for the United States: Firstly, the south-eastern flank of NATO could collapse, NATO could be destabilised and the cohesion of the Western alliance could be damaged severely and weakened in facing the enemy camp. Secondly, the political, military and economic co-operation between the United States, Greece and Turkey could be undermined, American relations with each state could deteriorate and thus the presence of American bases and facilities in these countries could be threatened. Thirdly, the Soviet Union could have the opportunity to involve itself in a matter concerning the NATO countries and to destabilise and destroy the south-eastern flank of NATO and the whole Western alliance. Finally, even if NATO was not damaged physically the prestige of the Western alliance could be harmed since the hostility would be a great embarrassment to the Western bloc and a symbol of the Western disunity.

As a part of this policy, American officials paid attention to the fact that the Cyprus question could lead Turkey and Greece to sever their ties with NATO and to improve their relations with the Soviet Union to the extent that they could fall under Soviet influence. Especially Turkey's efforts to have a closer relationship with the Warsaw pact and the Third World attracted the attention of American rulers and led them to be more careful in not alienating Turkey with their attitude on the Cyprus question. They sought assurances from Turkish leaders that their new efforts would not weaken Turkey's ties with the Western alliance.

The United States had strategic concerns over Cyprus in the 1960s. Like Greece and Turkey, Cyprus, too, was strategically located. It was located at the cross-roads of the three

---

[65] H. J. Psomiades, "the United States and the Mediterranean Triangle: Greece, Turkey and Cyprus: a New Phase" in M. A. Attalides (ed.), *Cyprus Reviewed*, p. 201.
[66] T. A. Couloumbis, *the United States, Greece and Turkey*, pp. 24, 28.

continents and the major routes connecting the West with the East. It is 44 miles south of Turkey, 64 miles west of Syria, 130 miles north-west of Israel, and 240 miles north of Egypt and the Suez Canal.[67] Cyprus commanded the outlets of the pipelines on the coasts of Syria, Lebanon, Israel and Egypt, the northern entrance of the Suez Canal and the line of containment of the Soviet Union along its southern borders.[68] Some developments in the 1960s seemed to increase the strategic importance of the island: "the growth of Soviet political and military missions in various Arab states, the growth of the Soviet fleet in the area; the continuing Arab-Israel crisis; the increasing American concern about Middle Eastern oil supplies and the protection of oil shipping routes; the prospect of a reopened Suez Canal and the loss of American bases and base rights in the area."[69] Cyprus could provide useful bases in the eastern Mediterranean, protecting Western and American interests in the region.

The British retained two sovereign Cyprus bases, Dhekelia and Akrotiri, and enjoyed the privileges of military use of Cypriot air space, transport and land. They could allow the United States to benefit from the same facilities whenever they wanted. Akrotiri especially was a very important RAF base and could be used by the United States and NATO to support operations in the Middle East and to defend NATO's south-eastern flank. "Warplanes leaving bases on Cyprus could reach deep into south Russian airspace and in a nuclear war no treaty could prevent other NATO members from using the bases."[70] Makarios had already "authorised the CIA to use the British airfield at Akrotiri as a base of operation for its U-2 spy planes, to set up radio monitors in Cyprus to eavesdrop on communications between Middle East and Iron Curtain countries, and to install secret antennas for its electronic intelligence network."[71] Thus, the United States had communication facilities in Cyprus, including radio listening and broadcasting stations and the horizon radar installations for the detection of ICBM launches in the Soviet Union.[72]

The strategic importance of Cyprus, which was mentioned above, led American officials to pursue a policy which would prevent the island from falling into the hands of enemies. They preferred that the Cypriot administration which pursued a non-alignment policy would be neutralised and the island would come under NATO control. But the priority of the American administration lay in having good relations with Greece and Turkey, and therefore the United States acted carefully not to alienate these two countries with its Cyprus policy. The American position in the eastern Mediterranean was more dependent on Greece and Turkey, in which there were many American bases.[73]

The American attitude to find a solution to the Cyprus question could be summarised as follows: The first thing which should be done was to bring the violence and clashes in Cyprus to an end. This could open a way to negotiations between the interested parties to find a political settlement. American officials pressurised the concerned parties from time to time to refrain from taking any actions which would worsen the situation in Cyprus and inflame the fighting. They particularly put pressure on the Turks to deter them from invading the island.

---

[67] Joseph S. Joseph, *Cyprus: Ethnic Conflict and International Concern*, (New York: Peter Lang, 1985), p. 119.

[68] Stephen G. Xydis, "Cyprus: What Kind of Problem?" in Michael A. Attalides (ed.), *Cyprus Reviewed*, p. 28.

[69] V. Coufoudakis, "United States Foreign Policy and the Cyprus Question", p. 109.

[70] M. A. Attalides, *Cyprus: Nationalism and International Politics*, p. 158.

[71] Pierre Oberling, *The Road to Bellapais: the Turkish Cypriot Exodus to Northern Cyprus*, (New York: Columbia University Press, 1982), p. 124.

[72] M. A. Attalides, *Cyprus: Nationalism and International Politics*, p. 13.

[73] John C. Campbell, "the United States and the Cyprus Question, 1974-1975" in Van Coufoudakis (ed.), *Essays on the Cyprus Conflict*, (New York: Pella Publishing Company, 1976), p. 14.

In order to maintain peace in the island, the United States also supported the United Nations peace-keeping force in Cyprus. She gave material support to the force, thinking that it would keep peace in Cyprus and avert a Greco-Turkish war. As for finding a solution to the Cyprus problem, the United States preferred all attempts to seek a solution to be made through quiet diplomacy with limited internationalisation of the question. American officials did not want a problem concerning Western states to be aired in international forums, thinking that it would provide an opportunity to the Soviets to destabilise the Western bloc and that it would cause the humiliation of the Western alliance in the international arena.

American leaders were generally reluctant to put forward a proposal for the Cyprus question since they feared that their proposal would alienate at least one ally. They frequently announced that the United States was in favour of a settlement which would protect the interests of all the interested parties. American officials were of the opinion that the best solution could be found through direct negotiations between the parties, especially between Greece and Turkey. They thought that only an agreed settlement between Greece and Turkey could bring a permanent solution to the problem because the two states had the power to influence the Cypriot communities. For this purpose, the United States pressed Turkish and Greek officials especially in the summer of 1964 to come together to find a peaceful way out of the Cyprus problem. During these bilateral talks, the United States came up with a proposal to be discussed by the two sides, which could be called Enosis, partition or double Enosis.

It seemed that the present position of independent Cyprus did not suit Western and American interests because it was very likely that it could attract Soviet influence to the region and cause a war between Turkey and Greece. The unification of the island with Greece (Enosis) with some concessions to Turkey could solve the problem in accordance with the Western interests. In this way, Cyprus would be put into NATO's ranks, a communist take over in the island would be prevented and Greece and Turkey would be kept happy. The Geneva talks and the Acheson plans were directed to achieving this aim. When it was understood that this scheme would not be successful, American policy shifted to the acceptance of a unitary independent Republic of Cyprus so long as the NATO alliance was not damaged by the situation in the island. But American politicians always kept the Enosis scheme as an alternative in case other solutions failed and encouraged the Greek and Turkish governments to hold secret bilateral talks on the question.

Another American concern related to the Cyprus question was to prevent communist influence advancing in the Mediterranean region. In the opinion of American officials, Cyprus could be another link in containing the Soviet Union in its southern borders. At that time it seemed that the Soviets had changed the balance of power in their favour and gained the upper hand in the Middle East by having a close relationship with non-aligned, anti-Western Arab regimes. If Cyprus fell under Soviet influence, the Western interests in the eastern Mediterranean and the Middle East could be damaged totally. To restore the balance of power in the region it was vital to keep the Soviet influence away from Cyprus. American officials had already been alerted by the policies of the Cypriot administration. It seemed that the Makarios regime had been flirting dangerously with the Soviet Union. It had appealed to the Soviet Union for support on the Cyprus question and showed readiness to rely on the Soviet support to protect its security. It signed trade agreements with the Soviet Union and made contacts to obtain Soviet weapons. The Cypriot government also pursued a non-aligned policy in its foreign relations and had close contacts with the non-aligned countries, especially with Nasser of Egypt, who seemed to pursue anti-Western policies. It rejected all Western designs for the Cyprus problem, gave communists a respectable political role in the state machinery, announced that it rejected all military alliances and even declared that it would not allow the use of Cypriot bases against the Arabs in case of a fighting between Arabs and Israel.[74]

Another worry of American officials was the strength of the Cyprus communist party, AKEL. The party was well-organised, had substantial popular support and was an influential factor in Cyprus politics. It was opposed to the presence of Western nuclear bases on the island and had tried to turn public opinion against Britain and the United States. If it gained political control, it could allow the Soviet fleet to use the Cyprus ports. Under these circumstances, American officials feared that Cyprus would be a Mediterranean Cuba. In order to prevent Cyprus from becoming a threat to Western interests, American policy was directed, to some extent, to the elimination or at least neutralisation of political capability of Makarios and the communist elements. American contacts with Greece and Cyprus aimed at finding a solution to the Cyprus problem, excluding Makarios and AKEL.

The overall US policy on Cyprus mentioned above made it necessary to prevent any Turkish intervention in Cyprus and to pressurise the Turks to act in a certain way when required. American authorities were not able to control the Greek Cypriots entirely to prevent their actions against Turkish Cypriots. But a Turkish intervention in Cyprus presented more dangers for them, i.e. a Greek-Turkish war and damage to NATO. It was therefore imperative for US rulers to check Turkish actions on Cyprus. It could be said that the United States did try to prevent a Turkish military intervention in Cyprus by using means of pressure. The most severe American pressure among them was the famous Johnson letter which was couched in an undiplomatic, threatening language and caused disappointment of Turkish rulers. However, Americans claimed that the United States did not prevent a Turkish military intervention directly, but only advised her close ally not take action because of possible dangerous results in the future. On 3 January 1966, American ambassador to Turkey Parker Hart told Turkish journalists that the United States had never prevented any Turkish initiative of military intervention in Cyprus but, as a close ally and friend of Turkey, only advised the Turkish government for the continuation of peace in the region.[75]

Objectively thinking, the American pressures, even if they were in the form of moral ones, became effective on the Turkish administration. In fact, the United States had been determined to stop any Turkish action and the Johnson letter of 1964 bore the character of an ultimatum. According to the article of H. W. Brands, Jr., in his discussion with George Ball on what the United States could do if Turkey seemed intent on invasion President Johnson asserted: "we are in a position to force them to settle the issue peacefully. If we told İnönü we'd cut off aid, he'd be forced to back down."[76] Four times after the Christmas of 1963 Turkey contemplated invading Cyprus and four times the Americans proved dissuasive. "Friendly advice about the superiority of peaceful negotiation was reinforced by apparent blocking manoeuvres of the American 6th Fleet."[77] Many authors and American statesmen labelled the Johnson letter, intended to prevent a Turkish intervention in Cyprus, as an ultimatum and even "the diplomatic equivalent of atomic bomb."[78] The statements of the

---

[74] M. A. Attalides, *Cyprus: Nationalism and International Politics,* p. 15.

[75] *Cumhuriyet,* 4 January 1966, p. 1.

[76] H. W. Brands, Jr., "America Enters the Cyprus Tangle, 1964", pp. 354-355.

[77] W. M. Dobell, "Division Over Cyprus", *International Journal,* vol. 22, No. 2, Spring 1967, p. 283.

[78] Ibid., p. 355.

American statesmen to Turkish journalist Haluk Þahin are interesting. George Ball said: "Secretary of State Dean Rusk believed that a strong warning was needed to stop the Turks. He feared that a warning which was not hard enough could fail to deter a Turkish action... It would be worse if a mild letter was sent and the Turks invaded Cyprus." Joseph Sisco said: "I know the letter gave a shock to the Turks, but to be honest it had been sent to the Turks to give them a shock."[79]

However, the Americans failed to predict how the Turks would respond to their warnings, which were, maybe unnecessarily, too harsh for an independent state. US officials might have been deceived by the fact that until that time the Turks always became the most loyal ally within NATO and always attributed great importance to pleasing their American ally with their actions. It seems that the Americans did not understand the pride of Turkish authorities. One reason for the severe US warning to Turkey might be that as a result of being a super-power the United States expected that a small country such as Turkey should listen to its advice in a matter which could concern the whole Western camp. Scolding of the Greek ambassador by Johnson strengthens this view. However, when US officials realised that they could alienate the Turks and eventually lose their alliance, which was important for US interests, they acted more cautiously.

TURKEY'S INTERESTS IN THE CYPRUS QUESTION

Since the second half of the 1950s the Cyprus question has been a constant factor and problem of Turkish foreign policy, affecting decisions of policy makers in other matters as well. For Turks, Cyprus is a matter of national honour and prestige, and polices towards it cannot be decided by a few top officials on their own without regard for public opinion.[80] In the 1960s the disappointment felt by the Turkish people towards Turkey's allies on the Cyprus question resulted in criticism and discussion of Turkey's general foreign policy which was considered taboo before 1960. When the Cyprus issue showed that Turkey was isolated in the international arena and betrayed by even her allies, foreign policy became subject to public debate perhaps for the first time in Turkish history. Thus, the Cyprus problem played a catalyst role in attracting people's attention to matters of foreign relations and encouraging them to express their views on foreign policy[81]. The developments on the Cyprus question also led the Turkish government to re-examine its foreign policy actions and pursue a more flexible foreign policy aiming at putting an end to Turkey's isolation in the international arena and gaining support of the Soviet bloc and Third World countries on the Cyprus issue.

The Cyprus question was a national cause for Turkey, concerning its national prestige, self-esteem and honour. The problem addressed deep-rooted feelings of the Turks. Since it gained its independence, Greece had expanded at the expense of Turkey's territories. The Turks had saved their mainland, Asia Minor, from the occupation of Greece but lost important Aegean islands to the Greeks. They strongly felt that they could not afford leaving

---

[79] Haluk Şahin, *Gece Gelen Mektup: Türk-Amerikan İlişkilerinde Bir Dönüm Noktası*, (İstanbul: Cep Kitapları, 1987), pp. 48, 50, 56.

[80] Ferenc A. Vali, *Bridge Across the Bosporus: The Foreign Policy of Turkey*, (Baltimore: the John Hopkins Press, 1971), p. 242.

[81] Mehmet Gönlübol, "NATO, USA and Turkey" in Kemal H. Karpat (ed.), *Turkey's Foreign Policy in Transition*, (Leiden: E. J. Brill, 1975), p. 32.

the most important island, Cyprus, to the Greeks. Vali describes these Turkish feelings as follows: "The Cyprus question was widely regarded in Turkey as point of national prestige and honour... Modern Turkey was no longer a sick man whose just claims could be ignored. Turks recalled that the island of Crete was gradually weaned away from Turkey under the pretext of self-government and finally surrendered to Greece; they did not want that precedent repeated with Cyprus. The surrender of Cyprus against Turkey's will would be inconsistent with national self-esteem."[82] The Turks were determined not to allow the same thing happen again. In their minds, modern Turkey was no longer a sick man whose just claims could be ignored. In his speech to the Turkish National Assembly on 5 May 1964, Turkish Prime Minister İnönü said: "Cyprus is a national cause for us, concerning each house and each individual in this country. We are right and we are determined to find a just solution for this problem. It will be solved in conformity with the honour and dignity of the Turkish nation. Any solution contrary to this will be beyond the capacity of any power to force us to accept."[83]

In the eyes of Turkish leaders, Cyprus had a great strategic importance to Turkey.[84] Cyprus is located in position overlooking the southern ports of Turkey, lying just over forty miles from the Turkish coast, and therefore it controlled Turkey's vital strategic approaches and consequently had fundamental importance to her security. The Turks argued that if Cyprus were controlled by an enemy power or a weak state such as Greece, in case of war Turkey would be in a dangerous situation, isolated from the outside world. Turkish officials also claimed that if Cyprus passed to Greece, Turkey's entire Aegean and Mediterranean coastlines would be controlled by an unfriendly Greece, who was almost a traditional enemy of the Turks, and thus the accepted Aegean and Mediterranean balance of power would be tilted into Greece's favour.

The Turks considered Cyprus an integral part of Turkey's defence system. The Turkish ports on the Mediterranean coast had a basic role in Turkish defence, harbouring main supply lines and defence facilities and support routes for the defence of Turkey's south. Cyprus had a commanding position over these vital defence facilities. The handover of Cyprus to Greece could not be accepted since it would weaken Turkey's total defence capability. Greece did not have enough military capabilities to defend the island and therefore could not prevent the island from falling into hands of an enemy state. Greece itself was the enemy of Turkey and had not renounced its traditional idea of the Megoli Idea, a Greater Greece at the expense of Turkey. Greece was totally unreliable for Turkey. These strategic considerations led Turkish leaders to maintain a firm stance against Enosis and the control of Cyprus by only Greek people. They were determined not to lose Cyprus.

In their dealings with the Cyprus question, Turkish officials always claimed that their main aim was to protect the lives and rights of Turkish Cypriots. They felt that this responsibility had been given to Turkey by the international agreements on Cyprus. In their view, Turkey had to act as protector of Turkish Cypriots who had the same ethnic origin,

---

[82] F. A. Vali, *Bridge Across the Bosporus*, p. 242.
[83] *Millet Meclisi Tutanak Dergisi*, vol. 30, term 1, sess. 3, 5 May 1964, p. 210.
[84] M. A. Ramady, "the Role of Turkey in Greek-Turkish Cypriot Communal Relations" in Van Coufoudakis (ed.), *Essays on the Cyprus Conflict*, p. 2, H. J. Psomiades, "the United States and the Mediterranean Triangle: Greece, Turkey and Cyprus: a New Phase", p. 203, Ferenc A. Vali, *Bridge Across the Bosporus*, p. 242, Suat Bilge, "the Cyprus Conflict and Turkey", in Kemal H. Karpat (ed.), *Turkey's Foreign Policy in Transition*, (Leiden: E. J. Brill, 1975), pp. 142, 183.

cultural and religious background and who had nobody else to rely on in saving them from discrimination by the Greek majority. For the Turks, the most suitable solution to the Cyprus problem was the partition of the island between the Turks and the Greeks and the separation of the two ethnic communities in Cyprus. In their view, the hatred between the two communities, which stemmed from having absolutely different national identities with different cultural, political and religious values, was so great that it would be dangerous and unreasonable not to separate them. The harrowing experiences which Turkish Cypriots suffered at the hands of Greek Cypriots in 1963 and the following years had showed that the Greek majority rule in Cyprus would not protect rights of the Turkish community. That was why Turkey accepted the first Acheson plan as the basis of negotiating a solution for Cyprus. The plan would have also satisfied Turkey's security concerns. The Turks were convinced that short of partition only federal government could give Turkish Cypriots security.[85]

In his speech to the Turkish Parliament on 3 September 1964 Prime Minister İnönü explained Turkey's idea on finding a solution to the Cyprus problem: "In order to show that we have no fixed idea in rejecting the independence of Cyprus, we put forward the formula of federation. If it is returned to the formula, we give consent to it. We agreed to negotiate a formula under which a portion of Cyprus meeting Turkey's military and administrative needs would be put under Turkey's sovereignty and rights of Turkish Cypriot community would be respected. If we agreed on this formula, we would have obtained the unification of a portion of Cyprus with Turkey in return for Enosis."[86] Turkish Foreign Minister İhsan Sabri Çağlayangil summarised Turkey's view on the solution of the Cyprus problem in his speech to the Turkish Senate on 1 February 1967: "We have four principles on the Cyprus question: The island cannot be unified with one state unilaterally. There are two communities in Cyprus and one of them cannot impose its own regime on the other. The international agreements which gave life to the Cypriot state cannot be abrogated unilaterally. Any solution of the Cyprus problem which will change the balance of power in the Mediterranean region cannot be accepted. The best solution for the problem which will contain these conditions is federation."[87]

Turkish leaders believed that their Cyprus cause was just and that it was the Greek side who caused all troubles and atrocities. They expected that their Western allies, especially the United States, would show a decisive reaction to the Greek attacks against the Turkish Cypriots and to pressurise Greece and Makarios to stop their violence. Turkey had supported its Western allies in all situations even by putting its own security into danger and it was now the West's turn to support its faithful ally Turkey in her just cause. This kind of action would also be a requirement of Western principles such as justice and human rights. But the Western states did not take decisive and effective actions. Instead of pressuring the Greek side Americans demanded more concessions from Turkey each time Makarios rejected a new proposal and the violence in Cyprus continued. Consequently Turkish leaders grew impatient.[88] In their view, this was an abandonment of Western principles by the West itself since the victims were non-Christian Turks.

American actions during the Cyprus crises were perceived by the Turks as preventing Turkey from taking actions to stop the massacre of the Turkish community in Cyprus. On this

---

[85] *Keesing's Contemporary Archives, 1965-1966*, vol. 15, p. 20267.
[86] Mehmet Gönlübol et al., *Olaylarla Türk Dış Politikası*, (Ankara: A.Ü., S.B.F. Yayınları, No. 407, 1977), p. 400.
[87] *Cumhuriyet Senatosu Tutanak Dergisi*, 1 February 1967, term 1, sess. 6, vol. 38-3, p. 376.
[88] Metin Toker, "Türkiye Yol Ağzında", *Akis*, 4 April 1964, p. 7.

ground, the Turkish rulers felt it necessary to obey demands of Americans and Turkish public opinion accused the Turkish government of being under the influence of America. In the parliamentary debate on 7 September 1964, Republican MP Nihat Erim, who represented the Turkish government in the Cyprus talks, said that on 4 June 1964 the government decided to land on Cyprus and made Turkish ships ready for an intervention. According to Erim, the government abandoned its action because of the American warning and when the situation was discussed in a secret parliamentary meeting no Turkish MP proposed to carry out the operation ignoring the American warning. Erim added that the Turkish government could not afford to intervene in Cyprus after the Soviet and American opposition became apparent.[89]

The disappointing attitude of the West and the United States led Turkish leaders to question Turkey's Western-oriented foreign policy which was thought to be the best policy up to that time. They began to think that the monolithic pro-US and pro-Western foreign policy did not meet Turkey's national interests entirely. It was understood that the interests of Turkey and the Western powers would not always be identical and that they could clash with each other in some situations. The Cyprus question created a conflict between Turkey's interests and her commitment to the NATO alliance and manifested that NATO was not enough to protect Turkey's interests but it restricted Turkey's capability of action in matters that concerned her. It also became apparent to Turkish leaders that Turkey was isolated in the international arena and had no support in her national causes. All these factors led Turkish policy-makers to reassess Turkey's foreign policy, her relations with the United States and her position within NATO and to improve Turkey's relations with non-Western states. Knowing that the ties between the West and Turkey were based on complementary interests rather than identical ones, they tired to be more flexible in their dealings with the West, the Warsaw Pact and the Third World. But it would be wrong to conclude that Turks really considered making radical changes in their traditional pro-Western foreign policy and in their relations with the USA. When such an interpretation circulated among Turkish political circles, Turkish leaders were quick to deny it.

Turkish Public Opinion on the Cyprus Question

First it will be useful to summarise the views of the Turkish political parties on the Cyprus question. Leaders of the main leftist party, the Republican People's Party, saw the main subjects of Turkish foreign policy such as the Cyprus question and Turkey's alliance with NATO as national matters rather than as matters concerning political competition. Both the party's general-secretary, Bülent Ecevit, and the party's leader, İsmet İnönü, made the Cyprus question a national issue, keeping the other party leaders informed of developments and seeking their advice on how to act. Their policy based on the validity of the Zurich and London accords on Cyprus in 1959 and aimed to stop the chaos in the island in order to ensure the security of the Turkish Cypriots.[90] RPP's leaders hoped that the United States and the West would support Turkey on the Cyprus question since Turkey was their ally and its stance on the matter was right. When they were disappointed with attitudes of the Western countries, particularly those of the USA, they bitterly criticised the West, but at the same time they did not want the breakdown of Turkey's ties with the West.

---

[89] *Millet Meclisi Tutanak Dergisi,* term 1, sess. 3, vol. 32, p. 326.

Like the Republican People's Party the Justice Party, the main rightist party, saw the Cyprus dispute as an important national issue of Turkey, which should be defended in the international arena by all the Turkish parties without being made a subject of domestic political rivalries. The JP's policy on Cyprus based on the validity of the Zurich and London accords in 1959 and the protection of the safety of the Turkish people on the island.[91] JP leaders claimed that they inherited the Cyprus question in its advanced phase and accused the previous İnönü cabinet of not solving the problem and of making the United States an indirect party to the dispute.[92] During the Cyprus crisis of 1967, to show its sensitivity towards the Cyprus question, the JP government threatened to invade Cyprus and therefore obtained authority from the Parliament to use the Turkish armed forces abroad if circumstances required it. But it preferred to use diplomatic methods to overcome the crisis.

As for the views of the leaders of the Turkish Labour Party, which represented the extreme leftist factions, they claimed that Britain had created the Cyprus problem and that this state and the United States had used it for their own political ends. In their opinion, the real solution to the Cyprus question could be found by arranging a conference between the powers which were directly concerned in the problem, excluding Britain and the United States.[93] The leaders of the far rightist and nationalist party, the Nationalist Action Party, believed that Cyprus belonged to the Turks since 1571 and it was geographically a part of Anatolia. A final solution could be found by giving the island to Turkey on the condition that it protected the rights of the Greek Cypriots. NAP politicians supported the Turkish military intervention in the island in 1974, but found it insufficient to secure the existence of the Turkish Cypriots. They were of the opinion that Turkey should have intervened militarily in the island during the 1964 and 1967 crises as well.[94] Turkey's religious and conservative party, the National Salvation Party, which arose in the political arena after 1970 and which succeeded to establish a coalition government with the leftist Republicans, played an active part in the Turkish military intervention in Cyprus in 1974. During the intervention the party leader, Necmettin Erbakan, seemed to favour a more aggressive and expansionist policy while Ecevit tried to pursue a moderate one not alienating the Western World. Some Salvationists and the right-wing press even claimed that it was Erbakan who had persuaded the government to intervene in Cyprus.[95]

Turkish military leaders believed that continuity of the London and Zurich accords of 1959 was the best solution for the problem. They were very sensitive towards the protection of rights and interests of the Turkish Cypriots and ensuring their security. During the Cyprus crisis of 1963-1964, the military was eager to intervene in the island militarily. Some high-ranking officers were strongly in favour of military intervention, but the harsh warning from President Johnson put a swift end to this ambition. Revelation of the contents of Johnson's

---

[90] N. Erim, *Bildiğim ve Gördüğüm Ölçüler İçinde Kıbrıs*, pp. 271-282.

[91] İsmail Arar, *Hükümet Programları 1920-1965*, (İstanbul: Burçak Yayınevi, 1968), pp. 477, 482, Süleyman Demirel, *Büyük Türkiye*, (İstanbul: Dergah Yayınları, 1975), p. 424, S. Bilge, "Cyprus Conflict and Turkey" p. 182.

[92] M. Sarıca et al., *Kıbrıs Sorunu*, p. 122, Feros Ahmad, *The Turkish Experiment in Democracy 1950-1975*, (London, Royal Institute of International Affairs, 1977), p. 223, George S. Harris, *Troubled Alliance*, (Washington D. C.: American Enterprise Institute, 1972), p. 134.

[93] Mehmet Ali Aybar, *Bağımsızlık, Demokrasi, Sosyalizm: Seçmeler 1947-1967*, (İstanbul: Gerçek Yayınevi, 1968), pp. 318-319, 342, 349, 406, 439-440, Hikmet Özdemir, *1960'lar Türkiye'sinde Sol Kemalizm: Yön Hareketi*, (İstanbul: İz Yayıncılık, 1993), pp. 213-214, 250.

[94] Alparslan Türkeş, *Temel Görüşler*, (İstanbul: Dergah Yayınları, 1975), pp. 310-320.

[95] F. Ahmad, *Turkish Experiment in Democracy*, p. 343.

letter in June 1965 served to direct popular anger against the Americans but some observers felt that İnönü had been secretly relieved at having the invasion option closed since shortage of landing craft and other military necessities would have rendered an invasion a highly perilous undertaking.[96]

The Cyprus question had a great impact on Turkish public opinion. For the first time, Turkey's foreign policy became a subject of public discussion, and anti-Americanism gained popularity among Turkish people. Leftist circles, university students, intellectuals and the press loudly criticised the United States. Mass demonstrations were arranged.[97] US personnel and buildings in Turkey were attacked and the shouting of "Yankee go home!" was heard in the Turkish streets for the first time. Turkish public opinion criticised the United States harshly on the ground that it prevented Turkey from launching a military operation against Cyprus, which was aimed at stopping Greek Cypriot attacks and saving lives of Turkish Cypriots. In the opinion of the Turks, the American action was an example of double-standard treating because the United States prevented Turkey's intervention in Cyprus, which was legal under international agreements while she herself bombed North Vietnam without having any right of intervention granted by any agreement. America was not doing anything to stop the bloodshed in Cyprus but was preventing those who wanted to do so as a part of their legal responsibility.[98] If their citizens were hurt, the Americans would react very harshly. When the American ships were attacked in the Southeast Asia, the United States launched a heavy bombardment against North Vietnam but she did not consider the same right for Turkey.[99] On this occasion American President Johnson had said that it was vital for peace that states that were right in their cause should struggle to gain their right but he threatened Turkey when she wanted to use its right.[100] The American prevention of Turkey's intervention was incompatible with justice, legality and international law because by acting in this way the United States had restrained Turkey from using its legal right granted by the international agreements on Cyprus.[101] The tone of American dissuasion was also not acceptable for a faithful ally like Turkey. The United States actually had threatened Turkey on its intervention intentions by resorting to methods reminiscent of the tactics of the eastern bloc countries and which gave the impression that America considered Turkey its colony.[102]

Another criticism of the United States by Turkish public opinion was that American leaders favoured Greece over Turkey on the Cyprus question. The Turks believed that all American actions on the Cyprus issue encouraged Greek and Greek Cypriots to arm themselves and to attack the Turkish Cypriot community. They were also of the opinion that the United States wanted the unification of Cyprus with Greece. Americans saw Enosis as the most suitable solution for the Cyprus problem, and the Acheson plan proved this American intention. The American leaders even changed the first version of the Acheson plan in favour

---

[96] G. S.. Harris, Troubled Alliance, p. 212.

[97] *Keesing's Contemporary Archives, 1965-1966*, vol. 15, p. 20627.

[98] M. F. Fenik, "Nazi Kampından Beter", *Son Havadis*, 31 March 1964 quoted by Duygu Sezer, *Kamuoyu ve Dış Politika*, (Ankara: SBF Yayını, No. 339, 1972), p. 184.

[99] Ali Rıza Alp, "Haçlı Zihniyetinin Yaşadığı Devirdeyiz", *Tercüman*, 21 September 1964.

[100] O. Z. Dorman, *Millet Meclisi Tutanak Dergisi*, vol. 32, term 1, sess. 3, 7 September 1964, p. 306.

[101] A. Bilgin, *Millet Meclisi Tutanak Dergisi*, vol. 40, term 1, sess. 4, 25 May 1964, p. 559, C. Odyakmaz, ibid., p. 561, A. Yıldız, *Cumhuriyet Senatosu Tutanak Dergisi*, 6 January 1966, term 1, sess. 5, vol. 31, p. 423.

[102] Cahit Talas, "Kıbrıs, Avrupa, NATO, Amerika", *Forum*, 15 September 1964, p. 9, Fahir Armaoğlu, "Dış Politikada Değişiklik Zorunludur", *Cumhuriyet*, 2 September 1964, p. 2, Ahmet Kabaklı, "Zararlı Faaliyetler", *Tercüman*, 29 September 1964.

of pure Enosis in order to please the Greek side[103] and then they tried to persuade Turkey to accept it. When the problem was solved through Enosis the United States would provide every kind of assistance to Turkey.[104] The United States could have brought Makarios and Greece into line if she had chosen to do so. But in spite of its economic, political and military power, the United States chose to stay inactive and tolerate the atrocities of Greek Cypriots. This American inactivity greatly encouraged the Greek side in their violence.[105] While threatening Turkey not to use force against Cyprus, the United States tolerated Greece's arms and troop shipment to Cyprus. Greece transferred large amounts of arms and men under the eyes of Americans.[106] While ignoring the fact that the Greek Cypriots used American weapons to attack Turkish Cypriots, the United States warned Turkey not to use American weapons in its operation against Cyprus.[107] American President Johnson came under the influence of Greece in his policy toward the Cyprus problem and tilted to the Greek position since he knew the importance of Greek American votes in the presidential election.[108]

Some Turkish critics of the United States, especially the rightist intellectuals, accused the American leaders of being indifferent to communist advance in Cyprus and the Middle East. They complained that the United States, who was opposed to communism all over the world, did not care about the increase of the strength of Cypriot communists under Makarios's political protection.[109] Rightist writers also accused the West of favouring Greece because of religious considerations. They claimed that the Western countries opposed Turkey's actions and tolerated Greek violence simply because the Greeks were Christian and owned the Greek-Hellenic civilisation.[110] The Western attitude demonstrated that Christians and communists were in the same position in being opposed to the Turks,[111] if the Christians had been attacked, the West would surely have shown a different reaction.[112]

Turkish public opinion also criticised the United States by making comparisons between the unwillingness of Washington in helping Turkey on the Cyprus question and Turkey's steadfast support for the United States in international crises such as the Korean, Cuban and Vietnam conflicts. Turkish critics of America recalled that Turkey always became a faithful ally of the West, fulfilling its responsibilities within the Western alliance and supporting the West in all international crises.[113] It was now America's turn to support Turkey, but its inactivity on the Cyprus question reached a degree which would disappoint the Turks greatly.

---

[103] "Başyazı", *Forum*, 15 September 1964, p. 3, O. Okyar, "Dış Politikada Revizyon", *Forum*, 15 September 1964, p. 10.

[104] C. Talas, "Kıbrıs, Avrupa, NATO, Amerika", *Forum*, 15 September 1964, p. 9, M. Toker, "İsmet Paşa ile 4 Buhranlı Yıl", *Milliyet*, 9 February 1969, p. 5.

[105] A. Artus, "Kıbrıs ve Amerika'nın Tutumu", *Milliyet*, 4 September 1964, "Durum", *Milliyet*, 2 September 1964, p. 1.

[106] Nihat Erim, *Millet Meclisi Tutanak Dergisi*, vol. 40, term 1, sess. 4, 25 May 1965, p. 550, A. Yıldız, *Cumhuriyet Senatosu Tutanak Dergisi*, 6 January 1966, term 1, sess. 5, vol. 31, p. 411, H. Uysal, "Tehlikeli Alakalar", *Akis*, 15 January 1966, p. 5.

[107] S. Ural, *Cumhuriyet Senatosu Tutanak Dergisi*, 4 February 1968, term 1, sess. 7, vol. 45-3, pp. 452-453.

[108] Ali Rıza Alp, "Kıbrıs Meselesinde Johnson'ın Hesabı", *Tercüman*, 4 September 1964.

[109] M. F. Fenik, "Bu Gafletin Cezasını Bütün Dünya Çeker", *Son Havadis*, 31 March 1964, M. F. Fenik, "Amerikan Nasihati", *Son Havadis*, 9 May 1964 quoted by D. Sezer, *Kamuoyu ve Dış Politika*, pp. 183, 184.

[110] O. S. Orhon, "Kıbrıs ve Ötesi", *Son Havadis*, 6.1.1964 quoted by D. Sezer, *Kamuoyu ve Dış Politika*, pp. 182-183, O. Z. Dorman, *Millet Meclisi Tutanak Dergisi*, vol. 30, term 1, sess. 3, 6 May 1964, p. 278.

[111] Ahmet Kabaklı, "Bakışlar", *Tercüman*, 4 January 1964.

[112] M. F. Fenik, "Biz Değişmedik Dostlar Değişti", *Son Havadis*, 13 June 1964, quoted by D. Sezer, *Kamuoyu ve Dış Politika*, pp. 184-185.

[113] O. Okyar, "Dış Politikada Revizyon", *Forum*, 15 September 1964, p. 10, Metin Toker, "Kral Kadar Kralcı", *Akis*, 9 September 1964, p. 7.

Turkey had sent troops to Korea to help the ideals of human rights and the United Nations but the United States did not show the same consideration for the Cyprus question.[114] Turkey steadfastly supported America during the Cuban crisis though it was in the forefront of the danger, but the Americans left Turkey alone when she confronted a danger because of the Cyprus problem and only watched the killings of Turkish Cypriots at the hands of Greek Cypriots.[115] The United States claimed that the Cuban situation would damage interests of NATO but seemed to ignore that the Cyprus events could affect NATO.[116]

Turkish public opinion, especially politicians and intellectuals, criticised the United States and other Western states, stating that the American and Western attitude towards the Cyprus question was not compatible with Western principles to which Turkish leaders attributed great importance. The main purpose of the Turkish Republic since its establishment had been integration with the West, which had exalted principles of human civilisation. Now on the Cyprus question the West betrayed its own principles and held a stance encouraging violators of great humanity principles. Western principles required respecting human rights, international law, international agreements, freedom, justice and independence. On the Cyprus question Greece and the Cypriot administration violated all these principles while Turkey did her best to respect them. But the West, especially the United States, restrained Turkey from stopping violations of Western principles and encouraged the Greek side in their actions by declaring neutrality.

How could the West watch the massacre of people and do nothing about it? How could the West allow the Greek side to violate international agreements openly? Was that not the moral collapse of the Western alliance? Why did the West not distinguish the guilty side from the innocent and pressurise the guilty one to stop its atrocities? How could the West declare neutrality while one side attacked the other side by ignoring all Western principles? How could NATO allow one of its members to violate all principles of NATO, damage the alliance and back the massacre of people? Did this not mean that NATO was powerless to protect international order and the order within itself? If the United States wanted to continue to be the leader of the West and if she did not want to deny its moral roots; she should stop acting neutrally, do something to stop the suffering of Turkish Cypriots, and thus show that she cared about exalted Western principles.[117]

Some Turkish intellectuals accused the United States of intervening in Turkey's internal affairs to find another prime minister who would comply with the American wishes on the Cyprus question, which İsmet İnönü rejected. They claimed that the CIA made enquiries in Turkey to find that who would be prime minister if İnönü resigned.[118] During the Geneva talks in August 1964, American mediator Acheson asked the Turkish delegation who would

---

[114] Ahmet Kabaklı, "Cepheler", *Tercüman*, 19 April 1964, O. Z. Dorman, *Millet Meclisi Tutanak Dergisi*, vol. 30, term 1, sess. 3, 6 May 1964, p. 278.

[115] R. Aşçıoğlu, "Böyle Oyun Olur mu?", *Tercüman*, 15 January 1965, Ecvet Güresin, "Amerika'nın Tutumu", *Cumhuriyet*, 6 June 1964

[116] I. Baran, *Millet Meclisi Tutanak Dergisi*, vol. 30, term 1, sess. 3, 5 May 1964, p. 244.

[117] Nihat Erim, *Millet Meclisi Tutanak Dergisi*, vol. 30, term 1, sess. 3, 5 May 1964, p. 223, C. Baban, *Millet Meclisi Tutanak Dergisi*, vol. 30, term 1, sess. 3, 5 May 1964, p. 236, O. Z. Dorman, *Millet Meclisi Tutanak Dergisi*, vol. 30, term 1, sess. 3, 6 May 1964, p. 278, Nihat Erim, *Millet Meclisi Tutanak Dergisi*, vol. 40, term 1, sess. 4, 25 May 1965, pp. 549-550, "Başyazı", *Forum*, 1 May 1964, p. 4, C. Talas, "Kıbrıs, Avrupa, NATO, Amerika", *Forum*, 15 September 1964, p. 9, Kayhan Sağlamer, "Dünyada Bugün", *Cumhuriyet*, 30 April 1964, p. 3, B. Savcı, "Amerika'nın Kısır, Haksız Politikası", *Cumhuriyet*, 8 September 1964, p. 2.

[118] "Başyazı", *Forum*, 1 September 1964, p. 3, A. Kabaklı, "Gün Işığında", *Tercüman*, 29 September 1964, M. Toker, "İsmet Paşa ile 4 Buhranlı Yıl", *Milliyet*, 11 February 1969, p. 5.

form a new government if İnönü resigned as prime minister and Nihat Erim had replied that he could not think of a politician or party who would replace İnönü if he resigned because he did not comply with pressures on the Cyprus question and that even if another person became prime minister, he would be much tougher.[119] For the same purpose, the United States had sent General Porter to Ankara in August 1964.[120]

Stimulated by this widespread criticism directed to the United States and the West, anti-American demonstrations took place in Turkish cities. Angry crowds formed by mainly university students shouted anti-American slogans in Turkish streets and attacked American officers, cars and official buildings. Frustrated with the attitude of the West, Turkish public opinion and the Turkish military believed that the Cyprus problem could be solved only through the Turkish military intervention in Cyprus and they pressurised the Turkish government to act in this direction. If the politicians did not partition the island by diplomatic means, a Turkish invasion could solve the problem permanently. An invasion, at least, could land a strong Turkish military force on Cyprus to protect the lives of Turkish Cypriots. Intervention appeals appeared frequently in the press and gained a substantial popular support. The hawks of the Turkish military such as General Cemal Tural, the chief of the Turkish land forces, too, felt that Turkey should take its own destiny into its own hands and resort to military force to solve the problem.[121] Considering the Western powers an obstacle in the way of a solution to the Cyprus problem, Turkish public opinion also felt that it was a mistake to involve the Western powers in the matter and they suggested that solutions to the problem should be sought outside NATO and the Western world.[122]

Developments on the Cyprus question led Turkish intellectuals and politicians to question Turkey's foreign policy orientation and its alliance with the West. In their view the Cyprus conflict demonstrated that membership in NATO was not enough to protect Turkey's national interests. NATO did not offer its help to Turkey to stop the fighting in Cyprus and on the contrary it restricted Turkey's freedom of action on the problem. Turkey was restrained by its NATO allies and was reminded that she could not use its weapons supplied by NATO. Putting all armed forces under the NATO command also was proved to be wrong by the Cyprus conflict.[123] It was high time for Turkey to reconsider its friendship, alliance and agreements with the West.[124] Turkey should stop expecting everything from the West and pursue an independent foreign policy from the West.[125] The Cyprus conflict had demonstrated disadvantages of a monolithic pro-Western foreign policy and showed its gaps and shortcomings.[126]

---

[119] N. Erim, *Bildiğim ve Gördüğüm Ölçüler İçinde Kıbrıs*, p. 405.

[120] M. Toker, "İsmet Paşa ile 4 Buhranlı Yıl", *Milliyet*, 11 February 1969, p. 5.

[121] G. S. Harris, *Troubled Alliance*, p. 112, T. A. Couloumbis, *the United States, Greece and Turkey*, p. 61.

[122] A. Oğuz, *Millet Meclisi Tutanak Dergisi*, vol. 32, term 1, sess. 3, 7 September 1964, p. 309.

[123] N. Erim, *Millet Meclisi Tutanak Dergisi*, 5 May 1964, term 1, sess. 3, vol. 30, p. 223, M. Karınca, *Millet Meclisi Tutanak Dergisi*, 24 February 1966, term 2, sess. 1, vol. 4, p. 469, S. Karaman, *Cumhuriyet Senatosu Tutanak Dergisi*, 7 May 1965, term 1, sess. 5, vol. 27-2, p. 185, Haydar Tunçkanat, *Cumhuriyet Senatosu Tutanak Dergisi*, 3 February 1967, term 1, sess. 6, vol. 38-3, pp. 568-570, *Forum*, 15 September 1964, p. 7.

[124] O. Z. Dorman, *Millet Meclisi Tutanak Dergisi*, vol. 32, term 1, sess. 3, 7 September 1964, p. 307, A. Bilgin, *Millet Meclisi Tutanak Dergisi*, vol. 40, term 1, sess. 4, 25 May 1964, p. 559.

[125] "Durum", *Milliyet*, 21 April 1964, p. 1, A. Oğuz, *Millet Meclisi Tutanak Dergisi*, vol. 32, term 1, sess. 3, 7 September 1964, p. 312.

[126] Ekrem Alican, *Millet Meclisi Tutanak Dergisi*, 7 September 1964, term 1, sess. 3, vol. 32, p. 314, Sadi Kocaş, *Cumhuriyet Senatosu Tutanak Dergisi*, 8 May 1965, term 1, sess. 5, vol. 27-2, p. 261.

There were also some Turkish critics whose approach to the Cyprus question was pro-American and pro-Western. They were of the opinion that Turkey should be very careful in criticising the Western states and that it should not change its main foreign policy line because of the Cyprus events. Turkey should not blame the United States and other Western states on the problems which stemmed from her own mistakes on the Cyprus question. The Turkish government should not hold the United States responsible for its own failures.[127] Acting emotionally Turkey should not change or even reconsider its foreign policy orientation and should continue to have close relations with the Western camp.[128]

EPILOGUE

To counter the public criticism directed against the United States and the West, the Turkish government tried to demonstrate that it was not under the influence of the West in its actions on the Cyprus question. It initiated some actions such as the bombardment of Cyprus in August 1964 and the withdrawal of Turkish forces from the proposed multilateral nuclear force, which were aimed at showing that Turkey could use its armed forces and weapons for Turkey's interests in Cyprus and that Turkey was independent in its foreign policy actions. However, Turkish authorities did not want to cause the deep resentment of the United States because they needed the alliance of this state. They tried to limit the damage done by public criticism to its alliance with the United States and NATO. While explaining the Acheson talks and the American attitude toward the Cyprus question to the Turkish Parliament on 4 September 1964, Turkish Prime Minister İnönü preserved a calm and detached tone. He said: "The United States has reconfirmed that it has tried sincerely to find a way of settlement for the Cyprus question, which could be accepted by both sides... We have wanted the United States to play an active role in finding a solution to the problem, not to be indifferent to it... The main American concern has been to prevent a war between two NATO allies... She believed that the problem would be solved through co-operating with the leaders of Turkey, Greece and Cyprus... The main reason for the failure of American efforts is that the United States misjudged the characteristics of the Greek and Cypriot administrations... and that the two governments misled the American leaders."[129]

US rulers, too, did not want to alienate the Turks and lose the alliance of Turkey completely, since the alliance served US interests. They tried to heal the wounds with Turkey and to appease the angry Turkish public opinion. The American administration issued public statements renewing the United States commitment to protect Turkey's security, and supplied extra American military assistance to the Turkish military. An American embassy spokesman assured the Turkish press that "the United States will be beside Turkey if it is attacked by the Soviet Union while using its treaty rights on Cyprus" and stated that the American Sixth Fleet had not intervened to prevent a Turkish landing on Cyprus. The chief of the American aid agency, AID, in Ankara denied the rumour that economic assistance was being cut to punish

---

[127] Fahir Armaoğlu, "Batı İttifakından Ayrılamayız", *Cumhuriyet*, 29 April 1964, Faruk Sükan, *Millet Meclisi Tutanak Dergisi*, 5 May 1964, term 1, sess. 3, vol. 30, pp. 231-232, Saadettin Bilgiç, *Millet Meclisi Tutanak Dergisi*, 7 September 1964, term 1, sess. 3, vol. 32, pp. 321-322.

[128] Faruk Sükan, *Millet Meclisi Tutanak Dergisi*, 5 May 1964, term 1, sess. 3, vol. 30, pp. 231-232, Gökhan Evliyaoğlu, *Millet Meclisi Tutanak Dergisi*, 6 May 1964, term 1, sess. 3, vol. 30, pp. 295-297.

[129] *Cumhuriyet*, 4 September 1964, p. 7.

Turkey for its Cyprus stand.[130] When the Turkish government rejected UN mediator Galo Plaza's plan on Cyprus and Galo Plaza himself as mediator[131] the United States did not raise any objection to Turkey. She tacitly agreed with Turkey that the UN mediation would bring no solution to the problem. When Galo Plaza resigned, the United States spent no effort to appoint another mediator.

In December 1965, the United States voted against the UN General Assembly resolution which appeared to support Makarios's claim for the independence of Cyprus and to discount the Turkish claim to the right of intervention in Cyprus based on the Treaty of Guarantee. The resolution recognised the fact that "the Republic of Cyprus, as an equal member of the United Nations, is, in accordance with the Charter, entitled to and should enjoy full sovereignty and complete independence without any foreign intervention or interference." It called upon all the states "to respect the sovereignty, unity, independence and territorial integrity of the Republic of Cyprus and to refrain from any intervention directed against it."[132] The resolution was passed by 47 votes to 6 with 54 abstentions. The Western and Eastern bloc countries abstained, while the Third World countries of Africa, Asia and South America voted in favour of the resolution. The countries who voted against it were Turkey, the United States, Albania, Iran, Pakistan, Libya and Afghanistan.[133]

The American opposition to the resolution was justified by American officials on the ground that it seemed to violate the existing treaties on Cyprus and to favour only one side of the problem. But the main American concern was to restore the prestige of the United State in Turkey, which was shaken by the Johnson letter. During the UN General Assembly talks on Cyprus between 11-17 December 1965, American Representative Charles W. Yost made the following points: "The Security Council had recognised that a solution to the Cyprus problem could not be imposed but should be reached by negotiation, accommodation and mediation. The Assembly should therefore refrain from any action inconsistent with the measures already taken by the Security Council, and it should in particular refrain from passing judgement on the positions of the parties or on the issues in dispute. The United States had no preferred formula for a settlement of the Cyprus problem. It merely hoped that the parties would move toward the agreed solution envisaged in the Council's resolution of March 4, 1964."[134]

In his speech to the UN Security Council in August 1965, Yost had reconfirmed the American consideration that the London-Zurich agreements were still valid. His main points were as follows: "The government of Cyprus had not been content with extending the mandate of its House of Representatives but had gone one step further and amended the electoral law. This was inconsistent with the London-Zurich agreements and the constitution of Cyprus. However, whatever legal rights any of the parties might claim, his delegation joined the Secretary General in urging all those concerned to refrain from any action or threat of action likely to worsen the situation in Cyprus or to endanger international peace."[135]

The American vote against the UN General Assembly resolution did not undo the negative impression in Turkey, created by the Johnson letter and general American policy

---

[130] G. S. Harris, *Troubled Alliance,* p. 120.
[131] *Keesing's Contemporary Archives, 1965-1966,* vol. 15, p. 20989.
[132] Ibid., p. 21237, *Foreign Policy (Dış Politika),* vol. 4, Nos. 2-3, February 1975, p. 217.
[133] M. Sarıca et. al., *Kıbrıs Sorunu,* pp. 109-112, *Keesing's Contemporary Archives, 1965-1966,* vol. 15, p. 21237.
[134] *International Organization,* vol. 20, 1966, pp. 308-309.
[135] *International Organization,* vol. 19, 1965, p. 987.

toward Cyprus. Anti-American demonstrations continued in Turkey. Some critics of the United States expressed their dissatisfaction with the American attitude, claiming that America could have influenced other states to vote against the resolution if she had wished, but American representatives in the UN did not spend any effort in this direction.[136] In fact, during the UN General Assembly talks the exercise of American influence on behalf of Turkey was not out of the question. The Greek and Greek Cypriot representatives feared that such an American initiative would be disastrous for their attempt to pass a resolution supporting their cause. Hence, they made strong representations to the US mission twice, when they thought that the United States was attempting to persuade Latin American states to support Turkey. These Greek actions were generally successful because the United States did not engage actively in the struggle to pass a resolution on Cyprus.[137]

---

[136] H. Uysal, "Tehlikeli Alakalar", *Akis*, 15 January 1966, p. 5, *Cumhuriyet,* 28 December 1965, p. 7.
[137] Robert O. Keohane, "the Study of Political Influence in the General Assembly", *International Organization*, vol. 21, 1967, p. 232.

Chapter 5

THE COURSE OF THE CYPRUS QUESTION IN THE 1965-1974 PERIOD AND THE US INFLUENCE ON THE PROBLEM AND ITS PARTIES

After the 1964 Cyprus crisis and after the failure its mediation effort on the Cyprus question, the American administration preferred to put a distance between itself and the problem. Its main purpose in this period was to avoid a major rift both in US-Turkish and US-Greek relations by keeping the Cyprus question under control through inter communal negotiations and pressures on the Turkish and Greek governments. On the other hand, the problem needed to be solved permanently because it could erupt at any time causing a serious blow to the Western security. It seemed from the American point of view that the unification of Cyprus with Greece with some concessions to Turkey could solve the problem to the advantage of the West. But to implement such a solution was not easy and required to pressurise all parties to the problem.

US INFLUENCE ON THE TURKISH AND GREEK GOVERNMENTS ON THE CYPRUS QUESTION

The United States and the Change of the Turkish Government

The claim that America played role in bringing down the İnönü government in February 1965 gained great credit among Turkish politicians, especially Republicans and far leftists. When the American Acheson plan on the Cyprus question was rejected by the Turkish government in August 1964, some rumours erupted in Turkey, claiming that the United States was looking for another prime minister in Turkey, who would accept American plans on Cyprus. Rightist columnist Ahmet Kabaklı gave this rumour a place in his column in daily *Tercüman*, stating that according to some terrible news, since the Turkish government resisted President Johnson's pressures on Cyprus, the United States carried out an investigation in Turkey to discover who could be prime minister and accept the Acheson plan if Prime

Minister İnönü resigned.[1] The editorial of weekly *Forum* accused the United States of carrying out underground activities to look for new prime ministers who could replace İnönü.[2] The son-in-law of İsmet İnönü, Metin Toker, claimed that in August 1964 American President Johnson sent American General Porter to Turkey in order to look for another prime minister who would accept some American proposals rejected by İnönü. According to Toker, at the same time the CIA was making enquiries about who could be prime minister if İnönü resigned in order to find a prime minister who would accept Johnson's new proposals on Cyprus. He also stated that the CIA was in aware of a radical change in Turkey's foreign policy and was trying to prevent it.[3]

In January 1965, Prime Minister İnönü himself rejected any claim that America was supporting one Turkish political party against another and said: "I myself do not worry about it. America has given definite assurances in this subject."[4] However, the visit of American Ambassador Raymond Hare to the opposition leaders just before the Parliamentary vote on 13 February 1965, which brought down the İnönü government, fuelled the accusations of American intervention in Turkish politics. Turkish politicians who were suspicious of American intervention claimed that the American ambassador was giving orders to the leader of the Justice Party, Süleyman Demirel, to bring down the İnönü government. Leftist writer Doğan Avcıoğlu wrote in *Yön* magazine that Washington naturally saw the pro-status quo Justice Party as an ally against İnönü, who was in favour of independent foreign policy. Avcıoğlu stated: "America certainly wanted to see the Justice Party in power. If America, who infiltrated to every part of Turkey, even want something, it is a great support for the rightist party."[5] Prime Minister İnönü himself rejected any American involvement in the fall of his government. In his speech in the Parliament on 1 March 1965, İnönü said: "I will not agree that a shadow be cast on honest and serious person because of a bad coincidence. In sum, at the time we relinquished our official duties we were in complete and mutual confidence with the American government and its ambassador."[6]

American Ambassador Raymond Hare, too, denied that he intended to affect opposition leaders for the fall of the İnönü government. He told Turkish journalists: "As decided long time ago, I paid ceremonial visits to the leaders of the two opposition parties. At the same time, an unexpected political crisis came about in Turkey. There is no relation between the two events apart from chronological coincidence. We, Americans, who are interested in Turkey's development, pursue the policy of keeping ourselves away from Turkey's internal politics. Internal politics is your business, not ours."[7] In his interview with daily *Milliyet*'s editor, Ambassador Hare stated that America never wanted to intervene in Turkey's internal politics which should be dealt by the Turks themselves. He denied any American involvement in Turkey's internal developments.[8]

---

[1] Ahmet Kabaklı, "Gün Işığında: Zararlı Faaliyetler", *Tercüman*, 29 August 1964.

[2] "Başyazı", *Forum*, 1 September 1964, p. 3.

[3] Metin Toker, "İsmet Paşa ile 4 Buhranlı Yıl", *Milliyet*, 11 February 1969, p. 5. See also A. Haluk Ulman and R. H. Dekmeijian, "Changing Patterns in Turkey's Foreign Policy 1959-1967", *ORBIS*, vol. 11, Fall 1967, p. 782.

[4] *Milliyet*, 8 January 1965.

[5] Doğan Avcıoğlu, "Asıl Muhalefet Şimdi Başlıyor", *Yön*, 19 February 1965, p. 3.

[6] Translated by George S. Harris, *Troubled Alliance: Turkish-American Problems in Historical Perspective 1945-1971*, (Washington D. C.: American Enterprise Institute, 1972), p. 132.

[7] *Cumhuriyet*, 24 February 1965, p. 1.

[8] *Milliyet*, 10 August 1965.

After the Justice Party came to power in the elections of 1965 the Turkish left accused it of having received American support during the election campaigns, and many leftist politicians and intellectuals continued to claim that America financially supported rightist groups against leftist ones and always wanted a rightist government in Turkey.[9] While explaining his doubts about American support for the right, Republican MP Bülent Ecevit, who would serve as prime minister in different periods in the 1970s, told his party's parliamentary caucus that America acted as if it was the ally of the Justice Party, not Turkey and that big American companies worked like JP's partners.[10] Ecevit mentioned the CIA's activities in other countries and hinted that it could do same thing in Turkey: "In America it has been disclosed with what dirty games the CIA is involved affecting domestic politics in friendly and allied countries. It pours money into elections in order to bring those it wants into power and to unseat those it does not want... In order to prepare a pretext for smashing legal and democratic opposition, it has claimed that there was a great communist danger; or else in order to prepare justification for armed American intervention it has claimed that there was a danger of unarmed and indirect aggression and has organised demonstrations, sabotage and civil war."[11] By mentioning the big increase in the number of rightist organisations, newspapers and magazines Ecevit hinted that their financial source had come from America.

It was also generally thought that the Justice Party was a pro-American party which worked for the protection of American interests in Turkey. Leftists claimed that JP voluntarily helped Americans in exploiting Turkey for their interests and intervening in Turkish domestic politics. When Süleyman Demirel was elected as the leader of the Justice Party, leftists presented him as an American lackey since he worked for an American company before entering politics. İlhan Selçuk wrote in his column: "Who could predict that a paid man of foreigners would become the leader of the biggest party in Turkey?".[12] In his speech in Parliament on 4 January 1967, the leader of the Nation Party, Osman Bölükbaşı, labelled Prime Minister Demirel as a man who worked for American interests more than Americans themselves did and accused the Demirel government of acting as an angel protecting American interests under her wings.[13]

The behaviour of the American ambassadors to Turkey, too, attracted the criticism of some Turkish politicians and intellectuals as acts of intervention in Turkey's domestic politics. We should state that as representatives of a super power, actions of American ambassadors to Turkey in the 1960s were always followed by the suspicious eyes of anti-American leftists. Therefore, when an American ambassador expressed his ideas on a subject of Turkish politics, great criticism was directed against him. When American ambassador Parker Hart claimed that America never prevented the planned Turkish military intervention in Cyprus[14] while a heated debate was going on between rival Turkish political groups on whether the government should explain the content of the Johnson letter in June 1964; the opposition groups attacked Hart, accusing him of joining an internal Turkish political debate. Cumhuriyet's columnist Ecvet Güresin wrote that by expressing his ideas on the subject, the

[9] İlhan Selçuk, "Hayallerden Silkinmek", *Cumhuriyet,* 22 June 1966, p. 2, İlhan Selçuk, "Bir, İki, Üç, Dört, Üstünü Ört", *Cumhuriyet,* 17 December 1968, p. 2.

[10] *Cumhuriyet,* 21 June 1966, p. 7.

[11] G. S. Harris, *Troubled Alliance,* p. 136.

[12] İlhan Selçuk, "Pencere: Bağımsızlık Ülküsü", *Cumhuriyet,* 26 December 1964, p. 2.

[13] *Millet Meclisi Tutanak Dergisi,* 4 January 1967, term 2, sess. 2, vol. 11, p. 38.

[14] *Dışişleri Bakanlığı Belleteni,* January 1966, pp. 37-38.

American ambassador joined a quarrel in internal politics at a very delicate time. He argued that the ambassador became a part of the debate by going beyond his official duties.[15]

Another Cumhuriyet columnist İlhan Selçuk wrote an open letter to the American ambassador in his column: "Dear Mr P. Hart,... It is understood from your speech that you support the thesis of the Justice Party, thus the Republican People's Party had the right to respond to your claims. I think in a near future the JP will completely leave the ground and you will start debating with the RPP."[16] The weekly *Forum* argued that the statement of the American ambassador was an open pressure on the government not to make public the Johnson letter which became a subject of a debate in Parliament. *Forum* labelled the ambassador's behaviour as the style of a high commissioner who intervenes in internal politics, far beyond an attitude of an ambassador.[17] MP Hayrettin Uysal stated in his article that Mr. Hart clearly intervened in Turkey's internal affairs and hurt the honour of the Turkish people. Uysal claimed that Hart acted like the prime minister of Turkey, fearlessly speaking about Turkey's internal problems.[18]

These unproved claims cannot be taken as facts since they were made by biased anti-American critics. Some of these critics such as Bülent Ecevit denied any foreign intervention in Turkish politics when they were in power. The only thing which can be said is that the United States wanted rightists to come into power in Turkey as she did in other countries because anti-Communist rightists were more likely to pursue policies which would be compatible with US interests. This does not necessitate direct US intervention. Since the Cyprus question became a national matter in Turkey outside political competition, the search of a new prime minister by the Americans to find a favourable solution to the problem is a remote possibility.

The United States and the Fall of the Papandreou Government

American rulers hoped that a small concession (probably a military base) by the Greeks to Turkey could solve the Cyprus problem to the advantage of all Western powers, including Greece and Turkey, with unification of the island with Greece. Therefore, they encouraged Greek and Turkish officials to have bilateral talks. The Americans certainly disliked the excessive Greek Cypriot opposition to such plans and Greek support for this opposition. This was probably the reason for apparent US pressures on the Greek side after 1965.

Some authors, especially Greek authors, claimed that between 1965 and 1967 the United States put enormous pressure on the Greek governments to have secret bilateral talks with Turkey to find a solution to the Cyprus problem along the Acheson plan lines. They were of the opinion that the United States played an important role in ousting the Papandreou government in July 1965 and the Greek military coup in April 1967. Those Greek authors argued that the main American intention in these incidents was to remove Papandreou from power since he supported Makarios' policies and did not comply with American demands on the Cyprus question such as having bilateral talks with the Turks. They further explained that the conservative minority governments between July 1965 and April 1967 and the Greek

---

[15] Ecvet Güresin, "Günün Notları: Amerika'nın Esef Verici Tutumu", *Cumhuriyet,* 5 January 1966, p. 1.
[16] İlhan Selçuk, "Pencere: Amerikan Elçisine Açık Mektup", *Cumhuriyet,* 6 January 1966, p. 2.
[17] "Amerikan Elçisinin Siyasi Komiser Edası", *Forum,* 15 January 1966, p. 6.
[18] Hayrettin Uysal, "Tehlikeli Alakalar", *Akis,* 15 January 1966, p. 5.

military junta which came to power in April 1967 relied primarily on American support for their survival and therefore, at American request, they embarked on secret talks with Turkey over the future of Cyprus. These Greek administrations themselves liked the Acheson plan-like schemes since they were in favour of Enosis even if it was to be implemented partially.

Several authors argued that American officials became increasingly antagonistic toward Andreas Papandreou, the son of Greek Prime Minister Papandreou, for several reasons. Firstly, Andreas Papandreou had leftist and neutralist ideas which could bring harm to American interests in Greece.[19] He "had openly advocated the abolition of the monarchy, the revision of the Greek foreign policy away from the NATO alignment and stronger control over the military."[20] There was a widespread rumour in Greece that Andreas Papandreou sponsored the so-called Aspida organisation to prepare the way for a left-wing military coup.[21] Another reason for the American antagonism toward Andreas Papandreou was claimed to be Andreas Papandreou's efforts to bring the Greek Central Intelligence service (KYP) under the effective control of the Greek government. As an adviser to the prime minister, he had nominal supervision over the KYP and discovered that the KYP had been funded directly by the CIA. When he demanded all funds of the KYP pass through the prime minister's office, the CIA blocked this attempt.[22]

The most emphasised reason for the American dislike of Andreas Papandreou was his attitude towards the Cyprus question. He supported the main policies of the Makarios government.[23] In Greece, the right wing press launched a series of attacks against Andreas Papandreou, claiming that he held the primary responsibility for the Greek rejection of one version of the Acheson plan which would bring the union of at least the major portion of Cyprus with Greece.[24] Andreas Papandreou himself claimed in his book that his ideas on the Cyprus question caused serious friction between the American and Greek governments. In his interview with Eric Rouleou of *Le Monde*, he had said: "Certain Western powers have attempted to create a rift between President Makarios and our government by asking us to condemn his policies... An agreement based on Enosis and a Turkish military base must be excluded as long as the Cyprus government is against it." The American services in Greece protested against this interview loudly. It was obvious that Andreas Papandreou was becoming a source of friction between the United States and the Greek government. In a short time he resigned from the post of Alternate Minister of Co-ordination. He wrote in his book: "While it was not true that the Americans had asked for my resignation, it was true that my clashes with them had created an atmosphere between them and our government that was working to the disadvantage of our government."[25]

---

[19] Theodore A. Couloumbis, *the United States, Greece and Turkey: the Troubled Triangle*, (New York: Praeger, 1983), p. 30.

[20] Halil İbrahim Salih, *Cyprus: the Impact of Diverse Nationalism in a State*, (Alabama: University of Alabama Press, 1978), p. 54.

[21] M. Goldbloom, "United States Policy in Post-War Greece" in Richard Clogg and George Yannopoulos (eds.), *Greece Under Military Rule*, (London: Secker and Warburg, 1972), p. 237.

[22] Ibid., p. 234.

[23] Michael A. Attalides, *Cyprus: Nationalism and International Politics*, (Edinburgh: Q Press Ltd., 1979), p. 72.

[24] Laurance Stern, *The Wrong Horse: The Politics of Intervention and the Failure of American Diplomacy*, (New York: Times Books, 1977), p. 33.

[25] Andreas Papandreou, *Democracy At Gunpoint: the Greek Front*, (London: Andre Deutsch, 1970), pp. 105-106.

According to Andreas Papandreou's account, in March 1965 the American embassy received information that a Greek ship carrying Soviet ground-to-air missiles had left Egypt and was on its way to Cyprus for delivery. The American officials in Greece expressed their great concern over the incident and American ambassador "Labouisse prepared a five-point program for pacification in Cyprus over a six-month period. The terms were intended to satisfy the pride of the Turks and to improve their relative military position." In mid-March 1965 Greek Defence Minister Garoufalias went to Cyprus to meet with the Cypriot cabinet and present the Labouisse ultimatum but achieved nothing.[26] Cypriot President Makarios disclosed that Garoufalias' action was ordered directly by American Secretary of Defence McNamara. He stated that obeying the Pentagon's instructions, Garoufalias prevented the delivery of Soviet missiles to Cyprus and withdrew from Cyprus all Greek officers who knew how to handle missiles and could have trained their Cypriot counterparts in those techniques.[27]

In early April 1965, stories began to appear in the Cyprus press that the Greek King was looking for a way to overthrow the Papandreou government, to establish a national unity cabinet and to find a permanent solution to the Cyprus problem on the basis of the Acheson plan.[28] In May 1965, at a meeting of the Crown Council of Greece, Makarios suggested that he would proclaim Enosis unilaterally if the Greek government supported him and were prepared to face the consequences of such an action. His move was a reaction to rumours that Greece was planning a partial Enosis on the basis of the Acheson plan. The Papandreou government was not ready to undertake such a responsibility. It was aware of the fact that complete Enosis was not possible without paying a price to Turkey.[29]

As a result of American pressures, Greek Foreign Minister Stavros Costopoulos and his Turkish counterpart Hasan Esat Işık held talks on the Cyprus question at the meeting of NATO foreign ministers in London in May 1965.[30] Makarios condemned the talks, stating that they could lead to the partition of Cyprus. After returning to Athens, Costopoulos and Greek Prime Minister Papandreou had to declare that "the talks in London did not touch the substance of the Cyprus issue. Greece will never deviate from the line that the Cyprus question is exclusively a matter within the competence of the United Nations and cannot be the object of Greek-Turkish negotiations."[31] A short time later Stephanos Stephanopoulos, the deputy premier and minister of co-ordination in the Greek cabinet, attacked Makarios by accusing him of preventing the success of the Acheson plan which would bring Enosis.[32] Meanwhile, the Cypriot press continued to carry stories that the overthrow of the Papandreou government was well under way.

In July 1965 a crisis came about between the Greek prime minister and the King. Prime Minister Papandreou decided to undertake the duties of the minister of national defence and asked the king to dismiss Defence Minister Petros Garoufalias but the king refused to do so. Many Greeks believed that the United States supported the King fully in his confrontation

---

[26] Ibid., p. 108.
[27] Ibid., p. 206.
[28] Ibid., p. 108, P. N. Vanezis, *Makarios: Pragmatism v. Idealism,* (London: Abelard-Schuman, 1974), p. 165.
[29] M. A. Attalides, *Cyprus: Nationalism and International Politics*, p. 66.
[30] A. Papandreou, *Democracy At Gunpoint*, p. 109, H. I. Salih, *Cyprus*, p. 54, Robert Stephens, *Cyprus: A Place of Arms*, (London: Pall Mall Press, 1966), p. 203, *Keesing's Contemporary Archives,* 1965-1966, vol. 15, p. 20809.
[31] A. Papandreou, *Democracy At Gunpoint*, p. 109.
[32] Ibid., p. 109, P. N. Vanezis, *Makarios*, p. 166.

with the prime minister over the defence post. Andreas Papandreou was one of them. In his account, on 13 July 1965 Norbert Anschuetz of the American embassy came to see him and tried to persuade him to follow a softer line toward the King. America was of the opinion that the King was right in denying George Papandreou the defence post. On the same day, American ambassador Henry Labouisse visited the Prime Minister, telling him that the King was right in not handing over the Ministry of National Defence to him.[33] When the King insisted on rejecting Papandreou's proposal, the Greek prime minister submitted his resignation on 15 July 1965.

Greek critics of the United States accused her of creating political destabilisation in Greece by supporting the King against Papandreou. They claimed that American attitude at least encouraged the King to dismiss the Papandreou government because he knew that he could be certain of considerable American sympathy.[34] It was claimed that the USA took part in this development by supporting the King mainly because of its dislike for Papandreou's Cyprus policy. Given the general US suspicion that leftist powers, including Papandreou's party, would harm American interests, this claim needs to be taken cautiously.

The Greek Minority Governments and the United States

The Stephanopoulos government which came to power after the resignation of George Papandreou was believed to be pro-American and to have ideas favoured by American officials on the Cyprus question. In the opinion of Goldbloom, even the formation of the Stephanopoulos government would not have been possible without American support. Members of the new administration were known for their close ties with the American embassy. Some of them broke away from Papandreou's Centre Union Party to support the King and some were believed to have CIA connections.[35] As for the Cyprus question the Stephanopoulos government seemed to favour a solution along the lines of the Acheson plan. In Andreas Papandreou's view, "Stephanopoulos and Makarios were bitter personal enemies, and that their mutual hostility sprang from their diametrically opposed views on the Cyprus question... Stephanopoulos belonged to that group of Greek politicians who advocated any solution that would satisfy the Western allies, promote the interest of NATO, and lay the foundations for a close co-operation between Turkey and Greece in the protection of those two countries from the communist menace. And it was on these commitments of Stephanopoulos that hope was built for the settlement of the Cyprus issue in a manner that would be satisfactory to the Pentagon and NATO."

It was claimed that Stephanopoulos inclined to solving the Cyprus problem through talks with Turkey for the sake of NATO's interests and sought union of Cyprus with Greece with some compensation to Turkey. American Secretary of State Dean Rusk was so encouraged by the attitude of the Stephanopoulos government that he called a conference on the Cyprus question to be attended by representatives of the United States, Britain, Greece and Turkey.[36] It was widely believed that Greek officials sought Enosis with some compensation for Turkey. On 18 February 1966 Greek General Grivas declared in Athens that Cyprus must be

[33] A. Papandreou, *Democracy At Gunpoint*, pp. 137-138.
[34] M. Goldbloom, ``United States Policy in Post-War Greece", p. 237.
[35] Ibid., pp. 237-238.
[36] A. Papandreou, *Democracy At Gunpoint*, p. 205.

united with Greece immediately. Since he did not clarify that the Enosis which he talked about included some price to Turkey, Turkish authorities protested against it.[37] In late March 1966, Makarios accused Grivas and Stephanopoulos of preparing a plot to assassinate him after a coup set for 25 March or 1 April 1966.[38] On 11 April 1966 Greek Foreign Minister Tsirimokos resigned because he was opposed to the partition plan for Cyprus which was being pursued by the Greek government under the influence of foreign powers.[39]

In May 1966 the Greek government announced its intention to hold direct negotiations with Turkey. Turkey responded favourably. Greek and Turkish representatives had talks in Brussels on 9 June 1966 under the auspices of NATO.[40] On 25 June 1966 the Turkish and Greek foreign ministers, Çağlayangil and Toumbas, met in Paris to discuss the Cyprus question and they agreed that Cyprus would be united with Greece in return for a base for Turkey in the island. But Toumbas did not give consent to Turkey's having full sovereignty over the base.[41] In December 1966, the Turkish and Greek foreign ministers exchanged a secret protocol along the lines of the Acheson plan. The Greek foreign minister proposed a form of Enosis and stated that the British base at Dhekelia would be made available for Turkey in case of an agreement. The Turkish foreign minister insisted on full sovereignty of that base, but the Greek foreign minister said that he could not answer immediately. Since the Greek government fell from office a few days later, nothing developed from this scheme.[42]

The Paraskevopoulos government, too, seemed to favour a solution of the Cyprus question along the lines of the Acheson plan. Paraskevopoulos called a Crown Council, inclusive of Makarios and George Papandreou, to search a solution for the problem. In Andreas Papandreou's words, "by stacking the council with ex-prime ministers who accepted the King's and the American embassy's directives, George Papandreou and Makarios could easily be put in a difficult situation, and be forced to give their blessing to the NATO-sponsored solution of the partition."[43] The Crown Council, which was convened on 6 February 1967 achieved nothing.

The Greek Military Coup and the United States

Many Greeks believed that the United States supported the Greek military coup of 21 April 1967. In their view, the United States was worried that a victory of Papandreou's Centre Union Party in the approaching elections, which seemed increasingly certain, would deprive the King of control over the Greek armed forces and threaten the monarchy itself.[44] Americans were also concerned that a Papandreou government would worsen the Cyprus question since Papandreou had supported the policies of the Makarios administration.

According to Stern, CIA station chief Maury in the American Embassy in Athens disclosed that "senior members of the CIA country team met in January 1967... We concluded

---

[37] Ibid., pp. 206-207.
[38] H. I. Salih, *Cyprus*, p. 55.
[39] A. Papandreou, *Democracy At Gunpoint*, p. 207.
[40] H. I. Salih, *Cyprus*, pp. 55-56, *Keesing's Contemporary Archives*, 1965-1966, vol. 15, p. 21540.
[41] Suha Bölükbaşı, *Superpowers and the Third World: Turkish-American Relations and Cyprus*, (New York: University Press of America, 1988), p. 132.
[42] M. A. Attalides, *Cyprus: Nationalism and International Politics*, p. 71, *Keesing's Contemporary Archives*, 1967-1968, vol. 16, p. 21947.
[43] A. Papandreou, *Democracy At Gunpoint*, pp. 207-208.
[44] M. Goldbloom, ``United States Policy in Post-War Greece'', p. 238.

that a victory by the Papandreous would seriously damage vital US interests in the eastern Mediterranean area, weaken the southern flank of NATO and seriously destabilise Greek-Turkish relations then severely strained by the Cyprus situation."[45] Allegedly, at the strong urging of the CIA station chief and some members of the American embassy staff, American ambassador to Greece Phillips Talbot recommended that the White House authorise the expenditure of 100,000 dollars in black funds to finance opposition to Papandreou.[46]

Reportedly, "American diplomatic and intelligence services expected an extra constitutional, military move in Greek politics in connection with the 1967 elections. The expectation was that this move would have been authorised by the King and put into operation by the hierarchy of the armed forces." Then American officials made a policy choice: The United States would not try to affect the 1967 elections in favour of Conservatives and pro-Royalist forces. That meant that the United States expected nothing from the elections and that it would not oppose an extra parliamentary initiative including a military take-over of power.[47] In Andreas Papandreou's account, American ambassador Talbot visited George Papandreou on 13 April 1967 and explained to him the importance of moderation at that critical time. Talbot also expressed the American administration's wish that George Papandreou would accept the national unity government solution.[48]

On 21 April 1967 a group of right wing military officers headed by George Papadopoulos overthrew the Greek government by carrying out the Plan Prometheus, which was a NATO plan formulated for use in case of a communist coup.[49] It seemed that American intelligence services were surprised by the particular timing of the coup and the specific structure of the military leadership which executed it. It appeared that the coup was not approved by the King beforehand. Nevertheless, the coup conspirators were not unknown to the Americans. George Papadopoulos, Nicolas Makarezos and Michael Roufogalis had all served with the Greek Central intelligence agency (KYP) which had close ties with the CIA. Papadopoulos had served as the liaison officer for a period between the KYP and the CIA.[50] According to the account of a disaffected member of the Greek military junta, which was quoted by Andreas Papandreou, after the coup began, "the CIA decided to move openly in order to counter the King's resistance. Through the American navy, army and air force attaches, the line was put forward that the Greek Armed Forces were on the side of the junta, and since the coup had succeeded, to oppose it now would encourage the communists to rise up. Thus, the King would be well advised to recognise the new regime."[51]

Some Greek authors claimed that the Greek junta was the agent of the United States and came under the American influence in its main policies, including its Cyprus stance. In Papandreou's words, the military regime "was supposed to settle the Cyprus issue [along lines prepared by the Pentagon and NATO], to make it possible for NATO to turn Greece into an important naval base, and to make it possible for the CIA to establish an enormous counter-espionage system in that part of the world."[52] On 28 April 1967 American Secretary of State Rusk hinted the American approval for the new regime: "I am encouraged to see that

---

[45] L. Stern, *the Wrong Horse*, p. 37.
[46] M. A. Attalides, *Cyprus: Nationalism and International Politics*, pp. 146-147.
[47] T. A. Couloumbis, *the United States, Greece and Turkey*, pp. 50-51.
[48] A. Papandreou, *Democracy At Gunpoint*, p. 187.
[49] Ibid., p. 191.
[50] T. A. Couloumbis, *the United States, Greece and Turkey*, p. 51.
[51] A. Papandreou, *Democracy At Gunpoint*, p. 192.
[52] Ibid., p. 201.

King Constantine in his first statement last Friday has called for an early return to parliamentary government... I am gratified that Greece will continue its strong support of NATO."[53] In August 1967, the Greek Prime Minister declared that Greece and Turkey were bound by the need "to confront jointly the common enemy -communism- and to consider all outstanding differences of view as secondary to this primary interest." At the same time, in order to promote a Cyprus solution, George Papadopoulos, the minister to the Prime Minister visited Cyprus. He was welcomed at the Nicosia airport by General Grivas, who shouted "long live Enosis."[54]

The Keşan-Alexandroupolis Talks

In September 1967, the Greek military regime called upon the Turks to have a meeting to consider a settlement of the Cyprus question. The prime ministers of Turkey and Greece, Süleyman Demirel and Kollies, met in the Turkish and Greek border towns, Keşan and Alexandroupolis (Dedeağaç), on 9 and 10 September 1967. The proposal of the Greek Prime Minister included the union of Cyprus to Greece, minority guarantees for Turkish Cypriots and territorial adjustments on the Greco-Turkish border in favour of Turkey. The Turks rejected Enosis and demanded either a return to the 1959 status quo or double Enosis.[55] The Greeks were still trying to achieve the second version of the Acheson plan, almost unconditional Enosis, but the Turks insisted on a sovereign base on the island. The talks ended with a complete failure.

After returning to Turkey, Turkish Prime Minister Demirel declared in his press conference that Turkey rejected Enosis and insisted on the validity of the existing London-Zurich agreements on Cyprus.[56] He said: "Security rights and interests of Turkish Cypriots will certainly be protected by Turkey... The importance of Cyprus from Turkey's security point of view will be taken into consideration while seeking a solution to the problem. The Turkish thesis is to solve the Cyprus problem under following conditions: The existing treaties cannot be changed without the consent of all participant states. One of the Cypriot communities cannot rule over the other. The balance of power in the region which was established by the Lausanne Treaty cannot be changed. Cyprus cannot be united to any country."[57] Demirel's statement was a serious blow to the Greek military junta. In Andreas Papandreou's words, "Demirel's statement fell like a bombshell in Greece. Papadopoulos and the junta government had had a resounding defeat."[58] The Enosis policy which was pursued by the Greek administration had openly been rejected by the Turkish government.

In Turkey, opposition MPs criticised the Keşan-Alexandroupolis talks on the ground that they were held under the influence of foreign powers and sought union of Cyprus with Greece. Turhan Feyzioğlu said that the most reasonable solution of the Cyprus problem was the partition of the island and the integration of a portion of Cyprus with Turkey. M. Ali

[53] Ibid., p. 200.
[54] Ibid., p. 208.
[55] Van Coufoudakis, ``United States Foreign Policy and the Cyprus Question" in Michael A. Attalides (ed.), Cyprus Reviewed: A Seminar on the Cyprus Problem, (Nicosia: Jus Cypri Association, 1977), p. 142n, Keesing's Contemporary Archives, 1967-1968, vol. 16, p. 22282.
[56] H. I. Salih, Cyprus, p. 57.
[57] Murat Sarıca et. al., Kıbrıs Sorunu, (İstanbul: İstanbul Üniversitesi Yayınları, No. 2071, 1975), p. 139.
[58] A. Papandreou, Democracy At Gunpoint, p. 209.

Aybar claimed that the talks were held because of American pressures and he stated that the problem could not be solved with leaving a small base to Turkey.[59] The general secretary of the Republican People's Party, Bülent Ecevit, declared that Turkey should not surrender itself to pressures of its Western allies who saw the Cyprus question from the point of their own interests. Turkey's representative in the Geneva talks, Nihat Erim, claimed that it was a mistake by the Turkish government to discuss the double Enosis with the Greeks because it would give impression that Turkey made bargains with Greece on Cyprus while at the same time she supported the thesis of federal system.[60]

THE 1967 CYPRUS CRISIS

The November 1967 Fighting in Cyprus

On 15 November 1967 a Greek Cypriot patrol under the command of Grivas entered the Turkish Cypriot village of Ayios Theodhoros (Boğaziçi) pretendly to carry out a routine inspection. Turkish Cypriots objected to this inspection and allegedly opened fire on Greek Cypriot forces. On the orders of Grivas, the Greek patrol occupied the village by the evening of the same day. At the same time, in a separate incident without having any relation with the patrol issue, Greek Cypriot forces attacked the Turkish Cypriot positions in the village of Kophinou (Geçitkale).[61] During these Greek Cypriot attacks, which were carried out by the Greek Cypriot National Guard and Greek Cypriot police, twenty-eight Turks and two Greeks were killed.[62] The United Nations forces in the region could not stop Greek Cypriot attacks and their call for a cease-fire was ignored by the Greek Cypriots until the two villages were completely overrun. National Guard troops dismantled the UN radio station in one position and disarmed UN soldiers in another.[63] As stated by Crawshaw, "the National Guard, under the command of Greek officers, tried to drive the UN soldiers away so that there would be no UN witnesses to the battle."[64]

The villages of Theodhoros and Kophinou were strategically located Turkish enclaves on the Nicosia-Limassol motorway and were controlled by the self-established Turkish Cypriot administration. Greek Cypriots apparently wanted to control these two strategic Turkish villages to weaken the strength of Turkish Cypriots. The Turkish side believed that Greek attacks were organised attempts to achieve Enosis as proved by their timing.[65] In 1967 the Cyprus government had established a new paramilitary unit in the police and imported large quantities of Czech arms. The National Guard had established its ties with the Greek army and had been virtually under the control of Greek officers. The doctrine of Enosis had been extremely vigorously propagated by these Greek officers from the mainland Greece.[66] On 26

---

[59] M. Sarıca et. al., *Kıbrıs Sorunu*, p. 138.

[60] Ibid., p. 140.

[61] A. Papandreou, *Democracy At Gunpoint*, pp. 209-210, S. Bölükbaşı, *Turkish-American Relations and Cyprus*, pp. 133-134.

[62] Rauf R. Denktash, *The Cyprus Triangle*, (London: K. Rüstem and Brother, 1988), p. 50.

[63] Thomas Ehlrich, *Cyprus: 1958-1967*, (London: Oxford University Press, 1974), p. 98.

[64] Nancy Crawshaw, *The Cyprus Revolt: an Account of the Struggle for Union With Greece*, (London, Boston: G. Allen and Unwin, 1978), p. 377.

[65] *Keesing's Contemporary Archives*, 1967-1968, vol. 16, p. 22435.

[66] Ibid., p. 373.

June 1967 the Greek Cypriot House of Representatives had unanimously passed a resolution declaring that the struggle for Enosis would continue until the union of Cyprus with the motherland, Greece, was achieved. And finally the Greco-Turkish dialogue on Cyprus, which had started in May 1965 and continued after the military take-over in Greece, had just come to an end with the failure of the talks between the Turkish and Greek prime ministers on 9-10 September 1967.[67]

It appeared that Greek Cypriots attacks were pre-planned. The report of UN Secretary-General U Thant suggested this conclusion: "The magnitude of the Ayios Theodoros operation and the speed with which it was carried out clearly indicate that the National Guard had planned in advance to carry out this operation in the event of any show of opposition by the Turkish Cypriots."[68] It was claimed that the Greek Cypriot offensive was arranged by General Grivas under the order of the Greek junta. Grivas had stated that he did not accept any commands from the Cyprus government but from the Greek administration.[69] On the night of November 15, Greek Prime Minister Collias cabled Makarios, advising him to order the evacuation of Greek Cypriot forces from the two villages in order to prevent the bombardment of Cyprus by the Turkish Air Force. But Makarios rejected his suggestion, claiming that the offensive had taken place with the consent of the Greek government.[70]

The Turkish Reaction to the Fighting

After the fighting began in Cyprus, the Turkish Ministry of Foreign Affairs issued a statement: "While there was still a possibility of reaching a negotiated solution, the attack launched against the Ayios Theodhoros constitutes a flagrant provocation by the Cyprus government. The United Nations force in Cyprus is requested to stop the fighting immediately and clear the Turkish Cypriot areas of Ayios Theodhoros and Kophinou of both Greek Cypriot and Greek armed forces. If this cannot be done, a crisis which will go beyond the borders of the island will be unavoidable."[71] In the evening of November 15, the Turkish foreign minister, İhsan Sabri Çağlayangil, called the UN force in Cyprus to bring about a cease-fire immediately.[72] In its meeting which continued all night, the Turkish National Security Council decided to send a note to Makarios, stating that the Turkish Air Force would bomb the positions of Greek Cypriots unless the Greek Cypriot forces withdrew from the two occupied villages. When the Greek forces started to evacuate the Turkish villages at 4.00 A.M. on November 16, the Turkish government cancelled its planned air strikes against Cyprus.[73] By the end of November 17, the UN force in Cyprus had achieved a cease-fire and the National Guard had withdrawn from the besieged areas.[74]

Meanwhile, the Turkish public opinion became increasingly pro-intervention, urging the government to launch a military operation against Greek Cypriot forces to save the Turkish

---

[67] R. R. Denktash, *The Cyprus Triangle*, p. 50.

[68] S. Bölükbaşı, *Turkish-American Relations and Cyprus*, p. 134.

[69] M. A. Attalides, *Cyprus: Nationalism and International Politics*, p. 98, A. Papandreou, *Democracy At Gunpoint*, p. 211.

[70] A. Papandreou, *Democracy At Gunpoint*, p. 211.

[71] T. Ehlrich, *Cyprus: 1958-1967*, p. 98.

[72] Ibid., p. 105.

[73] S. Bölükbaşı, *Turkish-American Relations and Cyprus*, p. 135, M. Sarıca et. al., *Kıbrıs Sorunu*, p. 143.

[74] T. Ehlrich, *Cyprus: 1958-1967*, p. 105.

community on the island. Public demonstrations, rallies and meetings were held in many Turkish cities. The Turkish government was widely criticised because of its apparent inactivity. The Turkish radio and especially the Turkish press created a war atmosphere, by publicising the news of Greek Cypriot atrocities and preparations of the Turkish armed forces. On 16 November 1967 in the closed session of the Turkish National Assembly, MPs from both opposition and government parties urged a military action against Cyprus. At the end, the National Assembly authorised the government to intervene in Cyprus if necessary by a vote of 432 to 1.[75] Under these pressures, on November 17, Turkish Prime Minister Süleyman Demirel sent an ultimatum-like note to Greece, demanding the following points: 1- The withdrawal of all Greek forces stationed in Cyprus since 1964 except those which were provided for in the 1959 London-Zurich agreements. 2- The recall of Greek general Grivas. 3- The disbandment of the National Guard. 4- The disengagement in areas of conflict. 5- Compensation for losses suffered by Turkish Cypriots. 6- The removal of pressure from the Turkish community by ensuring freedom of movement. 7- The enlargement of the UN force in Cyprus. 8- The formation of local Turkish governing bodies in the Turkish enclaves.[76]

It seemed that Turkey was poised to invade Cyprus if Greece did not accept its demands and the situation in Cyprus deteriorated further. The Turkish armed forces continued their preparations for a landing in Cyprus. Turkish jet fighters flew over the island daily. Turkish war ships were sent to the port of Mersin, the closest harbour to Cyprus. Between November 17-22, the situation grew rapidly to a war atmosphere. On 20 November 1967 Turkish Foreign Minister Çağlayangil sent a strong warning to the Greek government, asking the Greek rulers to ensure security of Turkish Cypriots: "The continuos threat directed at the Turkish community should be lifted."[77]

Washington Post's editorial on 21 November 1967 described the situation: "In response to the last week's shooting, Turkey prepared for war. The Parliament unleashed the military move on Greece if more harm came to Turkish Cypriots, the press published frightful atrocity pictures, troops boarded vessels of war, and Turkish jets screamed over Cyprus. American and British diplomats are frantically trying to avert war... At the end of the road in any Cyprus crisis lies the possibility of a collision between the interests of the USSR, which can be expected to encourage anything that weakens NATO, and the vital interests of the United States."[78] *The Daily Telegraph*'s editorial on November 24 suggested: "Perhaps a quick operation [by Turkey] with a minimum of bloodshed is the only way to solve this chronic problem to the advantage of all except Makarios and the Russians -who naturally want to keep Cyprus as an apple of discord within NATO. Things might soon settle down under some partition agreement."[79]

The Turkish armed forces were not ready for a landing in Cyprus though the Turkish government seemed committed to a military operation if its demands were not met. When military commanders and government officials began making plans for a military intervention, it was realised that the Turkish military had not enough military equipment and

---

[75] S. Bölükbaşı, *Turkish-American Relations and Cyprus*, p. 136, Erol Mütercimler, *Kıbrıs Barış Harekatının Bilinmeyen Yönleri*, (İstanbul: Yaprak Yayınevi, 1990), p. 117, *Keesing's Contemporary Archives*, 1967-1968, vol. 16, p. 22435.

[76] V. Coufoudakis, ``United States Foreign Policy and the Cyprus Question" p. 142n, A. Papandreou, *Democracy At Gunpoint*, pp. 211-212.

[77] A. Papandreou, *Democracy At Gunpoint*, p. 211.

[78] Ibid., p. 211.

[79] Ibid., p. 212.

personnel. Nevertheless, Turkish leaders decided to resort to military force if necessary. Military preparations were made as if Turkey would intervene in Cyprus.[80] However, Prime Minister Demirel and opposition leader İnönü were thinking that Turkey should avoid a military intervention and act very cautiously. Demirel told İnönü that he "would be satisfied to solve the crisis in a manner that would more or less save his and Turkey's prestige." Turkish intervention would lead to a Greek-Turkish war and he "did not want a war at all." İnönü said to Demirel and Foreign Minister Çağlayangil that the Turkish army had no overseas fighting experience and that a military defeat would mean disaster for Turkey.[81]

The Vance Mission

As it was in the former Cyprus crises, the main American concern during the November 1967 crisis was to restore peace on the island and thus to prevent an outbreak of a Greco-Turkish war because of the Cyprus problem. American officials tried to restrain both sides from taking any action which would worsen the situation. While they put pressure on Greece to comply with Turkish demands, they urged the Turkish rulers not to intervene in Cyprus. From the beginning of the crisis, the American ambassador to Turkey, Parker Hart, maintained constant contact with Turkish Foreign Minister Çağlayangil. He told Çağlayangil that American President Johnson requested Turkey not to intervene in Cyprus but chose not to send a written message because of the Turkish public's reaction to the Johnson letter in 1964.[82] A task force of the American Sixth fleet was deployed close to the shores of Cyprus. It was widely believed that this American action was directed to deterring the Turkish forces from launching a military operation against Cyprus.[83]

On 22 November 1967, the American administration joined with Britain and Canada in proposing a settlement formula: "1- Greek and Turkish troop strengths would be reduced to the Treaty of Alliance levels. 2- The UN force would be enlarged. 3- Turkish Cypriots who suffered losses in the attacks would be compensated and the future security of the Turkish Cypriot areas would be assured. 4- Turkey would guarantee not to intervene militarily in the future."[84] When the Greek government rejected the Turkish demands on 22 November 1967 and the possibility of armed combat seemed very high, American President Johnson appointed Cyrus Vance, the former deputy secretary of defence, as his special envoy to mediate between the parties to the Cyprus question. UN Secretary General U Thant and his special representative Rolz Bennett also became actively involved in mediating between the sides.

When the Greek note was sent to the Turkish government on November 22, the American intelligence reports predicted that Turkey would initiate military action within twenty-four hours. The American State Department concluded that the United States had two options to prevent a Turkish military operation. 1- To invite Greek King Constantine and Turkish President Sunay to Washington to discuss the crisis with Johnson. 2- To send a special envoy to the area to mediate between the sides. Secretary of State Rusk advised Johnson to dispatch

---

[80] S. Bölükbaşı, *Turkish-American Relations and Cyprus*, p. 135, E. Mütercimler, *Kıbrıs Barış Harekâtının Bilinmeyen Yönleri*, p. 120.
[81] S. Bölükbaşı, *Turkish-American Relations and Cyprus*, p. 137.
[82] Ibid., p. 137.
[83] Ibid., p. 137, M. Sarıca et. al., *Kıbrıs Sorunu*, p. 144.

a special envoy since he believed this option would be more beneficial. Cyrus Vance "was told that Turkish troops were already at the embarkation port and were expected, according to intelligence, to invade Cyprus the next morning. This would mean war between Greece and Turkey." President Johnson instructed Vance: "Do what you have to to stop the war. If you need anything, let me know."[85]

As a first step, Cyrus Vance manoeuvred to gain time to be able to mediate between the sides. In his meeting with Turkish Prime Minister Demirel on November 23, Vance obtained the Turkish government's promise that it would not invade Cyprus in next few days.[86] Then Vance shuttled between Athens and Ankara to find a settlement formula agreed by both sides. His main tactic was "to press Greece and Turkey to some settlement, and then to put the Archbishop in the position of either accepting the settlement or being the isolated cause of a continuing crisis that threatened to explode at any moment."[87] Although Vance pressed the Turkish side as well as the Greek side, this time there would be no repetition of the Johnson letter in 1964. A Johnson letter-like threat could cause total alienation of Turkey from the United States. This time, it was the Greek side which caused the instability that threatened the cohesion of NATO. The Greek side had caused the crisis, therefore it should make major concessions to end the crisis. Nevertheless, Greece should be approached properly to encourage her in making concessions. Some reports indicated that Cyrus Vance developed a formula which would provide the weaker side with a ladder it could climb down. In Adams and Cottrell's words, "the United States was prepared to use as much diplomatic persuasion as possible short of military intervention to head off what appeared to be an inevitable military conflict. However, since it intervened against Turkey diplomatically in the 1964 crisis in rather sharp terms, the United States would do nothing further to worsen its relations with the Turkish government in the present crisis."[88]

The official American position was that Vance acted only as a mediator and did not threaten sanctions against either side. But there were some rumours that the United States would cut off its military aid to both sides. Ehlrich suggests that "even if Vance did not directly discuss future military assistance for Greece and Turkey, the issue must have been very much in the minds of leaders in those countries, for both depended on American assistance to maintain their armed forces."[89] In Ankara, according to some reports, Vance reminded Turkish officials of the American view that the use of US-supplied weapons and military equipment by Turkey in its operation against Cyprus was not compatible with the assistance agreements between the two countries. He put diplomatic pressure on the Turks not to resort to military force.[90] In Athens, Vance pressed the Greeks to reach a settlement by saying that the United States was unwilling to continue deterring the Turks from invading Cyprus.[91]

---

[84] T. Ehlrich, *Cyprus: 1958-1967*, p. 110.

[85] S. Bölükbaşı, *Turkish-American Relations and Cyprus*, p. 139.

[86] T. Ehlrich, *Cyprus: 1958-1967*, p. 111.

[87] Ibid., p. 112.

[88] Thomas W. Adams and Alvin J. Cottrell, *Cyprus Between East and West*, (Baltimore: John Hopkins Press, 1968), p. 72.

[89] T. Ehlrich, *Cyprus: 1958-1967*, pp. 111-112.

[90] M. Sarıca et. al., *Kıbrıs Sorunu*, pp. 146-147, E. Mütercimler, *Kıbrıs Barış Harekatının Bilinmeyen Yönleri*, p. 124.

[91] H. I. Salih, *Cyprus*, p. 59.

The Greek colonels seemed prepared to compromise because they did not want to worsen their already uneasy position in NATO by a conflict with Turkey.[92] By 25 November 1967, Cyrus Vance had persuaded the Greek junta to withdraw its troops from Cyprus. On 28 November 1967, Cyprus President Makarios entered the scene and informed the United States that he would consent to the withdrawal of Greek troops provided all foreign troops in Cyprus would be withdrawn. Despite Makarios' opposition, on November 30, Vance persuaded the Greek junta to accept an immediate withdrawal of Greek forces from Cyprus and disbandment of the Greek Cypriot National Guard and the recall of its commander Grivas.[93] The main points which were agreed by Greece and Turkey were as follows: 1- The demobilisation of Turkish armed forces that had been poised for war. 2- The gradual withdrawal of Turkish and Greek forces over the number authorised by the 1959 London-Zurich agreements. 3- Compensation to the Turkish Cypriots in Ayios Theodhoros and Kophinou for their losses resulting from the Greek Cypriot attacks. 4- Expansion of the size and powers of the UN force in Cyprus to prevent repetition of fighting. 5- The disbandment of the 20,000 member Greek Cypriot National Guard. 6- The recall of Greek General Grivas to Athens. 7- The authorisation for Turkish Cypriots to form their own local governments and police forces in their enclaves. 8- Disengagement where the fighting was taking place.[94]

On the same day, November 30, Cyrus Vance took his plan to Makarios. Makarios mainly agreed with the plan but refused to dismantle the National Guard, which was largely equipped with Soviet arms. Vance was unable to persuade Makarios on this point.[95] The crisis was over when both Greece and Turkey announced on 3 December 1967 that they would comply with the appeal of UN Secretary General U Thant, which called for the withdrawal of all foreign troops illegally introduced into Cyprus and the dismantling of paramilitary forces on the island.[96] One important result of the settlement of the crisis was that Greece lost its major leverage in Cyprus against a Turkish military intervention, i.e. the Greek forces in Cyprus and Grivas. Since then, the Greek junta became more open to American and Turkish pressures to have bilateral talks on the Cyprus question.

After the November 1967 Cyprus crisis, on 28 December 1967 the Turkish Cypriot leadership established the Provisional Turkish Cypriot administration. In the words of Turkish Cypriot leader Rauf Denktaş, "this arrangement... illustrates the way in which the Turkish Cypriot administration took over or assumed its share of functions under the 1960 constitution, thus showing its intention to give a constructive hand in reshaping the 1960 bi-communal partnership. As the prospects of the restoration of the 1960 constitution receded, the word "provisional" was dropped and the Turkish Cypriot administration continued to function as a fully fledged government catering for all the needs of the Turkish

---

[92] G. S. Harris, *Troubled Alliance*, p. 123.

[93] S. Bölükbaşı, *Turkish-American Relations and Cyprus*, p. 140.

[94] H. I. Salih, *Cyprus*, 59, A. Papandreou, *Democracy At Gunpoint*, pp. 212-213, Metin Tamkoç, *The Turkish Cypriot State: the Embodiment of the Right of Self-Determination*, (London: K. Rüstem and Brother, 1988), p. 94, *Keesing's Contemporary Archives*, 1967-1968, vol. 16, p. 22436.

[95] S. Bölükbaşı, *Turkish-American Relations and Cyprus*, pp. 140-141, Joseph S. Joseph, *Cyprus: Ethnic Conflict and International Concern*, (New York: Peter Lang, 1985), pp. 141-142.

[96] S. Bölükbaşı, *Turkish-American Relations and Cyprus*, p. 141, T. Ehlrich, *Cyprus: 1958-1967*, pp. 114-115.

community."[97] The American administration did not recognise the new Turkish political arrangement as legal.[98]

Concerns, aims and tactics of the Americans during the 1967 Cyprus crisis were almost same as those in 1964, when Turkey threatened to resort to military force. The only difference was that US rulers acted more cautiously this time in order not to alienate Turkey. They succeeded in preventing Turkish intervention in 1967 without causing deterioration of US-Turkish relations but their mediation effort increased the Turks' determination to solve the Cyprus question in their own way because US intervention brought no important change in the Cyprus situation from their own point of view. The Turkish intervention in 1974 was the eventual outcome.

The Reaction of Turkish Public to the US Mediation

Since the memory of the American prevention of Turkish military intervention in Cyprus in 1964 had not yet faded from the minds of Turkish people, when the United States became involved in the November 1967 crisis to mediate between the interested parties, Turks, especially Turkish leftist circles, assumed that the United States would press Turkish rulers not to invade, and block Turkish action again. During the crisis, leftist university students organised anti-American demonstrations. American mediator Vance could not land on the civilian Esenboğa airport in Ankara because of demonstrations but had to land on the military Mürted airport.[99] Leftists claimed that the Americans forced Turkish rulers not to launch military intervention for which a real opportunity was created by the Greek Cypriot attacks and thus prevented a permanent solution of the Cyprus problem. Rumours spread in Ankara that the American Sixth Fleet interposed itself between Cyprus and Turkey to block the way of Turkish ships.

Leftist writer İlhan Selçuk put forward the following claims in his articles: This time Turkey had a real opportunity to intervene in Cyprus and thus to solve the Cyprus problem permanently, providing guarantee for security and rights of Turkish Cypriots. But the United States intervened in the matter again by dispatching Cyrus Vance as a mediator. Johnson and his special envoy put obstacles in front of Turkish military intervention and restricted Turkey's capacity to act during the crisis. While America was mediating between Greece and Turkey, time passed and Turkey lost a golden opportunity to intervene in Cyprus. Turkish people realised again that Turkey was not free in its actions and that it could not act in any matter without the approval of the United States.[100]

In the Turkish Parliament, Turkish Labour Party MP Behice Boran criticised the American attitude during the Cyprus crisis. She admitted that this time the United States did not send its fleet and did not warn that Turkey could not use US-supplied weapons but she claimed that the United States did pressurise the Turkish government to accept an unsuitable settlement for Turkish interests but did not put any pressure on Makarios when he refused the final version of the settlement formula. In her view, the Cyprus problem could not be solved

---

[97] R. R. Denktash, *the Cyprus Triangle*, p. 35.
[98] Ellen B. Laipson, ``Cyprus: A Quarter Century of US Diplomacy" in John T. A. Koumoulides (ed.), *Cyprus in Transition 1960-1985*, (London: Trigraph, 1986), p. 66.
[99] S. Bölükbaşı, *Turkish-American Relations and Cyprus*, p. 140.
[100] İlhan Selçuk, ``Pencere", 26-28 November 1967, *Cumhuriyet*, p. 2.

under the auspices of NATO and the United States because they preferred Enosis which would provide for the presence of British bases and the establishment of new NATO bases on the island.[101]

The majority of general Turkish public opinion, especially press and politicians, thought that this time the American attitude favoured the Turkish position. Daily *Cumhuriyet*'s columnist Ecvet Güresin's opinion was that the United Stated had a totally different stance from its attitude during the 1964 Cyprus crisis because she feared that she would provoke the reaction of Turkish people and lose Turkey completely. Güresin claimed that through its slow reaction the United States had given a green light for Turkish intervention but Turkey did not succeed in doing so.[102] The editorial of Turkish newspaper *Milliyet* described the American attitude as follows: "Johnson's special envoy did not threaten Turkish officials not to intervene but brought a peace plan which was entirely suitable to Turkish interests. This time the United States distinguished the guilty from the innocent and pressed Athens to accept the Turkish demands."[103]

In the Parliamentary discussions on the Cyprus question, Turkish MPs generally did not voice criticism against the United States. Reliance Party MP Coşkun Kırca stated that if the Western states implemented forceful measures to prevent a Turkish military action against Cyprus, they should not expect that Turkey would stay in NATO and comply with their warnings. In his opinion, Turkey's interests in Cyprus were more important than its alliance with the West. However, Kırca admitted that Turkey's Western allies acted more reasonably during the last Cyprus crisis in November 1967.[104] The leader of the Reliance Party, Turhan Feyzioğlu, held a view fully supporting the Turkish government's position on the last Cyprus crisis. In his opinion, the claim that Turkey could not intervene in Cyprus by using its weapons supplied by NATO countries since it would be prevented by the West proved to be wrong by the last Cyprus crisis. It became clear that Turkey could use its weapons and all NATO bases on its territory for its interests outside NATO such as the Cyprus question. Nobody could any more dare to send a Johnson letter or a similar threat to Turkey.[105]

The Turkish government claimed that it acted independently during the November 1967 Cyprus crisis and it did not come under American pressure on its actions. Foreign Minister Çağlayangil made the following points in Parliament: Turkey's alliance with the West did not prevent her from pursuing a policy on the Cyprus question, which was suitable for her interests. The last Cyprus crisis was fortunately solved through peaceful means and American mediator Vance played an important role. Some people claimed that Turkey was deceived by the United States again and that the American mediator pacified Turkey but did not put pressure on Makarios. These people also said that Turkish intervention was prevented once more by the Americans. All these claims were categorically wrong. Turkey had the willingness, power and right to intervene in Cyprus, she could intervene any time if she wished, nobody could stop her.[106] Defence Minister Ahmet Topaloğlu compared the latest Cyprus crisis with the one in 1964: "This time we used more forces than the İnönü

---

[101] *Millet Meclisi Tutanak Dergisi*, vol. 22, term 2, sess. 2, 4 December 1967, pp. 330-331, *Millet Meclisi Tutanak Dergisi*, vol. 25, term 2, sess. 3, 20 February 1968, p. 468.

[102] Ecvet Güresin, "Günün Notları", *Cumhuriyet*, 23 November 1967, p. 1.

[103] "Durum", *Milliyet*, 11 December 1967, p. 1. See also A. H. Ulman, R. H. Dekmeijian, "Changing Partners in Turkey's Foreign Policy 1959-1967", *ORBIS*, vol. 11, Fall 1967, p. 784.

[104] *Millet Meclisi Tutanak Dergisi*, vol. 25, term 2, sess. 3, 20 February 1968, p. 454.

[105] *Millet Meclisi Tutanak Dergisi*, vol. 31, term 2, sess. 4, 23 January 1969, p. 425.

[106] *Millet Meclisi Tutanak Dergisi*, vol. 25, term 2, sess. 3, 20 February 1968, pp. 482, 487.

government used in 1964 but President Johnson did not send any warning letter to us. The Turkish government took every kind of measure to use the Turkish armed forces for Turkey's interests and when it acted in this way it did not care about the possibility of receiving any American warning."[107]

GREEK-TURKISH SECRET TALKS ON CYPRUS 1967-1974

After the November 1967 Cyprus crisis, both the Turkish and Greek governments were still willing to have secret bilateral talks to find a political settlement to the Cyprus problem. The Greek junta, which was largely dependent on the United States for its survival, seemed to attribute more importance to its membership in NATO. The Greek colonels were willing to find a solution to the Cyprus question, based on the lines of the Acheson plan, i.e. Enosis in return for some compensation to Turkey. This kind of solution would satisfy their traditional aim of unifying Cyprus with Greece and please their American allies.

In his interview with *Le Monde* and *The Times* on 29 November 1968, Greek president Caramanlis explained Greece's ideas: "Turkey knows that the natural solution of the problem is the union of Cyprus with Greece. Greece, on the other hand, understands that such a union cannot be realised without granting to the Turks certain concessions... The London-Zurich agreements possess great advantages. The threat of war which existed during that period was eliminated; after many years of slavery, Cyprus became a free country; those treaties would permit the re-establishment of a honest friendship between Greece and Turkey and open the way to a permanent solution of their problem."[108] This Greek gesture found a positive response in the Turkish side. The Turkish government, too, pursued a moderate policy which would not displease the Greek rulers. By late 1969 Greece and Turkey had resumed their secret talks on the Cyprus question.[109] On 30 May 1971 another Greek gesture came. In his statement to the Turkish newspaper *Milliyet* on 30 May 1971, Greek Prime Minister Papadopoulos said that he believed in a Greco-Turkish federation and that the two countries "should convince our communities in Cyprus that we are not disposed to spoil the relations between us and quarrel for their sake; consequently they should settle their differences in a manner acceptable to us also."[110]

The most important achievement in Greek-Turkish talks came during the negotiations of the Turkish and Greek foreign ministers, Osman Olcay and Palamas, during the Lisbon meeting of NATO foreign ministers on 3-4 July 1971. The two foreign ministers agreed that the Cyprus question should be solved through negotiations.[111] Although Olcay and Palamas did not reach a formal agreement their meeting seemed rather promising, the two sides had moved closer to a consensus on some form of double Enosis.[112] However, extreme pro-

---

[107] *Cumhuriyet Senatosu Tutanak Dergisi*, 4 February 1968, term 1, sess. 7, vol. 45-3, p. 489.
[108] A. Papandreou, *Democracy At Gunpoint*, pp. 219-220.
[109] V. Coufoudakis, ``United States Foreign Policy and the Cyprus Question'' p. 125.
[110] M. A. Attalides, *Cyprus: Nationalism and International Politics*, p. 132, Stephen G. Xydis, ``the Military Regime's Foreign Policy'' in R. Clogg and G. Yannopoulos (eds.), *Greece Under Military Rule*, p. 203.
[111] S. Bölükbaşı, *Turkish-American Relations and Cyprus*, pp. 172-173. M. Stearns, former US ambassador to Greece, describes the Lisbon meeting as "the closest the two communities have come to an agreement." Monteagle Stearns, *Entangled Allies: US Policy Toward Greece, Turkey and Cyprus*, (New York: Council on Foreign Relations Press, 1992), pp. 113-115.
[112] L. Stern, *the Wrong Horse*, p. 90, T. A. Couloumbis, *the United States, Greece and Turkey*, p. 78.

enosist elements in Greece and Cyprus resorted to terrorist acts at this time, and prevented the achievement of a solution[113] because their activities soured relations between the Greek and Greek Cypriot governments and as well as between the Turkish government and the Greek regime. Some writers suggest that the Greek and Turkish foreign ministers agreed on terms of partitioning Cyprus on the double Enosis formula.[114] Attalides interprets the agreement between Olcay and Palamas as follows: "The basic aim was to resolve the Cyprus problem on the basis of independence but with very substantial regional and communal autonomy for the Turkish Cypriots. The aim was that the monolithic Turkish Cypriot community lacking an organised left would provide an avenue for NATO and US influence in Cyprus. This would be further reinforced by a strong Turkish military presence. The trend of such a constitutional settlement was partition."[115]

THE GREEK JUNTA - THE CYPRIOT ADMINISTRATION RELATIONS

Greek contacts with the Turks did not please the Greek Cypriots. In fact, the relationship between the Makarios regime and the Greek junta between 1967 and 1974 was one of the strong enmity toward each other. Their main disagreement point arose from their different approaches to the Cyprus question. The Greek junta mainly aimed at unifying Cyprus with Greece but it thought that any solution of the Cyprus problem should be acceptable to the Turkish and American governments as well. Hence the Papadopoulos government was ready to make some concessions to the Turkish side.[116] It seemed that in this policy the Greek government was "motivated by anti-communism; the fear of losing American support; the concern that the United States would not indefinitely block the threatened Turkish invasion of Cyprus; and the need to remove Cyprus from the list of problems affecting Greek and allied interests."[117]

Makarios, too, was a strong believer in Enosis. As it is believed by the Turkish side, Greek Cypriot President Makarios always aimed to achieve Enosis but as a tactical and temporary choice he propagated for a unitary and independent Cyprus. On 18 October 1970 he told the representatives of Dutch and Belgian radio and television: "I have always been in favour of union with Greece. I realise, though, that because of extraneous difficulties such a solution is not attainable now."[118] At the end of 1967, Makarios had said that a solution must be sought "within the limits of what is feasible which does not always coincide with what is desirable."[119] In Makarios' language, desirable meant Enosis, and feasible meant constant Hellenization of Cyprus in accordance with the Akritas Plan, eventually leading to Enosis.[120]

---

[113] M. Stearns, *Entangled Allies*, pp. 113-115.

[114] V. Coufoudakis, ``United States Foreign Policy and the Cyprus Question'' p. 126, M. A. Attalides, *Cyprus: Nationalism and International Politics*, p. 132.

[115] M. A. Attalides, *Cyprus: Nationalism and International Politics*, pp. 153-154.

[116] T. A. Couloumbis, *the United States, Greece and Turkey*, p. 78, P. N. Vanezis, *Cyprus: the Unfinished Agony*, (London: Abelard-Schuman, 1977), p. 46.

[117] Van Coufoudakis, ``the Dynamics of Political Partition and Division in Multiethnic and Multireligious Societies: the Cyprus Case'' in Van Coufoudakis (ed.), *Essays on the Cyprus Conflict*, (New York: Pella Publishing Company, 1976), p. 46.

[118] Pierre Oberling, *The Road to Bellapais: the Turkish Cypriot Exodus to Northern Cyprus*, (New York: Columbia University Press, 1982), p. 147.

[119] N. Crawshaw, *The Cyprus Revolt*, pp. 378-379.

[120] M. Tamkoç, *The Turkish Cypriot State*, p. 82.

Makarios also said on 14 March 1971: "Cyprus is Greek. Cyprus has been Greek since the dawn of her history, and will remain Greek; Greek and undivided we have taken over; Greek and undivided we shall preserve her; Greek and undivided we shall deliver her to Greece."[121] Makarios told a mass rally in Nicosia on 8 February 1973: "As I have declared in the past, all the Greeks of Cyprus are enosists. It is to Greece that our soul and heart will always be turned. If factors and situations beyond our control do not make Enosis possible, this does not mean that we shall cease to be Greeks... But since we are enosists, why are we carrying out talks with the Turkish Cypriots and speaking about an independent, unitary and sovereign state? Because this is necessitated by grim reality to which neither the Greek nor the Cyprus governments can close their eyes."[122]

However, Makarios was opposed to paying any price to Turkey such as a Turkish military presence on the island in return for Enosis. He refused giving greater local autonomy to Turkish Cypriots. Given the Greek policy toward the Cyprus question and impossibility of Enosis for that time, Makarios chose to pursue a policy directed to protecting the independence and the unitary state character of Cyprus. To the Greek junta, "Makarios was a traitor to Enosis, a red priest who flirted with the local communist party, championed non-alignment, and consorted with... Tito of Yugoslavia and Nasser of Egypt."[123] The Athens' colonels also believed that Makarios supported anti-junta elements in Greece.[124]

An example of Makarios-Greek junta enmity occurred in February 1972. A supply of Czech weapons for the Cyprus police arrived in Cyprus in late January 1972. On 11 February 1972 the Greek government issued a nine-point ultimatum to Makarios, asking him to hand over Czech weapons to the UN force and to take strong measures against the Cyprus communist party, AKEL. Makarios resisted the Greek pressures while the Soviet Union warned the Athens government not to attempt to overthrow Makarios.[125] The United States moved to calm the Greek junta down since the incident would have looked like a direct intervention in Cyprus by Greece.[126] It is claimed by many observers that in order to achieve its Enosis aim Greece tried to overthrow the Makarios regime and therefore actively supported the pro-Enosis terrorist organisations in Cyprus. It is also widely believed that Greece was behind the many assassination attempts against Makarios. After Makarios was re-elected in 1968, right-wing groups established several organisations such as the National Front, the Organisation Akritas, and the Enosist Youth Phoenix whose main aim was to bring about union of Cyprus with Greece. The Greek junta officers who commanded the Greek Cypriot National Guard actively supported these organisations.[127]

The National Front (Ethnikon Metopan), whose declared aims were union to Greece and the ouster of anti-union elements from the Cypriot government, launched a series of terrorist activities against the Cyprus administration in late 1969 and 1970. On 8 March 1970 Makarios' helicopter was shot down but Makarios escaped unhurt. This assassination attempt was claimed to be a part of a wider plan which was called the Operation Hermes and aimed at overthrowing Makarios, separating Greek and Turkish Cypriots and finally partitioning

---

[121] R. R. Denktash, *The Cyprus Triangle*, p. 55.
[122] *Keesing's Contemporary Archives,* 1973, vol. 19, p. 25778.
[123] L. Stern, *The Wrong Horse*, p. 86.
[124] T. A. Couloumbis, *The United States, Greece and Turkey*, p. 77.
[125] Ibid., p. 78, V. Coufoudakis, "United States Foreign Policy and the Cyprus Question", p. 127, M. A. Attalides, *Cyprus: Nationalism and International Politics*, p. 134.
[126] M. A. Attalides, *Cyprus: Nationalism and International Politics*, p. 157.
[127] S. Bölükbaşı, *Turkish-American Relations and Cyprus*, p. 168.

Cyprus between Greece and Turkey. It was believed that the attack was carried out by the National Front, which had links with the Greek government, and that the plan Hermes was prepared by Colonel Ioannides, an influential member of the Greek junta.[128] There were other assassination attempts against Makarios, which were thought to be organised by the Greek rulers.

In September 1971 George Grivas escaped from his house arrest in Athens and secretly entered Cyprus to head the fight for Enosis. He reactivated the terrorist organisation EOKA in the form of EOKA-B and assumed its leadership.[129] The Greek Cypriot leadership believed that Grivas had been allowed to escape to Cyprus in order to provide a check on Makarios and communist elements on the island. They were of the opinion that Grivas would not have returned without the approval and knowledge of the Papadopoulos regime.[130]   On 26 October 1971 Grivas denounced the Makarios administration as unworthy of the Greek community. He declared that he had come back to fulfil the long-held aspiration of the Greek community to unite Cyprus with Greece.[131] Under Grivas' leadership, EOKA-B organised terrorist activities against the Cyprus government. Its two coup attempts in February and July of 1972 were foiled by the police. Although Grivas favoured struggle for Enosis he did not want a full-scale war with the Makarios administration, there were some reports that he disagreed with the Greek junta in some points.[132] In Greece in November 1973, Dimitros Ioannides, who was known as extremely pro-Enosis, replaced Papadopoulos as the head of the junta. On 27 January 1974 Grivas died of a heart attack and since then EOKA-B came under the direct control of the Greek junta.[133] Terrorist activities against the Cypriot administration continued.

TURKEY'S CYPRUS POLICY (1967-1974)

Before 1968, Turkish Prime Minister Süleyman Demirel and Foreign Ministry officials made statements explaining the Turkish government's main principles on the Cyprus question. These principles were as follows: 1- Turkey's security concerns had to be protected. 2- Cyprus could not be unified with another state unilaterally. 3- The international agreements on Cyprus could not be abrogated or changed by one side unilaterally. 4- One community in Cyprus could not impose its own regime over the other. 5- The power balance in the Mediterranean and the Aegean region which was established by the Lausanne treaty could not be changed in favour of one side.[134] As explained by Demirel on 5 December 1967, the Turkish government also insisted on its right to intervene in Cyprus, granted by the London-Zurich agreements. Turkey could not give up this right which was vital to protect its interests in Cyprus and rights of Turkish Cypriots.[135] In his press conference on 22 April 1967 Turkish

---

[128] V. Coufoudakis, ``United States Foreign Policy and the Cyprus Question'', pp. 125-126, M. A. Attalides, *Cyprus: Nationalism and International Politics*, p. 131.

[129] *Keesing's Contemporary Archives*, 1971-1972, vol. 18, p. 25033. For the EOKA terror see *Keesing's Contemporary Archives*, 1973, vol. 19, pp. 25778, 25979-25980, 26115, 1974, vol. 20, p. 26603.

[130] V. Coufoudakis, ``United States Foreign Policy and the Cyprus Question'', p. 126.

[131] R. R. Denktash, *The Cyprus Triangle*, pp. 60-61.

[132] S. Bölükbaşı, *Turkish-American Relations and Cyprus*, p. 169.

[133] R. R. Denktash, *The Cyprus Triangle*, p. 64, M. A. Attalides, *Cyprus: Nationalism and International Politics*, p. 163.

[134] M. Sarıca et. al., *Kıbrıs Sorunu*, pp. 129, 139.

[135] Ibid., p. 150.

Prime Minister Demirel described the Turkish government's main aims on the Cyprus question as follows: 1- To gain international support for its policies toward the Cyprus issue. 2- To increase the resistance strength of Turkish Cypriot community. 3- To try all means to solve the Cyprus problem through negotiations. 4- To block any unilateral solution of the Cyprus problem and to prevent change of the status quo in Cyprus to the disadvantage of Turkey and Turkish Cypriots.[136]

Makarios had lifted restriction on the Turkish Cypriot community on 7 March 1968 and removed the barricades and road blocks surrounding the Turkish areas. In Denktaş's words, "he had consolidated his military position and could afford to relax" now.[137] At the beginning of 1968 Makarios also proclaimed new presidential elections and asked for a mandate to negotiate with the Turkish side a new constitutional settlement on the basis of independent, unitary state. The inter-communal talks between the representatives of the two communities began on 6 June 1968 and continued for the next six years. Although substantial progress was made, the talks eventually got bogged down.

After the withdrawal of Greek forces from Cyprus in 1967, Makarios' lifting of the blockade around Turkish Cypriot enclaves and the commencement of talks between Greek and Turkish Cypriots; the Turkish government paid very little attention to developments in Cyprus. It devoted its attention mainly to domestic problems such as economic development and increasing terrorist activities. The Demirel government tried to give the impression to Turkish public opinion that normalcy was restored in Cyprus and the situation of Turkish Cypriots improved greatly. While strongly supporting the inter-communal negotiations, Prime Minister Demirel seemed to accept the unitary position of Cyprus state in return for local autonomy for Turkish Cypriots. In a speech at the Turkish Parliament on 7 November 1969, Demirel said: "The Cyprus question is a problem which concerns many parties. Therefore, the crisis cannot be solved according to the wishes... of only one party... The legitimate interests and rights of all parties have to be taken into account... The only way to do this is through negotiations..."[138]

The military-supported Turkish governments between 1971 and 1973, too, were preoccupied with domestic problems. As governments lacking popular support, they were not willing to take any initiative in foreign policy issues including the Cyprus question. However, during their time Turkish officials held bilateral talks with Greek representatives to find a solution to the Cyprus problem. But nothing serious was achieved. The Ecevit-Erbakan coalition government, which came to power at the beginning of 1974, considered that the most suitable solution for the Cyprus question was federation giving autonomy to Turkish Cypriot enclaves but excluding territorial separation of the two ethnic communities in Cyprus. The coalition government's programme, which was read in the Turkish Parliament on 1 February 1974, stated that the coalition partners believed that the most reasonable solution of the Cyprus problem, which would protect the equal sovereign status of the Turkish community and which would bring co-operation of the two communities in the administration of the state, was a federal system.[139] Foreign Minister Turan Güneş said on 23 May 1974: "The Cyprus talks will be conducted on the basis that two communities exist on Cyprus, that both communities have rights over Cyprus, that they would be subject to different legislation

---

[136] *Dışişleri Bakanlığı Belleteni*, April 1967, p. 85.
[137] R. R. Denktash, *The Cyprus Triangle*, p. 53.
[138] S. Bölükbaşı, *Turkish-American Relations and Cyprus*, pp. 147, 171.
[139] M. Sarıca et. al., *Kıbrıs Sorunu*, p. 173.

in the fields [where] they differ from each other, and that there would be no unilateral amendment of legislation. This means that our government will not accept the idea of a unitary state, that is to say, changing the status of the Turkish Cypriot community into a minority."[140]

US POLICY TOWARD CYPRUS (1967-1974)

After the November 1967 Cyprus crisis, the United States stopped its diplomatic efforts to find a solution to the Cyprus problem. The negotiations between the representatives of Greek and Turkish Cypriots, Glafkos Clerides and Rauf Denktaş, which began on 24 June 1968,[141] seemed to suit American interests since they brought a relative calm to the Cyprus issue. Thanks to the inter-communal talks whose main aim was to make the 1960 constitution work in a way that would protect Turkish minority rights and also permit the Cyprus government to function, an international conflict would disappear from the agenda of the American administration at least for the time being. Therefore, the United States endorsed and gave support to the inter-communal negotiations held under the auspices of the United Nations.[142] This American policy brought about supporting the Makarios regime and the independence of Cyprus.[143] The long-held anti-Makarios American view seemed to be replaced with a favourable attitude to the Archbishop. In Laipson's words, Americans thought that "Soviet and American governments might have convergent interests in a stable Cyprus, and that the communist party on the island, AKEL, was not an effective instrument of subversion for Soviet aims... The image of President Makarios as the Castro of the Mediterranean was replaced, at least temporarily with the notion that Makarios was a popularly supported leader whose involvement in the non-alignment movement need to be inimical to American interests and Cyprus under Makarios was tolerable."[144] Makarios, too, seemed to be willing to cooperate with the American administration. He allowed the United States to use the British bases on Cyprus for its espionage flights, intelligence gathering and for other communication aims.[145]

The United States also seemed to favour the Turkish side's position. During Turkish President Cevdet Sunay's visit to Washington in April 1967, President Johnson officially supported "the two-communities" concept of the Turkish side, tending to accept that there were two equal communities in Cyprus, and reject the terms of "majority" and "minority" for these groups.[146] The joint Turkish-American communiqué which was issued at the end of this visit stated that the two Presidents agreed that the existing treaties on Cyprus had binding

---

[140] S. Bölükbaşı, *Turkish-American Relations and Cyprus*, p. 178.

[141] For the inter communal talks see *Keesing's Contemporary Archives*, 1967-1968, vol. 16, p. 22883, 1969-1970, vol. 17, pp. 23635, 24041, 24117, 1971-1972, vol. 18, pp. 24398, 24673-24674, 25032-25033, 25367, 1973, vol. 19, pp. 25700, 25979, 1974, vol. 20, pp. 26310, 26603.

[142] V. Coufoudakis, ``United States Foreign Policy and the Cyprus Question", pp. 119-120, 123, M. A. Attalides, *Cyprus: Nationalism and International Politics*, p. 153, L. Stern, *the Wrong Horse*, p. 91.

[143] V. Coufoudakis, ``United States Foreign Policy and the Cyprus Question", p. 127.

[144] E. B. Laipson, ``Cyprus: A Quarter Century of US Diplomacy", p. 67.

[145] L. Stern, *The Wrong Horse*, pp. 106-107.

[146] M. A. Attalides, *Cyprus: Nationalism and International Politics*, p. 153, T. W. Adams and A. J. Cottrell, *Cyprus Between East and West*, p. 68.

effects and would continue to be an essential element in seeking a settlement formula.[147] American rulers also supported bilateral talks between Greece and Turkey on the Cyprus question. They believed that it was in American interests to let Greece and Turkey solve the problem between them. It would reduce American involvement in the conflict, put greater responsibility on the regional powers[148] and make it easier to reach a settlement since Greek and Turkish Cypriot communities were dependent on Greece and Turkey. While the inter communal talks and Greek-Turkish bilateral talks continued but reached nowhere, American officials became more worried about the situation in Cyprus. In 1973 there were reports that the United States pressurised the parties to the conflict to reach a quick solution. Otherwise the United States would not make any effort to prevent a possible Greco-Turkish war.[149] American officials were also concerned over the mounting deficit of the UN Force in Cyprus. By December 1972 UNFICYP had been reduced fifty percent from its original strength of 6500 men.[150]

Some researchers claimed that during the 1967-1974 period the United States still favoured double Enosis and the partition of Cyprus and gave support to attempts to overthrow the Makarios regime. According to Attalides and Coufoudakis, in June 1971 American State Department analysts concluded that Greece and Turkey were favourably disposed to double Enosis proposals. They proposed that the United States should restrain Turkey and Greece from any premature moves toward partition but the possibility of an eventual double Enosis should not be ruled out. These American officials believed that Makarios would accept double Enosis if confronted with something worse as an alternative. Consensus was reached among these officials that the Makarios problem must be left to Greece. They also suggested that partition plans should be implemented quickly to face the Soviets with a *de facto* situation.[151]

In the opinion of some authors, the United States decided to settle the Cyprus crisis permanently at any price. The most favourable solution to American officials was partition of Cyprus between Greece and Turkey. This solution would bring Cyprus under the control of NATO and eliminate the communist danger in Cyprus. As a NATO territory the United States would be able to use the island for strategic and military purposes. An important dispute between the two NATO allies would disappear and thus the cohesion of NATO would be saved. Both Greece and Turkey would be kept happy and their ties with the West would not be weakened. A large proportion of the island would do for the Greek junta's prestige and any proportion would do for Turkey's strategic need to control access to its southern ports.[152] Cyprus President Makarios was seen as the most important obstacle to partition designs. Although his removal from power was dangerous at least for the time being since it would harm the relative calm in Cyprus, State Department officials still regarded him as a disturbing factor and recommended that his power should be weakened and that he should be made to

---

[147] *Dışişleri Bakanlığı Belleteni*, April 1967, p. 61, *Amerika'da Onbir Gün*, Ankara: Yarın Yayınları, 1967, p. 32. During Turkish P. M. Erim's visit to the USA in March 1972 US authorities reiterated the same opinion. *Resmi Temaslar: Sayın Başbakan ve Bn. Erim'in Amerika'yı Ziyareti*, 18-23 March 1972, p. 63.

[148] E. B. Laipson, ``Cyprus: A Quarter Century of US Diplomacy'', p. 66.

[149] M. A. Attalides, *Cyprus: Nationalism and International Politics*, p. 103.

[150] V. Coufoudakis, ``United States Foreign Policy and the Cyprus Question'', p. 120.

[151] Ibid., p. 126, M. A. Attalides, *Cyprus: Nationalism and International Politics*, p. 154.

[152] M. A. Attalides, *Cyprus: Nationalism and International Politics*, pp. 132, 183-184, S. G. Xydis, ``the Military Regime's Foreign Policy'', pp. 202-203.

realise the strength of his opponents in Cyprus. He had to be forced to take a more moderate stance.[153]

In the opinion of mainly Greek authors, the United States together with the Greek junta, and pro-Enosis elements in Cyprus, were involved in the plans aimed at destroying the independence of Cyprus and overthrowing the Makarios regime.[154] They claimed that American intelligence services were highly active in Greece and Cyprus, supporting terrorist activities and trying to destabilise the Cypriot administration. Even Israel, which had no sympathy for Makarios' neutralism and friendship with the Arabs, was thought to be involved in anti-Makarios activities.[155] When an unsuccessful assassination attempt was made against Makarios in March 1970, several circles attacked the United States because of its alleged involvement in the plot. The Soviet official newspaper *Pravda* claimed that the United States had used Greek colonels to remove the Cypriot administration from power. The English newspaper *The Guardian* commented that the CIA could be involved in terrorist activities in Cyprus since the overthrow of Makarios and the materialisation of Enosis would be in American interests. Andreas Papandreou, the leader of the Pan-Hellenistic movement, declared in Toronto that the Greek junta with the consent and help of Turkey and the United States prepared new plans to overthrow Makarios, thus to bring Cyprus under NATO control.[156] Critics of the United States claimed that American officials at least were well-informed of anti-Makarios terrorist activities and the involvement of the Greek junta in these attempts but chose to do nothing about it. According to Attalides, in 1971 the Greek dictator informed the American government of his intention to remove Makarios through a coup if he did not capitulate to the pressures mounted against him.[157] The American ambassador to Cyprus appealed to the State Department to condemn the assassination attempts against Makarios but the appeal was ignored by Secretary of State Henry Kissinger and was opposed by the American ambassador to Greece.[158]

It was a fact that the Greek junta was completely isolated internationally and desperately needed American support and therefore it was open to pressures from the United States. Allegedly, American officials, benefiting from this fact, put much more pressure on the Greek side than they put on the Turkish side to find a solution to the Cyprus problem along the lines of American accepted plans such as double Enosis and partition.[159] In the summer of 1968, Greek Foreign Minister Pipinellis had told the Cyprus government that Enosis was impossible without making concessions to Turkey. He had informed Greek Cypriot rulers that the United States had pointed out to the Greek dictatorship that a Greek-Turkish war over Cyprus would bring an irreversible Soviet intrusion into the region and that the United States would do nothing, either in the event of a Greek-Turkish war or in case Turkey invaded Cyprus.[160]

---

[153] V. Coufoudakis, ``United States Foreign Policy and the Cyprus Question'', p. 128.

[154] M. A. Attalides, *Cyprus: Nationalism and International Politics*, pp. 155, 156-157. As early as March 1965, Greek Cypriot newspaper *Agon* alleged that US intelligence agents and certain Greek Cypriots had plotted to overthrow Makarios. *Keesing's Contemporary Archives*, 1965-1966, vol. 15, pp. 20630-20631.

[155] V. Coufoudakis, ``United States Foreign Policy and the Cyprus Question'', pp. 128, 144n, P. M. Kitromilides, ``From Coexistence to Confrontation: the Dynamics of Ethnic Conflict in Cyprus'' in M. A. Attalides (ed.), *Cyprus Reviewed*, pp. 58-59.

[156] M. Sarıca et. al., *Kıbrıs Sorunu*, pp. 165-166.

[157] M. A. Attalides, *Cyprus: Nationalism and International Politics*, p. 133.

[158] Ibid., p. 131.

[159] Polyvious G. Polyviou, *Cyprus: Conflict and Negotiation 1960-1980*, (London: Duckworth, 1980), p. 127.

[160] M. A. Attalides, *Cyprus: Nationalism and International Politics*, p. 99.

In order to understand future Cyprus crises, the special relationship between Greece and the United States in the 1967-1974 period should be mentioned briefly. In this period, because of its military regime, Greece became increasingly isolated in international arena, especially within the Western world and NATO. In NATO more than half of the member countries repeatedly questioned the Greek regime and its participation in NATO.[161] Greek rulers knew that the most important source of support for their regime's survival was the United States. They were aware of that by emphasising Greece's military ties with the West and the United States and their loyalty to NATO obligations they would get the American support and strengthen the hands of American officials who took their side against the critics urging the United States to put pressure on them. In every opportunity Greek colonels announced their total attachment to NATO and the United States and they attacked world communism and Soviet totalitarianism. The junta-controlled press praised NATO and created an image of Greece as the leading, the most faithful, the most committed ally of the West and the USA.[162] In order to secure American support, the Greek junta offered vast privileges and facilities to the United States.

For the United States, the most important thing was to use the Greek territory and bases in connection with the NATO strategy and in connection with dealing the Arab-Israel conflict. For Americans, "Greece was a point for the storage and shipment of supplies, for naval replenishment and repair, and a refuge for Americans brought out of the Middle East countries, in time of emergency."[163] In the 1967-1974 period the United States enjoyed complete freedom to use its naval and air bases in Greece such as the US Sixth Fleet base at Pireaus which was considered to be imperative to NATO in the eastern Mediterranean.[164]

In Andreas Papandreou's opinion, the United States transformed Greece into a key naval and air communications and supply centre for the NATO command and an espionage and counterespionage base in the Near and Middle Eastern region.[165] As stated by Xydis, in September 1970, the United States asked the Greek junta to grant facilities for passage and refuelling not only for planes flown to the Middle East to evacuate American nationals from Jordan, but also for military reconnaissance planes that would naturally have flown mainly over Arab countries.[166] In fact, Greek territorial and air space and Greek bases remained open and available to the United States during major Middle East crises.[167] In return for Greek favours, the United States supplied military and economic assistance to Greece and supported her in international forums. It countered anti-Greek criticism within the Western alliance. The American State Department resisted repeated Western European moves against the Greek junta.[168] Although a military embargo was imposed on Greece from time to time because of its anti-democratic regime,[169] the embargo was loosely enforced and frequently violated. The American administration supplied military aid to Greece and enlarged favourable foreign credit terms for the Greek colonels. In Couloumbis's words, "the Nixon administration

---

[161] S. G. Xydis, "The Military Regime's Foreign Policy", pp. 195-196.
[162] A. Papandreou, *Democracy At Gunpoint*, p. 294.
[163] John C. Campbell, "The United States and the Cyprus Question 1974-1975" in V. Coufoudakis (ed.), *Essays on the Cyprus Conflict*, pp. 16-17.
[164] H. I. Salih, *Cyprus*, p. 71.
[165] A. Papandreou, *Democracy At Gunpoint*, p. 295.
[166] S. G. Xydis, "The Military Regime's Foreign Policy", p. 204.
[167] T. A. Couloumbis, *The United States, Greece and Turkey*, p. 54.
[168] S. G. Xydis, "The Military Regime's Foreign Policy", pp. 195, 200.
[169] M. Goldbloom, "United States Policy in Post-War Greece", pp. 244, 246.

swiftly adopted the role of apologist for the blunt and tactless military regime, shielding it from political and economic pressures from circles in the Council of Europe and the European communities." To show its support for Greece, the United States also authorised high level military and political visits to Greece.[170] American admirals, generals and Vice President Agnew visited Greece and made statements praising the Greek rulers.[171]

---

[170] T. A. Couloumbis, *The United States, Greece and Turkey*, p. 52.
[171] M. A. Attalides, *Cyprus: Nationalism and International Politics*, p. 130.

Chapter 6

THE MILITARY COUP IN CYPRUS, THE TURKISH MILITARY INTERVENTION IN THE ISLAND AND THE AMERICAN REACTION (JUNE 1974-JULY 1974)

The military coup in Cyprus, which seemed to be organised by the Greek junta to unite Cyprus with Greece, and the subsequent Turkish military intervention, which allegedly aimed at ending the oppression of the Turkish Cypriots at the hands of the Greek Cypriots, changed the character of the Cyprus question completely and brought about the present situation more or less. The American role in and the American reaction to the critical events on Cyprus in June and July 1974 were intensively questioned and the American government came under the fire of accusations from all the sides. Were there any grounds to accuse the United States for mishandling the events; did the USA have the power to prevent the tragic developments on Cyprus; did the American rulers worked deliberately to the disadvantage of the one side? All these are the questions need to be answered. The answers to them will also give clues to the situation of the Turkish-American relationship at that time.

THE MILITARY COUP IN CYPRUS

The Greek-Greek Cypriot Relationship

As mentioned in the section on the 1967-1974 period, the relations between the Greek junta and the Cypriot administration were not easy before the 1974 Cyprus crisis. Especially after General Grivas died and the terrorist organisation EOKA-B came under the direct control of Greek colonels in Athens, the enmity between the two administrations increased. This enmity was finally fuelled by Cypriot President Makarios's attempts to reassert his control over the Cypriot National Guard and its Greek army officers. As early as 1972 Makarios had imported Czech arms apparently to create a private paramilitary unit to counter-balance those forces which were set up by the constitution and which were under the Greek control. In 1974 Makarios increased his attempts to bring the National Guard under his control since he believed that if he did not act swiftly the National Guard's Greek officers would overthrow him. On 25 April 1974 the Cypriot administration declared EOKA-B an illegal organisation and opened an undeclared war against it.[1] On 26 June 1974 the Cypriot administration's spokesman claimed that EOKA-B was directed from Athens and co-operated with the Greek intelligence service.[2]

The Greek-Greek Cypriot disagreement reached its peak at the beginning of July 1974 when Cypriot President Makarios sent a letter to the Greek President, General Phaedon Gizikis. Some points which were raised by Makarios in his letter on 2 July 1974 are as follows: "It is certain that from the first days of his arrival here, Grivas was in touch with officers from Greece serving the National Guard from whom he received help and support in his effort to set up an unlawful organisation and allegedly to fight for Enosis. And he established the criminal EOKA-B organisation, which has become the cause and source of many sufferings in Cyprus... The National Guard, which is staffed and controlled by Greek officers, has been from the outset the main supplier... to EOKA-B... My co-operation with the Greek government for time being is for me a national duty. The national interest dictates harmonious and close co-operation between Athens and Nicosia. No matter what Greek government was in power it was to me the government of the mother country and I had to cooperate with it... The Cyprus state could be dissolved only in the event of Enosis. However, as long as Enosis is not feasible it is imperative that Cyprus should be strengthened as a state. By its whole attitude toward the National Guard issue, the Greek government has been following a policy calculated to abolish the Cyprus state... I would ask that the Greek officers staffing the National Guard be recalled."[3] Makarios' letter was released to the press on 6 July 1974.[4]

The Cypriot Coup and the United States

According to many authors, especially Greek ones, the United States was well informed about the plottings in Cyprus and in Greece against Makarios and had enough information to predict that a coup against the Makarios regime would be launched. The American intelligence service, the CIA, had close and constant contact with the Greek intelligence and therefore had known what was going on in Athens. Makarios himself and the Cypriot press publicised the fact that a coup against the Cypriot administration was being prepared.

Reportedly, in March 1974 the Cypriot ambassador to the United States, Nikos Dimitriou, visited the American State Department where he said to Assistant Secretary of State for Near Eastern Affairs Rodger Davies and Cyprus Country Director Thomas Boyatt: "I have reliable intelligence that a serious effort will be made to assassinate Makarios before Greek Easter." If a coup was carried out against Makarios, the Turks would move in and a crisis with unforeseeable outcomes would develop. Davies replied that American services were able to confirm nothing.[5] After this incident some working level State Department

---

[1] Murat Sarıca et. al., *Kıbrıs Sorunu*, (İstanbul: İstanbul Üniversitesi Yayınları, No. 2071, 1975), p. 178.

[2] Ibid., p. 179.

[3] Rauf R. Denktash, *The Cyprus Triangle*, (London: K. Rüstem and Brother, 1988), pp. 174-179, *Keesing's Contemporary Archives*, 1974, vol. 20, pp. 26661-26662.

[4] Theodore A. Couloumbis, *the United States, Greece and Turkey: the Troubled Triangle*, (New York: Praeger, 1983), p. 30.

[5] Laurance Stern, *The Wrong Horse: The Politics of Intervention and the Failure of American Diplomacy*, (New York: Times Books, 1977), p. 94, Michael A. Attalides, *Cyprus: Nationalism and International Politics*, (Edinburgh: Q Press Ltd., 1979), p. 166.

officials, particularly from the American Embassy in Nicosia and from the Cyprus Desk in Washington, attempted to generate a policy response which might prevent a coup against Makarios. They appealed to the higher level officials in the State Department to express their opposition to assassination attempts against Makarios. But higher level officials ignored their warnings since they "considered the alarm-ringing the work of cry-babies or boys crying wolf."[6] In fact at that time high-level officials of the State Department focused their attention on the tension between Greece and Turkey, stemmed from their disagreement over oil exploration rights in the Aegean Sea.

When Ambassador Belcher visited Cyprus in May and June of 1974, he was told by very senior officials of the Cypriot administration that the United States was involved in attempts to overthrow Makarios. These officials also claimed that they had documentary evidence proving that the CIA was financing the terrorist organisation EOKA-B via Greek dictator Ioannides and the National Guard officers.[7] On 20 June 1974 General Ioannides, the head of the Greek junta, informed a CIA officer in Athens that his administration decided to overthrow the Makarios regime and asked what the United States would think about this.[8] Subsequently, a CIA report was dispatched to Washington in the third week of June 1974. Based on a direct contact with Ioannides, the highly classified report made it clear that Ioannides was seriously considering a move against Makarios in order to settle the Cyprus problem once and for all.

Within two days, the State Department sent new instructions to its ambassador to Greece, Henry Tasca, signed by Under-secretary of State for Political Affairs, Joseph Sisco. Tasca was requested to meet with Ioannides personally and convey Washington's opposition to the use of violence in Cyprus.[9] Tasca had not been well informed about the intelligence reports. He did not know the details of the CIA report about Ioannides' message on 20 June. Sisco did not tell him that the situation was urgent. Hence Tasca did not regard the situation as critical and chose not to see Ioannides personally but to send a middle grade CIA officer to see him.[10] Tasca himself passed the message through the formal Greek government channels.[11] He saw Prime Minister Androutsopoulos, who assured him that the coup rumours were inaccurate.[12] There is disagreement among authors about whether Tasca really made an attempt to dissuade Ioannides from embarking on his plot in Cyprus.

On 3 July 1974 the CIA passed a message to Washington from a new and untested source that Greek General Ioannides decided to abandon his coup action against the Cypriot administration. It seemed that Ioannides' new decision was a response to American pressures against such an action.[13] On 8 July 1974 Greek Foreign Minister Tetenes and two other high

[6] Ellen B. Laipson, "Cyprus: A Quarter Century of US Diplomacy" in John T. A. Koumoulides (ed.), *Cyprus in Transition 1960-1985*, (London: Trigraph, 1986), p. 68, M. A. Attalides, *Cyprus: Nationalism and International Politics*, pp. 166-167.

[7] M. A. Attalides, *Cyprus: Nationalism and International Politics*, p. 169.

[8] Ibid., p. 163.

[9] T. A. Couloumbis, *the United States, Greece and Turkey*, p. 86, L. Stern, *the Wrong Horse*, pp. 99-100.

[10] M. A. Attalides, *Cyprus: Nationalism and International Politics*, p. 167.

[11] T. A. Couloumbis, *the United States, Greece and Turkey*, p. 86, John C. Campbell, "the United States and the Cyprus Question, 1974-1975" in Van Coufoudakis (ed.), *Essays on the Cyprus Conflict*, (New York: Pella Publishing Company, 1976), p. 18.

[12] Suha Bölükbaşı, *Superpowers and the Third World: Turkish-American Relations and Cyprus*, (New York: University Press of America, 1988), p. 182.

[13] M. A. Attalides, *Cyprus: Nationalism and International Politics*, pp. 167-168, L. Stern, *the Wrong Horse*, pp. 101-102.

level Greek Foreign Ministry officials resigned apparently for health reasons. This new development did not cause any substantial concern in high level American State Department officials. Later it became clear that the Greek officials resigned because of their opposition to Ioannides' coup plan against Makarios.[14]

On the eve of the Cypriot coup, on July 14, the CIA reported again that Ioannides had been dissuaded from attempting a coup in Cyprus. British military intelligence also believed that Ioannides had been forced to back off by diplomatic pressures.[15] Bell suggests that "it is possible that Ioannides believed that the warnings from Washington, which came to him only via the CIA,... were talking for record." In Bell's opinion, the British military intelligence report "strengthens the reasons for supposing that the CIA was deceived rather than deceiving, and that Ioannides believed himself to have enough diplomatic leverage to induce Washington to restrain the Turks, just as they had done in the crises of 1964 and 1967."[16] Karpat supports Bell's opinion by stating that "the junta in Greece seemed to have reached the conclusion that the United States would not allow Turkey to land troops on Cyprus... The granting of new facilities to the American Navy, the use of some seven bases by American personnel in Greece and the fervent pro-Greek attitude of the American ambassador in Athens were some of the factors supporting the Greek junta's belief that the United States would continue to oppose and if necessary even use force to prevent Turkish landing on Cyprus."[17]

In the opinion of some writers, the American attitude encouraged the head of the Greek junta, Ioannides, in organising a coup against Cyprus. After the coup Ioannides told the chiefs of the Greek navy and air force that he had assurances from Americans that there would be no Turkish intervention in Cyprus. It was even reported that Sisco himself assured Ioannides that Turkey would not invade Cyprus.[18] There is also a report that Peter Koromilas, a Greek American officer of the CIA in Greece, met several times with Ioannides shortly before the coup and gave assurances to him that if Makarios were to be removed the United States would not react.[19]

It was argued that the USA could prevent the Cyprus coup if it took a strong action against the Greek junta in the early stages when rumours erupted. American Secretary of State Henry Kissinger was criticised because of his inactivity against the reports predicting a coup in Cyprus. In spite of all evidences showing that Greece would initiate a military coup in Cyprus neither Kissinger nor Sisco took any initiative to register their disapproval of the Greek junta's plot. They did not call the Greek ambassador in Washington, Constantine Panayotakos, to express the American government's severe opposition to a military coup in Cyprus.[20] There is one report stating that in early June 1974 Chairman of the Senate Foreign Relations Committee William Fulbright visited Kissinger to tell him that he had received information that Ioannides was preparing for a Cyprus coup. When Fulbright suggested that

---

[14] S. Bölükbaşı, *Turkish-American Relations and Cyprus*, p. 183, Paul Y. Watanabe, *Ethnic Groups, Congress and American Foreign Policy: The Politics of the Turkish Arms Embargo*, (London: Greenwood Press, 1984), p. 88.

[15] Coral Bell, *Diplomacy of Détente: The Kissinger Era*, (London: Martin Robertson, 1977), pp. 146-147, L. Stern, *the Wrong Horse*, p. 102.

[16] C. Bell, *Diplomacy of Détente*, pp. 146-147.

[17] Kemal H. Karpat, "War on Cyprus: the Tragedy of Enosis" in Kemal H. Karpat (ed.), *Turkey's Foreign Policy in Transition 1950-1974*, (Leiden, Netherlands : E. J. Brill, 1975), p. 195.

[18] M. A. Attalides, *Cyprus: Nationalism and International Politics*, p. 170.

[19] S. Bölükbaşı, *Turkish-American Relations and Cyprus*, p. 185.

[20] L. Stern, *the Wrong Horse*, p. 101, M. A. Attalides, *Cyprus: Nationalism and International Politics*, p. 167, P. Y. Watanabe, *Ethnic Groups, Congress and American Foreign Policy*, p. 88.

he should avert the coup, Kissinger rejected his idea by saying that the United States should not interfere in the internal affairs of the Greeks.[21] But after the Cyprus coup Kissinger denied that his department had any prior knowledge of the Greek junta's plans for a coup against Makarios. At a press conference on 22 July 1974 Kissinger said: "The information concerning an impending coup was not exactly lying around the streets."[22]

After the Cyprus coup on 15 July 1974, the United States was subjected to the severe criticism that it failed to try and forestall the coup against Makarios government. It was claimed that the United States could have taken strong and effective preventive action which could have dissuaded the Greek junta from carrying out the coup.[23] In Polyviou's opinion, "the United States had an opportunity to prevent the fatal coup against President Makarios, but let it pass because of a long held dislike and distrust of the Archbishop and unwillingness to offend the then military rulers of Greece, whom the United States had helped and assisted throughout their repressive rule of Greece."[24] Bell's view is that the United States tried to persuade Makarios not to push his quarrel with the Greek junta too far and put pressure on Ioannides to prevent his coup plan but both American efforts failed.[25] The Cyprus Country Director in the State Department, Thomas Boyatt, later denied the accusations that the United States deliberately did not prevent the Cyprus coup. In a conference on 22 February 1975 he said: "I am prepared to accept that US policy was inadequate... and that there have been mistakes made... [But] I absolutely reject the devil theory, the proposition that this government, through any of its arms, somehow bluntly and clandestinely developed a situation with General Ioannides that he would take an action which in the last analysis would have the result which is so totally disastrous for the United States."[26]

It seems that US rulers had continued their policy of leaving the Makarios problem to the Greeks. In spite of enough warnings on the Greek junta's action, they did not want to get involved in disagreements between the Greek and the Greek Cypriot administrations by condemning the one side. The Americans would pay more attention not to alienate the Greek junta because of US interests in Greece. However, they might have failed to predict the exact time of the Cypriot coup to take effective action to prevent it.

Anyway, on 15 July 1974, the Greek Cypriot National Guard, aided by units of EOKA-B and led by Greek officers, attacked the Cypriot presidential palace with heavy weapons to achieve the death of President Makarios and thus to overthrow the Makarios regime. The palace was totally destroyed and reduced to rubble by artillery fire. Nevertheless, Makarios escaped from death and fled to the British base at Akrotiri. With British help he was able to leave the island.[27] It was believed that the coup d'état was planned and supported by Greek military junta leader Dimitros Ioannides. Allegedly it was also the Greek regime which

---

[21] S. Bölükbaşı, *Turkish-American Relations and Cyprus*, pp. 183-184.

[22] P. Y. Watanabe, *Ethnic Groups, Congress and American Foreign Policy*, p. 87.

[23] T. A. Couloumbis, *the United States, Greece and Turkey*, p. 88.

[24] Polyvious G. Polyviou, *Cyprus: the Tragedy and the Challenge*, (Washington D. C.: American Hellenic Institute, 1975), p. 85.

[25] C. Bell, *Diplomacy of Détente*, p. 149.

[26] "US Foreign Policy Toward Greece: Panel Discussions" in Theodore A. Couloumbis and Sallie M. Hicks (eds.), *US Foreign Policy Toward Greece and Cyprus: the Clash of Principle and Pragmatism*, (Washington D. C.: Center for Mediterranean Studies, 1975), p. 140.

[27] T. A. Couloumbis, *the United States, Greece and Turkey*, p. 88, P. G. Polyviou, *Cyprus: the Tragedy and the Challenge*, p. 55, *Keesing's Contemporary Archives*, 1974, vol. 20, p. 26662. Makarios told the UN Security Council on 19 July that the coup was organised by the Greek junta. *Keesing's Contemporary Archives*, 1974, vol. 20, pp. 26664-26665.

replaced Makarios with Nikos Sampson, a rightist journalist and a leading figure in EOKA-B whose aims were to overthrow Makarios and achieve the unity of Cyprus with Greece.[28] After gaining power Sampson promised general elections within a year and the continuation of inter-communal talks. But since he had a reputation for his terrorist activities against the Turks, his promises were not convincing for the Turkish side. In fact, Sampson later admitted that his ultimate aim was Enosis and that if the Turkish invasion had not taken place he would have proclaimed the unification of Cyprus with Greece.[29]

American Attitude Toward the Cyprus Coup

In the first few days of the Cypriot coup, the United States seemed to follow a wait-and-see policy, avoiding to show any reaction to the developments in Cyprus. The American administration did not condemn the coup and its organisers, did not criticise the Athens junta for its alleged involvement in the coup and did not call for the withdrawal from Cyprus of the Greek officers who had organised the coup.[30] The United States generally expressed its opposition to violence in Cyprus, and supported the territorial integrity of Cyprus but did not openly criticise the Athens junta, which was considered by the other states the violator of the sovereignty of Cyprus.[31] American officials did not make it clear whether the Greek junta was responsible for the coup in Cyprus and seemed to give the impression that they regarded it as purely internal affair.[32] They were also not clear about who represented Cyprus. Unlike other states which recognised Makarios still as official representative of the Cypriot state, the United States equivocated on whether Sampson or Makarios represented the official authority in Cyprus.[33] According to Makrides, some State Department and Pentagon experts urged Secretary of State Kissinger to issue an open statement similar to that issued by the British government, announcing that the United States still recognised Makarios as the legitimate ruler of Cyprus but Kissinger ignored their advice.[34] Soon it seemed that the United States was ready to accept the new situation in Cyprus as an accomplished fact, to recognise the new regime and to prevent the restoration of the constitutional government. It was even claimed that the United States welcomed the coup in Cyprus, which overthrew Makarios. Allegedly American officials felt great relief when they learned the removal of Makarios, who had been long regarded by American authorities as an untrustworthy person because of his neutralist

---

[28] Theodore A. Couloumbis and Sallie M. Hicks, "the Impact of Greek Americans Upon United States Foreign Policy: Illusion or Reality?" in Michael A. Attalides (ed.), *Cyprus Reviewed: A Seminar on the Cyprus Problem,* (Nicosia: Jus Cypri Association, 1977), p. 145.

[29] S. Bölükbaşı, *Turkish-American Relations and Cyprus,* pp. 185-186.

[30] J. C. Campbell, "the United States and the Cyprus Question, 1974-1975", p. 19.

[31] Nikolas A. Stavrou, "Kissinger's Tilt on Cyprus, the New Style of Crisis Diplomacy" T. A. Couloumbis and S. M. Hicks (eds.), *US Foreign Policy Toward Greece and Cyprus,* p. 100.

[32] E. B. Laipson, "Cyprus: A Quarter Century of US Diplomacy", p. 69, Polyvious G. Polyviou, *Cyprus: Conflict and Negotiation 1960-1980,* (London: Duckworth, 1980), p. 156.

[33] E. B. Laipson, "Cyprus: A Quarter Century of US Diplomacy", p. 69, T. A. Couloumbis, *the United States, Greece and Turkey,* p. 88.

[34] Kryriacos C. Markides, *The Rise and Fall of the Cyprus Republic,* (New Haven, Conn. and London: Yale University Press, 1977), p. 180.

and pro-Soviet ideas.[35] It was reported that a high US official, upon learning that Makarios had escaped assassination on July 15, said: "How inconvenient!"[36]

Statements by American State Department Spokesman Robert Anderson in the first week of the Cyprus coup were confusing and did not make the American position clear. On the day of the coup, July 15, Anderson declared: "The United States has long been on record as opposed to any resort to violence on the island. Our policy remains that of supporting the independence and territorial integrity of Cyprus and its constitutional arrangements, and we urge all other states to support a similar policy."[37] While the coup was condemned throughout Europe, Anderson did not criticise the Athens junta for its involvement and did not express American sadness for the reported assassination of Makarios. In the first few days, Ambassador Anderson refused to comment on the questions about American recognition of the Sampson regime. On 16 July he said that "the present situation on Cyprus is unclear, and in our view, as of the moment, the question of recognition does not arise." When a reporter asked if the Makarios government was the government of Cyprus at that moment as far as the United States was concerned, Anderson replied: "I would rather just not comment on it at all."[38] The American administration announced that the overall situation was being evaluated, and a decision on which regime would be recognised would only be made when clearer reports arrived from the American embassies.[39] On 17 July 1974 Robert Anderson maintained that "in our view, there has been no outside intervention."[40]

American ambassador to Turkey, William B. Macomber, who had been reportedly called to Washington as a protest against the Turkish decision to resume poppy cultivation, returned hurriedly to his post in Ankara. On 17 July, he brought a message from Kissinger to Turkish Prime Minister Bülent Ecevit. The United States was opposed to the violation of the constitutional order in Cyprus. But it avoided criticising the Greek junta and clarifying its position on the recognition of the Sampson regime. The United States was only proposing negotiations to prevent the outbreak of a war between Greece and Turkey.[41] The American administration also failed to give support for the Turkish prime minister's compromise demand for the resignation of Sampson and the establishment of a federation in Cyprus to be negotiated by the Greek and Turkish representatives in the inter-communal talks.[42]

On 19 July 1974, American ambassador to the United Nations Scali said that "it will be a serious error to rush to judgement on an issue of this gravity" (meaning the recognition of the Sampson regime).[43] It was claimed that in the United Nations the US representative tried to block and soften resolutions which would have explicitly condemned the Greek military junta for the events in Cyprus. The US representative in NATO was successful in softening the criticism of the Greek government by the NATO members on its involvement in Cyprus.[44] The attitude of the American ambassador to Cyprus, Rodger Davies, reinforced the suspicions

---

[35] P. Y. Watanabe, *Ethnic Groups, Congress and American Foreign Policy*, pp. 90-91, A. Haluk Ulman, "Geneva Conferences, July-August 1974", *Foreign Policy (Dış Politika)*, vol. 4, Nos. 2-3, February 1975, p. 50.

[36] T. A. Couloumbis, *the United States, Greece and Turkey*, pp. 88-89.

[37] C. Hackett, "Ethnic Politics in Congress: the Turkish Embargo Experience" in Abdul A. Said (ed.), *Ethnicity and US Foreign Policy*, (New York: Praeger Publishers, 1977), p. 21.

[38] L. Stern, *the Wrong Horse*, p. 112.

[39] P. G. Polyviou, *Cyprus: Conflict and Negotiation*, p. 156.

[40] L. Stern, *the Wrong Horse*, p. 112, S. Bölükbaşı, *Turkish-American Relations and Cyprus*, p. 186.

[41] M. Sarıca et. al., *Kıbrıs Sorunu*, p. 186.

[42] M. A. Attalides, *Cyprus: Nationalism and International Politics*, p. 171.

[43] Ibid., p. 171.

[44] N. A. Stavrou, "Kissinger's Tilt on Cyprus", p. 101.

on the American approval for the coup in Cyprus. On 18 July 1974 Davies received the foreign minister of the Sampson regime, Dimis Dimitrou, at the latter's request. Thus the United States became the only state which established official contact with the short-lived Sampson regime.[45]

Attalides claims that the American secret services gave assurances to the Greek dictators that there would be no Turkish intervention and that this American attitude took the pressure off the Greek rulers to restore the status quo in Cyprus. Attalides cites in his book: The American ambassador to Cyprus "told Glafkos Clerides that if Sampson did not resign and the Greek officers [were not] withdrawn, there would be a [Turkish] invasion. Clerides warned the foreign minister of Cyprus appointed by the junta. He communicated with Athens and told Clerides: "What the ambassador told you does not worry us, because we have different assurances from Athens."[46]

It seems that the main American concern after the Cyprus coup was to prevent the outbreak of a war between Turkey and Greece rather than to restore the status quo in Cyprus. American officials concentrated their efforts in this front so that a conflict within NATO could be avoided.[47] Keeping the Soviet Union away from the Cyprus dispute was another American concern. But the main American interest which affected its policy toward the Cyprus coup was to keep good relations with Greece because of Greece's importance for American strategic interests. James Reyton's article in *International Herald Tribune* on 18 July 1974, "Cyprus Crisis and NATO's Flank", voiced this opinion: "Washington deplores the authoritarian military regime in Athens, but it is dependent on the Greek mainland and at Soudhas Bay on the island of Creete for its supply routes from Europe to the unstable Middle East... The official view here is that it would be extremely difficult to support the US Sixth Fleet in the eastern Mediterranean without the Greek bases... The Nixon administration faces one more dilemma. It is embarrassed not only by the internal policy of the Greek government, but by Greek subversion of the Makarios regime. Still for strategic reasons it needs the co-operation of Athens in order to defend its vital interests in the Middle East."[48]

It was reported that American Secretary of State Kissinger feared that if the United States alienated the Ioannides regime in Greece by condemning the Cyprus coup, the Greek military government might be overthrown by a new clique of younger officers with anti-Western and anti-American positions.[49] The American President's crisis-reaction team headed by Kissinger, the Washington Special Action Group (WASAG), reached the conclusion from the day of the Cyprus coup that the United States depended on its air and naval bases in Greece and would do nothing to jeopardise them with the present or any future government.[50] Allegedly Kissinger did not work for the restoration of the status quo in Cyprus because he considered Archbishop Makarios politically dead and regarded him as a loser. The Sampson

---

[45] Ibid., p. 101, T. A. Couloumbis, *the United States, Greece and Turkey*, p. 89, E. B. Laipson, "Cyprus: A Quarter Century of US Diplomacy", p. 69.

[46] M. A. Attalides, *Cyprus: Nationalism and International Politics*, pp. 170-171.

[47] K. H. Karpat, "War on Cyprus: the Tragedy of Enosis", p. 197.

[48] Seyfi Taşhan, "Turkish-US Relations and Cyprus", *Foreign Policy (Dış Politika)*, vol. 4, Nos. 2-3, February 1975, p. 172.

[49] K. C. Markides, *The Rise and Fall of the Cyprus Republic*, p. 180, Pierre Oberling, *The Road to Bellapais: the Turkish Cypriot Exodus to Northern Cyprus*, (New York: Columbia University Press, 1982), p. 161.

[50] L. Stern, *The Wrong Horse*, p. 113.

regime, its radio and television stations loudly and repeatedly echoed Kissinger's words as evidence of his support for the new regime in Cyprus.[51]

Later Kissinger claimed that he opposed making any public proclamation against the Sampson regime since he feared that his statements and statements of other American officials condemning the coup could be used by the Turks to justify their military intervention in Cyprus.[52] Kissinger stated in his memoir that many American groups and the State Department wanted the United States to adopt a stance against the Cyprus coup that would accelerate the fall of the Greek military regime. He wrote: "Greece was a military dictatorship; hence all groups critical of our approach to human rights urged us to turn on it as the instigator of the upheaval; failure in Cyprus would, it was hoped, produce the overthrow of the hated Greek colonels... This view was the dominant conviction in the State Department; the Secretary of Defence moved toward it increasingly as the week progressed."[53] Kissinger claimed that he had different views: "Turkey's demands left little doubt that it was planning to intervene... My view... was that the Greek government was unlikely to survive its follies. That made it all the more necessary that the United States not to be seen in Greece as the agent of its humiliation."[54]

The Turks believed that the American attitude toward the Cyprus coup was working in the interest of the Greek side. They feared that if they did not act quickly the United States would recognise the Sampson regime and the fait accompli in Cyprus would be legalised.[55] The Greek side was of the opinion that the American attitude worked to the Turks' advantage, encouraging and giving them a good pretext for their invasion of Cyprus.[56] In Polyviou's words, "the early equivocation and hesitation of the American administration were interpreted by the Turkish government as signs that recognition of the new Cyprus regime was imminent, and that unless immediate military action was taken the stage might be set for eventual unification of Cyprus with Greece."[57] Greek critics of the United States claimed that Turkey could be persuaded to hold back on military intervention if the United States gave public support to the British government's refusal to recognise the Sampson regime and its demand that Athens should immediately recall the Greek officers in Cyprus, who directed the coup operation.[58]

In Campbell's opinion, the result would have not been different even if the United States had acted differently: "It is not probable that if the United States had condemned the coup and verbally supported the position of Makarios, the outcome would have been different from what it was. Nor was Makarios such a favourite in Ankara that his restoration would be seen there as a solution to the problem. It is doubtful that the Turks could have been held back short of drastic change, not just promise of it... The Turkish military leaders, after ten years of frustration, were probably bent on moving in anyway, once they had such a heaven-sent

---

[51] K. C. Markides, *The Rise and Fall of the Cyprus Republic*, pp. 180-181.
[52] P. Oberling, *The Road to Bellapais*, p. 162, L. Stern, *The Wrong Horse*, p. 113.
[53] Henry Kissinger, *Years of Upheaval*, (London: Weidenfield and Nicolson and Michael Joseph, 1982), p. 1190.
[54] Ibid., pp. 1190-1191.
[55] P. Oberling, *The Road to Bellapais*, p. 162, Mehmet Ali Birand, *30 Sıcak Gün*, 4th Edition, (İstanbul: Milliyet Yayınları, 1976), p. 30.
[56] N. A. Stavrou, "Kissinger's Tilt on Cyprus", p. 101.
[57] P. G. Polyviou, *Cyprus: Conflict and Negotiation*, pp. 156-157.
[58] P. G. Polyviou, *Cyprus: the Tragedy and the Challenge*, p. 85, T. A. Couloumbis, *the United States, Greece and Turkey*, p. 89.

pretext for it."[59] While explaining the reasons for the American ineffectiveness on the Cyprus crisis in 1974, Hackett states: "Partly, it was simple neglect by a US government preoccupied with the domestic turmoil of a possible presidential impeachment. More importantly, it was a self-inflicted paralysis of policy, which, by making military bases the measures of a country's worth, now found itself unable to influence that country's government as it embarked on an evil course against a third country."[60] Attalides gives the State Department's reasoning for the American attitude: The United States had neither the right nor the possibility of checking the coup or the invasion in Cyprus. It was impossible to hold anyone responsible for a complex course of events such as that in Cyprus.[61]

It is difficult to say under these circumstances that the US attitude aimed to encourage a Turkish intervention which could cause the loss of Greece for America and could bring unpredicted grave dangers for US interests. Anyway, the US attitude pleased neither the Turks nor the Greeks. The Turks claimed that if they did not act quickly the United States would recognise the Sampson regime and the fait accompli in Cyprus would be legalised. The Greek side was of the opinion that the US inactivity against the Cyprus coup gave Turkey a good pretext for its invasion of Cyprus.

Turkey's Reaction to the Coup in Cyprus

When he received the news of the coup in Cyprus on 15 July 1974, Turkish Prime Minister Bülent Ecevit was about to board a plane for his journey to the city of Afyon, where he would explain the Turkish government's decision to lift the ban on poppy cultivation. In spite of the serious development in Cyprus Ecevit went to Afyon but immediately returned to Ankara on the same day to head the Turkish National Security Council's emergency session on the Cyprus crisis. Ecevit declared that Turkey would "never accept any fait accompli of any kind in Cyprus. We will not permit anyone to intervene in the rights of the Cypriot Turks."[62] During the National Security Council (NSC) meeting some Turkish ministers and Ecevit argued that Turkey should respond strongly to the Cyprus coup, including resort to military force. In their opinion, the coup was product of the Athens junta and Cyprus would fall into the hands of the Greeks if not confronted. As a result of the détente atmosphere in the international arena, the world powers seemed inclined to accept fait accomplis. Some ministers questioned the readiness of the Turkish armed forces to undertake a military intervention in Cyprus. The Chief of the General Staff assured them that this time Turkey was ready for a military operation against Cyprus. Although some ministers talked about the disadvantages of a military intervention, the NSC unanimously decided to land forces in Cyprus on 20 July 1974. Vice-Prime Minister Necmettin Erbakan insisted on an immediate invasion but finally it was agreed to consult with the British first as a requirement of the Treaty of Guarantee.[63]

After the NSC meeting, Ecevit issued a statement: "The coup in Cyprus is a Greek intervention in Cyprus. The constitutional system in Cyprus was destroyed and an illegal

---

[59] J. C. Campbell, "the United States and the Cyprus Question, 1974-1975", p. 20.
[60] C. Hackett, "Ethnic Politics in Congress", p. 22.
[61] M. A. Attalides, *Cyprus: Nationalism and International Politics*, p. 165.
[62] T. A. Couloumbis, *The United States, Greece and Turkey*, p. 90.
[63] S. Bölükbaşı, *Turkish-American Relations and Cyprus*, pp. 188-190.

military government was established. Turkey considers this act a violation of international agreements and guarantees on Cyprus."[64] The Chief of Turkey's General Staff, Semih Sancar, announced that the Turkish armed forces were placed in a state of readiness.[65] Meanwhile, Turkish Foreign Ministry authorities informed the British and American representatives in Ankara of Turkey's opinion on the Cyprus crisis. The Cyprus coup was an intervention of Greece and Turkey would not accept it.[66] The Turkish diplomatic note to the British charge d'affaires on July 15 proposed a joint action in Cyprus in accordance with Article 4 of the Treaty of Guarantee.[67] Turkish Prime Minister Ecevit believed that Britain would not accept Turkey's proposal for a joint military intervention in Cyprus to restore the status quo but he felt that he had to follow the procedure provided for in the Treaty of Guarantee in order to convince the world public opinion that Turkey's cause was just.[68] However, the Turkish government did not consider Greece a party which had to be consulted according to the Treaty because, in Turkish eyes, Greece had violated the international agreements through her action in Cyprus.[69] On July 16 the British government replied to Turkey's note and informed Ecevit of their readiness for bilateral consultations as proposed by Ecevit. In his statement before leaving for Britain Ecevit said: "We will consult with the British authorities in accordance with the Treaty of Guarantee. If we achieve no result, we will have to fulfil the requirements of the agreements. The independence of Cyprus and Turkey's security and interests compel us to act in this way."[70]

In London, Ecevit met with British Prime Minister Harold Wilson and Foreign Minister James Callaghan on 17 and 18 July 1974 and proposed to them to take a joint military intervention in Cyprus. The British authorities rejected Ecevit's proposal by arguing that peaceful alternatives had not been exhausted and that there was still time for further consultations, including consultation with the Greek government.[71] In his statement to the public about his meetings with the British authorities Ecevit said: "We want to use Turkey's right to intervene in Cyprus as a guarantor state together with the British government. We demand that necessary measures be taken to restore the status quo in Cyprus."[72]

It is claimed by mainly Greek authors that Turkey was determined and prepared to intervene in Cyprus and that Turkish rulers were just looking for an excuse to carry out their plan. The Turkish army had made preparations between 1968 and 1974 as if Turkey would intervene in Cyprus at any moment. The Cyprus coup on 15 July 1974 was a golden opportunity for the Turks to move against Cyprus and they would not miss it in any situation. It was reported that a Turkish diplomat in Washington said: "The Greeks committed the unbelievably stupid move of appointing Sampson, giving us the opportunity to solve our problems once and for all. Unlike 1964 and 1967, the US leverage on us was minimal. We

---

[64] M. Sarıca et. al., *Kıbrıs Sorunu*, p. 180.

[65] Ibid., p. 181, T. A. Couloumbis, *The United States, Greece and Turkey*, p. 90.

[66] M. Sarıca et. al., *Kıbrıs Sorunu*, p. 181.

[67] T. A. Couloumbis, *The United States, Greece and Turkey*, p. 90.

[68] S. Bölükbaşı, *Turkish-American Relations and Cyprus*, p. 191.

[69] Ümit Haluk Bayülken, "The Cyprus Question and the United Nations", *Foreign Policy (Dış Politika)*, vol. 4, Nos. 2-3, February 1975, p. 119.

[70] M. Sarıca et. al., *Kıbrıs Sorunu*, p. 186.

[71] Ü. H. Bayülken, "The Cyprus Question and the United Nations", pp. 119-120, *Keesing's Contemporary Archives*, 1974, vol. 20, p. 26663.

[72] M. Sarıca et. al., *Kıbrıs Sorunu*, p. 186.

could no longer be scared off by threats of the Soviet bogeyman."[73] The Treaty of Guarantee was a good instrument for the Turks to justify their intervention.[74]

Makarios' Statement in the UN Security Council

On 19 July 1974 Archbishop Makarios made a speech before the UN Security Council, explaining the nature of the Cyprus coup. It will be useful to cite some of its points here to be able to judge the reactions of other states such as the United States and Turkey to the coup: "The military regime of Greece has callously violated the independence of Cyprus. Without trace of respect for the democratic rights of the Cypriots, without trace of respect for the independence and sovereignty of the Republic of Cyprus, the Greek junta has extended its dictatorship to Cyprus... I knew all along that the illegal organisation [EOKA-B] had its roots and supply resources in Athens... As things developed I considered the danger from Turkey of a lesser degree than the danger from them [the Greek junta]... I was surprised at the way they [the Greek junta] are trying to deceive world public opinion. Without a blush, the Greek junta is making efforts to simplify the situation, claiming that it is not involved in the armed attack and that the developments of the last few days are an internal matter of the Greek Cypriots... It is clearly an invasion from outside, a flagrant violation of the independence and sovereignty of the Republic of Cyprus. The so-called coup was the work of the Greek officers staffing and commanding the National Guard... There is no doubt that the coup was organised by the Greek junta... The invasion is continuing so long as there are Greek officers in Cyprus."[75]

THE TURKISH MILITARY INTERVENTION IN CYPRUS

The Sisco Mission

On the night of 17 July 1974, when Turkish Prime Minister Ecevit and the British authorities were having talks on the Cyprus crisis, American Under-Secretary of State Joseph Sisco was dispatched by Secretary of State Henry Kissinger to the crisis zone. In Kissinger's words, "Sisco's mission was to help Britain start a negotiating process that might delay a Turkish invasion and enable the structure under Sampson in Cyprus to fall of its own weight."[76] Sisco would shuttle between Athens and Ankara to defuse the Cyprus crisis and to find a solution to it. He would also try to prevent the worst possible development from the American point of view: outbreak of an armed conflict between two allies of the United States; Greece and Turkey. Such a development could threaten the American military bases in these two countries.

In Couloumbis' view, the American move, dispatching Sisco to Athens and Ankara, was too little and too late to prevent a Turkish intervention in Cyprus. The Turks at that stage were virtually unstoppable.[77] As stated by Watanabe, "Sisco was weakened by the fact that the previous decisions not to condemn the Greek junta's actions and Sampson installation robbed

---

[73] T. A. Couloumbis, *The United States, Greece and Turkey*, pp. 89-90.
[74] T. A. Couloumbis and S. M. Hicks, "the Impact of Greek Americans Upon United States Foreign Policy", p. 145.
[75] R. R. Denktash, *The Cyprus Triangle*, pp. 180-185.
[76] H. Kissinger, *Years of Upheaval*, p. 1191.

the administration of much needed leverage in dealing with the Turkish leaders."[78] Thus in many people's view, the Sisco mission was an ineffective American response which was from the outset bound to fail. In Kissinger's opinion this outcome arose from the fact that "Turkey was not interested in a negotiated settlement; it was determined to settle old scores."[79] The Turks were of the opinion that they showed good will and conciliatory attitude by accepting to wait American mediation effort before intervening in Cyprus. They had agreed to show restraint until the end of Sisco's mission to Greece.[80]

When Turkish Prime Minister Ecevit learned on 17 July 1974 that Sisco was coming to London to join the Turco-British talks on the Cyprus crisis, he rejected the proposal of trilateral talks by arguing that the United States was not a guarantor power. However, he said that he was ready to have separate talks with Sisco. Ecevit later claimed that he refused a trilateral meeting because he did not want the Soviet Union to think that a NATO plan was being prepared to settle the Cyprus crisis.[81] During their meeting in London on 18 July 1974 Sisco assured Ecevit that American military assistance to Turkey, which was reduced during the last weeks as a result of American displeasure over Turkey's decision to resume poppy cultivation, would be resumed in full.[82] Then Sisco warned Ecevit about possible results of a Turkish intervention in Cyprus. A war between Greece and Turkey might break out and Turkish-American relations might be damaged as well. The Soviet Union would oppose the Turkish move and might take advantage of a Greco-Turkish war. The American assistance to Turkey could be cut off if Turkey went ahead without complying with American warnings.[83] Ecevit seemed unimpressed by Sisco's arguments. He told Sisco that if the United States tried to prevent a Turkish action great damages could be done to Turkish-American relations. The United Stated had restricted Turkey on the Cyprus problem since 1964, therefore there was an anti-American atmosphere in Turkey.[84] Reportedly, Ecevit "told Sisco that he could cancel the intervention provided that 1- Sampson and putschist Greek officers were withdrawn by Greece; 2- Turkey sent as large an armed force to Cyprus as Greece currently had; 3- Turkish Cypriots were given control of a coastal region; and 4- negotiations to create a federal system of government started immediately between the two Cypriot communities."[85]

It seemed that Ecevit was determined to intervene militarily unless Britain ensured the reversal of the Sampson coup and the restoration of Makarios to power. But Britain would not promise any such guarantee unless she had the full support of the United States. Sisco, speaking for Washington, where President Nixon faced impeachment, had no authority to promise any American commitment in an event which would cause confrontation with the Greek junta and its Cypriot puppets. Nevertheless, Sisco promised Ecevit to try to persuade the Greek junta to accept Turkish demands and asked him not to undertake military action until he brought the Greek junta's answer to Turkey.[86] Ecevit accepted his demand but he was

[77] T. A. Couloumbis, *The United States, Greece and Turkey*, p. 91.
[78] P. Y. Watanabe, *Ethnic Groups, Congress and American Foreign Policy*, p. 94.
[79] H. Kissinger, *Years of Upheaval*, p. 1191.
[80] Ü. H. Bayülken, "The Cyprus Question and the United Nations", p. 120.
[81] S. Bölükbaşı, *Turkish-American Relations and Cyprus*, p. 191.
[82] M. A. Birand, *30 Sıcak Gün*, p. 48, N. A. Stavrou, "Kissinger's Tilt on Cyprus", p. 102.
[83] S. Bölükbaşı, *Turkish-American Relations and Cyprus*, p. 192.
[84] M. A. Birand, *30 Sıcak Gün*, p. 48.
[85] S. Bölükbaşı, *Turkish-American Relations and Cyprus*, p. 192.
[86] C. Hackett, "Ethnic Politics in Congress", p. 19.

convinced after the talks in London that the only way to oust the Sampson regime was Turkey's military intervention.

In Athens Sisco had difficulty in finding the Greek military officials.[87] Only after spending a good deal of time he was able to meet with the Greek junta's head, Ioannides, and Prime Minister Adamantios Androutsopoulos on 19 July 1974. Sisco pressurised the Greek colonels to replace Sampson with a more moderate Greek Cypriot and to withdraw Greek officers from Cyprus.[88] The Greek authorities rejected Sisco's suggestion but offered only to replace rather than withdraw the Greek officers on Cyprus on a phased timetable.[89] Apparently Sisco did not threaten the Athens colonels by saying that the United States would not take action against the Turkish military intervention in Cyprus.[90]

Sisco then flew to Ankara on the same day to inform Ecevit of the Greek answer. Ecevit insisted on his demands and did not accept the Greek concession. Sisco reportedly told Ecevit: "You have given all your life to humanitarianism, to the spirit of liberty. Now as a result of your decision a lot of people are going to be dead."[91] Allegedly, Sisco also threatened Ecevit by using the following logic: If Turkey intervened in Cyprus Greece would fight against Turkey and this would bring great damages to NATO. The United States would not allow the destruction of NATO and its southern flank.[92] Sisco asked Ecevit for a forty-eight hour delay in Turkish operation. Ecevit replied that Turkey would not repeat the mistakes of 1964 and 1967: "The United States and Turkey both made mistakes in the past - the United States by preventing Turkish military action and Turkey by complying with the American advice. We should not make the same mistakes again."[93] Sisco flew to Athens back to persuade the Greek dictators but he returned to Ankara empty-handed. At 3.00 A.M. on 20 July 1974 Ecevit received Sisco again, together with American Ambassador William B. Macomber. The Turkish prime minister informed them of Turkey's decision to intervene in Cyprus militarily: "We have done it your way for ten years, and now we are going to do it our way."[94]

Later, in the summer of 1987, Joseph Sisco made following points on his interview with Turkish journalist Haluk Şahin: I believed at that time and I still believe that Turkey had the legal right to intervene in Cyprus... We all agreed that the Sampson coup was a casus belli (reason for war)... I told Ioannides that there was one way to prevent Turkish intervention: "You should restore the status quo in Cyprus, bring Makarios back to power and dismiss Sampson..." During in our meetings in London and Ankara Ecevit told me the same thing more than one dozen times: "Mr Sisco, we will do it our way this time, we will not act as we acted in 1964." In 1974 Turkey was determined to intervene. No American intervention like the Johnson letter in 1964 could prevent the Turks from landing on Cyprus because Greece had changed the status quo unilaterally...[95]

---

[87] Ibid., p. 17.
[88] Halil İbrahim Salih, *Cyprus: the Impact of Diverse Nationalism in a State*, (Alabama: University of Alabama Press, 1978), p. 91.
[89] T. A. Couloumbis, *The United States, Greece and Turkey*, p. 92, L. Stern, *The Wrong Horse*, pp. 118-119.
[90] T. A. Couloumbis, *The United States, Greece and Turkey*, p. 91.
[91] Ibid., p. 92.
[92] M. A. Birand, *30 Sıcak Gün*, p. 62.
[93] Ibid., p. 64, T. A. Couloumbis, *The United States, Greece and Turkey*, p. 92, L. Stern, *The Wrong Horse*, p. 119.
[94] T. A. Couloumbis, *The United States, Greece and Turkey*, p. 93, L. Stern, *The Wrong Horse*, p. 120.
[95] Haluk Şahin, *Gece Gelen Mektup: Türk-Amerikan İlişkilerinde Bir Dönüm Noktası*, (İstanbul: Cep Kitapları, 1987), pp. 57-59.

US Ineffectiveness to Prevent the Turkish Intervention

Writers who mainly supported the Greek cause accused the United States of not being sincere in trying to prevent the Turkish intervention in Cyprus. They claimed that despite having information about the certainty of the Turkish intervention the United States did not have the slightest intention to avert the Turkish aggression and avoided taking decisive actions to deter the Turks from invading Cyprus.[96] In the opinion of these writers, statements of Turkish officials proved how the United States encouraged the Turks through its insufficient efforts.[97]

In his press conference in Ankara on 16 August 1974 Turkish Prime Minister Ecevit strongly praised the American role during the Cyprus crisis. He applauded the United States for being less emotional than Britain. Ecevit said that the American administration had evaluated the problem objectively, and refrained from taking sides and putting pressures on the parties to the problem.[98] In his statement to the Associated Press agency in September 1974, Ecevit praised the American policy toward the Cyprus question again. He remarked that Washington acted responsibly and in moderation.[99] Turkish Foreign Minister Turan Güneş later acknowledged that the United States resorted to diplomatic methods to persuade Turkish rulers not to intervene but did not use any threats because she knew that if she acted on this way she would lose Turkey completely. Güneş also stated that the American National Security Council had almost the same ideas as Turkey on the Turkish landing in Cyprus and decided not to prevent Turkish intervention.[100]

Authors who supported the Greek cause also accused the United States of not pressurising Turkey despite she had the power to influence Turkish rulers. In their opinion, during their discussions with Greek and Turkish authorities, American officials did not raise the possibility of an aid cut off, except in the context of a war between Greece and Turkey. American officials themselves declared that they did not threaten Turkey to deter her from intervening in Cyprus. In his informal news conference on 22 July 1974, American Secretary of State Kissinger said: "I made clear on Saturday in San Clemente [at a July 20 news briefing] that no war would be fought between NATO allies with an open American supply line so this put a limit to the escalation that could be conducted. As to the other steps that were taken, there were no specific threats made. It was very clear that we would consider a continuation of a military confrontation between NATO allies as a very grave matter." When one reporter asked whether the United States had warned the Turkish government before its invasion that it would lose aid if it moved, Kissinger replied: "No, but we made very clear that we were strongly opposed to a military action."[101]

In another press conference on 19 August 1974 Kissinger said: "The United States did not threaten to cut off military aid to Turkey for these reasons: 1- It was considered that such

---

[96] P. G. Polyviou, *Cyprus: the Tragedy and the Challenge*, p. 83, P. Y. Watanabe, *Ethnic Groups, Congress and American Foreign Policy*, p. 93.

[97] M. A. Attalides, *Cyprus: Nationalism and International Politics*, p. 172.

[98] P. Y. Watanabe, *Ethnic Groups, Congress and American Foreign Policy*, p. 119.

[99] *Cumhuriyet*, 8 September 1974, p. 7.

[100] *Cumhuriyet*, 25 July 1975. In his interview with the author, former Turkish foreign minister Osman Olcay made almost the same comment.

[101] A. A. Fatouros, "How To Resolve Problems by Refusing to Acknowledge They Exist: Some Legal Parameters of Recent U. S. Policy Toward Greece and Cyprus" in T. A. Couloumbis and S. M. Hicks (eds.), *US Foreign Policy Toward Greece and Cyprus*, p. 46n, *Milliyet*, 24 July 1974.

an action would be ineffective and would not prevent the threatening eventuality. 2-... We are giving economic and military aid as a reflection of our common interest in the defence of the eastern Mediterranean. Once such a decision is taken, it will have the most dramatic consequences... It was judged that the United States would be both ineffective and counter-productive to threaten the cut off aid. Short of this, however, we made the most repeated and urgent representations to Turkey in order to prevent the military action that happened."[102] State Department Spokesman Anderson said in August 1974: "We supply military aid to Turkey and Greece not only for their interests but for our interests as well. We did not cut off aid to both countries because of the Cyprus crisis but we openly informed both states that they should not rely on American assistance if they fought with each other."[103]

According to some Turkish authors, during the days between the Cyprus coup and Turkish intervention the United States made great efforts to prevent Turkish landing in Cyprus.[104] It was claimed that the United States threatened Turkey to cut off its all economic and military aid in order to persuade Turkish rulers not to resort to military force.[105] Allegedly this threat was raised by Joseph Sisco during his meetings with Turkish authorities. But, "the flow of US supplies to Turkey had during recent months already been reduced to a bare minimum for budgetary reasons and possibly because of Congress' attitude on the poppy question. This was not a sufficient weapon to stop Turkish action and it would have reopened probably to an incurable degree the scar created by President Johnson's letter in 1964."[106] In the opinion of Turkish authors the United States could not threaten Turkey in 1974 with cutting off aid or any other forceful method and that even if she had done so her threats would not have been effective. It was claimed that any American effort in the direction of preventing Turkey from using its right to intervene would create a great shock in Turkey, cause alienation of Turks and thus bring incalculable damage to Turkish-American relations.

In Karpat's opinion, "to prevent Turkey from intervening under treaty rights would turn Turks against the United States and NATO... Turkey controlled the Straits and had a common frontier with the Soviet Union as well as with Syria and Iraq. A slight move by Turkey toward the Soviet bloc would have drastically altered the balance of power in the Mediterranean."[107] Turkish-American relations had already been strained because of the dispute over the poppy issue, any American pressure on the Turks on the Cyprus question could cause the total breakdown of relations. Meanwhile, the Turks were determined to resist any outside pressure. According to Arthur Hartman, Assistant Secretary of State for European Affairs, Turks told them that the 1964 Johnson threat was the last time that they were going to listen to the advice from the United States. American officials accepted that conclusion.[108]

Bell relates American ineffectiveness on Turkey's actions with the détente atmosphere in 1974: "The local decision-makers in... Turkey believed themselves able to defy the advice from their great and powerful friends, in a way that would have been unlikely during the cold war years... There was not really much of an "or else" to be put on the Turks in the circumstances of 1974: only the American arms aid, against which they could and did bargain

---

[102] A. A. Fatouros, "How To Resolve Problems by Refusing to Acknowledge They Exist", pp. 34-35.
[103] *Cumhuriyet,* 19 September 1974, p. 1.
[104] A. H. Ulman, "Geneva Conferences, p. 50.
[105] H. I. Salih, *Cyprus,* p. 92.
[106] S. Taşhan, "Turkish-US Relations and Cyprus", p. 173.
[107] K. H. Karpat, "War on Cyprus: the Tragedy of Enosis", p. 198.
[108] P. Y. Watanabe, *Ethnic Groups, Congress and American Foreign Policy,* p. 95.

the US bases. So the widespread assumption that the American pressures on the Turks, which worked in 1964 and 1967 could have been made to work again in 1974, seems rather questionable."[109]

There was one report that, desperate to prevent the Turkish invasion, American Ambassador to Greece Henry Tasca urged the Pentagon to deploy the Sixth Fleet to the Mediterranean to discourage Turkey. Secretary of State Kissinger intercepted the message and cabled Tasca that the idea was "hysterical." This would have undermined Turkish-American relations and would have made the United States the supporter of the Sampson regime.[110] It was claimed by some authors that Kissinger concluded after the Cyprus coup that a Turkish invasion was inevitable and that any American pressure which was brought to bear on the Turks would be counter productive in terms of wider American strategic interests.[111]

Kissinger himself wrote in his memoirs that "it had become... an article of faith in Turkish politics that this submission to American preferences [in 1964 and 1967] had been unwise and would never be repeated. I had always taken it for granted that the next communal crisis in Cyprus would provoke Turkish intervention... I thought it was most unlikely that Turkey would tolerate the union of Cyprus with Greece. That Turkey was driving toward a showdown was obvious... It would be difficult to imagine a foreign leader more unpopular in Turkey than Makarios... Suddenly Ankara put forward the demand that Makarios be returned to office. The motivation had be that Ankara calculated Athens was even more reluctant to see Makarios restored; Ankara presumably was counting on using the Greek refusal as a pretext to move its army into Cyprus."[112]

On the possibility of prevention of the Turkish invasion by the United States Kissinger wrote: "There was nothing we needed less than a crisis -especially one that would involve two NATO allies. Whomever we supported and whatever the outcome, the eastern flank of the Mediterranean would be in jeopardy. And our government was neither cohesive enough, nor did the president have sufficient authority, to sustain a prolonged period of tension... We could not without cost resist a Turkish invasion because that would be considered as objectively supporting the Greek junta... In any case, only the threat of American military action could have prevented a Turkish landing on the island; this was impossility. My consultations with Congressional leaders produced the unanimous advice that we should not get involved at all. We could not avoid diplomatic engagement in a NATO crisis, but in the last three weeks of Nixon's Presidency we were in no position to make credible threats or credible promises."[113]

US failure to prevent the Turkish intervention in Cyprus seems to be the most important example of the United States' inability to influence Turkey to act in a certain way. The Americans had not opposed secession of a Cypriot territory (a base) to Turkey and even thought about a controlled invasion of a part of Cyprus by the Turks. However, they certainly did not want an uncontrolled Turkish intervention in Cyprus, which was very likely to lead to a Greco-Turkish war. Therefore, US rulers applied diplomatic pressures, which were

---

[109] C. Bell, *Diplomacy of Détente*, p. 149.
[110] K. C. Markides, *The Rise and Fall of the Cyprus Republic*, p. 181, M. A. Birand, *30 Sıcak Gün*, p. 58, K. H. Karpat, "War on Cyprus: the Tragedy of Enosis", pp. 198-199.
[111] P. G. Polyviou, *Cyprus: Conflict and Negotiation*, p. 156, L. Stern, *The Wrong Horse*, p. 113.
[112] H. Kissinger, *Years of Upheaval*, pp. 1189-1190.
[113] Ibid., pp. 1190-1191.

eventually unsuccessful, to stop the Turks. But as was apparent from the events, the Americans were not altogether determined to prevent the Turkish intervention. They had shown the same attitude toward the Greek coup, which weakens the claim that the Turks effectively defied the US influence. The US regime at that time was preoccupied with the Watergate scandal and impeachment of the president, so it was not in powerful position to deter the Turks. Moreover, the Turkish intervention in Cyprus was likely to bring less damage to general US interests than the Turkish alienation by US intervention provided that the USA could prevent a Greco-Turkish war whose possibility was reduced by the Greek unpreparedness.

The Turkish Military Intervention in Cyprus

The Turkish naval and aerial landing on Cyprus started at 5.30 A.M. on 20 July 1974.[114] In his public statement on the same day Turkish Prime Minister Ecevit announced Turkey's military operation as follows: "The Turkish Armed Forces have started a peace operation in Cyprus this morning to end decades of strife provoked by extremist and irrendist elements... [The Cyprus coup] was the forceful and flagrant violation of the independence of the Cyprus Republic and of the international agreements on which this Republic was based. Turkey is a co-guarantor of the independence and constitutional order of Cyprus. Turkey is fulfilling her legal responsibility by taking this action. The Turkish government did not resort to armed action before all the other means were tried, but to no avail..."[115] In his speech on the Turkish radio Ecevit praised peace efforts of the United States and Britain and stated that these two countries were not responsible for the failure of peaceful methods to end the crisis.[116]

The Turkish government's statement on 20 July explained Turkey's reasoning for its intervention as follows: "A coup d'état has been carried out in Cyprus by both the Greek contingent stationed in the island and the unconstitutional Greek National Guard which is under the complete command and control of officers from the mainland Greece. Since the forces involved in the coup are the military units under the direct command of a foreign state, the independence and the territorial integrity of Cyprus have been seriously impaired as a result of this action... After having fully evaluated the recent events which took place in the island and in view of the failure of the consultations and efforts it undertook in accordance with the Treaty of Guarantee of 1960 as one of the guarantor powers, the government of the Republic of Turkey has decided to carry out its obligations under Article 4;2 of the said Treaty, with a view to enable Cyprus to survive as an independent state and to safeguard its territorial integrity and the security of life and property of the Turkish community and even that of many Greek Cypriots who are faced with all sorts of dangers and pressures under the new administration... The purpose of our peaceful action is to eliminate the danger directed against the very existence of the Republic of Cyprus and the rights of all Cypriots as a whole and to restore the independence, territorial integrity and security and the order established by the basic articles of the constitution... Our purpose in Cyprus, a bicommunal state, is to get

---

[114] *Keesing's Contemporary Archives,* 1974, vol. 20, pp. 26663-26664.
[115] *Foreign Policy (Dış Politika),* vol. 4, Nos. 2-3, February 1975, pp. 226-227.
[116] M. Sarıca et. al., *Kıbrıs Sorunu,* p. 192.

the inter-communal talks to start as rapidly as possible in order to restore the situation prior to the coup and the legitimate order...”[117]

In the opinion of authors who supported the Turkish cause, the Cyprus coup on 15 July 1974 compelled Turkey to resort to military intervention in Cyprus.[118] The coup had brought an end to the independence of Cyprus and its constitutional order. If Turkey did not act swiftly, the fait accompli in Cyprus would be legalised and the unification of the island with Greece would be realised in a short time.[119] Turkey was obliged to protect the Turkish Cypriots with whom she had ethnic, religious, cultural and political ties. She was also one of the legal guarantors of the Cyprus Republic and therefore she could not accept the Greek action against the independence and sovereignty of Cyprus nor could she stand by and watch Turkish Cypriots being killed or put under the Greek colonial rule.[120] It was apparent that the Cyprus coup and its expected bad results could be reversed only through Turkey's military intervention. In conformity with the 1959 Guarantee treaty, Turkey had consulted with other guarantor powers and tried peaceful ways to solve the crisis but had received no positive response. By intervening in Cyprus “Turkey not only protected its own national interest but also demonstrated its respect for international treaties... [Its action] simultaneously put an end to the civil war among the Greek Cypriots, protected the existence of the Turkish community and prevented the extension of the military junta regime to Cyprus... [and] discouraged the Athens junta from new adventures and put a bloodless end to their regime.”[121]

According to the research of Bölükbaşı, during its military operation against Cyprus, Turkey used only 30 percent of its landing craft because Turkish commanders thought that Greece would declare war on Turkey and that the main area of confrontation between Greece and Turkey would be Thrace and the Aegean islands, not Cyprus. 70 percent of the Turkish landing craft were stationed in the Aegean. Hence Turkey had great difficulties at the beginning of its operation. On 22 July the Turks controlled less territory than they did before the intervention.[122] Meanwhile the UN Security Council met to discuss the Cyprus crisis and adopted resolution 353 on 20 July 1974. The resolution, “deeply deploring the outbreak of violence and continuing bloodshed, gravely concerned about the situation which led to a serious threat to international peace and security” and “equally concerned about the necessity to restore the constitutional structure of the Republic of Cyprus, established and guaranteed by international agreements.” It called upon all states to respect the sovereignty, independence and territorial integrity of Cyprus; called upon all parties to cease all firing and to exercise the utmost restraint and to refrain from any action which might further aggravate the situation; demanded an immediate end to foreign military intervention in Cyprus; requested the withdrawal without delay from Cyprus of foreign military personnel present otherwise than under the authority of international agreements; and called on Greece, Turkey and the United Kingdom to enter negotiations without delay for the restoration of peace in the area and constitutional government in Cyprus.[123]

---

[117] *Foreign Policy (Dış Politika)*, vol. 4, Nos. 2-3, February 1975, pp. 224-225.
[118] Kamran İnan, “Cyprus, 1974 Crisis”, *Foreign Policy (Dış Politika)*, vol. 4, Nos. 2-3, February 1975, p. 67.
[119] Ü. H. Bayülken, “The Cyprus Question and the United Nations”, p. 119, Metin Tamkoç, *The Turkish Cypriot State: the Embodiment of the Right of Self-Determination*, (London: K. Rüstem and Brother, 1988), p. 99.
[120] M. Tamkoç, *The Turkish Cypriot State*, p. 105, R. R. Denktash, *The Cyprus Triangle*, p. 68.
[121] K. İnan, “Cyprus, 1974 Crisis”, p. 67.
[122] S. Bölükbaşı, *Turkish-American Relations and Cyprus*, pp. 195-196.
[123] *Foreign Policy (Dış Politika)*, vol. 4, Nos. 2-3, February 1975, pp. 218-219, *Keesing's Contemporary Archives*, 1974, vol. 20, p. 26665.

American Efforts to Contain the Fighting

After the Turkish military operation started the Greek junta's head, Ioannides, seemed determined to widen the conflict by declaring war on Turkey. The danger of a major war between Greece and Turkey was so acute that American officials concentrated all their efforts on averting this possibility. The main American aim at that stage was to prevent the further intensification of the conflict and the outbreak of an all-out war between the two NATO allies. Joseph Sisco was ordered to continue his shuttle diplomacy between Athens and Ankara to secure a quick cease-fire on the ground in Cyprus and to begin a process of negotiation. Reportedly General Ioannides informed Sisco on 20 July of that Greece would declare war on Turkey unless Ankara accepted a cease-fire and withdrew from Cyprus.[124] While Sisco and the American embassy staff in Greece struggled to establish contact with the Greek government ministers to arrange a cease-fire, Ioannides and his closest advisers were preparing orders for submarine and aerial attacks on the Turkish forces landing on Cyprus.[125] On 21 July Sisco went to Ankara to secure cease-fire. In Athens Ioannides decided to attack Turkey on all fronts and ordered total mobilisation for an all-out war.[126] He had hoped to establish a national front consisting of all political parties and groups to confront Turkey[127] but his efforts failed.

On 21 July American Ambassador Tasca met with the Greek junta and took a very strong stance against their intention to attack Turkey.[128] There was considerable confusion and unpreparedness in the Greek war plans. Greek senior generals realistically evaluated the situation. The Greek military was unprepared and relatively weak for a major military struggle with Turkey. Such a struggle would have resulted in the loss of the undefended Greek islands in the Aegean, which were close to the coast of Turkey.[129] On 22 July the chiefs of the Greek army requested President Gizikis to depose Ioannides and call the civilian politicians back to power.[130] Gizikis agreed and a civilian government headed by Constantine Caramanlis was brought to power on 23 July.[131] Meanwhile, soon after the signing of the Cyprus cease-fire and the fall of the Athens junta, the puppet Sampson regime in Cyprus collapsed, Sampson went into hiding and Glafkos Clerides, the President of the Cyprus House of Representatives, assumed the duties of president.[132] In Laipson's opinion, "Clerides, well-liked by the Americans, was subsequently viewed by American officials in Nicosia as a satisfactory alternative to Makarios, whose political fortunes they thought and/or hoped were finished."[133] According to Attalides, shortly after these developments, Arthur Hartman, Assistant Secretary of State for European Affairs, went to Athens and informed the new

---

[124] H. I. Salih, *Cyprus*, p. 93.
[125] L. Stern, *The Wrong Horse*, p. 120.
[126] Ibid., p. 122, T. A. Couloumbis, *The United States, Greece and Turkey*, p. 94.
[127] M. Sarıca et. al., *Kıbrıs Sorunu*, p. 198.
[128] S. Bölükbaşı, *Turkish-American Relations and Cyprus*, p. 198.
[129] T. A. Couloumbis, *The United States, Greece and Turkey*, p. 94, J. C. Campbell, "the United States and the Cyprus Question, 1974-1975", pp. 20-21, H. I. Salih, *Cyprus*, p. 93.
[130] L. Stern, *The Wrong Horse*, p. 124.
[131] *Keesing's Contemporary Archives*, 1974, vol. 20, pp. 26666-26668.
[132] P. G. Polyviou, *Cyprus: the Tragedy and the Challenge*, p. 56, T. A. Couloumbis, *The United States, Greece and Turkey*, p. 95, *Keesing's Contemporary Archives,* 1974, vol. 20, p. 26666.
[133] E. B. Laipson, "Cyprus: A Quarter Century of US Diplomacy", p. 70.

Greek government that it was important in the interests of the future settlement of Cyprus that Makarios should not return to Cyprus.[134]

After the Turkish intervention started, American Secretary of State Henry Kissinger himself made intensive efforts to secure a cease-fire. He asked his European colleagues to help and made a lot of phone calls to Ankara, Athens, London, Paris and Bonn. In their telephone conversation, Ecevit told Kissinger that Turkey would accept a cease-fire as soon as it captured a bridgehead in northern Cyprus. Turkish Foreign Minister Turan Güneş refused Sisco's cease-fire offer on 21 July for the same reason.[135] Kissinger publicly said that the United States and its allies expressed urgency so that both Turkey and Greece knew "this was a matter that was not taken lightly... and that there was total unanimity of view between Europe and the USA."[136] In the evening of 22 July Turkey's decision to agree to a cease-fire was announced by Prime Minister Ecevit in a press conference: "We have considered it our duty to respond to the UN call for cease-fire in Cyprus. Cease-fire in Cyprus will be effective as from now. The Turkish military operation there has reached its objective of three days. Effective Turkish presence on the island is now irrevocably established. This will create new possibilities for finding viable and fair solutions for the Cyprus problem. The task before us now is peace..."[137]

There are different views on why Turkey accepted the cease-fire on 22 July 1974. Kissinger claimed in his memoirs: "During the night of July 21-22, we forced a cease-fire by threatening Turkey that we would move nuclear weapons from forward positions -especially where they might be involved in a war with Greece. It stopped Turkish military operations while Turkey was occupying only a small enclave on the island."[138] Bölükbaşı cites in his book Kissinger's threat and the American de facto arms embargo against Turkey (the United States slowed the delivery of arms and spare parts to Turkey and avoided signing new arms contracts with the Turkish government); gives the fact that the cease-fire went into effect only after Turkey secured a bridgehead in Cyprus and concludes that the American pressures on Turkey did not play a decisive role in the adoption of the cease-fire.[139] In Birand's opinion, Turkey was able to intervene in Cyprus since the United States and the Soviet Union did not give a red light but when the fighting continued Turkey feared that the two superpowers could agree on a settlement and stop the Turkish intervention collectively as they did in the Suez crisis against Britain. Therefore Turkey accepted the cease-fire offer.[140]

In his press conference on 22 July 1974 Turkish Prime Minister Ecevit praised the American and British efforts to secure a cease-fire: "During our efforts to reach, to find a solution to the immediate crisis in Cyprus, we have received friendly co-operation from many countries. We have been in close and almost constant contact with our friends, the United States and the United Kingdom, on this issue, and they certainly have contributed a lot to the establishment of conditions for a cease-fire."[141] When a reporter asked whether there was an outside intervention in the adoption of the cease-fire, Ecevit replied: "There has been no

---

[134] M. A. Attalides, *Cyprus: Nationalism and International Politics*, p. 173.

[135] S. Bölükbaşı, *Turkish-American Relations and Cyprus*, p. 199.

[136] J. C. Campbell, "the United States and the Cyprus Question, 1974-1975", p. 20.

[137] *Foreign Policy (Dış Politika)*, vol. 4, Nos. 2-3, February 1975, pp. 228-229.

[138] H. Kissinger, *Years of Upheaval*, p. 1192.

[139] S. Bölükbaşı, *Turkish-American Relations and Cyprus*, pp. 199-200.

[140] Mehmet Ali Birand, *Diyet: Türkiye ve Kıbrıs Üzerine Uluslararası Pazarlıklar*, (İstanbul: Ağaoğlu Yayınevi, 1979), p. 28.

[141] *Foreign Policy (Dış Politika)*, vol. 4, Nos. 2-3, February 1975, p. 229.

pressure from any country. Pressure tactics are and should be out of the question between friendly countries. I had a friendly conversation with Kissinger, whom I have known for a long time. We made joint effort for peace and agreed on the necessity of establishing peace in the region. I highly appreciate Kissinger's peace efforts."[142] It is, however, almost certain that Turkey stopped its operations before achieving its real aims because of international opposition, especially the US opposition.

US Attitude Toward the First Phase of the Turkish Intervention

The general American policy in the aftermath of the first phase of the Turkish intervention in Cyprus was to avoid actions which would alienate its two NATO allies, Turkey and Greece. After the Cyprus coup the United States had refrained from condemning the Greek rulers and the puppet Sampson regime to protect its strategic interests in Greece. When Turkey intervened in Cyprus the American administration showed more or less the same attitude toward the Turkish action not to harm its strategic interests in Turkey. In both incidents the United States chose passivity and avoided taking radical actions. The American administration's weakness stemmed from the president's impeachment at that time also played an important role in the US attitude.

During and after the Turkish military intervention, the United States did not directly and officially condemn the Turkish action and apparently did not put substantial pressure on Turkish rulers to reverse their action. The State Department did not issue any official statement critical of the Turks and Secretary of State Kissinger did not openly denounce the Turkish landing in Cyprus in his press conferences devoted to the Cyprus crisis.[143] It seemed that American policy tilted in favour of Turkey to minimise losses within NATO and to safeguard American strategic interests.[144] The Turkish intervention had already caused the alienation of Greece. Any American response would not stop the Turks but would alienate them. Hence it was wise not to lose Turkey as well to preserve the American foothold in a strategic region. This opinion was voiced by Oberling: "When it became clear that the Turks had every intention of staying on the island until a viable solution to the Cyprus conflict could be worked out, the United States showed a growing inclination to accept the status quo. The fact was that the United States did not want to risk a confrontation with Turkey, its principal ally in the eastern Mediterranean, especially when Greece was facing an uncertain political future. Kissinger now merely sought, by diplomatic means, to limit the scope of the Turkish operation in the hope that the Greeks and the Greek Cypriots would accept it as a fait accompli."[145] In Ulman's opinion, after Kissinger realised that the Turkish intervention could not be reversed, he "modified his efforts by establishing a dialogue with the Turks to confine the Turkish military operation in Cyprus within limits acceptable to Greece and Cypriot Greece, while at the same time attempting to find a new status for the island that would have a chance of acceptance by all parties concerned, especially Turkey."[146]

---

[142] M. Sarıca et. al., *Kıbrıs Sorunu*, p. 197.
[143] P. G. Polyviou, *Cyprus: the Tragedy and the Challenge*, p. 86, P. Y. Watanabe, *Ethnic Groups, Congress and American Foreign Policy*, p. 97.
[144] Kamran İnan (former Turkish diplomat and MP) and Seyfi Taşhan (Turkish academic) told the author that America's position favoured the Turkish side.
[145] P. Oberling, *The Road to Bellapais*, pp. 169-170.
[146] A. H. Ulman, "Geneva Conferences, p. 50.

According to Kissinger's account, the main American concern was "to keep both Greece and Turkey in the alliance." He was opposed to views suggesting forceful actions against Greece and Turkey. Defence Secretary Schlesinger, two days after the Turkish intervention, had "urged a conspicuous dissociation from the Greek government, a withdrawal of American nuclear weapons from Greece, and an end to home-porting arrangements in Greece for the US Sixth Fleet." Kissinger was "convinced that the junta in Athens would not last out the week" but he was "certain that if [the Americans] were perceived as the cause of Greece's debacle [they] would pay for it for years to come."[147] Kissinger was also opposed to turning against Turkey. After the Turkish intervention and the establishment of a civilian government in Greece, in Kissinger's words, "the very groups that had castigated us for our reluctance to assault Greece now wanted us to go into all-out opposition to Turkey. We were being asked to turn against Turkey over a crisis started by Greece,... to take a one-sided position regardless of our interest in easing the conflict between two strategic allies in the eastern Mediterranean and to do all this in the very weeks that the US government was on the verge of the collapse."[148] The American presidential crisis had restricted American action capability. In Kissinger's words, "while I briefed Nixon regularly, he was in no position to concentrate or decide between my basic point and Schlesinger's... The preoccupation with Watergate had reached a point where we were losing even the ability to transmit papers bearing on vital foreign policy matters... between the president and the White House."[149]

To assess developments on the Cyprus crisis correctly, the other super power's attitude, too, should be mentioned very briefly. The main Soviet concern on the Cyprus question was to prevent the island from becoming a NATO territory. Hence the Soviet Union was opposed to the annexation of Cyprus to Greece, Enosis, or its partition between Greece and Turkey, double Enosis. Soviet rulers regarded the Sampson coup in Cyprus as a first step toward Enosis and therefore strongly condemned it. They denounced the overthrow of Makarios, accused the Athens junta of armed aggression and demanded reinstallation of Makarios' power and the independence of Cyprus. Their accusations were directed much more toward the Greek military regime and its patrons, the United States and NATO.[150] Soviet rulers did not condemn but welcomed and backed the first Turkish intervention in Cyprus in the beginning because they thought that the Turkish action would prevent Enosis and lead to Makarios' return to power.[151] However, after the Turkish intervention seemed to partition the island permanently, Soviet officials began to criticise Turkey and demanded the withdrawal

---

[147] H. Kissinger, *Years of Upheaval*, p. 1191.

[148] Ibid., p. 1192.

[149] Ibid., pp. 1191-1192.

[150] A. H. Ulman, "Geneva Conferences, p. 50, Fahir Armaoğlu, "the 1974 Cyprus Crisis and the Soviets", *Foreign Policy (Dış Politika)*, vol. 4, Nos. 2-3, February 1975, p. 180, Joseph S. Joseph, *Cyprus: Ethnic Conflict and International Concern*, (New York: Peter Lang, 1985), pp. 146-147.

[151] F. Armaoğlu, "the 1974 Cyprus Crisis and the Soviets", p. 180, J. S. Joseph, *Cyprus*, p. 147, K. H. Karpat, "War on Cyprus: the Tragedy of Enosis", pp. 199, 202.

of all foreign troops from Cyprus and respect for the independence, sovereignty and territorial integrity of Cyprus.

Chapter 7

THE SECOND PHASE OF THE TURKISH INTERVENTION IN CYPRUS AND THE AMERICAN ARMS EMBARGO AGAINST TURKEY (JULY 1974-OCTOBER 1975)

In contrast to the first phase, the second phase of the Turkish military intervention in Cyprus attracted the great criticism of the American administration and especially of the American Congress and resulted in a sad episode in the Turkish-American relationship, that is the US arms embargo on Turkey. The American role in Turkey's resuming her military activities in Cyprus and the failure of the US administration to stop the Turks attracted great criticism and brought about different explanations from the different sides. The struggle between the US administration and the Congress on imposing an arms embargo on Turkey to punish this state for using the American weapons in Cyprus necessitated a broad analysis of the subject, including the views of the sides on the matter and the real reasons behind the episode. There is no doubt that the arms embargo and more importantly the Cyprus question, which was the apparent cause of it, constituted and still constitutes a critical test of the US-Turkish relationship.

THE GENEVA CONFERENCES

The First Geneva Conference

The first Geneva conference on the Cyprus crisis was held between 25 and 30 July 1974 and was attended by the foreign ministers of Turkey, Greece and Britain; Turan Güneş, George Mavros and James Callaghan. The United States sent to the conference a special representative, Assistant Secretary of State William Baffum. According to Ulman, who joined the conference in the Turkish delegation, Baffum and the representative of the Soviet Union "avoided creating an impression that they might be suggesting to the parties specific solutions and trying to get them accepted; they merely tried to create the feeling that they had no purpose other than obtaining first hand information regarding the intentions of the parties and monitoring what was taking place in the conference halls and in the lobbies. However,... they made various approaches to the parties concerned to further their aims [on the Cyprus question]."[1]

During the conference, such subjects as arranging a cease-fire, the establishment of a security zone between the opposing forces and a lifting of the siege around Turkish villages remaining in the Greek sector were discussed.[2] It should be noted that while the Geneva conference took place, the Turkish expansion on Cyprus continued at a lower scale and Greek forces carried on occupying new Turkish enclaves.[3] On 27 July 1974 the conference reached a deadlock over the issue of violating the 22 July cease-fire. American Secretary of State Kissinger intervened at this stage by phoning to the Greek and Turkish prime ministers and persuaded them to adopt a new cease-fire line which recognised the expansions of both Greek and Turkish forces.[4]

On the evacuation of the Turkish landing forces in Cyprus, the Greek side argued that genuine peace and security could not be established unless Turkish troops left the island. The Turkish side stated that the Turkish forces would not be withdrawn unless peace and security was established and the constitutional order was reinstalled. They claimed that Turkish forces were in Cyprus under the authority of the Treaty of Guarantee.[5] On the issue of the constitutional order in Cyprus, the Greeks argued that there was no need to search for a new order since the order established by the 1960 constitution was still there. The entire problem was to make it operative again. The Turkish representative claimed that the 1960 constitutional order, which had been violated by the Greek Cypriots since 1963, no longer provided enough safety for the Turkish Cypriot community. Therefore, it was not possible to return to that order, which was destroyed completely by the Sampson coup. A new realistic order which would recognise the existence of two separate communities should be introduced.[6]

At the end of the first Geneva conference, on 30 July 1974, the foreign ministers of Turkey, Greece and Britain signed a declaration.[7] In the opinion of the Turkish side, the declaration approved their viewpoint. At least they thought that they did not make any substantial compromise in Geneva. In Ulman's view, this was because of Greek Foreign Minister Mavros' attitude. "Since his primary concern at the time was to arrange a cease-fire which would halt the Turkish advance on the island, he could not put up much resistance against the Turkish demands."[8] According to the Turkish interpretation of the declaration, Article 4 linked the withdrawal of Turkish forces from Cyprus to the achievement of "a just and lasting solution acceptable to all parties concerned and thus implicitly recognised the Turkish military presence on the island.[9] The most important gain for the Turks was that Article 5 accepted the legitimacy of the Turkish Cypriot administration: "The ministers noted the existence in practice in the Republic of Cyprus of two autonomous administrations, that of

---

[1] A. Haluk Ulman, "Geneva Conferences, July-August 1974", *Foreign Policy (Dış Politika)*, vol. 4, Nos. 2-3, February 1975, pp. 49-50.

[2] Ibid., pp. 52-59.

[3] Suha Bölükbaşı, *Superpowers and the Third World: Turkish-American Relations and Cyprus*, (New York: University Press of America, 1988), p. 200.

[4] Ibid., p. 201.

[5] A. H. Ulman, "Geneva Conferences", p. 55.

[6] Ibid., p. 57.

[7] For the text of the declaration see *Foreign Policy (Dış Politika)*, vol. 4, Nos. 2-3, February 1975, pp. 230-232, *Keesing's Contemporary Archives*, 1974, vol. 20, p. 26709.

[8] A. H. Ulman, "Geneva Conferences", p. 47.

[9] S. Bölükbaşı, *Turkish-American Relations and Cyprus*, p. 201.

the Greek Cypriot community and that of the Turkish Cypriot community. Without any prejudice to the conclusions to be drawn from this situation the ministers agreed to consider at their next meeting the problems raised by their existence."[10]

The Second Geneva Conference

The Second Geneva conference was held between 8 and 14 August 1974 and was also attended by Turkish Cypriot leader Rauf Denktaş and Greek Cypriot President Glafcos Clerides apart from the foreign ministers of Turkey, Greece and Britain. When the conference started, Turkey was still reinforcing its troops on the seven percent of Cyprus it controlled and the Greek Cypriot National Guard still occupied Turkish enclaves on the other parts of the island although the Geneva declaration required their immediate evacuation.

The Turkish side, both the Turks and the Cypriot Turks, had come to the conference with the solution of a federal system in their mind, which would be based on the geographical separation of the two ethnic communities in Cyprus. The first Turkish proposal of a federal system of government prepared by Rauf Denktaş was given to the Greek and Greek Cypriot delegation on 10 August through British Foreign Secretary Callaghan.[11] According to the proposal, the Republic of Cyprus, "shall be composed of two federal states with full control and autonomy within their respective geographical boundaries" and "the area of the Turkish Cypriot Federated State shall cover 34 percentum of the territory of the Republic."

The Greek and Greek Cypriot delegation categorically rejected Denktaş's proposals. In the opinion of the Turkish side, the Greek and Greek Cypriot representatives showed an uncompromising attitude in the second conference largely because of Makarios' opposition to negotiations with Turkey. Makarios was opposed to the conference, therefore Greek Cypriot leader Clerides lost his manoeuvring capability because he did not have as much popular support as Makarios and Sampson had in Cyprus. Greek Foreign Minister Mavros, who had good relations with Makarios, also became uncompromising because of Makarios' opposition to any concession to Turkey and the attitude of British Foreign Secretary Callaghan.[12]

After the refusal of the Turkish proposal by the Greek side US Secretary of State Kissinger intervened to prevent a deadlock. In his telephone conversation with Ecevit on 12 August Kissinger requested him to put a cantonal system proposal on the table.[13] According to Ulman, Kissinger and other Western diplomats informed Turkey of the following: "It would be difficult for both the Greek government and for the Greek Cypriot leaders to accept a federation based on two separate regions for it would appear as a division of the island into two, placing one part under Turkish hegemony. Both the Greek government and the Greek Cypriot leaders were worried about their public opinion and feared to lose their posts if they accepted the Turkish proposals. In fact both Karamanlis and Clerides were the most reasonable leaders Turks would find to deal with and if they were dismissed from their offices it was not known who would replace them. Moreover, a federation based on two separate regions would require large population shifts and this would be both a difficult operation and

---

[10] *Foreign Policy (Dış Politika)*, vol. 4, Nos. 2-3, February 1975, p. 231.
[11] A. H. Ulman, "Geneva Conferences", pp. 60-61.
[12] Ibid., pp. 47-48, S. Bölükbaşı, *Turkish-American Relations and Cyprus*, pp. 203-204.
[13] Mehmet Ali Birand, *Diyet: Türkiye ve Kıbrıs Üzerine Uluslararası Pazarlıklar*, (İstanbul: Ağaoğlu Yayınevi, 1979), p. 27.

would breed new frictions... Turkey... should contemplate a cantonal system that would ensure geographical separation but would not require big population exchanges."[14]

On the same day, 12 August, Ecevit brought Kissinger's proposal to the Turkish National Security Council and persuaded the NSC members to accept it. Despite the fact that Turkish Foreign Minister Güneş and Turkish Cypriots did not like the cantonal formula, Turkey submitted the proposal to the Greek and British delegation in the evening of the same day.[15] According to the proposal, the Republic of Cyprus would consist of a Turkish autonomous region having six districts and one autonomous Greek region, covering the remaining areas. The total surface area of Turkish districts would be around 34 percent of Cyprus. This proposal, too, was rejected by the Greek side. On 13 August, Callaghan conveyed Kissinger's attitude to Clerides and Mavros: He was in constant communication with Kissinger. Kissinger could not undertake to exert any further pressure on Turkey in order to prevent a further expansion of the area under the control of the Turkish landing forces. The United States was not even prepared to threaten a halt in American military aid to Turkey. Callaghan also said that Britain was ready to use its forces in Cyprus to prevent Turkey's expansion on the condition that the US and the UN favoured such an action. But since Kissinger would not approve a British intervention, Clerides would have to accept Turkey's federation thesis. If Clerides accepted it, Kissinger and Callaghan himself would pressurise Turkey to limit the Turkish zone to 20 to 22 percent of Cyprus.[16]

All the developments at Geneva mentioned above took place in private talks behind the scenes, not in the plenary sessions. Meanwhile, the Turks began to think that time was running against them. In their opinion, the safety of the Turkish troops and the Turkish Cypriots was coming under greater danger. In order to bring the conference to an early conclusion, Turkish Foreign Minister Turan Güneş asked for a plenary session of the conference on 13 August and put forward all Turkey's proposals openly. Both Greek and Greek Cypriot representatives, Mavros and Clerides, asked for an adjournment of 36 hours to consider the Turkish proposals. According to the Turks, this was a delaying tactic of the Greek side. The proposals were not unknown to the Greeks, they had rejected them from the beginning of the conference.[17] They were now trying to gain time in order to regroup their forces in Cyprus.[18] In the afternoon session, Güneş rejected the Greek request and demanded an immediate yes-or-no answer, arguing that further delays would create security problems for the Turkish troops in Cyprus.[19] Thus the negotiations broke down.[20]

Meanwhile, toward the end of the second Geneva conference the American attitude seemed increasingly favouring the Turkish position. In Couloumbis' words, "the judgement of Washington was that a Turkish presence in Cyprus was now a fait accompli and that no future settlement could be arrived at without some disaggregation of the ethnic populations and the attainment of considerable autonomy rights for the Turkish Cypriots in territorially

---

[14] A. H. Ulman, "Geneva Conferences", p. 62.
[15] Ibid., p. 63, M. A. Birand, *Diyet*, p. 29, S. Bölükbaşı, *Turkish-American Relations and Cyprus*, p. 205.
[16] Polyvious G. Polyviou, *Cyprus: Conflict and Negotiation 1960-1980*, (London: Duckworth, 1980), pp. 175-176.
[17] S. Bölükbaşı, *Turkish-American Relations and Cyprus*, pp. 206-207, A. H. Ulman, "Geneva Conferences", pp. 59-60, 64.
[18] Rauf R. Denktash, *The Cyprus Triangle*, (London: K. Rüstem and Brother, 1988), p. 73.
[19] Theodore A. Couloumbis, *The United States, Greece and Turkey: the Troubled Triangle*, (New York: Praeger, 1983), p. 97.
[20] *Keesing's Contemporary Archives*, 1974, vol. 20, pp. 26709-26710.

distinct regions of Cyprus."[21] It seemed to many people that Kissinger was encouraging the Turkish "belligerence" to consolidate their gains. The Turkish proposal, which was called the Güneş plan, had been drawn up at Kissinger's request and contained heavy inputs from Kissinger. Kissinger was not taking a strong stance against Turkey, which was expected by the Greek side. The American State Department's statement on 13 August, in many people's opinion, encouraged the Turks to launch their second intervention in Cyprus: "US position is as follows: we recognise that the position of the Turkish community in Cyprus requires considerable improvement and protection. We have supported a greater degree of autonomy for them. The parties are negotiating on one or more Turkish autonomous areas. The avenues of diplomacy have not been exhausted and therefore the United States would consider a resort to military action unjustified. We have made this clear to all parties."[22] Washington's statement seemed to regard the Turkish policy as a just and fair attitude and to support Turkey's cantonal proposal.

This apparent pro-Turkish American policy originated from the American thinking that Turkey was a much more important military ally for NATO and the American defence structure than Greece was.[23] In Stern's words, Turkey "had a standing army of half a million. It lay astride the southern border of the Soviet Union, and it contained some two dozen installations including a number of powerful electronic monitoring stations that provided military intelligence from within the Soviet Union. Turkey was also the most forward base for the stationing of US and NATO nuclear weapons."[24] Moreover, the United States was not in the position to take effective actions to deter the Turks because the American administration was experiencing the last stages of the Watergate scandal. President Nixon had just resigned and intensive efforts were being carried out to establish the Ford administration. Secretary of State Kissinger had no time to deal with foreign policy issues since he was largely preoccupied with helping the formation of the new American government.[25]

Turkish Prime Minister Ecevit later explained that the cantonal federation proposal was not the last proposal of Turkey in the second Geneva conference and that after the Greek side rejected the Turkish proposal he made a further interim proposal to prevent the breakdown of the conference. In his letter to Turkish Cypriot leader Rauf Denktaş on 12 July 1982, Ecevit made this clear by quoting from M. Ali Birand's book called *30 Sıcak Gün*: "Ecevit made a brand new proposal to Kissinger: The Greek side should declare that they accepted the basic aim [proposals for either cantonal or bi-zonal federation]. At the same time a buffer zone should be determined around the area under the control of the Turkish armed forces and Greeks should withdraw their armed forces from 17-18 percent of the area of the island and leave its administration to the Turkish Cypriots... "Would you recognise them 36 hours if they accept this proposal of yours?" asked Kissinger. Ecevit's reply was: "I can wait not 36 hours but 36 days. On condition that the demilitarised zone will be immediately evacuated by Greek armed elements..."

---

[21] T. A. Couloumbis, *The United States, Greece and Turkey*, p. 96.

[22] Ibid., pp. 96-97, P. G. Polyviou, *Cyprus: Conflict and Negotiation*, p. 181.

[23] John C. Campbell, "the United States and the Cyprus Question, 1974-1975" in Van Coufoudakis (ed.), *Essays on the Cyprus Conflict*, (New York: Pella Publishing Company, 1976), p. 22.

[24] Laurance Stern, *The Wrong Horse: The Politics of Intervention and the Failure of American Diplomacy*, (New York: Times Books, 1977), p. 130.

[25] M. A. Birand, *Diyet*, p. 34.

"Kissinger was pleased with this attitude; it was a realistic and constructive proposal... Kissinger began a wide ranging political activity. He visited everyone one by one. He explained to them the advantages of accepting Ecevit's proposals... Callaghan did not take part in this effort by Kissinger, which continued all day long... Callaghan's negative attitude on this subject, his lack of effort to convince Greece and Greek Cypriots to accept these proposals is considered by the Americans as one of the reasons which opened the way to the second Turkish peace operation."[26] Ecevit also stated in his letter: "In 1976,... when I went to the United States, while talking with Kissinger in the State Department, and while assessing the Cyprus incidents in retrospect, Kissinger confirmed this observation of Birand. He openly complained of the negative and indifferent attitude of Callaghan... at the second Geneva conference, and especially in relation to our interim solution proposal. He pointed out that he considered this British attitude as one of the main factors which prevented the success of the conference."[27]

On the reasons for the second Geneva conference's failure, Campbell states: "It may well be that the talks were poorly handled by Mr Callaghan. It may be that the United States underestimated the intransigence of the Turks. The maps and proposals for settlement which the Greek and Turkish foreign ministers exchanged at Geneva were far apart, and the latter had no flexibility in his instructions from Ankara."[28] However, Campbell also admits that "the Turks' impulse to act was surely not as strong as before the first invasion, and there was more time to put together a combination of pressures and rewards that might have deterred them..."[29] In many Greek authors' opinion, the United States was the main guilty party since it did not work to stop the Turks but on the contrary encouraged them. Polyviou condemns this American attitude as follows: "American policy over Cyprus was at best one of hasty improvisation, its diplomatic efforts being throughout incredibly naive, insensitive and ineffective, and a coldly calculating one, aiming exclusively at a minimisation of disturbances within NATO and showing total disregard for the true dimensions, both political and human, of the crisis."[30]

The Turkish determination to secure long-lasting substantial gains after committing their armed forces certainly played an important role in the failure of the second conference. Campbell suggests in his book: "It is difficult to avoid the conclusion... [that] the outcome was foreordained by decisions taken by Turkey's military leadership and concurred in by a prime minister increasingly aware of the political potency of emotional nationalism... The military leadership regarded the [military] operations as unfinished. The experience of the international reaction to the first invasion led to a rather clear conclusion: if Turkey's bargaining position was strengthened by the first bite, it would be further strengthened by a second bite."[31] From the beginning, the second operation had been considered by Turkish rulers an integral part of the Turkish strategy.[32] By the end of 13 August, the Turks had realised that the negotiations would bring no favourable results and that if they did not act

---

[26] R. R. Denktash, *The Cyprus Triangle*, pp. 369-373.

[27] Ibid., p. 373.

[28] J. C. Campbell, "the United States and the Cyprus Question, 1974-1975", p. 21.

[29] Ibid., p. 22.

[30] P. G. Polyviou, *Cyprus: Conflict and Negotiation*, p. 199.

[31] J. C. Campbell, "the United States and the Cyprus Question, 1974-1975", p. 21.

[32] S. Bölükbaşı, *Turkish-American Relations and Cyprus*, p. 207.

swiftly international public opinion would totally turn against them and they had to be content with the seven percent of Cyprus without being able to initiate further actions.

THE SECOND PHASE OF THE TURKISH INTERVENTION IN CYPRUS

The Military Actions of 14-17 August 1974

The Second Geneva Conference ended with failure at 2.20 A.M. on 14 August 1974 and the second Turkish military operation in Cyprus began two hours later, at 4.19 A.M.[33] Turkish Prime Minister Ecevit explained the Turkish action in his statement to the press: "Having reached the conclusion that there is no use but only harm in maintaining the appearance of continuing a conference that is intentionally obstructed and whose deliberations are unilaterally violated, Turkey has considered it her duty to fulfil by herself her prerogatives and duties as a guarantor power and her responsibilities concerning the independence of Cyprus as well as the rights and security of the Turkish Cypriot people."[34]

The Turkish government's statement on the same day explained the reasons for the Turkish intervention as follows: "Under the disguise of taking into custody, unarmed and defenceless people were being kept as prisoners or hostages under the conditions that would drive the civilised consciences to revolt. The Turkish community in the island can no longer tolerate this situation which offends the human dignity and threatens the lives and the very existence of its greater majority, and they, therefore, anticipate Turkey, as a guarantor power, to liberate them as soon as possible... During the second Geneva conference... it was understood once again that Greece had continued to see the Cyprus state as a Greek island and had no intention whatsoever to give up its high aspirations of annexing the island to its mainland when an opportunity so avails. It has also become very clear that Greece wanted to prevent the recognition of equal rights and well deserved security to Turkish community... It was also observed that Greece had not refrained from resorting to various delaying tactics in the conference. Greece as a guarantor state has not carried out its obligations incumbent upon by the Security Council Resolution 353,... did not abide by the responsibilities it undersigned and has accepted by the Geneva Declaration of 30th July 1974... [and] refrained from serious negotiations for the whole six days since the beginning of the second Geneva conference at 8th August, and has adopted an uncompromising attitude... Under these circumstances, it has become obvious that all the peaceful representations that has been carried out by Turkey with utmost goodwill and patience would not culminate in a positive result. Turkey has been compelled to take unilateral action to establish a legal order in which the existence, independence and territorial integrity of the State of Cyprus will never be threatened again and the rights and security of the Turkish community will be duly protected..."[35]

The second Turkish operation was much more successful than the first one since the Turks had enough tanks and troops to complete the intervention. By 16 August, the Turkish forces had captured 36 percent of the territory of Cyprus. The Turkish action created an

---

[33] Murat Sarıca et. al., *Kıbrıs Sorunu*, (İstanbul: İstanbul Üniversitesi Yayınları, No. 2071, 1975), pp. 207-208, *Keesing's Contemporary Archives*, 1974, vol. 20, p. 26710.

[34] Ümit Haluk Bayülken, "The Cyprus Question and the United Nations", *Foreign Policy (Dış Politika)*, vol. 4, Nos. 2-3, February 1975, p. 122.

[35] *Foreign Policy (Dış Politika)*, vol. 4, Nos. 2-3, February 1975, pp. 233-234.

enormous refugee problem by displacing thousands of mainly Greek Cypriot people. The Greek losses during the fighting far exceeded the Turkish ones. But the Turks reasoned that "most of the Greek casualties were military personnel, whereas Turkish casualties included hundreds of civilians who were massacred by the Greek forces."[36] On 16 August 1974, the UN Security Council adopted Resolution 360 on the latest Cyprus crisis: "The Security Council,... gravely concerned at the deterioration of the situation in Cyprus, resulting from the further military operations which constituted a most serious threat to peace and security in the eastern Mediterranean area, records its formal disapproval of the unilateral military operations against the Republic of Cyprus; [and] urges the parties to comply with all provisions of previous resolutions of the Security Council, including those concerning the withdrawal without delay from the Republic of Cyprus of foreign military personnel present otherwise than under the authority of international agreements..."[37]

US Position in the Aftermath of the Second Operation

The first American reaction after the second Turkish operation started was to issue a statement announcing that if Turkey and Greece fought with each other the United States would cut off its military aid and arms sales to both countries.[38] Officially the United States did not take a firm stance against the Turkish intervention in Cyprus. The American administration did not state that the territorial integrity, sovereignty and independence of Cyprus was violated by the Turkish forces' action in capturing a substantial part of the island.

The Greek side accused the United States of being biased toward Turkey by tolerating the Turkish expansion and seeming to accept a biregional settlement, some kind of geographical federation, on Cyprus. In Polyvious' opinion, "when the Turks landed a substantial force in Cyprus..., American policy tilted decisively and conclusively in favour of Turkey as it was thought that only in this way could losses within NATO be minimised and American strategic interests safeguarded."[39]

According to the Greeks, American Secretary of State Kissinger chose to support Turkey by refusing serious attempts to restrain the Turks in furthering their military gains in Cyprus. Allegedly he told some diplomats that he would not try to stop the Turks until they had reached their territorial objectives.[40] In his statement on the American policy on Cyprus on 19 August 1974, Kissinger stated that there was no doubt that the extent of the Turkish zone to be demarcated was negotiable. This meant, in Greek eyes, the American acceptance that there should be some kind of geographical federation.[41] Kissinger's statement in Miami in August 1974 was further increased the Greek alienation. He reportedly stated that the United States would not launch a military intervention in Cyprus by giving in to pressures because she was not the policeman of the world.[42]

---

[36] S. Bölükbaşı, *Turkish-American Relations and Cyprus*, p. 211.
[37] *Foreign Policy (Dış Politika),* vol. 4, Nos. 2-3, February 1975, p. 221.
[38] M. A. Birand, *Diyet*, p. 39.
[39] P. G. Polyviou, *Cyprus: Conflict and Negotiation*, p. 201, Polyvious G. Polyviou, *Cyprus: the Tragedy and the Challenge,* (Washington D. C.: American Hellenic Institute, 1975), p. 87.
[40] Michael A. Attalides, *Cyprus: Nationalism and International Politics*, (Edinburgh: Q Press Ltd., 1979), p. 176.
[41] P. G. Polyviou, *Cyprus: the Tragedy and the Challenge,* pp. 195-196n.
[42] *Cumhuriyet,* 22 August 1974, p. 1.

The only criticism of the Turkish action by the American administration came from Secretary of Defence Schlesinger. In a television interview on 18 August 1974 Schlesinger said that "we have understood the desire of the Turks to protect the minority Turkish problem, but the Turkish moves at this point have gone beyond what any of its friends or sympathisers would have accepted." He raised the possibility of an aid cut-off as a real one by stating that his department was reviewing US military aid to Turkey in view of the Cyprus events. He added that at future negotiations Turks could be asked to return some of the Cyprus territory which they captured.[43]

It should be noted again that when the second Turkish intervention took place, American officials were still preoccupied with the resignation of President Nixon and the change of the administration. At that stage Kissinger could do nothing but recommend immediate resumption of talks between the concerned parties and to offer his services as mediator. His opinion was that the current Cyprus crisis could best be solved through negotiations among the directly concerned parties. He encouraged the parties to hold talks and offered to play the role of mediator between them. In September 1974 Kissinger said: "The sovereignty, political independence and territorial integrity of Cyprus must be maintained. It will be up to the parties to decide on the form of government they believe best suited to the particular conditions of Cyprus."[44]

American strategic concerns played an important role in the accommodating US attitude toward the Turkish intervention. American strategic interests in the eastern Mediterranean led American officials to try to remove Cyprus as a source of friction in the region by forcing both sides to compromise rather than condemning only one side. In Coufoudakis' words, "the prospects of a reopened Suez Canal; the strong Soviet presence in the Eastern Mediterranean; and the need to protect the oil shipping routes and guarantee energy supplies have given great urgency to the quest for stability in this critical region."[45] American interests in the eastern Mediterranean could best be served by the reconciliation between Greece and Turkey through the solution of the Cyprus problem in a way acceptable to both sides. In this way Greece and Turkey could resume their co-operation in NATO and allow the use of American bases in their countries. Nevertheless, the Turkish bases were more important to the American administration. As Bell pointed out, Turkey, in addition to being a substantial conventional military power sitting astride the Black Sea, played an important part in the overall nuclear relationship by virtue of the monitoring devices on Turkish territory.[46] Hence it was imperative to the American government not to alienate Turkey by condemning its action in Cyprus.

The other super power, the Soviet Union, strongly opposed the second Turkish intervention unlike its supportive attitude toward the first Turkish action. Turkey's federation thesis on the basis of geographical separation and its capturing substantial part of Cyprus seemed to lead to double Enosis (partition of Cyprus) and the extension of NATO to Cyprus, this situation was not compatible with Soviet interests. The decision of the Greek government

---

[43] *Cumhuriyet*, 19 August 1974, Thomas M. Franck and Edward Weisband, *Foreign Policy by Congress*, (New York, Oxford: Oxford University Press, 1979), p. 36, M. A. Attalides, *Cyprus: Nationalism and International Politics*, p. 177.

[44] Halil İbrahim Salih, *Cyprus: the Impact of Diverse Nationalism in a State*, (Alabama: University of Alabama Press, 1978), pp. 97-98.

[45] Van Coufoudakis, "United States Foreign Policy and the Cyprus Question" in Michael A. Attalides (ed.), *Cyprus Reviewed: A Seminar on the Cyprus Problem*, (Nicosia: Jus Cypri Association, 1977), p. 131.

[46] Coral Bell, *Diplomacy of Détente: The Kissinger Era*, (London: Martin Robertson, 1977), p. 153.

to withdraw from the military structure of NATO led the Soviet Union to soften their hard-line attitude toward Greece and to shift their support to Greece. The Soviet statement on 22 August 1974 claimed that the Guarantee Agreement was no longer valid and that Britain, Turkey and Greece no longer had the authority to intervene in Cyprus because the Cyprus problem had ceased to be a matter of concern for the three states.[47] The Soviet Union also proposed an international conference to be attended by all interested parties and members of the UN Security Council to settle the Cyprus question.[48] The Soviet proposal was totally against Turkey's viewpoint on the issue.

The American failure to stop the second Turkish intervention caused great disappointment in Greece and Greek Cyprus. The Greeks were angry against the United States because it had failed to come to the help of Greece in its hour of need. They "found Kissinger's offer of mediation an offensively mild reaction to what had been a criminal action on Turkey's part."[49] Kissinger was blamed by the Greeks for not pressurising the Turks since he decided that Turkey was more important than Greece for the American interests and policies in the eastern Mediterranean. Especially in the eyes of Greek Cypriots, the main cause of the occupation of Cyprus was "American imperialism" which helped Turkey through the CIA and NATO, armed her and encouraged her to invade the non-aligned Republic of Cyprus.[50] As a demonstration of their anger toward NATO and the United States and as a measure to defuse the explosive state of public emotions, on 14 August 1974 Greek rulers announced Greece's withdrawal from the military area of NATO.[51] In this negative atmosphere, apparently to lower the American profile in Greece, the United States decided to discontinue the Sixth Fleet home-porting arrangements in Greece that had been established in 1972 in a comprehensive and open-ended agreement with the Athens junta.[52]

Meanwhile, large public demonstrations against the United States were organised in Greece and Cyprus. In the anti-American demonstration in Nicosia on 19 August 1974, Greek-Cypriot Guards opened fire on the American embassy and killed American Ambassador Rodger P. Davis and an embassy secretary.[53] In August and September 1974, Americans of Greek extraction arranged two large and emotional demonstrations in front of the White House. The demonstrators condemned Kissinger's passivity toward the Turkish actions and demanded sanctions against Turkey because of its military operation against Cyprus which had been carried out with American weapons.[54]

After the Turkish intervention in Cyprus, Turkish Cypriot and Greek Cypriot representatives held bilateral talks to find a solution to the Cyprus problem. The only realistic solution from the Turkish point of view was a federation composed of two ethnic zones. They proposed a new constitutional order based on two autonomous communal units. The Turkish Cypriots would have the northern part of the island and the Greeks the southern part of the

---

[47] Fahir Armaoğlu, "the 1974 Cyprus Crisis and the Soviets", *Foreign Policy (Dış Politika)*, vol. 4, Nos. 2-3, February 1975, pp. 181-182.

[48] Kemal H. Karpat, "War on Cyprus: the Tragedy of Enosis" in Kemal H. Karpat (ed.), *Turkey's Foreign Policy in Transition 1950-1974*, (Leiden, Netherlands : E. J. Brill, 1975), p. 202.

[49] Pierre Oberling, *The Road to Bellapais: the Turkish Cypriot Exodus to Northern Cyprus*, (New York: Columbia University Press, 1982), p. 182.

[50] Zenon Stavrinides, *The Cyprus Conflict: National Identity and Statehood*, (Loris Stavrinides Press, 1976), p. 92.

[51] T. A. Couloumbis, *The United States, Greece and Turkey*, p. 97, H. I. Salih, *Cyprus*, p. 98, *Keesing's Contemporary Archives*, 1974, vol. 20, p. 26710.

[52] T. A. Couloumbis, *The United States, Greece and Turkey*, p. 98.

[53] H. I. Salih, *Cyprus*, p. 98, *Keesing's Contemporary Archives*, 1974, vol. 20, p. 26753.

[54] T. A. Couloumbis, *The United States, Greece and Turkey*, p. 98.

island, but Cyprus would be united under one federal government. The central government would handle foreign affairs and some minor internal policies. The Turks claimed that this arrangement would safeguard the integrity and independence of Cyprus and emphasised that they had no intention of partitioning Cyprus and annexing the Turkish Cypriot unit. They were opposed to the return of refugees to their homes because they believed that separation of the two ethnic groups was the best way of reducing tensions and of safeguarding rights of the communities. On 13 February 1975 Turkish Cypriots proclaimed the Turkish Federated State of Cyprus. In the opinion of Turkish Cypriot leader Denktaş, "the principle of a federal solution had already been accepted and the Turkish Cypriots' action was merely to establish the Turkish wing of the envisaged Federal Republic of Cyprus. In spite of repeated assurances that this was not a unilateral declaration of independence, the Greek Cypriots walked out of the talks."[55]

THE ARMS EMBARGO AND TURKISH-AMERICAN RELATIONS

Imposition of the Arms Embargo

Turkey's second military operation in Cyprus and its capturing a substantial part of the island caused a long battle between the American administration and the Congress over whether an arms embargo should be imposed on Turkey since she used American weapons in carrying out her military operations in Cyprus. Even before the Turks had completed their second advance, on 15 August 1974, a delegation of Greek-American congressmen led by Representative John Bredamas visited Secretary of State Kissinger to request sanctions against Turkey. Bredamas told Kissinger: "We are placing the blame squarely on you, sir. We are not assigning responsibility for the failure of US policy in Greece and Cyprus to President Ford. We feel it is yours." Bredamas asked why there had been no public protest from the State Department when Makarios was overthrown or when Turkey intervened in Cyprus. He also questioned why the State Department did not issue public statements of support for Callaghan in his efforts to prevent the Turks from leaving the bargaining table in Geneva. Finally Bredamas requested that the United States cut off its military assistance to Turkey until its troops were withdrawn from Cyprus.[56]

In Kissinger's eyes, the Greek-American Congressmen were merely instruments of the Greek foreign office. He could not accept their intervention in the formulation of American foreign policy since he regarded foreign policy making as a prerogative of the executive branch.[57] Kissinger put the blame for the failure of the second Geneva conference largely on Callaghan and claimed that some positive developments were achieved in the Cyprus tragedy because of American pressures.[58] He assured the visiting Congressmen that the United States was engaged in very active diplomacy with the Turks and was insisting on assurances from Ankara that the troops would move no further.[59]

---

[55] R. R. Denktash, *The Cyprus Triangle*, p. 80.
[56] L. Stern, *The Wrong Horse*, pp. 140141, M. A. Birand, *Diyet*, pp. 42-43.
[57] K. R. Legg, "Congress as Trojan Horse, the Turkish Embargo Problem, 1974-1978" in John Spanier and Joseph Hogee (eds.), *Congress, the Presidency and American Foreign Policy*, (New York: Pergamon Press, 1981), p. 117, M. A. Birand, *Diyet*, p. 41.
[58] M. A. Birand, *Diyet*, p. 42.
[59] L. Stern, *The Wrong Horse*, p. 141.

At a news conference on 19 August 1974 Kissinger was asked about the legality of Turkish use of US-supplied military equipment in Cyprus. Did the military assistance acts require an embargo on military aid to countries using US-supplied equipment for aggressive purposes? Could these acts be applied to Turkey? Kissinger replied: "I will have to get a legal opinion on that subject, which I have not done" and he promised a legal analysis of the question.[60] The next day, on 20 August, a team of lawyers in the Legal Advisor's Office under the chairmanship of Carlyle J. Maw, former legal advisor and by then Under-Secretary of State for Security Assistance, was asked to prepare a legal memo on Turkey's action.[61] The study of the legal team was completed but their eventual report was not made public. This secrecy which was applied to legal findings on the Turkish action led to the suspicion that the State Department's legal sources were being manipulated. However, the legal memo was soon leaked to Senate staffs by the American administration. On 3 September 1974 a State Department official came on a secret mission to the office of Senator Thomas Eagleton and told Eagleton's chief foreign policy aide Brian Adwood that the legality study of the Turkish military aid question had been completed. Its conclusion was that by no stretch of the statues or the legal imagination of the State Department's attorneys could military aid to Turkey be continued.[62] Turkey's action was not capable of being justified by lawful and defensive purpose, and therefore was interpreted as a breach of the agreements under which arms were provided.[63]

When Eagleton heard this account he decided to plunge into battle with the American administration on the issue of law and order in the context of the legality of the military aid to Turkey. To persuade Congressmen not to impose an arms embargo on Turkey, Kissinger addressed the Senate Democratic caucus on 19 September 1974. He urged the Democrats not to write restrictions into the law that would tie President Gerald Ford's hands in dealings with the Cyprus issue.[64] According to the senators, the Turkish use of American weapons in Cyprus violated the bilateral agreements between the United States and Turkey in 1947 and 1960 and the American Foreign Assistance Act in 1961.[65] When Senator Eagleton asked whether Kissinger had knowledge of the legal memorandum claiming Turkey's August action could not be legally justified, Kissinger replied that the "dominant interpretation within my legal department" agreed with Eagleton's view that further aid to Turkey was illegal since she used in Cyprus US-supplied weapons which could be used only for defensive purposes under provisions in military aid legislation.[66] Kissinger accused Eagleton of not understanding the foreign policy priorities. It appeared that while he accepted the illegality of the Turkish action he was opposed to the enforcement of the law in this specific incident. Some other things

---

[60] C. Hackett, "Ethnic Politics in Congress: the Turkish Embargo Experience" in Abdul A. Said (ed.), *Ethnicity and US Foreign Policy,* (New York: Praeger Publishers, 1977), p. 23, K. R. Legg, "Congress as Trojan Horse, the Turkish Embargo Problem, 1974-1978", p. 117.

[61] Ellen B. Laipson, *Congressional-Executive Relations and the Turkish Arms Embargo,* (Washington: U. S. Government Printing Office, June 1981), p. 14, A. A. Fatouros, "How To Resolve Problems by Refusing to Acknowledge They Exist: Some Legal Parameters of Recent U. S. Policy Toward Greece and Cyprus" in Theodore A. Couloumbis and Sallie M. Hicks (eds.), *US Foreign Policy Toward Greece and Cyprus: the Clash of Principle and Pragmatism,* (Washington D. C.: Center for Mediterranean Studies, 1975), p.35.

[62] L. Stern, *The Wrong Horse,* pp. 143-144.

[63] E. B. Laipson, *Congressional-Executive Relations and the Turkish Arms Embargo,* p. 14.

[64] L. Stern, *The Wrong Horse,* p. 145.

[65] M. A. Birand, *Diyet,* p. 56.

[66] E. B. Laipson, *Congressional-Executive Relations and the Turkish Arms Embargo,* p. 19, C. Hackett, "Ethnic Politics in Congress: the Turkish Embargo Experience", p. 23.

such as the continued access to the US bases in Turkey were more important than the law. Kissinger explained that if Congress cut off aid to Turkey the US bases in this country would be jeopardised.[67]

The chronological events of the Turkish arms embargo are as follows:[68] On 19 September 1974 the Senate passed the Eagleton-Stevenson amendment to the Export-Import Bank Bill. The amendment urged the president to end the shipment of US arms to Turkey. On 24 September 1974 the House of Representatives voted 307 to 90 to adopt the Rosenthal-Du Pont amendment to the Continuing Appropriations Bill for the fiscal year 1975. The amendment favoured an arms embargo on US military assistance to Turkey until the president certified that substantial progress toward agreement was made regarding military forces in Cyprus. On the same day, Kissinger met with Turkish Foreign Minister Güneş in Washington, telling him that Turkey could make some territorial concessions in Cyprus to create a favourable atmosphere for bilateral negotiations between the concerned parties because she had the upper hand. Güneş stated that some minor alterations could be made.[69] In his press conference on 25 September 1974, Turan Güneş condemned the Congress decision to stop American aid to Turkey and said: "Turkey is not going to change its Cyprus policy under the pressure of the American Congress's decision... We will not accept any pressure from any power or state and will not change our policy... If the aid is ended Turkey will have to reconsider the mutual defence co-operation to establish the balance of interests."[70]

On 30 September 1974, the Senate adopted an amendment which called an embargo on US military assistance to any country that used US arms and aid in contravention of US laws. On 14 October President Ford vetoed the spending authorisation bill including the cut-off in the American aid to Turkey. When the House failed to override the president's veto on 15 October, the White House and Congress made bargaining on a compromise solution. As a result, on 16 October the Senate passed a new amendment permitting the president to continue military assistance to Turkey until 10 December 1974 if it was determined as useful in promoting a peaceful solution on Cyprus. But on the same day the House adopted the Rosenthal amendment which favoured an immediate withdrawal of US military assistance to Turkey if the latter violated US laws by using equipment for military operations on Cyprus. The next day President Ford vetoed the second authorisation bill but when the House failed to override the president's veto with only a two-vote margin, the president had to sign a compromise version of the bill on 18 October, thus he agreed to cut off aid on 10 December 1974 if Turkey still did not make substantial concessions to settle the Cyprus problem.[71]

Meanwhile, Turkey accepted the UN General Assembly resolution on 1 November 1974, which called on all parties to respect the sovereignty, independence and territorial integrity of Cyprus, to withdraw all foreign armed forces from Cyprus and to allow for the return of refugees to their homes.[72] Turkish Prime Minister Ecevit's coalition partner Necmettin Erbakan, the leader of the National Salvation Party, severely criticised Turkey's acceptance of

---

[67] C. Hackett, "Ethnic Politics in Congress: the Turkish Embargo Experience", p. 26.

[68] For the Congress actions on the Turkish arms embargo see Theodore A. Couloumbis and Sallie M. Hicks, "the Impact of Greek Americans Upon United States Foreign Policy: Illusion or Reality?" in M. A. Attalides (ed.), *Cyprus Reviewed*, pp. 165-171.

[69] M. A. Birand, *Diyet*, pp. 65-66.

[70] *Cumhuriyet*, 26 September 1964, p. 1.

[71] M. A. Birand, *Diyet*, p. 72.

[72] *Foreign Policy (Dış Politika)*, vol. 4, Nos. 2-3, February 1975, pp. 222-223.

the resolution.[73] On 5 November 1974 the Turkish National Security Council decided to make some territorial concessions in Cyprus and to withdraw 5,000 Turkish soldiers from the island. But Erbakan's refusal to approve the concessions led to the resignation of Ecevit on 7 November 1974. Consequently, the planned visit of Kissinger to Turkey in November 1974 to discuss the Cyprus issue had to be cancelled for lack of a responsible counterpart.[74] After Ecevit's resignation, Turkey was ruled by the caretaker government of Sadi Irmak, which failed even to receive a vote of confidence from the parliament. Hence the Turkish administration did not have the power and authority to make concessions on the Cyprus issue.

The Senate decision on 4 December allowed the president to delay the ban on military aid to Turkey until 5 February 1975 if Turkey abided by the cease-fire agreement and did not send more troops and equipment to Cyprus. Between 12 and 14 December 1974 Kissinger held talks with the Turkish and Greek foreign ministers to speed up efforts to find a solution to the Cyprus problem. According to Birand, in his meeting with Turkish Foreign Minister Melih Esenbel, Kissinger threatened that if inter communal talks did not began it would be impossible to prevent the Congress from imposing an arms embargo.[75] On 31 December 1974 President Ford signed the military and economic assistance bill which delayed the aid cut-off to Turkey until 5 February 1975. In spite of intense efforts of the American administration, the American Congress did not change its decision to impose an arms embargo on Turkey. At the beginning of February 1975, according to Birand, Kissinger phoned Melih Esenbel to inform him that the arms embargo's coming to effect was inevitable. The administration had failed to block the Congress' action. If Turkey reacted harshly, the administration would face more difficulties to persuade Congressmen.[76] After learning that the embargo would certainly be implemented Melih Esenbel said in the Turkish Senate that the American aid was not a favour for Turkey but a requirement of the NATO system, and declared that Turkey would not make any concessions on the Cyprus problem in return for the resumption of American aid.[77]

On 5 February 1975 the Congress' action came into effect. The provisions of section 620(x) of the Foreign Assistance Act went into effect, freezing deliveries for over 200 million dollars in arms purchases and grants which had been scheduled for transfer to Turkey.[78] "All military assistance, all states of defence articles and services (whether for cash or by credit, or any other means), and all licences with respect to the transformation of arms, ammunitions, and implements of war" to the Turkish government were suspended.[79] The ban included 78 million dollar worth of equipment already paid for.[80]

The American action led the Turkish government to stiffen its resolve on the Cyprus issue rather than making concessions. On the same day the Turkish government announced that it was suspending talks with the Americans on agreements relating to the joint defence bases and installations in Turkey.[81] Turkey's National Security Council accused the American

---

[73] M. A. Birand, *Diyet*, p. 79.

[74] Ibid., pp. 81-82.

[75] Ibid., pp. 90-94.

[76] Ibid., pp. 99-100.

[77] *Cumhuriyet*, 18 December 1974, p. 7.

[78] T. A. Couloumbis, *The United States, Greece and Turkey*, p. 105.

[79] *Legislation on Foreign Relations Through 1979: Current Legislation and Related Executive Orders*, vol. 1, US House of Representatives and Senate, (Washington: US Government Printing Office, 1980), p. 113.

[80] K. R. Legg, "Congress as Trojan Horse, the Turkish Embargo Problem, 1974-1978", p. 121.

[81] P. G. Polyviou, *Cyprus: the Tragedy and the Challenge*, p. 210, M. A. Birand, *Diyet*, p. 100.

Congress of committing a very grave mistake and indulging in an experiment of putting pressure on Turkey. Prime Minister Sadi Irmak said that the Turkish government would review its relations with the United States and NATO and added: "Turkey is determined to protect the legitimate rights of Turkish Cypriots under all circumstances until the end."[82] He also told journalists that the American aid was not a privilege for Turkey but a part of mutual responsibilities derived from the NATO alliance. Irmak stated that the Turkish government was expecting the United States to fulfil its responsibilities as Turkey did.[83] In Birand's opinion, Irmak and Esenbel opposed the closure of some American bases in Turkey as a response to the American action because they thought that the presence of the American troops and installations in Turkey was in Turkey's interest and that once they were withdrawn it would be very difficult to recall them. There was no need to act emotionally, Kissinger had promised that the embargo would not last long.[84]

After the implementation of the embargo decision began, the criticism of the Turkish authorities against the United States sharpened. Foreign Minister Melih Esenbel stated in Parliament that the embargo decision would force the Turkish government to reconsider its contribution to the mutual defence co-operation and added: "if the American Congressmen were thinking that Turkey would be affected by their pressures, they were making a serious mistake."[85] On 22 March 1975, Esenbel warned the Americans again that Turkish-American relations would be affected badly if the implementation of the embargo, which could be considered a hostile act between the two allies, continued."[86]

In March 1975 the American State Department issued a statement explaining American policy: "We believe that the Cyprus question can only be resolved through a fair and freely negotiated settlement which preserves the sovereignty, territorial integrity and independence of Cyprus... We have sought to discourage unilateral actions by either side that would complicate efforts to achieve a peaceful settlement. We will do all we can to support political negotiations between the two communities on the island, and to play an active role in assisting them to reconcile their differences and to achieve a peaceful conciliation."[87] On 10 March 1975 Kissinger was in Ankara to talk to Turkish leaders on the Cyprus issue. According to Birand, he pressed Esenbel to make territorial concessions in Cyprus, otherwise the American Congress would not be persuaded to reverse the arms embargo decision.[88] American Under-Secretary of State for European Affairs Arthur Hartman came to Ankara on 22 April 1975 to obtain concessions from Turkey in return for lifting the arms embargo. If Turkey wanted the arms embargo to be lifted, she should work for the achievement of positive results in the inter communal negotiations which would start in Vienna and for the restoration of normal relations between Greece and herself.[89]

On 19 May 1975 the American Senate passed a bill with a thin margin of 41 to 40 authorising the president to lift the embargo if US security interests were at stake. On 23 May 1975 Kissinger held talks with Turkish Prime Minister Süleyman Demirel and Foreign Minister İhsan Sabri Çağlayangil in Ankara where he was attending a CENTO meeting.

---

[82] P. G. Polyviou, *Cyprus: the Tragedy and the Challenge*, pp. 210-211.
[83] *Cumhuriyet*, 4 and 5 February 1975, p. 7.
[84] M. A. Birand, *Diyet*, p. 100.
[85] *Millet Meclisi Tutanak Dergisi*, 21 February 1975, term 4, sess. 2, vol. 9, p. 460.
[86] *Cumhuriyet*, 23 March 1975, p. 1.
[87] H. I. Salih, *Cyprus*, p. 186n.
[88] M. A. Birand, *Diyet*, pp. 118-119.
[89] Ibid., p. 120.

According to Birand, Kissinger requested from Turkish rulers territorial concessions again and stressed that Turkey had to make a move on the Cyprus problem.[90] In the NATO meeting in Brussels on 30 May 1975 Kissinger told the Turkish prime minister and the foreign minister again that if Turkey made a concession on Cyprus the American administration would have a better chance to get the embargo lifted. Demirel replied that there would be no solution in Cyprus as long as the embargo continued.[91] On 9 June 1975 Turkey's ambassador to Washington, Melih Esenbel, told Kissinger that the most important reason for the failure of the inter communal talks on Cyprus was the arms embargo. The Turkish government could make no move under the pressure of the embargo.[92]

In his speech in Parliament on 12 June 1975, Turkish Foreign Minister Çağlayangil used bitter language while criticising the continuation of the American embargo. He said: "America's attempt to use the military aid as a means of political pressure on Turkey is baseless and dangerous decision which is also incompatible with the defence co-operation between the two countries. No Turkish government will yield to these kinds of pressures... If the embargo decision is not changed, we will take some counter measures... History shows that getting positive results with pressure is not an effective way which can be used against the Turks."[93] In his press conference on 15 June 1975 Turkish Prime Minister Süleyman Demirel severely criticised the United States and said that Turkey could not implement bilateral agreements which were violated by the United States. Demirel went so far to say that Turkey would not need the states which did not need Turkey.[94] In his statement to journalists on 25 June 1975, the language of Demirel's criticism was much more severe: "Turkey has always remained as a proud and loyal friend to the United States. If the Americans try to punish Turkey, they will never find such a loyal friend again."[95]

Toward the end of June 1975, the American administration started a fresh campaign to persuade the Congress to lift the arms embargo completely. But when the White House realised that its campaign would fail, it began to work for the partial lift. The Greek lobby launched a rival campaign to prevent the lift and organised mass demonstrations against Ford and Kissinger.[96] On 24 July 1975 the House of Representatives defeated a similar bill to the Senate bill on 19 May, which authorised the president to restore aid to Turkey, by a close vote of 223 to 206. The next day the Turkish government announced that the Defence Co-operation Agreement of 1969 and all other related agreements between the United States and Turkey had lost their legal validity. It also declared that all the joint Turkish-American bases and defence installations except the İncirlik air base came under the control and custody of the Turkish armed forces. The İncirlik air base was to be used for only direct NATO purposes. Operations at the four American intelligence-collecting centres at Karamürsel, Sinop, Diyarbakır and Belbaşı were suspended.[97]

---

[90] Ibid., pp. 123-124.

[91] Ibid., pp. 126-128.

[92] Ibid., p. 164.

[93] *Millet Meclisi Tutanak Dergisi,* 12 June 1975, term 4, sess. 2, vol. 12, pp. 579-580.

[94] *Cumhuriyet,* 16 June 1975, p. 7.

[95] *Cumhuriyet,* 26 June 1975, p. 7.

[96] M. A. Birand, *Diyet,* pp. 166-168.

[97] Ibid., p. 175, T. A. Couloumbis, *The United States, Greece and Turkey,* p. 151, *Cumhuriyet,* 26 July 1975, *Keesing's Contemporary Archives,* 1975, vol. 21, p. 27337, Richard F. Grimmett, *Turkish-US Defense Relationship: the Arms Embargo Issue,* the Library of Congress, Congressional Research Service, (Washington: U. S. Government Printing Office, 1978), pp. 43-44, *The Military Aspects of Banning Arms Aid*

During the talks between Ford, Kissinger and Demirel in Helsinki on 31 July 1975, Kissinger requested concessions from Turkish rulers on Cyprus to ease the American administration's job on the arms embargo. Demirel replied that Turkey could not make any move and the Cyprus question could not be solved unless the American Congress stopped pressurising Turkey. President Ford proposed to use his authority to release a special 50 million-dollar NATO fund for Turkey but Demirel rejected it by saying that Turkey's aim was not to get money but to know whether the United States was a friendly country or not.[98] On 2 October 1975, the House of Representative voted 237 to 176 to lift the embargo partially, exempting from the embargo military deliveries contracted for before the effective day of the embargo (arms worth 185 million dollars)[99] but this move was not enough for Turkish rulers, they did not reconsider the closure of American defence installations in Turkey.

According to the statement of US Defence Secretary Harold Brown, between 1975 and 1979 Turkey was authorised credits of $425 million, under the Foreign Military Sales (FMS) Financing Program.[100] In this period Turkey also purchased US military repair parts, maintenance services and spares totalling $31.2 million through the NATO Maintenance and Supply Agency (NAMSA) and received about $265 million worth of military equipment from other Western powers.[101] On 26 March 1976 Turkey and the United States signed a new Defence Co-operation Agreement, providing $800 million in FMS and $200 million in grant aid over a four-year period. But it was not approved by the Congress and was never implemented.[102]

The complete abolition of the embargo on US assistance to Turkey was realised in 1978. On 26 July 1978 the Senate voted to repeal the embargo and the House followed through on 1 August.[103] The embargo repeal legislation was presented to the president on 26 September 1978, the president signed it on the same day and the embargo was then lifted. Shortly thereafter Turkey announced the termination of the suspension measures which were applied to US bases and facilities in Turkey.[104] On 29 March 1980 Turkey and the United States signed an updated Defence and Economic Co-operation Agreement (DECA).[105] It was a five-year executive agreement, renewable annually, which would implement the NATO treaty. The United States undertook to provide defence equipment, services, and training to the Turks; Turkey, in return, authorised the United States to maintain forces and carry out

---

to Turkey, hearing before the Committee on Armed Services, US Senate, 95th Congress, 2nd session, June 28, 1978, (Washington: US Government Printing Office, 1978), pp. 8, 72.

[98] M. A. Birand, *Diyet*, p. 182.

[99] *Keesing's Contemporary Archives*, 1975, vol. 21, p. 27450, US Public Law 94-104 in *Current Legislation and Related Executive Orders*, pp. 247-249, Richard C. Campany, *Turkey and the United States: The Arms Embargo Period*, (New York: Praeger, 1986), p. 63, Bruce R. Kuniholm, "Turkey and NATO: Past, Present and Future", *ORBIS*, Summer 1983, p. 440.

[100] *The Military Aspects of Banning Arms Aid to Turkey*, pp. 21-22, 32, 76, R. C. Campany, *Turkey and the United States*, p. 63, B. R. Kuniholm, "Turkey and NATO: Past, Present and Future", p. 440.

[101] *The Military Aspects of Banning Arms Aid to Turkey*, pp. 33, 35, 48, 79.

[102] R. F. Grimmett, *Turkish-US Defense Relationship: the Arms Embargo Issue*, pp. 44, 88-93, R. C. Campany, *Turkey and the United States*, p. 63, L. Stern, *The Wrong Horse*, pp. 155-156.

[103] US Public Law 95-384 in *Current Legislation and Related Executive Orders*, p. 320.

[104] T. A. Couloumbis, *The United States, Greece and Turkey*, p. 106, B. R. Kuniholm, "Turkey and NATO: Past, Present and Future", p. 427n.

[105] For the texts of the main agreement and supplementary agreements see R. C. Campany, *Turkey and the United States*, pp. 103-123.

military activities at specified installations. A US-Turkish Joint Commission was created as a mechanism for discussing how to use Turkey's resources for its security objectives.

To conclude we should say that the American embargo did not influence the Turkish government to change its policies vis-à-vis Cyprus, which was the original aim of the Congressmen. George S. Harris, an American expert on Turkey, stated this fact as follows: "At no time, under pressure of the embargo did Turkey significantly soften its stand on maintaining military force in Cyprus, nor on the need for a bizonal solution, nor on refusing to give large amounts of territory from the Turkish zone."[106] The arms embargo and suspension of functioning of military bases in Turkey represented a serious cut-off on US-Turkish military relations though the two states remained allies within NATO. The embargo did not achieve its original declared aim, Turkish concessions on the Cyprus question, but it reminded the Turks that their defence was heavily dependent on the United States. By nullifying the 1969 agreement, the Turks showed that they were not merely a stooge of the United States. But they could not save themselves entirely from military dependence on the USA. US imposed conditions on aid in the following years continued to be a headache for Turkish authorities.

Arguments of the US Congress on the Arms Embargo

In the eyes of the American Congress, the second Turkish military operation in Cyprus was an unacceptable aggressive act whereas its first action could be justified as a defensive act aimed at protecting lives of Turkish Cypriots and restoring the status quo in the island. American Congressman Donald Riegle voiced this opinion on 2 July 1975: "To this point [the aftermath of the first Turkish operation] the Turks had achieved the goals intended by their military intervention: they stopped the illegal coup on Cyprus, restoring that island's legitimate government. The intervention had also caused indirectly the fall of the 7-year Athens dictatorship. Whether this first Turkish military action was legal under American law is debatable. Turkey had right under the London accords of 1959, to intervene in Cyprus if the other guarantor powers failed to act jointly but only for the purpose of restoring the state of affairs under the treaty. If Turkey had moved militarily for that purpose and had ended its actions when such restoration occurred, the tragedy of Cyprus would not exist today... When the Congress assessed these events, it concentrated on the August expansion of Turkish occupation of Cyprus. No Congressional attempt came in the period of July 20 to August 14 to cut aid to Turkey. But the August moves by Turkey were so flagrant in their violation of both American law and the bilateral agreements Turkey had made with the United States on the use of military aid that no other choice than ending aid was available to the Congress."[107] In Hackett's words, "[the second Turkish military action] fit every definition of aggression. There was no military danger to the Turkish troops beyond their capability for self-defence. They had secured lines of supply and communication with Turkey. Their limited political goal authorised under the London-Zurich accords -to restore order- was attainable. Yet

---

[106] George S. Harris, "Turkey Between Alliance and Alienation", *Foreign Policy (Dış Politika)*, vol. 8, Nos. 3-4, 1980, p. 120.

[107] Paul Y. Watanabe, *Ethnic Groups, Congress and American Foreign Policy: The Politics of the Turkish Arms Embargo*, (London: Greenwood Press, 1984), p. 100.

Turkish domestic political considerations... caused Turkey to abandon its prudence by forcing a military solution... upon an essentially helpless country."[108]

The main thesis of Congressmen who was in favour of imposing an embargo on US assistance to Turkey was that Turkey used in its military operations in Cyprus US arms and military equipment contrary to the American law and the provisions of the agreements under which these arms had been granted or sold to it. These agreements and laws which were thought to be violated by Turkey were the Foreign Assistance Act of 1961, the Military Sales Act of 1968 and the bilateral agreements signed between the United States and Turkey in 1947 and 1959. Under these laws, military arms and defence equipment given by the United States to any country should be furnished solely for legitimate self-defence, internal security or collective arrangements consistent with the UN Charter and any substantial violation of these provisions should render the violator immediately ineligible for further assistance.[109] Contending that American arms had been illegally used by Turkey in its operations in Cyprus, the American Congress favoured an arms embargo against Turkey until progress toward a peaceful settlement of the Cyprus issue could be demonstrated.

In the opinion of pro-embargo Congressmen, an arms embargo was necessary to force Turkey to make concessions to the Greek side and thus to accelerate the process of finding a peaceful settlement to the Cyprus question. Turkey had committed an aggressive act in Cyprus with the aid of American equipment and tried to create a new system in the island. If the United States did not cut off its aid to Turkey, it would be rewarding the Turkish aggression and allowing the Turks to dictate their solution of the Cyprus problem by the force of arms. The American administration failed to identify the Turkish intransigence as the key obstacle to progress and therefore refrained from pressurising Turkish rulers. An arms embargo could be an effective and strong means to force Turkey to make meaningful concessions on the Cyprus issue and could dramatically affect the situation in Cyprus.[110] Even George Ball and Cyrus Vance, the former American mediators on the Cyprus question, testified in favour of retaining the linkage between Turkey's security assistance program and demonstrated progress on Cyprus.[111] One of the main embargo activists, Representative Benjamin Rosenthal, argued in the House of Representatives: "If we pass this resolution..., it is a signal to the government of Turkey that they cannot have military equipment to continue and maintain this kind of aggressive action. It is, indeed, a signal to the Greek government, which says, "why don't you come on along in the negotiations because we are going to use all the effort and muscle we can vis-à-vis the Turkish government."[112]

The pro-embargo forces in Congress claimed that if the United States remained indifferent to Turkey's use of force in Cyprus by not imposing an embargo, Greece, a strategically vital ally of the United States, would be alienated and thus the American interests in that region would be harmed. Representative Rosenthal argued: "It is, in my view, indispensable that Greece be able to enter negotiations on an improved basis. Otherwise, the risk is very great that the provisional Karamanlis government will succumb to pressures from

---

[108] C. Hackett, "Ethnic Politics in Congress: the Turkish Embargo Experience", p. 25.
[109] T. A. Couloumbis and S. M. Hicks, "the Impact of Greek Americans Upon United States Foreign Policy", p. 146, T. A. Couloumbis, *the United States, Greece and Turkey*, p. 104.
[110] R. F. Grimmett, *Turkish-US Defense Relationship: the Arms Embargo Issue*, p. 4.
[111] Ellen B. Laipson, "Cyprus: A Quarter Century of US Diplomacy" in John T. A. Koumoulides (ed.), *Cyprus in Transition 1960-1985*, (London: Trigraph, 1986), p. 73.
[112] S. Bölükbaşı, *Turkish-American Relations and Cyprus*, pp. 216-217.

the right or the left. This, in turn, would make a Cyprus compromise extremely unlikely and the Greek drift away from the United States more acute."[113] Some congressmen went so far to say that the United States did not need Turkey any more because its strategic value and benefits to NATO and the United States had sunk to almost zero.[114]

However, it should be noted that the main reasons for Congressmen opposing the American administration on the embargo issue stemmed from the uneasy relationship between the legislative and executive branches. The American policies toward Vietnam, Cambodia, Chile, the Soviet Union and Pakistan had caused the gradual loss of Congressional confidence in the practices of the administration. As the years passed, Congress became more and more suspicious of the motives and practices of the executive branch. Finally the Watergate scandal resulted in an almost complete breakdown of Congressional confidence in the Presidency. In the eyes of Congressmen, the American administration had become a body which did not care about the rule of law and the power of Congress. Congressmen believed they had to give a lesson to the executive branch to break its arrogance. The Cyprus issue provided this opportunity. "The attempt by Kissinger to downplay the legal aspects of the Turkish situation, and his attempt to convince Congress that the administration was in the best position to evaluate US national interests in the Turkish situation, backfired."[115] In Laipson's words, "Cyprus touched a nerve for members who were concerned about congressional authority, the executive branch's seeming lack of respect for the rule of law, and the arrogance of Henry Kissinger."[116]

In the summer of 1974 and in the first half of 1975 Congress was simply unwilling to accept any executive direction and act "with many recent discoveries of lies and misstatements made by the administration to Congress to justify various foreign and domestic issues fresh in its memory."[117] The administration's soft approach toward the Turkish action which violated American laws was intolerable for Congressmen in the context of abhorring domestic abuses of law. In Laipson's words, "many congressmen felt that American credibility and self-respect had been badly tarnished by Watergate, and thought that the Nixon administration's lack of concern for possible violations of US law by Turkey was another manifestation of the corrupt and lawless character of the administration. In their view, it was up to Congress to restore the image of the United States... as a law-abiding society."[118]

The opposition to Kissinger as a former member of the now discredited Nixon administration, too, played an important role in the Congress' insistence on the arms embargo. At that time, it was very common for Congressmen to criticise and oppose Kissinger's views and acts. Kissinger's opposition to the embargo, in a sense, increased Congress' determination to impose it. Laipson explains the anti-Kissinger attitude of Congressmen as follows: "Kissinger's highly visible profile in the final days of the Nixon administration triggered in many minds an association between Kissinger and what was considered the arrogance of power demonstrated by the discredited president... Kissinger's

[113] Ibid., p. 217.
[114] Duygu Sezer, "Turkey's Security Policies" in Jonathan Alford (ed.), *Greece and Turkey: Adversity in Alliance,* (Aldershot: Gower, International Institute for Strategic Studies, 1984), p. 63, George E. Gruen, "Ambivalence in the Alliance: US Interests in the Middle East and the Evolution of Turkish Foreign Policy", *ORBIS,* vol. 24, No. 2, Summer 1980, p. 372.
[115] R. C. Campany, *Turkey and the United States,* p. 78.
[116] E. B. Laipson, "Cyprus: A Quarter Century of US Diplomacy", p. 71.
[117] R. C. Campany, *Turkey and the United States,* p. 78.
[118] E. B. Laipson, *Congressional-Executive Relations and the Turkish Arms Embargo,* p. 30.

words and actions throughout the fall of 1974 reinforced the perception that he had little regard for Congress, for the role of consultation in making foreign policy, and for the legal question raised by the law-makers."[119] The Turkish arms embargo issue offered an opportunity for Kissinger's congressional critics to question some major tenets of his domestic and foreign policies, his methods and his style of careful manipulation of Congress and public opinion.

For many Congressmen, to work for imposing an arms embargo on Turkey was a part of the struggle to have a greater voice in foreign affairs. In reality what Congress challenged was the strong executive dominance over the foreign policy process and the enhanced executive role in foreign policy, which became more apparent with the American administration's actions in Vietnam and Cambodia. In many cases including the Cyprus issue, the White House had determined major policies with maximum secrecy and without consulting Congress. In Campany's words, "Congress was [now] attempting to restore its role, and the role of public law, in the conduct of US foreign policy to the extent any infringement of the executive on Congressional authority was the target of strong reaction."[120] Thus the arms embargo was a case in which Congress worked hard to have a greater control and voice on foreign policy decisions intimately affecting American interests.

For some Congressmen who were highly critical of the Turkish government's decision to resume poppy cultivation, the arms embargo was a good opportunity to express their disapproval over the Turkish decision and punish Turkey. Several attempts had been made by Congress to cut off military assistance to Turkey because of her uncompromising attitude on the opium issue. On 6 August 1974 the House of Representatives voted to urge that foreign aid to Turkey be cut off unless safeguards were devised to prevent the smuggling of Turkish heroin. Even after Turkey's second military operation in Cyprus, the House was still concerned with poppy growing, therefore it amended legislation concerning the Export Import bank to ban further business with Turkey.[121] Once the initiative was launched to cut off US assistance to Turkey on the ground of her action in Cyprus, some Congressmen supported this move largely because of their displeasure with the Turkish decision to renew the poppy production.

Arguments of the US Administration on the Embargo

Some of the American administration's arguments in opposing an arms embargo against Turkey can be seen in American officials' statements which are mentioned below. On 5 October 1974 President Ford said of the continuing Congress act to impose an arms embargo: "It is my conviction that approval of the continuing resolution, containing the Eagleton Amendment or similar language, would destroy any hope for the success of the initiatives of the United States has already taken or may take in the future to contribute to just settlement of the Cyprus dispute... If the Eagleton Amendment or similar language is adopted by the Congress, the United States will have lost its negotiating flexibility and influence."[122] In his veto message to both houses of Congress on 15 October 1974, Ford stated that cutting off aid

---

[119] Ibid., p. 29.
[120] R. C. Campany, *Turkey and the United States*, p. 78.
[121] K. R. Legg, "Congress as Trojan Horse, the Turkish Embargo Problem, 1974-1978", p. 119.
[122] P. Y. Watanabe, *Ethnic Groups, Congress and American Foreign Policy*, p. 107.

to Turkey was entirely destructive to the United States efforts to bring about Cyprus peace negotiations. He said that this ban might imperil the US relations with Turkey and consequently weaken the United States in the crucial eastern Mediterranean.[123] A White House statement stated that the suspension of military aid to Turkey was likely "to impede the negotiation of a just Cyprus settlement" and "could have far reaching and damaging effects on the security, and hence the political stability, of all countries of the region"; the ban would "adversely affect not only Western security but [also] the strategic solution in the Middle East" and might "jeopardise the system on which [American] relations in Eastern Mediterranean have been based for 28 years."[124]

Kissinger wrote in his memoirs: "While Ford struggled to restore executive authority over the next months, a freewheeling Congress destroyed the equilibrium between the parties we had precariously maintained; it legislated a heavy-handed arms embargo against Turkey that destroyed all possibility of American mediation..."[125] On 7 December 1974 Kissinger said: "The US military assistance to Turkey is not, and has never been, granted as a favour. It has been the view of the US government since 1947 that the security of Turkey is vital to the security of the Eastern Mediterranean, to NATO, Europe and to the security of the Atlantic community."[126]

The Senate majority leader, who supported the administration's stance on the arms embargo, said in a speech to his colleagues: "If we adopt an amendment aimed directly and specifically against Turkey... we might see a tilt on the part of Turkey toward the Soviet Union. They have a thousand-mile frontier, and within that area they have nuclear warheads and US installations... The Turks are Moslem people. Perhaps there might be a tilt on the part of Turkey toward... the Middle East."[127] On 31 January 1975 State Department Spokesman Anderson stated that the Congressional aid deadline was undermining the prospects for a settlement in Cyprus "because it puts pressure on one of the parties" and could well drive Turkey from the Western alliance.[128]

President Ford issued a statement on 5 February 1975. He said: "legislation enacted by Congress requires that arm deliveries to Turkey must be suspended from February 5. The administration will comply fully with the law. However, it should be made clear that military aid to Turkey is not given in the context of the Cyprus issue, nor has it been granted as a favour to Turkey. Rather it is based on our common conclusions that the security of Turkey is vital to the security of the eastern Mediterranean and to the security of the United States and its allies... A suspension of military aid to Turkey is likely to impede the negotiation of a just Cyprus settlement. Furthermore, it could have far-reaching and damaging effects on the security and hence the political stability of all the countries in the region. It will affect adversely not only Western security but also the strategic situation in the Middle East. It cannot be in the interests of the United States to take action that will jeopardise the system on which our relations in the eastern Mediterranean have been based for 28 years... "When it is seen that the US is taking action which is clearly incompatible with its own interests, this will raise grave doubts about the conduct of American foreign relations, even among countries

---

[123] H. I. Salih, *Cyprus*, p. 100.
[124] P. G. Polyviou, *Cyprus: the Tragedy and the Challenge*, p. 211.
[125] Henry Kissinger, *Years of Upheaval*, (London: Weidenfeld and Nicolson and Michael Joseph, 1982), p. 1192.
[126] H. I. Salih, *Cyprus*, pp. 100-101.
[127] L. Stern, *The Wrong Horse*, p. 152.
[128] Ibid., p. 152.

that are not directly involved in that area. The Administration judges these adverse effects of suspension of aid to Turkey to be so serious that it urges the Congress to reconsider its action and authorise the resumption of our assistance relationship with Turkey."[129]

In his speech before a joint session of Congress in April 1975 President Ford said: "I earnestly ask Congress to weigh the broader considerations and consequences of its past actions on the complex Greek and Turkish dispute over Cyprus... US military assistance to an old and faithful ally -Turkey- has been cut off by action of the Congress. This has imposed an embargo on military purchases by Turkey, extending even to items already paid for -an unprecedented act against a friend... We are continuing our earnest efforts to find equitable solutions to the problems which exist between Greece and Turkey. But the results of the congressional action have been to block progress toward reconciliation, thereby prolonging suffering on Cyprus; to complicate our ability to promote successful negotiations; to increase the danger of a broader conflict... Our long-standing relationship with Turkey is not simply a favour to Turkey; it is a clear and essential mutual interest. Turkey lies... [next to] the Soviet Union and at the gates of the Middle East. It is vital to the security of the Eastern Mediterranean, the southern flank of Western Europe, and the collective security of the Western alliance. Our US military bases in Turkey are critical to our own security as they are to the defence of NATO."[130]

In his letter to Congressman Thomas Morgan, Chairman of the House Committee on International Relations, in the summer of 1975, President Ford wrote: "I am convinced that immediate congressional action is needed to relax the embargo on arms shipments to Turkey if US security interests in the Eastern Mediterranean are not jeopardised beyond repair... The affected facilities [in Turkey] are vital to US and Western security... It [the embargo] is a major impediment to negotiations toward a constructive settlement of the tragic Cyprus problem..."[131]

The arguments of anti-embargo forces, the American administration and some congressmen, could be summarised as follows: Firstly, putting pressure on only one side in a complicated problem would not help its solution. Imposing an arms embargo on Turkey would be destructive to US efforts to bring about a peaceful solution of the Cyprus problem. In Couloumbis' words, "leverage on Turkey [on the Cyprus issue] could be applied better through persuasion and positive reinforcement measures rather than by penalties and sanctions [such as an arms embargo which] would offend the proud and independent-minded Turks, rendering them less flexible on future Cyprus negotiations."[132] An arms embargo would never force the Turks to make concessions but would cause the loss of the US administration's leverage on Turkey.

Secondly, an arms embargo against Turkey would bring about great damage to US security interests. It would cause alienation of Turkey, whose strategic importance with respect to the Soviet Union and the Middle East was vital to NATO and Western security designs and Turkey would seek non-NATO resources to satisfy its defensive requirements.[133]

---

[129] *Keesing's Contemporary Archives, 1975,* vol. 21, p. 27035.

[130] H. I. Salih, *Cyprus,* p. 187n.

[131] P. Y. Watanabe, *Ethnic Groups, Congress and American Foreign Policy,* p. 109.

[132] T. A. Couloumbis, *The United States, Greece and Turkey,* p. 105.

[133] *The Military Aspects of Banning Arms Aid to Turkey,* pp. 8, 62. In this reference, US Secretary of State Cyrus Vance, Secretary of Defence Harold Brown, Chairman of the Joint Chiefs of Staff David C. Jones, Commander in Chief in US European Command Alexander Haig, five former supreme allied commanders and Colonel Phelps Jones presented arguments for the necessity of lifting the arms embargo.

Consequently, the Western alliance would be damaged greatly, the United States would lose its strategic military and communication facilities in Turkey and the American position in the strategic eastern Mediterranean region would weaken.

Thirdly, the suspension of the US activities in some Turkish installations because of the embargo resulted in the loss of some intelligence information on Soviet space, missile and military systems development, operations and training. It hampered the US capability to develop counter-measures to Soviet weapons systems under development and degraded intelligence acquisition used to monitor and verify compliance with the SALT agreements.[134] The embargo had impaired the cohesion and strength of the south-eastern flank of NATO.[135] The fighting capability, deterrent posture and material readiness of the Turkish armed forces had been diminished and the Turkish NATO forces had been weakened.[136] The unavailability of Turkish ports for the US 6th Fleet visits had created morale and other problems for the fleet.[137] In the final analysis, the embargo had degraded NATO's overall military capabilities and adversely affected US national security interests.[138]

Fourthly, the arms embargo was an act of Congress which represented an abuse of congressional prerogative in foreign policy and violated the principle of separation of power in the state structure. Foreign policy making and its tactical (day-to-day) applications were largely the prerogative of the administration. Congress' excessive involvement in foreign policy making in the example of the arms embargo was an unacceptable act which restricted the administration's executive capabilities in protecting US interests. Congressmen could not be trusted to preserve global American interests because they might come under the influence of more specific and narrower interests and influential groups. While imposing an arms embargo against Turkey, congressmen could not take a responsible, statesmanlike posture in an important issue because they were influenced and manipulated by an agitated group of politically active Greek Americans. "Congress trapped by its parochial concerns, responding first to Greek sensitivities, only secondly to the major national interests of the strategic balance in the Eastern Mediterranean."[139] Congress should take her hands off major foreign policy issues and leave the arms embargo and the Cyprus issues in the hands of the administration.

Finally, apparently to prompt the opposition of the mighty Israeli lobby and to persuade congressmen not to legalise the arms embargo, the American administration claimed that an arms embargo against Turkey could also hurt Israel. Israel, too, might be caught by a strict interpretation of the non-defensive use provisions of the law because Israel had used American weapons in its struggle against the Arabs.[140] Moreover, the US bases in Turkey, which were threatened by the arms embargo, were important for Israel's defence.[141]

Grimmett summarises the arguments of anti-embargo congressmen as follows: "The nature of the Turkish intervention in Cyprus in 1974 was not clear-cut in legal terms... The

---

[134] *The Military Aspects of Banning Arms Aid to Turkey*, pp. 8, 26, 48, 49, P. Y. Watanabe, *Ethnic Groups, Congress and American Foreign Policy*, pp. 109, 131, L. Stern, *The Wrong Horse*, pp. 152-154.

[135] *The Military Aspects of Banning Arms Aid to Turkey*, pp. 4, 11, 12, 15.

[136] Ibid., pp. 4-5, 7, 9-10, 12, 23-24, 39, 48.

[137] Ibid., p. 48.

[138] Ibid., pp. 4, 10, 62, P. Y. Watanabe, *Ethnic Groups, Congress and American Foreign Policy*, p. 109.

[139] E. B. Laipson, *Congressional-Executive Relations and the Turkish Arms Embargo*, p. 30.

[140] C. Hackett, "Ethnic Politics in Congress: the Turkish Embargo Experience", p. 26, K. R. Legg, "Congress as Trojan Horse, the Turkish Embargo Problem, 1974-1978", p. 118, M. A. Birand, *Diyet*, p. 70.

[141] C. Hackett, "Ethnic Politics in Congress: the Turkish Embargo Experience", p. 26.

Turks have been faithful NATO allies and their friendship should not be jeopardised by the action of embargo. The Cyprus dispute can be dealt with outside of the NATO context. The embargo unwisely places the United States in the position of choosing one side over the other in Cyprus conflict -a very complicated and long-standing dispute... The Turks may have much less leverage over their clients, the Turkish Cypriots, than may appear to be case. In this context, it may be very difficult for Turkey to force concessions out of their clients and thus to comply with the US desire to compel a resolution of the Cyprus issue. If so, the embargo punishes the Turks unfairly."[142]

Role of Greek Americans in the Imposition of the Embargo

The Greek Orthodox Church in North America was very active in communicating a deep concern over Cyprus to its members and in activating Greek American population to force American officials and legislators for anti-Turkish actions. In Couloumbis and Hicks' words, "when questions concerning the morality and legality of continuing American aid to Turkey first arose, it was the [Greek] priests, in their dual role as preservers of religious traditions and guardians of Hellenism, who began using their sermons to rouse the Greek American communities to action. Money for Greek Cypriot refugee relief was collected during services and petitions urging US congressmen and senators to impose a military embargo on Turkey were circulated among the congregation."[143]

In the combined meeting of the Archdiocesan Council of the Greek Orthodox Archdiocese of North and South America and presidents of Greek associations, which was convened by Archbishop Iakovos on 30 July 1974, it was decided that a public relations office be established to ask Congress to cut all military and economic aid to Turkey. During church sermons Greek Orthodox priests read from the pulpit the names of the "damned" congressmen who voted with the administration against the Turkish embargo and urged Greek Americans to pressurise their representatives to change their votes. The Orthodox church also organised letter-writing and telegram, telephone campaigns.[144]

The expected role of the Orthodox Church on the arms embargo was so great that in October 1974 Ford and Kissinger met with Archbishop Iakovos in the Oval Office in order to win the support of the Archbishop and his Greek American flock. Reportedly Kissinger tried to convince Iakovos that neither Greek Prime Minister Karamanlis nor Foreign Minister Mavros were opposed to the continuation of the US military aid to Turkey. Allegedly Kissinger told the Archbishop: he should and could ease Greek American pressure on Congress by informing his congregation that US military aid to Turkey was not contrary or harmful to Greek national interests.[145]

Greek American lobby groups, too, played a crucial role in activating Greek American population and putting pressure on congressmen and the American administration on the arms embargo issue. In spite of their small numbers Greek Americans were well organised and able to exert political pressure. Some Greek Americans had reached high ranks in American

---

[142] R. F. Grimmett, *Turkish-US Defense Relationship*, p. 4.

[143] T. A. Couloumbis and S. M. Hicks, "the Impact of Greek Americans Upon United States Foreign Policy", p. 152.

[144] S. Bölükbaşı, *Turkish-American Relations and Cyprus*, p. 214.

politics. The former vice president, several state governors, representatives, including the majority whip, and several influential congressional staff members were Greeks. Greek American lobby groups; the American Hellenic Educational Progressive Association (AHEPA); the American Hellenic Institute, which was established in the late summer of 1974, and its lobbying arm American Hellenic Institute Public Affairs Committee (AHIPAC); the United Hellenic American Congress and other groups which were established in response to the Cyprus crisis unanimously condemned the Turkish military intervention in Cyprus and put pressure on congressmen to impose the arms embargo and to maintain it.[146] These organisations urged Greek Americans to write personal letters to congressmen on the embargo issue and organised mass demonstrations. They put pressure on congressmen each time Congress seemed to decide to weaken or abolish the embargo. Before each congressional vote on the embargo they mounted massive telephone campaigns across the United States to apply additional pressure on those who were still undecided.

It was claimed by some people and the American administration that congressmen were influenced by the efforts of Greek Americans in their votes on the embargo issue because they wanted to secure the support of Greek Americans in the approaching congressional elections in November 1974. No congressmen would like the agitated Greek-American groups, which constituted a politically and socially activated segment of the US population, lobbying against him. Many congressmen would incline toward accommodating such an important ethnic group in a symbolic vote. According to Bölükbaşı, Greek Americans affected the votes of representatives of some congressional districts in New York, Massachusetts, Indiana and Illinois, where Greek Americans and other ethnic minorities constituted a body of electoral significance. None of the 16 congressmen in these districts voted against the embargo in any of the five votes in the House. Anti-embargo votes of both Republicans and Democrats usually came from southern states with little or no Greek electorate.[147]

In the opinion of Couloumbis and Hicks, Greek Americans had little or no effect on congressmen's votes. They argue: "Critics who have claimed that there were and are no Greek American groups or constituent pressures are incorrect... Critics who have claimed that a Greek lobby was the determining factor in the congressional decision to cut off military aid to Turkey are also incorrect... The Greek American lobby and considerations of voter repercussions were only one of many factors in a senator's or congressman's decision to vote in favour of an arms embargo on Turkey."[148] Laipson suggests a mutual influencing between congressmen and Greek Americans: "While the efforts of some Greek American groups were prodigious in 1974, the ultimate legislative achievement of the arms embargo reflected multiple motives... Members of Congress expressed support for and worked to achieve the goals of the so-called Greek lobby, but also used the lobby as an outside network of political support for legislative action."[149]

---

[145] T. A. Couloumbis and S. M. Hicks, "the Impact of Greek Americans Upon United States Foreign Policy", p. 155.

[146] Ibid., pp. 162-163, S. Bölükbaşı, *Turkish-American Relations and Cyprus*, pp. 214-215, K. R. Legg, "Congress as Trojan Horse, the Turkish Embargo Problem, 1974-1978", pp. 117, 120, C. Hackett, "Ethnic Politics in Congress: the Turkish Embargo Experience", p. 29.

[147] S. Bölükbaşı, *Turkish-American Relations and Cyprus*, pp. 215-216.

[148] T. A. Couloumbis and S. M. Hicks, "the Impact of Greek Americans Upon United States Foreign Policy", p. 174.

[149] E. B. Laipson, *Congressional-Executive Relations and the Turkish Arms Embargo*, p. 5.

Hackett admits that the issue of ethnic voters' influence on congressmen on the embargo voting is very complicated: "On one hand, the absolute number of Greek Americans is quite small, about 1 percent of the total US population. Yet, on the other, they are a socially and politically active segment... There are few congressional districts or states where elections are decided regularly or even often by the percentage of votes represented by the Greek American votes in that electoral unit. Yet the political and social activism of Greek Americans gives them a weight beyond their one percent in the population. No elected official likes to have an agitated group, however small, lobbying against him. Many such officials would incline toward accommodating an important ethnic group like Greek Americans in a symbolic vote."[150] Legg claims that constituency pressures from Greek Americans were a significant factor in the arms embargo issue.[151] Thus, it may be said that Greek American pressures influenced the votes of Congressmen in the arms embargo issue. But it should be noted that congressmen were also affected by other factors and they used efforts of Greek Americans for their own political aims.

Whatever its reasons were, the arms embargo was the most important action of the United States after the Johnson letter to force Turkey to act in a certain way. The Turks felt the negative consequences of the embargo but they did not change their policies toward Cyprus. The US administration's opposition to the embargo might have played a role in this Turkish attitude. But it is also a fact that US officials asked the Turks to make concessions in Cyprus to help the lifting of the embargo. The Turkish reaction was to suspend US activities in military bases in Turkey rather than yield to US pressures.

Arguments of Turkish Rulers Against the Embargo

The Turkish rulers were generally pleased with the attitudes of the American administration during and after the military intervention in Cyprus. But when the American Congress introduced bills ending the American aid to Turkey, Turkish authorities strongly condemned the decision as an open violation of bilateral agreements between the two countries. Although they did not accuse the American administration directly, they expressed their strong opposition to the embargo and said that their policies on Cyprus would not be affected by this pressure, but they would take counter measures against the United States. After some hesitation and delay, it was ironically the rightist coalition government which took the decision to abolish the Turkish-American bilateral agreement of 1969 and terminate the activities of American forces in American bases in Turkey in response to the insistence of the American Congress on the continuation of the embargo.

Firstly, Turkish authorities claimed that their military operations in Cyprus were just and in conformity with international law and agreements and that therefore the arms embargo which aimed at punishing Turkey for its Cyprus action was unjust. Their arguments on the legality and the rightness of the Turkish military action were mentioned in the previous sections.

Secondly, Turkish authorities argued that the arms embargo, which was defended by its supporters as an action that would bring positive developments in the Cyprus issue, would not help solving the problem but would cause its deterioration. In their opinion, the arms embargo

---

[150] C. Hackett, "Ethnic Politics in Congress: the Turkish Embargo Experience", p. 29.

was an obstacle to the negotiation process in Cyprus in many ways: 1- It encouraged the uncompromising attitude, intransigence of Greek leaders in Athens and Nicosia on the Cyprus issue. 2- It brought Turkey under psychological pressure not to make any concessions because if Turkey acted in this way it would look like a puppet of the United States and it would seem yielding under pressure. The embargo forced Turkish rulers to declare that Turkey would make no changes in its Cyprus policy under the pressure of the American Congress.[152] 3- The Cyprus problem could be solved through free negotiations with the equal participation of both sides but the embargo changed the balance between the positions of the two sides by putting pressure on only one side and thus it undermined the peace negotiations from the outset.[153] 4- The embargo decreased the possibility of solving the Cyprus question by abolishing the American leverage on the parties to the problem.

Thirdly, Turkish rulers always stressed that the Cyprus question and the bilateral defence co-operation between Turkey and the United States were separate issues and could not be linked with each other.[154] There should be no linkage between progress toward a settlement of the Cyprus dispute and the US military assistance to Turkey. "The Cyprus controversy had nothing to do with Turkey's roles and responsibilities as a member of NATO and its requirement to keep its military strong for self-defence and NATO defence purposes."[155] The American Congress violated the essence and functioning of the defence co-operation between Turkey and the United States by making an outsider element, the Cyprus issue, a part of this co-operation and forced Turkey to reconsider its co-operation with the USA[156]

Fourthly, Turkish officials pointed out that the supply of American arms to Turkey was not a favour but an essential obligation under a military defence alliance. Both Turkey and the United States had undertaken obligations under their bilateral alliance. The arms embargo meant that the United States refrained from fulfilling its responsibilities and thus violated the alliance unilaterally. Turkish rulers stated that the Congress' action constituted a unilateral violation of defence co-operation accords between the two countries.[157] They perceived the embargo as a hostile act that undermined the capability, preparedness and effectiveness of the Turkish armed forces. The new condition compelled Turkey to reconsider and to rearrange its defence co-operation with the USA and NATO.[158]

Fifthly, Turkish authorities argued that the arms embargo would bring harm to the NATO defence system by causing the destruction of its south-eastern flank and the weakening one of its members. If the United States wanted to keep NATO strong it should continue its

---

[151] K. R. Legg, "Congress as Trojan Horse, the Turkish Embargo Problem, 1974-1978", p. 118.
[152] Speeches of the Turkish foreign ministers, Turan Güneş and Melih Esenbel, in Turkish Parliament in *Cumhuriyet*, 26 October 1974, p. 1, 18 December 1974, p. 7.
[153] Turkish Foreign Minister Melih Esenbel, *Millet Meclisi Tutanak Dergisi*, 21 February 1975, term 4, sess. 2, vol. 9, pp. 459-460.
[154] Turkish Prime Minister Süleyman Demirel's talk to Kissinger in M. A. Birand, *Diyet*, p. 124.
[155] R. F. Grimmett, *Turkish-US Defense Relationship*, p. 2.
[156] Melih Esenbel, *Millet Meclisi Tutanak Dergisi*, 21 February 1975, term 4, sess. 2, vol. 9, pp. 459-460, Foreign Minister I. S. Çağlayangil, *Millet Meclisi Tutanak Dergisi*, 12 June 1975, term 4, sess. 4, vol. 12, p. 579.
[157] In *Millet Meclisi Tutanak Dergisi*: M. Altınsoy, 20 February 1975, term 4, sess. 2, vol. 9, p. 369, I. Müftüoğlu, 21 February 1975, term 4, sess. 2, vol. 9, p. 444, S. Öztürk, 21 February 1975, term 4, sess. 2, vol. 9, p. 452, Haluk Ulman, 21 February 1975, term 4, sess. 2, vol. 9, p. 457, H. Savaşçı, 28 April 1976, term 4, sess. 2, vol. 19, p. 120.
[158] M. Esenbel, *Millet Meclisi Tutanak Dergisi*, 21 February 1975, term 4, sess. 2, vol. 9, p. 460, Turkish P. M. Sadi Irmak's statement to journalists in *Cumhuriyet*, 4 February 1975, p. 7, Turkey's National Security Council's statement in *Cumhuriyet*, 17 June 1975, p. 9.

assistance to Turkey, one of NATO's important members.[159] Otherwise the effectiveness of Turkey's military contribution to NATO would be weakened. Sixthly, Turkish rulers warned that the arms embargo could cause the total breakdown of US-Turkish relations and that if this happened both countries would suffer from this result.

Finally, Turkish officials claimed that the arms embargo was a discriminatory act of the United State toward Turkey because the United States did not apply the same US laws against other countries which used US-supplied weapons and military equipment for non-defensive purposes. The embargo was a pro-Greek move resulting from pressures applied by the Greek lobby in Congress. The Greek Cypriots and Greek officers in Cyrus had used US-supplied military equipment against Turkish Cypriots and they had also carried out the anti-Makarios coup in mid-July 1974 with American weapons. But the United States did not put a similar pressure on the Greek side.[160] On the contrary, the United States continued to strengthen the defence capability of Greece while crippling the Turkish defence power with the embargo decision.[161]

Turkish Public's Reaction to the Military Intervention and the Arms Embargo

Some Turkish people, especially leftist ones, believed that the Cyprus coup was a plot organised under the auspices of the United States. According to Birand, even Turkish Prime Minister Ecevit suspected a CIA hand when he first heard of the Cyprus coup.[162] Some columnists in the daily *Cumhuriyet* claimed that the Greek junta and their puppets in Cyprus received full support and a green light from American rulers in launching their coup.[163] In the opinion of these columnists, the United States expected the following results from the Cyprus coup: 1- Anti-American Makarios would be replaced by a person who would be more inclined toward American policies. 2- Enosis would be more feasible and as a result the pro-American Greek junta would be strengthened. 3- The United States would consolidate its position in Greece and the whole Eastern Mediterranean region. It would establish strategic military bases in Cyprus and thus it would be able to control the Suez Canal route which was important for oil shipping. 4- Turkish Prime Minister Bülent Ecevit with anti-American and leftist inclinations would not be able to resist the Cyprus coup, and thus he would lose his credibility at home and would be replaced by a more pro-American politician. 5- The chronic Cyprus problem would be solved permanently.

The Turkish military intervention in Cyprus received unanimous support from Turkish public opinion. There was no other issue, domestic or foreign, on which there was such unanimity in Turkey. All Turkish major parties and the domestic press supported the Turkish military action. There were no MPs and no editorials in any major newspapers and magazines criticising the move and calling for the withdrawal of Turkish troops from Cyprus. No

---

[159] Turkish Prime Minister Süleyman Demirel's talk to President Ford in M. A. Birand, *Diyet*, p. 126.
[160] Turkish Defence Minister Hasan Işık's statement on the Turkish state television in *Cumhuriyet*, 27 September 1974.
[161] Turkish Prime Minister Süleyman Demirel's talk to Kissinger in M. A. Birand, *Diyet*, p. 182.
[162] Mehmet Ali Birand, *30 Sıcak Gün*, 4th Edition, (İstanbul: Milliyet Yayınları, 1976), p. 30.
[163] Ibid., p. 80, Oktay Akbal, "Paylaşmaya Doğru mu?", *Cumhuriyet*, 20 July 1974, İlhan Selçuk, "Pencere", *Cumhuriyet*, 24 July 1974, p. 2, Ali Sirmen, "Dünyada Bugün", *Cumhuriyet*, 26 July 1974, p. 3.

important or well-known religious or business leader even made a public statement opposing the continued occupation of Cyprus.

The arms embargo was unanimously condemned by the whole public opinion as an anti-Turkish move and nobody suggested withdrawing from Cyprus or making any compromise. Even the Turkish armed forces, which were the most affected element of the Turkish society by the arms embargo, did not favour any concessions under the American pressure but condemned the embargo as a tool of influence; they felt that withdrawal from Cyprus would betray their honour. Rightists were naturally in favour of maintaining the Turkish presence in Cyprus to protect Turkish people in spite of American pressures. Leftists rejected the embargo as a means of foreign influence, which they saw as a similar act to the capitulations. Only a small group of leftist radicals, intellectual Marxists, opposed Turkey's military intervention because they felt that Turkey was acting as an imperialist state.[164]

The arms embargo was subjected to severe criticism in Turkish Parliament, too.[165] According to Turkish MPs, the main motivation of the American Congress in imposing an arms embargo on Turkey was to please Greece and Greek Americans at home. Congressmen came under the influence of Greek lobbyists in voting for the embargo, their main concern was to get the support of Greek voters in the approaching elections. The embargo action clearly showed that the United States preferred Greece to Turkey. However, the Americans should not forget that Turkey was a very important country for the NATO defence system. If they wanted to keep NATO strong for the defence of the whole Western world, they should not alienate Turkey. The embargo action could bring grave dangers to NATO, it could even cause its destruction.

The embargo decision demonstrated the real face of the United States and the West, who were thought to be friends of Turkey. It showed that the West would not support Turkey in its just causes and in its difficult times but would betray her. The arms embargo was a clear violation by the United States of the bilateral alliance and co-operation between Turkey and the USA. American rulers had failed to fulfil their obligations toward Turkey. It seemed that they did not care about the alliance between the two countries and they did not need it any more. It seemed that the US-Turkish friendship ended. If this was the case, there was no need for Turkey to continue the bilateral alliance relationship with the USA. Turkey should make radical changes in its military relations with the United States and teach the American Congress that it could not get away with its hostile action against Turkey.

---

[164] R. C. Campany, *Turkey and the United States,* pp. 52-53.
[165] *Millet Meclisi Tutanak Dergisi,* 20 February 1975, term 4, sess. 2, vol. 9, pp. 367-372, 21 February 1975, pp. 444-457.

Chapter 8

THE CYPRUS QUESTION IN THE 1974-2002 PERIOD AND TURKISH-AMERICAN RELATIONS

INTRODUCTION

The future of Cyprus has always been determined by the outside powers. After being ruled by the Ottomans and the British for centuries, the powers of the Western camps set out the structure of Republic of Cyprus and became its guarantors. Turkey, Greece, the United States, NATO and the European Union are the powers, which will have some kind of, impact on a future Cyprus solution. The views and interests of these powers on the Cyprus question also inevitably affect the developments in this important matter. On the other hand, the Cyprus issue is an important factor that will be able to shape the mutual relations among the United States, Greece and Turkey. The interactions between these three powers have importance to the extent that they will take part in the establishment of the new world order. It is, therefore, necessary to analyse the Cyprus question in the context of conflicting and varying interests of the concerned powers. Especially the vital importance of the Cyprus issue for Turkey and the American involvement in the matter has the potential to affect the future of Cyprus. The Turkish side's reaction to the Greek and Cypriot-Greek side's co-operation with the European Union in shaping the future Cyprus state representing the whole island and the American intervention in this development might create repercussions not only for Cyprus, but also for the region and the whole world. In this article, the recent events related to the Cyprus issue will be studied with constant references to views, interests and interventions of the concerned powers. Especially the Turkish and American actions and approaches will be the main focus of the study.

THE BACKGROUND

During the Ottoman Empire period the Turks had lost Cyprus to Britain in a tricky way. The founders of the Republic of Turkey, too, surrendered the island with the Treaty of Lausanne to Britain officially as a part of their policies aiming at completing internal reforms and ending their problems with the European countries. With some help from the British and the Americans, Turkish rulers managed in a sense to regain Cyprus through the London and

Zurich Agreements in 1960; this is still considered one of the major achievements of Turkish foreign policy-makers in the history of the Turkish Republic. The fact that Turkish Cypriots, whose rate within the total population of Cyprus dropped to 18 percent because of the policies of the Ottoman Empire and the British administration and under the effect of other factors, became co-founders of the Republic of Cyprus and were allowed to share the rule with the Greek Cypriots was really a big success for the Turkish side.

However, after the Greek Cypriots ousted the Turks from the state mechanism by resorting to force in 1963, the Cyprus issue became one of the most important problems of Turkish foreign policy and Turkey's relations with big powers as well as its main foreign policy tendencies stayed under the influence of this matter. In 1964 Turkey could not intervene in Cyprus to protect the lives of Turkish Cypriots by using its rights given by the international treaties because of the pressures of the United States and the other Western countries. But there were also other facts showing that accusing the others was not a right attitude. In 1964, Turkey did not have the ability to launch a military intervention in Cyprus and Prime Minister İsmet İnönü tried to ensure the American opposition to such a Turkish intervention in order to be able to explain the non-intervention to his people. Turkey itself recognised the resolution of the UN Security Council in March 1964 on Cyprus, which brought about the international recognition of Greek Cypriots' administration as the official representative of Cyprus. Turkey also did not spend serious efforts in the 1964-1974 period to reverse this resolution and it did not bring up the issue in international meetings to express its own views seriously. It was also Turkey, which took into consideration the American-sponsored proposals, called double enosis and suggesting the unification of Cyprus with Greece in return for some kind of concession to Turkey. But Turkey insisted that a territory which will be large enough to meet Turkish security needs should be put under Turkish sovereignty. Given these negative points, the coup carried out by the Greek Cypriots on 15 July 1974 was a golden opportunity for Turkey. If the coup did not occur, Turkey would not have been able to intervene in the island militarily and Greek Cypriots would not have come to accepting a solution of the Cyprus problem based on federation. It was highly likely that inter-communal talks would have continued without bringing any concrete results and the situation of Turkish Cypriots, who did not attract any sympathy of the international public opinion in spite of all their sufferings and miseries, would have been forgotten totally.

The Turkish intervention in 1974 assured the security of Turkish Cypriots and made it possible for them to establish their own autonomous administration. The failure of the Americans to show an enforcing reaction to the Turkish action played to the hands of the Turkish rulers. But it should not be forgotten that the Americans did not show a severe reaction to the Cypriot coup, too. Moreover, the American administration was about to collapse because of the Watergate scandal, and therefore, it was not in the position to launch a serious initiative in foreign policy. The general American policy in this period was to avoid taking actions which would bring about losing Turkey and Greece and to accept the de facto situation, the separation of Cypriot Turks and Greeks from each other. The American embargo, which was implemented against Turkey from the early 1975, was mostly a product of a struggle between the American administration and the Congress. For the American Congress, the embargo was a golden opportunity to teach a lesson to the administration, which abused and went beyond its original authorities since 1969. With the implementation of the embargo, a troublesome period began for Turkey, in which the Cyprus issue became the main problem and menace of Turkish foreign policy. The embargo also made the Cyprus issue a constant trouble point in Turkish-American relations and Turkey was put under pressure by the American authorities in this matter.

THE 1974-1990 PERIOD

In the aftermath of the 1974 events, the American administration continued to recognise the Greek government as the sole representative of Cyprus and the USA and the other members of the UN Security Council accepted the constitutional demands of the Turkish Cypriots to join the Cypriot administration in a partnership project.[1] Although the United States did not favour the Cypriot Greek side openly in the Cyprus issue, Turkey came under the heavy American pressure. When Turkish rulers were demanded to initiate some positive developments in the Cyprus issue in return for the removal of the embargo, they felt the pressure of the Turkish public not to act in this direction. Even if they wanted to fulfil demands of the Americans, they could not have done so because in this case they would have given the impression that they were retreating under pressure.

In the American elections in 1976, the Cyprus issue became an important matter attracting the attention of the whole American nation. After the Nixon and Ford administrations failed to reverse the partition of Cyprus, the candidate of the Democrat Party for the presidency, Jimmy Carter, stated that a positive approach should be adopted toward the Cyprus issue. The unexpected demonstration of interest by the American people in the matter led President Carter to send former defence minister Clark Clifford to Ankara, Athens and Cyprus to find out the realities on the Cyprus question and to make contribution to a peaceful solution. In this way, Carter tried to prevent weakening of NATO's southern flank and to reduce the tensions between Turkey and Greece.[2] The proposal of Clifford was that the disagreements in the Aegean, Cyprus and making a defence agreement with Turkey should be dealt with collectively. In 1977, the representatives of the Greek Cypriots and the Turkish Cypriots, Denktash and Clerides, signed a document, which demonstrated that they agreed on important basic points. But the severe Greek Cypriot reaction to the American initiative in 1978 led the American authorities to take a relatively passive attitude on the matter in the following years. Meanwhile, the meeting of American State Secretary Cyrus Vance in 1978 with the leader of the Turkish Cypriots, Rauf Denktash, as the successor of Dr. Fazil Kutchuk, who had been elected as the vice-president of the Republic of Cyprus, showed that the Americans might extend some kind of recognition to the Turkish Cypriot side.[3]

In the following period, the Cyprus question lost its position as a matter having the potential to affect the American elections for the presidency. Beginning with the Reagan administration, it was no longer an issue which the American president would consider worthwhile to attract his attention and to affect its development. The Cyprus issue was handled and policies were produced about it not by high-level policy makers, but by experts and special envoys. The Reagan administration evaluated in a narrow regional context and never saw it a first-class problem which would concern the American interests seriously. As a

---

[1] James H. Wolfe, "United States and the Cyprus Conflict" in Kjell Skjelsbaek (ed.), *The Cyprus Conflict and the Role of the United Nations*, Norwegian Institute of International Affairs, November 1988, p. 51.

[2] Brian Mandell, "The Cyprus Conflict: Explaining Resistance to Resolution" in Norma Salem (ed.), *Cyprus: A Regional Conflict and its Resolution*, New York: St. Martin's Press, 1992, p. 213.

[3] Wolfe, "United States and the Cyprus Conflict", pp. 52, 53, 55.

parallel to this American approach, the American and Soviet representatives did not consider the Cyprus issue when they met to deal with regional problems.[4] Reagan did not choose to resort to personal diplomacy by assigning the task of mediating for the Cyprus issue to a special envoy. But State Secretary Alexander Haig created a permanent desk within the State Department, which would deal with the Cyprus issue: the special co-ordinator for Cyprus. Among the remarkable American diplomats who served as the special co-ordinator were Reginald Bartholomew, Christian Chapman, Richard Haass, James Wilkinson and Thomas Weston. At the beginning, the special co-ordinators were interested only in the Cyprus question, but as the matter receded to secondary importance these diplomats began to undertake other tasks.[5]

American Special Co-ordinator for Cyprus Richard Haass was opposed to launching dramatic initiatives on the Cyprus issue. In his opinion, the United States should take modest actions to normalise the relations between the two communities in Cyprus and should focus on the confidence building measures. The Turkish side's proclamation of its own independent republic on 15 November 1983 constituted a radical development contradicting the American attitude of recognising the Greek Cypriot government as the official representative of Cyprus. The White House expressed its displeasure over the Turkish action and the State Department prevented the recognition of the new state by the Muslim countries by warning them one by one. However, the American reaction did not amount to taking forceful measures and American authorities continued to give support to holding negotiations between the two communities to find a solution.[6] In the period following 1985, the apparent war between the American administration and the Congress on the Cyprus issue began to be replaced by the opinion that the two organs of the state should launch joint actions to persuade the parties to the Cyprus problem.[7]

The proximity talks in 1984-1986 were considered especially by American Secretary of State George Shultz as the best and last chance for the sides to reach a solution.[8] As a result of this thinking American President Reagan sent a special letter on 22 November 1984 to Turkish President Kenan Evren, calling for serious efforts to reach a speedy solution in Cyprus. In Reagan's opinion, the ultimate aim should be to establish a federal republic, which would end the partition of the island. It was reported that the apparent American pressures led the Turkish rulers to persuade the Turkish Cypriots in moderating their attitude toward the Greek Cypriots.[9] In this conjunction, the American administration promised the Turkish rulers that it would end its pressures if they accepted the UN written proposals on 17 January 1985 and 29 March 1986, the Turkish side gave its approval to the documents, but the Americans directed their pressures toward the Turks again instead of criticising the Greek Cypriots, who rejected the proposals.[10] The Turkish side was further alienated in September 1986 because of the treatment of their leader by the Americans. In contrast to their attitude in

---

[4] Ellen Laipson, "The United States and Cyprus: Past Policies, Current Concerns" in Salem (ed.), *Cyprus*, pp. 96, 97.

[5] Wolfe, "United States and the Cyprus Conflict", p. 56.

[6] Mandell, "The Cyprus Conflict...", p. 215.

[7] Laipson, "The United States and Cyprus...", p. 96.

[8] Mandell, "The Cyprus Conflict...", p. 216.

[9] Glen D. Camp, "Island Impasse: Peacemaking on Cyprus 1980-1994" in Vangelis Calotychos (ed.), *Cyprus and Its People: Nation, Identity and Experience in an Unimaginable Community 1955-1997*, Boulder: Westview Press, 1998, p. 143.

[10] Sabahattin İsmail, *Kıbrıs Üzerine Bildiriler*, Lefkoşa: CYREP, 1998, p. 287.

the aftermath of the 1974 events, which considered the Turkish Cypriots as the co-partners of the Cypriot states, the Americans now avoided giving the slightest impression that they recognised the Turkish Cypriot administration. However, the Turkish Cypriot bureau in New York, which was opened in spite of intensive Greek opposition, was able to become one of the players of the diplomatic game. While the Turkish Cypriot representative established contact with American authorities and foreign missions in New York, Harold Rhode, an official of Pentagon did not hesitate in visiting this bureau.[11]

In the 1988 American presidential elections, an American having Greek origin won the candidacy for the presidency for the first time, but the Cyprus issue never became an important matter for discussion between the candidates. The organisers of the Dukakis campaign issued a statement on 11 May 1988, calling for implementing principles of law in Cyprus and withdrawal of the foreign troops from the island, but Dukakis did not see it necessary to make another statement on the Cyprus issue.[12] This apparent American indifference to Cyprus would begin to change with the successes achieved in the solution of regional problems in 1988.

THE STRATEGIC FACTOR

Before passing to the analysis of events in the 1990s, it will be useful to study the relationship of the Cyprus issue with the Cold War. The Americans always approached to the Cyprus question from the perspective of their global leadership in the context of their global interests and security. Their main concern was to prevent the outbreak of a war between the two NATO allies, namely Greece and Turkey, and thus to hinder the weakening of NATO's southern flank. The Americans had to intervene in the Cyprus crises not to allow them to bring strategic losses for the United States and the Western bloc.[13] The non-aligned policies pursued by Greek Cypriot leader Makarios and the strength of the Cypriot communist party, AKEL, concerned the Americans greatly. The Cold War mentality of the Americans required that the Cyprus question should be resolved in accordance with interests of the USA, NATO, Greece and Turkey. Makarios could not be allowed to make Russian influential on the Cyprus issue. He should be irritated or removed from power by the Greek junta. The most suitable solution could be the unification of the island with Greece in return for some concessions to Turkey. In this way, Cyprus could be opened to the unrestricted use of NATO and the United States. When the Greek Cypriot opposition and the Turkish insistence on the size of the territory which would be given to Turkey prevented the success of this scheme, the Americans tried to keep the issue under control with its present situation not to allow an outbreak of Greek-Turkish war on the matter.[14] If the Cold War conditions did not exist, the enmity of the non-aligned bloc toward the West did not help Makarios and the hands of the

---

[11] Wolfe, "United States and the Cyprus Conflict", p. 52, Yılmaz Polat, *Washington Entrikaları*, İstanbul: Milliyet, 1999, pp. 150-152.

[12] Wolfe, "United States and the Cyprus Conflict", p. 58, Laipson, "The United States and Cyprus...", p. 96.

[13] John Roper, "The West and Turkey: Varying Roles, Common Interests", *The International Spectator*, vol. 34, No. 1, January-March 1999, pp. 93, 101.

[14] Mehmet Hasgüler, *Kıbrıs'ta Enosis ve Taksim Politikalarının Sonu*, İstanbul: İletişim, 2000, p. 147.

Americans were not bound with the Cold War restrictions, a solution could have been reached in Cyprus on the basis of granting limited autonomy to the Turkish Cypriots.[15]

The strategic importance of Cyprus still affects the approach of the Americans toward the Cyprus issue and their approach, in return, has the potential to affect the future of the problem. Cyprus is located in the crossroads of the routes reaching the Middle East, which is the most important and the most troublesome region of the world. It has the potential to serve as a suitable base to intervene in serious developments in the region. The Gulf War demonstrated that the military bases which will be established on Cyprus, the ports, which will provide great help to the American navy and weapon systems and reconnaissance facilities, which will be installed on the island, will have great importance for the United States. The Americans use at the moment the sophisticated military support and intelligence gathering stations in the south of the island, which serves security interests of the Western world in the eastern Mediterranean, the Middle East and the northern Africa. There are also antenna of the US Federal Broadcast Information Service on Cyprus. These installations, which are the property of the British, had no task related to NATO, but they serve the American and Western interests with their capacity of gathering electronic intelligence.[16] In the past, Makarios, who pursued non-aligned policies, permitted the use of these bases by the US forces for such purposes as minesweeping operations or high-altitude intelligence gathering flights.[17] The Americans naturally do not want to endanger these facilities by pursuing harmful policies. Even it can be said that since it is the Greek Cypriot side, which provides various services to the USA, the Americans do not act completely in accordance with the principle of equality by favouring the Greek Cypriots.[18] However, in the last analysis, the American authorities attribute more importance to their relations with Greece and Turkey and do not want to alienate these two countries with their Cyprus policies. In this context, the USA is criticised on the ground that it prevents the emergence of more practical and realist choices with its policies based on strategic thinking.[19]

The strategic concerns are also apparent in the American attitude of not pursuing completely anti-Turkish policies and not applying excessive pressures on Turkey regarding the Cyprus issue.[20] Even in the periods when the Congress applied pressures against Turkey, the American state and defence departments and the National Security Council emphasised that Turkey should not alienated from the USA by underlying the strategic importance of this country. The end of the Cold War did not reduce this importance, but, on the contrary, Turkey became a strategic partner of the United States in a period in which new threats emerged in the surrounding region of Turkey, concerning the Americans closely. In the opinion of American Deputy Secretary of State Strobe Talbott, US-Turkish relations have even more of a hardheaded geopolitical, strategic rationale in the Post-Cold War period than during the Cold War.[21] Since the Americans considered Turkey as a base and antidote against radical

---

[15] Monteagle Stearns, *Entangled Allies: US Policy Toward Greece, Turkey and Cyprus*, New York: Council on Foreign Relations Press, 1992, p. 17.

[16] Stearns, *Entangled Allies*, pp. 107, 125.

[17] Wolfe, "United States and the Cyprus Conflict", p. 48.

[18] Clement H. Dodd, *The Cyprus Imbroglio*, Huntingdon: The Eothen Press, 1998, p. 116.

[19] Laipson, "The United States and Cyprus...", p. 93, Ronald J. Fisher, "Conclusion: Path Towards a Peaceful Cyprus" in Salem (ed.), *Cyprus*, p. 245.

[20] SİSAV Dış Politika ve Savunma Grubu, *1997 Yılı Sonu İtibariyle Kıbrıs Sorunu*, İstanbul: SİSAV, March 1998, p. 31.

[21] Alan Makovsky, "New Activism in Turkish Foreign Policy", *SAIS Review*, Winter-Spring 1999.

religious movements and as a democratic, secular model for the regional states and as an ally for Israel, they prevent the total condemnation of Turkey and the enactment of forceful measure against Turkey in the UN Security Council on the Cyprus issue.[22]

INTENSIVE INITIATIVES AND INCREASING TENSIONS ON THE CYPRUS ISSUE (THE EARLY 1990S)

The Background of the Initiatives

In spite of the apparent American inclination toward Turkey in the early Post-Cold War period, it was not guarantee that the United States would consent to the non-solution of the Cyprus problem eternally and that it would not force Turkey for a solution when it considered the situation suitable. The American pressures on its closest ally, Israel, in the aftermath of the Gulf War to persuade it to make peace with Palestinians showed that the United States might resort to pressure tactics to force its allies to act in a certain way.[23] The Cyprus issue could not be an exception in this regard. While the détente became the dominant phenomenon in the world politics and local problems were solved one by one, the United States would not allow that the Cyprus problem, which was closely related to the Western alliance, would continue to exist and thus to harm the American prestige in the eyes of world public opinion. NATO did not want to see any longer the Cyprus question as a source of discord among the allies, but it preferred to see it as an area of co-operation with its solution as soon as possible. The Greek-Turkish confrontation was one of the most important obstacles to the efforts of increasing NATO's effectiveness and reliability and of consolidating the new world order. It was, therefore, necessary not allow the Cyprus issue to take Turkish-Greek relations as a hostage and to solve this problem in order to strengthen the solidarity of the Western alliance.[24]

In a period in which the Middle East gained more importance as a centre of crisis, allowing the weakening of the south-eastern flank of NATO in the field of military effectiveness because of the Cyprus question could bring about much more serious consequences than it could have brought during the Cold War period. It was reported that the American ambassador in Nicosia, Robert Lamb, said the following things on 18 February 1993: the UN Secretary-General and the Security Council were so busy with other international problems that it was not right to trouble them with the Cyprus issue. If the Cypriots wanted a solution, they should know that the solution would come out as a result of the negotiations held between the two sides.[25] In this period, the United States was pressurising the sides continuously, was trying to keep the inter-communal talks activated and was putting more pressure on the side which seemed to avoid negotiations. Since Turkey and the Turkish Republic of Northern Cyprus were perceived as the sides causing difficulties in

---

[22] Mustafa Aydın, "Cacophony in the Aegean : Contemporary Turkish-Greek Relations", *The Turkish Yearbook of International Relations*, No. 27, 1997, p. 124, Mandell, "The Cyprus Conflict...", p. 222.

[23] Nasuh Uslu, "Körfez Savaşı ve Amerika'nın Politikaları", *Ankara Üniversitesi SBF Dergisi*, vol. 54, No. 3, July-September 1999, pp. 165-199.

[24] Hasgüler, *Kıbrıs'ta Enosis ve Taksim...*, pp. 148, 297, 307.

[25] Mehmet Arif Demirer, *Türkün Onur Sorunu: Kuzey Kıbrıs Türk Cumhuriyeti*, Ankara: Turhan Kitabevi, 1993.

negotiations in the early 1990s, they were subjected to more American pressures.[26] Meanwhile, with the active participation of the European Union into the process of trying to find a solution to the Cyprus problem, it was inevitable that Turkey would come under more pressures because Turkey was not a member of the EU and was considered the absolute criminal side in the matter. The EU would appoint a permanent envoy on the Cyprus issue and would be one of the most important parties of the problem by accepting the application of the Greek Cypriot side for the EU membership. The Turkish side only could hope that the tendency in the early 1990s of giving consent to the secession of ethnic groups from their state to maintain the regional balances might help the position of the Turkish Cypriots.[27]

The Ledsky Initiative

At the end of the 1980s, the Americans were continuing their efforts not to allow the interruption of the dialogue between the Cypriot communities. They were more eager to support the UN initiatives since they considered Greek Cypriot leader Vasiliou as a more modest politician. They appointed Nelson Ledsky as the special co-ordinator for Cyprus. The American president met with the Greek Cypriot leader in the White House in June 1989. The president called the Cypriot communities to hold new negotiations. As a part of the new American attitude, the American administration gave full support to the Resolution 649 of the UN Security Council.[28]

In the eyes of Turkish Cypriots, the real motive behind the new American initiative was to promote the candidacy of Cyprus for the European Union. The EU members and the United States were hastening to solve the problems relating to Cyprus and thus to remove the obstacles to the membership of Cyprus into the EU. According to Turkish Cypriots, Ledsky had come to Cyprus to save Vasiliou, who faced a difficult situation when Turkish leader Denktash proposed on 11 October 1989 declaring an "announcement of joint good will". In fact, Ledsky's statements during his visit contributed the stubbornness of Greek Cypriots in solving the problem by seeming to support their views. He voiced the following views: The Cyprus wall should fall down as the Berlin wall fell down. The Americans did not accept a Turkish state in Cyprus and we would not so in the future. The Turkish Cypriot community had one alternative: negotiating with the Greek Cypriot community with a new understanding. The Turkish Cypriots should not spend their time and money in vain for legal arguments to prove the legitimacy of the Turkish Republic. The American administration would never recognise their state.[29]

In the eyes of the Americans Turkish Cypriot leader seemed the most important obstacle in finding a solution for Cyprus. Since they were not able to control him through direct

[26] SİSAV Dış İlişkiler ve Savunma Araştırma Grubu, *Kıbrıs Sorunu: Gelişmeler ve Görüşmeler*, İstanbul: SİSAV, September 1990, pp. 74-75.

[27] Aydın, "Cacophony in the Aegean...", pp. 123-124, Ecmel Barutçu, *Hariciye Koridoru*, Ankara: 21. Yüzyıl Yay., 1999, p. 274.

[28] Van Coufoudakis, "Domestic Politics and the Search for a Solution of the Cyprus Problem" in Salem (ed.), *Cyprus*, pp. 31, 33, 34-35.

[29] Sabahattin İsmail, *Self-Determinasyon ve Kıbrıs Türk Halkı*, İstanbul: Kastaş Yay., June 1990, pp. 28, 53, 86, 185, 186-187, 199, 232, 286, 290, 292, 293, Mustafa Evran, "Türkiye-Avrupa Birliği İlişkileri Çerçevesinde Kıbrıs'ın Avrupa Birliği Üyeliğine Başvurusu" in Çiler Eminer and Gülden İlkman (ed.), *Avrupa Birliği ve Kıbrıs*, Lefkoşa: KKTC Dışişleri ve Savunma Bakanlığı, pp. 19-20, Demirer, *Türkün Onur Sorunu*, pp. 48-49, Orbay Deliceırmak (ed.), *Haklılık ve Kararlılık*, Lefkoşa, February 1993, p. 40.

pressures, they only could ask the Turkish authorities to persuade Denktash in holding more moderate attitude. But, in a meeting held in the American State Department, the drawbacks of pressurising Turkey in this regard were mentioned. Since the situation of the Turkish-American relationship at that time was not in a desired level, the Americans only could only support the initiatives of the UN Secretary-General and could hope that the EU would be influential on the Turkish side in moderating their approach. Meanwhile, Turkish President Turgut Özal seemed to come under the influence of the Americans and to apply pressures on Denktash in accordance with the request of American authorities. Turkish Foreign Minister Mesut Yılmaz, who did not join Özal's to visit the United States, must have been disturbed from the talks in Washington; he made a non-scheduled speech in the Turkish Parliament, criticising the United States and emphasising that "no Turkish government can make concessions which the nation cannot accept."[30]

The Cyprus question was also discussed in the summit meeting between American President George Bush and Soviet leader Gorbachev on 2 June 1990. Commenting on the summit, American Secretary of State James Baker gave the following information: Bush and Gorbachev discussed the all aspects of the Cyprus issue. The two world leaders, who shared the opinion that the two countries should do their best to help the solution of the problem, stated that they would continue to support the efforts of the UN Secretary-General on finding a solution.[31] In the same month (June), the Cyprus question came to the forefront again, this time because of the Defence Co-operation Agreement signed between the United States and Greece. The Greek governments, as a traditional policy, had perceived a threat from Turkey on the integrity of their territory; and in order to overcome their insecurity in this regard, they had sought guarantees from the United States in various forms, ensuring that no attempt would be made to solve Greek-Turkish differences through other than peaceful means. As an extension of this policy, some sentences requiring the protection of the military balance of power in the region and expressing that the United States gave some assurances in this direction were included in the preamble to the US-Greek Mutual Defence Co-operation Agreement (DCA). This worried Turkish authorities. Ankara had interpreted those sentences to the meaning that they would encourage Greece to initiate fait accomplices in the Aegean and in Cyprus with the help of Greek Cypriots. Turkish authorities voiced their displeasure in their highest level contacts with the American officials. The fact that the Turkish attendance at the US ambassador's reception on 4 July 1990 stayed in a very limited level was nothing more than expressing this pleasure in an open way. At the end, Turkish officials managed to get assurances from the Americans that the preamble was not directed against Turkey.[32]

The Set of Ideas

After the inter-communal talks failed in March 1990, the American administration considered that in the positive atmosphere created by the success in the Gulf War, the Turkish-Greek dialogue on Cyprus could be given a new push. It was believed that American President Bush was in favour of holding an international conference on Cyprus, but he could not apply pressures in this matter not to alienate Turkey, which provided great help to the

---

[30] Polat, *Washington Entrikaları*, p. 97.
[31] SİSAV, *Kıbrıs Sorunu*, p. 55.
[32] Ibid., p. 56, Stearns, *Entangled Allies*, pp. 99-100.

USA during the Gulf War.[33] Nevertheless, the American insistence on solving the Cyprus problem brought about serious negotiations under the auspices of the UN. In the American eyes, the most important obstacles in this regard were the Turkish Cypriot stubbornness and the Turkish failure to establish a stable government.[34] They could trust in their close friend Turkish President Özal in overcoming the first obstacle.

The proposal of holding a four-partite meeting between the representatives of Turkey, Greece, and the communities in Cyprus, which was put forward by Turkish President Özal on 30 May 1991, represented a diversion from Turkey's traditional policy of not involving in Cyprus negotiations. In Özal's view, if the four leaders came together in the style of the Camp David negotiations and discussed the problem, a serious progress could be achieved in the solution of the Cyprus question. But Greek and Greek Cypriot authorities rejected the proposal. Their counter-proposal was that an international conference should be held with the participation of the nine states including the five permanent members of the UN Security Council apart from the sides of the problem. This time the Turkish side objected to the conference proposal, believing that the real intention of the Greek side was to put Turkey under the pressure of the great powers.[35]

The next event, the meeting between Turkish Prime Minister Yıldırım Akbulut and Greek Prime Minister Mitsotakis on 6 July 1990, demonstrated that the attitude of Turgut Özal did not change. Mitsotakis suggested that the Greco-Turkish dialogue should be focused on the Cyprus issue. If a sufficient progress was achieved in the solution of the Cyprus problem, then the other problems could be negotiated by the two states. Akbulut gave his consent to the proposal. However, the meeting between Turkey's new Prime Minister Süleyman Demirel and Mitsotakis at the end of 1991 showed that the attitude of the Turkish side changed. Mitsotakis asked Demirel to put pressure on Denktash to persuade him in making more concessions. But Demirel refused to intervene in Denktash's handling the inter-communal talks. It seemed that the Turkish government readopted its previous attitude that only the Cypriot leaders could find a solution to the Cyprus problem through bilateral talks.[36]

In 1992, intensive initiatives were launched on the Cyprus issue. The inter-communal talks under the auspices of UN Secretary-General Butrous Butrous Ghali reached a serious point with the proclamation of the Set of Ideas put forward by the Secretary-General. The UN Security Council ratified that the Set of Ideas constituted a suitable framework for finding a solution to the Cyprus problem. At the beginning, Turkish Cypriots were pleased with the UN's speaking of a sovereignty which would be established with the joint participation of the two sides. On the other hand, the Greek Cypriot side emphasised the idea of "a state of Cyprus with a single sovereignty and a single citizenship", which was formulated in the Set of Ideas. Later the UN Security Council combined the opinions of the two sides and proposed a federal republic which would have "one sovereignty which is indivisible and which emanates equally from the Greek Cypriot and Turkish Cypriot communities", but the Greek side objected this formulation.[37] As we return to the Set of Ideas, Turkish Cypriots found it

[33] Süha Bölükbaşı, "The Turco-Greek Dispute: Issues, Policies and Prospects" in Clement H. Dodd (ed.), *Turkish Foreign Policy: New Prospects*, Huntingdon: The Eothen Press, 1992, p. 51.

[34] Ian O. Lesser, "Bridge or Barrier? Turkey and the West After the Cold War" in Graham Fuller et al., *Turkey's New Geopolitics: From the Balkans to Western China*, Boulder, 1993, p. 112.

[35] Dodd, *The Cyprus Imbroglio*, p. 43, Bölükbaşı, "The Turco-Greek Dispute...", pp. 32-33.

[36] Bölükbaşı, "The Tuco-Greek Dispute...", p. 48.

[37] Clement H. Dodd, "Confederation, Federation and Sovereignty", *Perceptions*, vol. 4, No. 3, September-November 1999.

acceptable the 91 articles of the package. They definitely rejected the remaining 9 articles since they proposed a federal system in which the Turkish Cypriots would not have their own sovereignty and the right of self-determination. This amounted to the refusal of the package of the UN Secretary-General.[38]

Some criticisms voiced by Turkish Cypriots on the Set of Ideas should be mentioned here since they reflected the attitude of the Turkish Cypriot leadership to a great extent and showed their distrust toward the United States and the United Nations. According those Turkish critics, by accepting the resolutions 649, 716, 750, 774 and 789, the UN Security Council tried to impose a solution, which would destroy the sovereignty of the Turkish community and which aimed at dissolving the TRNC and putting Turkish Cypriots under the authority of the Greek Cypriot state. The members of the UN Security Council not only recognised the Greek Cypriot government as the official representative of the island, but they also tried to impose their own choice of solution by joining the negotiation table on behalf of the Greeks in a sense and thus they violated the principle that the sides should continue the talks with their free will. The diplomats of the UN and the United States lobbied intensively among journalists, businessmen, industrial and commercial unions, political parties and people in TRNC. They aimed to give damage to the prestige of President Denktash, the Turkish Cypriot Parliament and the government and to impose their own proposal of solution on the Turkish side by intervening in internal affairs of Turkish Cypriots. The American officials and UN Secretary-General Ghali, who was under the great influence of the Americans, tried to reduce the size of TRNC as a condition of establishing a federation and focused only on the situation of the Greek Cypriot refugees as if they were the only refugees on the island. Their efforts of imposing on the Turkish side an agreement which would lead to the establishment of the Greek Cypriot authority on the island and which would bring back the dark days of the period before 1974 would cause nothing more than turning the island to a battle field. The thing which upset Turkish Cypriots the most was that Turkish President Özal accused them of not continuing the talks after the UN Security Council Resolution 649, preventing the four-partite summit and causing the enactment of the UN Security Council Resolution 716. However, this was not the truth. The United States tried to impose an agreement by bringing the sides to New York before the preparations were not completed. When it was failed to do so, the anger it felt led it to agree with the Greek side on passing an anti-Turkish resolution in the Security Council.[39] It was unfortunate that the enmity the Americans felt against Denktash spread to the Turkish leadership as well. Denktash himself stated that he was sure on the existence of an organised effort directed to humiliate him and to replace him with another person.[40]

The speech made by Denktash in the Turkish Grand National Assembly during his return journey from the New York talks, in which he felt suffocated under duress, was rather interesting. He made the following points. The Security Council member had focused on the Varosha issue. If Turkish Cypriots acted in the way they wanted by yielding to their pressures, it was inevitable that further concessions would be demanded. By hurling threats such as "if you do not accept our proposal, we will impose an embargo on you and Turkey will be held responsible from your attitude", they would take up other issues. Since they knew

---

[38] İsmail, *Kıbrıs Üzerine Bildiriler*, p. 227.

[39] Ibid., pp. 226-227, 228, 229, 238, 244, 246, 273, 275, 287, Sabahattin İsmail, *Egemenlik, Konfederasyon ve Kıbrıs Türk Halkı*, November 1993, pp. 168, 177-178, 179.

[40] Deliceırmak (ed.), *Haklılık ve Kararlılık*, p. 34.

that Turkish Cypriots were sensitive on not causing any harm to Turkey, the representatives of the five great powers considered this situation a weakness of the Turkish side and continued their threats basing on this fact. The representative of each power made speeches in front of the negotiators, supporting the report read by the Secretary-General and gave the sides a certain time to sell the proposals to their people. Denktash himself witnessed for the first time that such a treatment was applied to the representative of a people under threats and restrictions. The members of the Security Council did not let Turkish Cypriots mention their sovereignty, diluted their equality, opposed taking executive decisions in a harmony existed in federations, and tried to recreate the dreadful situation before 1964 by snapping territory from the Turkish side and allowing settlement of Greek Cypriots on other parts of the Turkish territory. The declaration issued on the same day in the Turkish Parliament with the participation of all the political parties was intended to show that Turkey would not yield to pressures of the great powers. The declaration stated: TGNA appreciated the peace efforts spent by Denktash. The Turkish nation would not accept a solution which was not accepted by the Turkish Cypriot nation. TGNA considered holding negotiations in an atmosphere distant from every kind of pressure as a dispensable condition of a lasting compromise.[41]

With the failure of the Set of Ideas, the Cyprus question continued to be an irritating point in Turkish-American relations. Ankara avoided taking actions which were seen by the Americans as the confidence building measures such as reducing the number of Turkish troops on the island. But the Turkish authorities had to persuade the Turkish Cypriot leadership in continuing the process of seeking a solution not to cause a crisis in relations with the United States. On the other hand, the American leaders were extremely displeased with the determination of Denktash in not accepting the plans put forward by the UN. In the opinion of the Turkish side, the Set of Ideas was based on giving territory in return for constitutional rights. This was normal for the Americans, who had the understanding of horse trade. But the Turkish Cypriots attributed more importance to basic principles such as the recognition of the equal status.

Following the failure of the Set of Ideas, the Americans began to focus on the confidence building measures again. With their initiative, the UN Secretary-General met with the representatives of the Turkish Cypriots to find a solution to the problems related to Varosha.[42] On 20 January 1995 Denktash issued a fourteen-point peace plan, explaining the views of the Turkish side on finding a solution to the Cyprus problem. The UN and the United Nations admitted that there were positive elements in the document, but Greek Cypriots rejected it.[43] On 23 January 1995, the American president's special emissary for Cyprus, Richard Beattle, conveyed a special message of President Clinton's to Denktash. In his message, Clinton mentioned the American support for the establishment of a bizonal and bicommunal federation in which the two political communities would live as a one state. He also emphasised that the only way of making progress in the Cyprus question was the implementation of the confidence building measures.[44] As it was understood from the message, the United States was still not pleased with the attitude of Turkish Cypriots. When

---

[41] Demirer, *Türkün Onur Sorunu*, pp. 54, 57, 58, 61-63.
[42] Dodd, *The Cyprus Imbroglio*, pp. 53, 58-59.
[43] Ibid., pp. 70, 91.
[44] The statements of the American authorities and the American government, which will be mentioned in the following section are taken from the web site of the American embassy in Cyprus if no footnote is used.

the Turkish side put more emphasis on their sovereignty and right of self-determination from the end of 1995, the Americans' fears increased further.

THE EUROPEAN UNION CONNECTION

With the application of Greek Cypriots for the membership of the European Union at the early 1990s, the Cyprus question gained importance for the EU and its enlargement as well. Thus the Cyprus question acquired a new aspect which could facilitate or bring new difficulties for the solution of the problem. The intervention of the EU in the problem, which was not a considerable factor up to that time, was also a development which could bring serious consequences for the Turkish-EU and Turkish-American relations. It was also inevitable that the approach of Turkey to the Cyprus question would change considerably.

On 17 September 1990, the Ministerial Council of the EU decided to transfer the application of the Greek Cypriot administration to the EU Commission. At that time, the American administration was opposed to such a development since it considered that it would complicate the problem. Some circles in the USA were of the opinion that the Cyprus question should be solved in accordance with the political and geopolitical interests of NATO and they were opposed to the intervention of the EU in the matter since Turkey was opposed to it.[45] Even Nelson Ledsky claimed that the membership of Cyprus in the EU would deteriorate the disagreements between the two communities rather than bringing them together.[46] But there were also Americans, who hoped that the EU aspect would lead Turkey to reconsider its standing in the Cyprus issue since it needed the American support for its membership in the EU.[47] Later the Americans would encourage the Turkish side to see the EU aspect as an opportunity in finding a solution to the Cyprus problem.

For the Turkish and Turkish Cypriot leaders, the application of the Greek Cypriots for the EU membership was nothing more than a Greek game launched to put the whole island under their rule. In their opinion, if the EU accepted the Greek Cypriot application, this would amount to the indirect enosis and the TRNC would not be able to continue its existence as it was. In this way, many principles, which the Turkish side defended insistently, such as sovereignty, the Turkish guarantee for Cyprus and bizonal state, would become non-functional and meaningless. After such a development, it would be impossible to prevent the likelihood of the Greek Cypriot domination over the Turkish community. Moreover, the Helenism would gain a great victory because the Treaty of Guarantee would not be used against a member of the EU. With the implementation of the EU laws, all the parameters, which emerged up to that time for the establishment of a bizonal and bicommunal state, would lose their meaning.[48] There was also a common view in the Turkish side that the European leaders would use the Cyprus issue and the Greek Cypriot application as a tool to

---

[45] Coufoudakis, "Domestic Politics...", p. 35, Nicholas Emiliou, "Knocking on the Door of the European Union: Cyprus' Strategy of Accession" in Heinz-Jürgen Axt and Hansjörg Brey (ed.) *Cyprus and the European Union: New Chances for Solving an Old Conflict?* Münih: Südosterapa-Gesellschaft, 1997, p. 128.

[46] Sabahattin İsmail, *150 Soruda Kıbrıs Sorunu*, İstanbul: Kaştaş Yay., August 1998.

[47] Laipson, "The United States and Cyprus...", p. 98.

[48] Barutçu, *Hariciye Koridoru*, p. 267, Mümtaz Soysal, *Aklını Kıbrıs'la Bozmak*, Ankara: Bilgi Yay., August 1995, p. 170, Denktash's letter to British Foreign Secretary Robin Cook, dated as 25 March 1998 (the official statements of the Turkish side in the following section is taken from the web site of the Turkish Foreign Ministry if no footnote is used).

keep Turkey outside the EU. In the following period, Turkey tried to prevent or soften the EU decisions in promoting the candidacy of the Greek Cypriots by approaching the EU countries and the USA. It also initiated some joint arrangements with the TRNC and declared from December 1995 that these arrangements would be expanded if the process of Cypriot application continued. In addition, Turkish authorities frequently stated that the continuation of the process torpedoed the Cypriot negotiations, which were held under the auspices of the UN Secretary-General.[49]

In spite of this apparent Turkish attitude, it was rather surprising that Turkey gave the green light to the continuation of the membership negotiations of the Greek Cypriots in return for signing the Customs Union agreement with the EU in March 1995. On 6 March 1995, the EU Council announced that the membership negotiations with the Greek Cypriots would start six months after the completion of the inter-governmental conference in 1996. In fact, behind this announcement lied a bargaining, which was carried out with the encouragement of the Americans. Greece withdrew its threat of vetoing the Customs Union agreement between the EU and Turkey, and in return, Turkey kept quiet about the EU decision to schedule the membership negotiations with Cyprus.[50] In the eyes of the Americans, the new moderate attitude of the Greek government was positive and valuable. Greece itself would benefit from supporting the Turkish bid to become a part of Europe. Keeping Turkey outside Europe might result in the establishment of a military or radical government in Turkey,[51] and such a development would create new problems for Turkish-Greek disagreements including the Cyprus issue. The American administration also encouraged the EU to include the Turkish Cypriots in the membership negotiations without staying under the fact that it recognised only the Greek Cypriot side as the official representative of Cyprus. Especially American Presidential Envoy for Cyprus Richard Holbrooke tried to persuade Turkish authorities on that Turkey had vital interests in the participation of the Turkish Cypriots to the membership negotiations. In his opinion, the most important obstacle in this regard could be overcome in the following way: Neither the Greek Cypriots should give up their claim of becoming the only representative of the island nor the Turkish Cypriots should withdraw their demand of the recognition of the TRNC. But the two sides should come together and should sit on the EU table together in spite of their conflicting attitudes.[52]

However, in the opinion of the Turkish side, their participation to the membership negotiations before their equal status was recognised would mean giving up their opinions, which they defended up to that time, and would result in the loss of their basic rights and powers. As their objections were not taken into consideration, Turkey and the TRNC signed an economic co-operation protocol and a financial support agreement on 3 January 1997. The two states also concluded a Partnership Council agreement on 20 July 1997, aiming at partially integrating the TRNC with Turkey. The new approach of the Turkish side was to carry out among themselves all the structural co-operation and adaptation arrangements, which were done between the EU and the Greek Cypriots. The Americans, who did not show

---

[49] SİSAV, *1997 Yılı Sonu İtibariyle Kıbrıs Sorunu*, p. 23.
[50] Andreas Theophanous, "Cyprus, the European Union and the Search for a New Constitution", *Journal of Southern Europe and the Balkans*, vol. 2, No. 2, 2000, p. 223, Soysal, *Aklını Kıbrıs'la Bozmak*, p. 169.
[51] Monteagle Stearns, "Yunan Güvenlik Meseleleri" in Graham T. Allison and Kalipso Nikolaydis (ed.), *Yunan Paradoksu*, (translated to Turkish by Bülent Tanatar), İstanbul: Doğan Kitap, October 1999, pp. 89, 90.
[52] Tözün Bahçeli, "Cyprus in the Post-Cold War Environment: Moving Toward a Settlement" in Calotychos (ed.), *Cyprus and Its People*, p. 109, Dodd, *The Cyprus Imbroglio*, pp. 111-112.

any serious objection to the EU-Greek Cypriot negotiations, stated that the Turkish-TRNC agreement would not help the solution of the Cyprus problem and warned that they did not want to see initiatives which would undermined the negotiation process held under the auspices of the UN.[53] On the other hand, Turkish authorities were adamant in extending to the Turkish Cypriots the suggestion that the integration with Turkey would always be available for them as an alternative.[54]

In spite of the initial EU and American unwillingness, it was the Greek and Greek Cypriot side, which managed to make the matter of membership to the EU an inseparable part of the Cyprus question with their insistent policies.[55] The plan of the Greek side was the following: "If the Greek Cypriots entered the EU as equal members even before a solution to the political division of Cyprus has been found, then – in Athens's view – there would be a more active and favourable European involvement. This would force Turkey, which is interested in close relations to the community, to accept a solution of the Cyprus problem in favour of Greek positions."[56] Regardless the motives of the parties were, some circles began to question whether the EU membership could play a catalyst role in bringing the two communities in Cyprus together. The UN Security Council and the EU Council had some hopes in this direction. They held the view that this new aspect could help the solution of the problem by putting pressures on both sides. But it was also asserted that the EU should work on the basis of what had been achieved by the UN Secretary-General and should remain in close touch with the American side. The European leaders also should "avoid a situation where facilitators competed with each other or are played off against one another."[57] Some argued that the prospect of negotiations for Cyprus admission to the EU challenged the relatively stable division of the island and was complicating rather than helping the resolution of the problems between the Greek and Turkish Cypriots.[58] Turkish Prime Minister Ecevit claimed that American special envoy Holbrooke stressed that the EU was largely responsible for the stalemate on the island.[59]

THE HOLBROOKE INITIATIVE

In early 1996, the Americans intensified their efforts to solve the Cyprus problem again. After ensuring the signing of the Dayton Agreement in Bosnia-Herzegovina, American President Clinton appointed the architect of this agreement, Richard Holbrooke, as his special envoy for Cyprus to benefit from the positive atmosphere in solving the Cyprus question. But Holbrooke, who spoke of applying the Dayton model to Cyprus, had to postpone his scheduled visit to Cyprus at the end of January 1996 because of the Kardak crisis between Turkey and Greece. Thus it was apparent in very start that the Cyprus question was not only

---

[53] SİSAV, *1997 Yılı Sonu İtibariyle Kıbrıs Sorunu*, pp. 13, 14.
[54] The statements of Foreign Minister İsmail Cem in his press conference during his visit to the TRNC.
[55] Emiliou, "Knocking on the Door...", pp. 127, 128.
[56] Peter Zervakis, "The Accession of Cyprus to the EU: The Greek Viewpoint" in Axt and Brey (ed.) *Cyprus and the European Union*, p. 139.
[57] Franz Eichinger, "Cyprus and the EU from the German Point of View" in Axt ve Hansjörg Brey (ed.) *Cyprus and the European Union*, p. 201.
[58] Roper, "The West and Turkey...", p. 93.
[59] Ahmet C. Gazioğlu (ed.), *Cyprus, EU and Turkey: Selected Extracts from the World Press*, Nicosia: CYREP, 1998, p. 101.

an ethnic conflict, but it was included in rather complicated problems and relations of the two important states of the region. In spite of apparent negative points of this problem, the Americans still believed that new initiatives would bring positive developments because of some factors. Firstly, the Greeks had started to pursue more pragmatic policies as it was proved by their attitude toward the EU-Turkish Customs Union agreement. Secondly, the European decision of starting the membership negotiations with Cyprus could lead the Turkish Cypriots to hold a more conciliatory attitude. Finally, the USA was in a better position in compared with its previous standing in playing the role of mediator between the sides.[60]

In the aftermath of the Kardak crisis, Turkish Foreign Minister Mesut Yılmaz offered "to the Greek government a package of solutions and proposals concerning all problems in the Aegean and set no precondition in order to create an atmosphere of confidence." The American administration expressed its pleasure with the Turkish proposal and announced that it was ready to participate into the negotiations as the third party.[61] However, the Greek indifference to the matter prevented the likelihood of a serious progress which might also help the Cyprus issue. The events of July 1996 in the Turkish-Greek frontier in Cyprus further aggravated the situation. When a Greek Cypriot was killed because he tried to lower the Turkish flag, the American administration showed a severe reaction to the incident. The spokesman of the American State Department, Nicholas Burns, stated that the flag was not important than human life whereas the coalition partner in the Turkish government, Tansu Ciller threatened "to break the hands which stretch to the Turkish flag". The effort of American Secretary of State Madelaine Albright to arrange a meeting between the military commanders of the two sides in order to reduce the tensions and prevent the events in the frontier, too, failed.[62]

In the following period, the American authorities were worried about the outbreak of a Turkish-Greek war and therefore they avoided taking the Greek side as the EU did in the disagreements between the two states.[63] The Cyprus question was one of the most important issues which the Americans handled sensitively in this regard. In May 1997, with the encouragement of the Americans, the Greek Cypriots announced that Greek warplanes would not fly over Cyprus during the Greek-Greek Cypriot joint military exercises. Turkey responded favourably to this action by declaring that it would not fly its warplanes over Cyprus. However, in October 1997 the Greeks and the Greek Cypriots carried out the joint military exercise of Nikiforos and Turkey and the TRNC retaliated by organising the exercise of Toros.[64]

Meanwhile, American special envoy for Cyprus Holbrooke intensified his initiatives in the second half of 1997. At first, he waited for the end of Denktash-Clerides meeting in Troutbeck on 9-13 July, which was their first face to face meeting after a three-year interval. In the meantime, the visit of Turkish Prime Minister to Cyprus to join the celebrations for the anniversary of the Turkish military intervention in 1974 agitated the Americans. In their eyes,

---

[60] F. Stephen Larrabee, "Yunanistan ve Balkanlar: Politika Önerileri" in Allison and Nikolaydis (ed.), *Yunan Paradoksu*, pp. 138-139.
[61] Hüseyin Bağcı, "Cyprus: Accession to the European Union- A Turkish View" in Axt and Brey (ed.) *Cyprus and the European Union*, p. 165.
[62] Dodd, *The Cyprus Imbroglio*, p. 95, Polat, *Washington Entrikaları*, pp. 163-164.
[63] Fotios Moustakis and Micheal Sheehan, "Greek Security Policy After the Cold-War", *Contemporary Security Politics*, vol. 21, No. 3, December 2000, p. 109.
[64] Roper, "The West and Turkey...", p. 93.

it was important not to harm the atmosphere of good relations between Turkey and Greece, which was brought about by the Madrid summit of NATO on 8-9 July,[65] through these kinds of actions.[66] During the Denktash-Clerides negotiations in Switzerland on 11-16 August, UN Special envoy Diego Cordovez presented two documents, one of which was a draft of joint statement, including the points the sides agreed. The other was about the negotiation process and principles. While Denktash declared he would not accept any document in the negotiations, Clerides stated that their attitude toward the document was positive though they had some reservations. This development led the UN Security Council members to hold the Turkish side responsible for the failure of the negotiations. On 26 September 1997, Denktash and Clerides met again, this time in Nicosia, to talk about the security matters, but nothing came out from the meeting.[67] In November, Holbrooke told Denktash during his visit to the United States that the participation of the Turkish Cypriots to the EU membership negotiations would be in the interest of Turkey. On 11 November, Holbrooke held a meeting in Ledra Palace on the Green Line with the leaders of the Cypriot communities. Apart from some progress on missing persons, nothing was achieved. Holbrooke was not upset because he did not expect serious outcomes from that kind of unofficial meeting.[68]

The end of 1997 witnessed serious developments on the Cyprus issue. In its Luxembourg summit, the European Union decided to start full membership negotiations with the Greek Cypriot administration whereas Turkey's name was not mentioned among the countries with which the EU would start membership negotiations in the future. The decision had been taken in spite of the opposition of the Americans, who believed that starting negotiations with the Greek Cypriots would be balanced with the acceptance of Turkey's candidacy for full membership. The Turkish side concluded that seeking for a bizonal federal state solution and continuing the inter-communal negotiations lost their meaning. The Turkish Cypriots would then try to acquire the recognition of the TRNC as having the status of equal and independent state before sitting the negotiation table. Turkey declared that it would not talk to and consult with the European Union any political matter including the Cyprus issue in the future. As it was stated by Turkish Foreign Minister İsmail Cem in his press conference on 30 March 1998, Turkey was in favour of the continuation of the TRNC's separate independent entity. If a federal state would be established in the future, this could be possible only with the continuation of the independent and equal status of the Turkish Cypriot side.[69]

In early 1998, Holbrooke launched a new peace initiative by talking to the authorities in Nicosia, Athens and Ankara. But his proposals were not satisfactory for both sides. When he accused the Turkish side of not taking the negotiations seriously, the Greek Cypriots felt pleasure. When he mentioned of the existence of the two communities, whose ethnic origins, languages and beliefs were different, the Turkish Cypriots considered it the approval of their viewpoints. Holbrooke's stated in his press conference on 4 May 1998: "I think it is very clear... that Glafcos Clerides does not represent or have control of the people of northern Cyprus." According to Holbrooke, the issues that were involved were all solvable, but the sides had to have a negotiation. If one of the sides did not wish to negotiate, that would not be

---

[65] Suat Bilge, *Büyük Düş: Türk-Yunan İlişkileri*, Ankara: 21. Yüzyıl Yay., October 2000, p. 269.
[66] Dodd, *The Cyprus Imbroglio*, pp. 101, 103.
[67] SİSAV, *1997 Yılı Sonu İtibariyle Kıbrıs Sorunu*, p. 15.
[68] *The Turkish Yearbook of International Relations*, No. 27, 1997, pp. 157-158, 160.
[69] Theophanous, "Cyprus, the European Union...", p. 223.

a catastrophe. Holbrooke did not consider his trip a failure. He was of the opinion that the problems he countered were part of the process.[70]

Turkish authorities did not feel any special resentment toward Holbrooke. The spokesman of the Turkish government, Şükrü Sina Gürel claimed that the failure of Holbrooke's initiative was due to the completely erroneous approach of the EU, which decided to start unilateral membership negotiations with the Greek Cypriots. According to Prime Minister Ecevit, there were some positive points in the attitude of Holbrooke. The American envoy had openly said that the southern Cyprus had no authority at all on the other part of the island and he, for the first time, referred to the north with its proper name (TRNC). Holbrooke also seemed to have realised that the Dayton model or the Irish model could not be applied to Cyprus. In the opinion of Turkish Cypriot leader Denktash, the Greek lobby in the USA started attacking Holbrooke after he referred Denktash as the elected leader of the Turkish Cypriots. If there were not the Greek lobby, Holbrooke would have spoken more openly.[71]

An important development which occurred during Holbrooke's term as special envoy for Cyprus was the initiative of the Greek Cypriots to purchase S-300 missiles from Russia. Turkish Foreign Minister Tansu Çiller responded severely to this development by declaring that Turkey would not hesitate in removing these missiles by force, if necessary. The spokesman of the American State Department, Nicholas Burns, did not approve this reaction and he emphasised that Turkey did not have the right to threaten Greece. But the Americans were also not happy about the Greek Cypriot initiative. Carey Cavanagh, the director of the Office of South European Affairs, toured the capitals of the sides to obtain the assurance that the missiles would not be deployed for next sixteen months. The threat to the stability to the eastern Mediterranean caused by the rapid armament of the Greek Cypriots and the severe Turkish response led the Americans to intervene in the matter.[72] On 6 January 1997, the American administration criticised the Greek Cypriots severely for their initiative of purchasing S-300 missiles. According to Yalçın Doğan, during his visit to Washington in the second half of 1998, Turkish Prime Minister Mesut Yılmaz obtained assurances from American President Bill Clinton that Russia would not sell those missiles. Clinton wanted to prevent the Turkish side, which was felt free itself in taking any action because of the EU's attitude on the candidacies of Turkey and the Greek Cypriots for full membership, from launching a radical action in Cyprus.[73]

In February 1998, the following development was mentioned in the press: the S-300 missiles was supposed to reach Cyprus in April, but the American pressures led the sides to promise that the delivery of the missiles would not be materialised at least until August.[74] In the eyes of the Americans, the initiative was a needlessly provocative effort complicating their diplomatic efforts on Cyprus. Russia, whose primary aim was to prop up their ailing military industry, might have other motivations such as extending their influence to the regions and creating problems for NATO. American authorities also believed that the deployment of the S-300 missiles would undermine the security of Cyprus. These weapons were effective enough to worry the Turks, but not effective enough to alter the basic military

---

[70] From the web site of the Turkish Foreign Ministry.
[71] Interviews with Denktash and Ecevit, *Turkish Daily News,* 12 and 17 May 1998.
[72] Dodd, *The Cyprus Imbroglio*, pp. 99, 101.
[73] SİSAV, *1997 Yılı Sonu İtibariyle Kıbrıs Sorunu*, p. 19.
[74] Steve Rodan, "Russia Asks Israel to Keep Out of S-300 Deal", *Defense News*, 23 February- 1 March 1998.

equation or prevent a Turkish invasion.[75] Meanwhile, some newspapers accused US officials of spreading rumours about the possibility of a serious incident in Cyprus. Their main aim was to raise local opposition to the deployment of the missiles and to undermine the morale of the Greek Cypriots in order to force them to accept any solution.[76]

In the end, the American pressures played role in the Greek decision of installing the missiles in the island of Crete instead of Cyprus. Although they did not admit their role publicly, the only reason for this attitude was not to annoy the Greek Cypriots for the sake of reaching a solution. The American spokesman stated in the Pentagon regular briefing on 4 February 1999 that the USA had long opposed the deployment of the S-300 missiles to Cyprus because it held the view that anything which increased the tensions between Turkey and Greece did not serve interests of these two countries, the USA or NATO. When he was asked whether American officials asked the Greeks to do got the missiles instead of Cyprus to the island of Crete, the spokesman answered: "I cannot tell you whether we played that active role in this issue or not." American Secretary of State Albright told Greek Cypriot Foreign Minister Kosoulides on 17 February 1999 that their courageous decision not to deploy the S-300 missiles to Cyprus opened up new opportunities to find a resolution for the Cyprus problem.

THE 1999-2001 PERIOD

The Events

The mutual sincere offers of help during the devastating earthquakes in Turkey and Greece in 1999 brought about a new period of détente in relations between the two countries. The mutual visits of the foreign ministers of Greece and Turkey, George Papandreou and İsmail Cem, to each other's country and their positive approach caused new hopes for the solution of the Cyprus problem as well. The problem had reached a point of deadlock because the EU membership process of the Greek Cypriots continued while Turkey was not granted even the candidacy status. The Turkish side was adamant that it would not negotiate with the Greek Cypriots unless its equal status was recognised. But the new positive atmosphere could not be missed. It was inevitable that the outside powers, especially the USA, would intervene and the sides would start proximity talks to meet the reservations of the Turkish side. In fact, American President Clinton informed the press members aboard Airforce One en route to Ankara for the OSCE meeting that Clerides and Denktash accepted an invitation to start proximity talks in New York on 3 December. The goals of the talks would be to prepare the ground for the meaningful negotiations leading to a comprehensive settlement of the Cyprus problem.

It appeared that the suitable conditions for a progress on Cyprus were present. Turkey and Greece were living through an extraordinary détente period. Turkey had the opportunity to demonstrate its strategic importance by hosting the meeting of the OSCE. American President Clinton, who considered Turkey as the centre of the world politics of the 21st century, was visiting Turkey. The high-level representatives of Turkey, the USA and the other

---

[75] Micheal R. Gordon, "Russia Planning to Ship Anti-Aircraft Missiles to Greek Cypriots", *The New York Times*, 29 April 1998.
[76] "Stop Playing Poker with the Missiles" (The Editorial), *The Cyprus Mail*, 14 May 1998.

concerned countries signed a document expressing their support for the realisation of the Baku-Ceyhan pipeline. In this important turning point, Turkey could bring about some progress in Cyprus to strengthen its increasing strategic importance in world politics. If the Cyprus issue were solved, Greece and Turkey would save their foreign policies from the restrictions of this problem and would be able to use their resources for their economic development. Moreover, President Clinton would increase his prestige greatly by solving an ages-old problem before the end of his presidency.

It seemed that with the encouragement of the Americans, Turkish authorities persuaded the Greek Turkish Cypriot leadership in joining the proximity talks in New York. The dialogue on Cyprus reached high points. American diplomats put forward proposals through their colleagues in the UN.[77] As an interesting coincidence, the proximity had started one week before the Helsinki summit of the EU. The EU's granting Turkey the status of candidacy for full membership with the removal of the Greek veto was a development which would boost the Cyprus negotiations. One reason for Turkey's adamant attitude on Cyprus had been abolished. It appeared that a different version of the Turkish-Greek bargaining on 6 March 1995 was put into practice again with the help of the Americans. This time, in return for gaining the candidate status, Turkey seemed to give implicit approval to the EU decision that a political settlement of the Cyprus problem would not be a precondition for Cyprus' accession to the EU.[78] Nevertheless, Turkish authorities seemed to feel more pleasure rather than enmity toward the EU decisions. President Clinton, too, was happy about the development; he thanked Greek Prime Minister Simitis for Greece's strong support for Turkey.[79]

The mutual visits of the Greek and Turkish foreign ministers to each other's capital in January and February 2000 (these visits were the first in their kinds, which were made after 37 and 40-year intervals respectively) were encouraging for the Cyprus issue as well. According to President Clinton's letter to the Speaker of the House of Representatives and the Chairman of the Senate Committee on Foreign Relations, dated as 7 March 2000, UN Secretary-General Annan reported that the Greek and Turkish Cypriots were engaged seriously on the whole range of issues that divided them. American President's Special Envoy for Cyprus, Alfred H. Moses and his team provided critical diplomatic support for the UN efforts. Moses, too, emphasised in his arrival statement at Larnaca Airport on 7 March 2000 that what constructive was that Denktash and his party were engaged in a negotiating process. In that point, the Americans did not comment on whether the position of one side or the other was constructive. They were not the party that had to decide on the agreement. Both sides encouraged them to come with fresh ideas. The sides had positions that were different, but there was recognition that what was ultimately in the interest of both sides was a comprehensive settlement on the island. Security was critical in the negotiations. The parties had to feel secure. Moses also stated on 10 March: he was encouraged by the commitment on both sides that this process was one that should be pursued to arrive a comprehensive settlement. In his opinion, they were moving in the right direction. Both sides were serious and both sides expressed to him that there was no alternative to a united Cyprus.

---

[77] *The Economist*, "Talks About Talks", 4 December 1999, vol. 353, No. 8148, p. 49.
[78] Theophanous, "Cyprus, the European Union...", p. 223.
[79] Moustakis and Sheehan, "Greek Security Policy...", s. 111.

The fourth round of the negotiations were held between 12 and 16 September 2000 in New York. In the opening of the talks, Kofi Annan made a speech emphasising that the communities on the island were politically independent parties not representing each other. He underlined the necessity that the parties should reach a comprehensive solution requiring a new partnership through negotiations, to which they would participate with their equal status. In his opinion, the equal status of the parties should be transformed to clear political provisions and should be included in the comprehensive solution clearly.[80] These statements were pleasing for the Turkish side while they attracted the reaction of the Greek Cypriots. In spite of the long-held negotiations, the failure in making any progress in solving the problem brought the worry again that it might have been returned to the fruitless efforts of the past. The Nikiforos-Toksotis military exercise of the Greeks and the Greek Cypriots between on 17 and 21 October 2000 strengthened this fear. According to the statement of the Turkish foreign ministry, the exercise was carried out on the basis of the scenarios of attacks against the Turkish side and Greek warplanes landed on the airbase in Paphos.[81] The statement of the UN Secretary-General on 8 November included points which attracted the reaction of the Turkish side. Annan emphasised that his statement constituted a basis for further negotiations and he called the sides to give a response to its content, but the Turkish side had already been alienated from the negotiation process. The negotiations were interrupted and it was not clear when they would resume.

On 11 January 2001, during his visit to Ankara, American President's Special Envoy for Cyprus Moses gave information on the negotiation process: In their discussions with the representatives of Turkey, Greece and the Turkish communities, he and his team emphasised the importance of continuation of the UN-led negotiations. All of the leaders with whom they met were of the opinion that a comprehensive settlement was preferable to the continuation of the status quo. Denktash and Turkish Prime Minister Ecevit had some objections to the current process. The American team discussed the issue of the Turkish side's coming back to the negotiating table with Denktash intensively. Although Denktash gave the assurances that he would carefully consider the views of the Americans, the ideas of the American were not finally agreed upon by the Turkish Cypriot side and there were also no commitments from the Turks to resume talks at that time. In the opinion of the Americans, the oral remarks of the UN Secretary-General on 8 November 2000 were not intended to be a framework agreement or something comparable to the Set of Ideas. They were not something definite that either party had to accept or that was intended to favour one side or the other. In short, from the American point of view, the Turkish side indicated their displeasure with the continuation of the proximity talks, proving that they were the side which did not want to dance.

According to Turkish Foreign Minister İsmail Cem, there was no interruption in the negotiation process, but it was entered into a period of waiting. The change of the American administration and the scheduled elections in the Greek Cypriot part of Cyprus on 27 May 2001 played role in this development. First of all, the new American administration would determine its Cyprus policy, then if the Americans insisted on the resumption of the negotiations after the Greek Cypriot elections, the parties would have to meet again. In his first Cyprus report, which he sent to the Chairman of the Senate Committee on Foreign Relations, Jesse Helms, and the Speaker of the House of Representatives, Dennis Hastert,

---

[80] *Dışişleri Güncesi: September 2000,* Ankara: TC Dışişleri Bakanlığı, p. 135.
[81] *Dışişleri Güncesi: October 2000.* Ankara: TC Dışişleri Bakanlığı, p. 197.

new American President George Bush mentioned the contacts of Clinton's Special Envoy for Cyprus Moses, Special Co-ordinator for Cyprus Tom Weston and American Ambassador in Nicosia Donald Bandler with the concerned parties. One important development in that conjunction was the abolishment of the office of President's Special Envoy for Cyprus by the Americans. This development might be interpreted as that the new American administration was not willing to put pressures on the parties to the Cyprus problem. Since the Turkish side felt more outside pressures, they could be pleased with this incident. But the eruption of heavy economic crises in Turkey and the TRNC underlined the possibility that the Turkish side might be open to more pressures on Cyprus because of their need for foreign economic help. Moreover, one possibility was that Cyprus would become a serious problem in Turkish-American relations. According to one scenario, Turkey would try to obtain the American opposition to the completion of the Greek Cypriot membership negotiations with the EU. Since they would know certainly that their efforts would not be successful, the Americans would only watch the Greek Cypriot side's becoming a full member of the EU. When the Turkish side, which was alienated totally, chose to integrate the TRNC with Turkey, their relations with the USA and the EU countries would deteriorate seriously and they would be isolated in the international arena. It can be derived from this scenario that the USA would not feel necessity to pressurise the sides of the Cyprus problem and to take the issue to the international agenda.

The Third Sides

One party which expressed its opinions on Cyprus to the disadvantage of the Turkish side is the Group-8. Especially the Americans are able to convey their opinions, which they cannot express openly because of the fear of alienating the Turks, to the international public opinion through the G-8 joint declarations. The G-8 generally asserts that the two sides should sit on the negotiation table without any precondition. Since the Greek Cypriots are the side, which are recognised officially, the attitude of the G-8 benefits them rather than the Turks. The Turkish Grand National Assembly, which believes that the G-8 considers the Cyprus issue with the initiative of Greece, has stated that the G-8 gives orders to the UN in the Cyprus issue and has condemned the intervention of the G-8 in the matter. In one of his interviews with a Turkish newspaper, Foreign Minister Cem stated the pressures of the external powers such as the G-8 escalated the situation in Cyprus and rendered a settlement more difficult.[82] The Turkish foreign ministry responded to the joint declaration of the G-8 on 23 July 2000 by emphasising that the G-8's proposals of solution did not have any opportunity to be accepted since they were not based on the consent of the sides.[83]

The decisions, actions and attitude of the UN Security Council, too, are generally in contradiction with the opinions of the Turkish side on the Cyprus issue. Recently, a serious disagreement has emerged between the two sides on the extension of the term of the UN Force in Cyprus. The Council's resolution on 14 June 2000 stated that the term of the force was extended with the consent of the government of Cyprus without mentioning the consent of the Turkish Cypriot side. On the contrary to the past practices, the Council did not issue this time an addendum which required that the UN Force sign an agreement with the TRNC

---

[82] Interview with İsmail Cem, *Turkish Daily News*, 28-29 July 1999.

regulating its activities on the north of the island. The reaction of the Turkish Foreign Ministry to the UN resolution was harsh: There was no government in Cyprus, representing the whole island as it was stated by the resolution. The UN Force was able to continue its activities with the co-operation of the TRNC government. The resolution was contrary to the principle of the equality of the sides in Cyprus. Turkey would not recognise this resolution and would reconsider the future of its relations with the UN Force. Turkish President Ahmet Necdet Sezer reacted to the resolution by stressing that the northern Cyprus was neither a no man's land nor a territory under the authority of the Greek Cypriots. If the UN Force wanted to continue its activities in Northern Cyprus, it had to obtain the consent and co-operation of the Turkish authorities.[84]

The resolution of the UN Security Council on 13 December 2000, too, mentioned only the consent of the Cypriot government. Thus, the UN established the practice of not taking the consent of the both sides. According to the Turkish side, this situation undermined the basis of the activities of the UN Force in Northern Cyprus. This was a dangerous development. The Turkish Foreign Ministry issued a statement asserting that the UN resolution was contrary to the text and spirit of the statement of the UN Secretary-General on 12 September 2000, which emphasised the political equality of the two communities. Turkey announced once more that it would not recognise such kind of resolutions. The American authorities did not share the views of the Turkish side on this matter. In the State Department's noon briefing on 14 December 2000, Spokesman Boucher clarified that the renewal resolution urged the Turkish side to rescind the restrictions that it had imposed on peacekeepers. He also added that the American administration would strongly oppose any additional measured to restrict the operations by the UN forces in Cyprus.

Another party whose opinions and actions on Cyprus are not approved by the Turkish side is the EU. In the opinion of the Turkish side, the EU has exhibited an unjust act violating principles of law and complicated the Cyprus question further by starting membership negotiations with the Greek Cypriot side. Statements, decisions and practices of different organs of the EU on the Cyprus issue as well as their attitude of considering this matter as a precondition of Turkey's becoming member of the EU annoy the Turkish authorities considerably. While responding to the acceptance of the report of Reporter Poos on the situation of Cyprus's membership negotiations by the General Assembly of the European Parliament on 4 October 2000, the Turkish Foreign Ministry stated that the members of the European Parliament approached the Cyprus issue by holding a biased view and leaving the realities aside. The EU's general attitude of considering the Turkish forces in Cyprus as the occupying forces, too, cannot be acceptable form the Turkish point of view.[85]

In the latter period of 1997-1999, the EU concerned that leaving Turkey outside the candidacy status for the EU membership might end the Cyprus diplomacy completely and might bring about serious crises between Greece and Turkey.[86] Ultimately, the EU ratified the candidacy status of Turkey in the Helsinki summit and thus the hopes for a progress in Cyprus were renewed. But the EU made no substantial change in its attitude toward the Cyprus issue, did not undertake any commitment on the membership of the Greek Cypriot

[83] *Dışişleri Güncesi: July 2000,* pp. 86-87.
[84] *Dışişleri Güncesi: June 2000,* pp. 71, 105-106.
[85] *Dışişleri Güncesi: October 2000,* pp. 39, 248.
[86] Alan Makovsky, "Turkey and the European Union: One More Try", Makovsky, "New Activism in Turkish Foreign Policy". (The articles of Makovsky are taken from the web site of The Washington Institute.)

and did not start membership negotiations with Turkey. The possibility of the Greek Cypriots' becoming member of the EU before Turkey was still high.[87] The new approach of the EU was that it would take into consideration all the relevant factors in deciding on the membership of Cyprus, but it would take its decision without being bound with the opinions of the sides. It was clear that the EU did not agree with the Turkish side's view that the international agreements and regulations of 1960 on Cyprus prohibited Cyprus's becoming member of the EU. The EU's announcement that the political solution of the Cyprus problem would not be a condition of the membership of Cyprus in the EU was also not in the interest of Turkey.

One idea which is put by some strategists is that through the policies which it pursues on the Cyprus issue, the EU will prove that it is an able power. In their opinion, the EU will also disprove in this way the claims that it cannot handle serious international problems such as Cyprus and cannot solve them without the help of the USA. If the EU pursues a coherent and strong foreign and security policy, it would be able to contribute to the solution of the Cyprus problem substantially. And if the EU solves this problem and completes the accession of Cyprus to its structure, this would symbolise its commitment to the security of the Mediterranean and the West decisively and would demonstrate its weight in world politics. On the contrary, if the EU fails to take such a determined attitude, its ability to influence developments in Cyprus would be reduced and it would appear that the EU is not a major power which is able to compete with other world powers. That kind of attitude would also have a negative impact on the interests of the EU itself in the eastern Mediterranean and beyond.[88] Such provocative opinions imply serious repercussions such as being isolated in the Cyprus issue for Turkey. It is assumed that in such likelihood, Turkey will expect that the Americans will resist the EU action to maintain its world leadership, but the Americans will not act in this way not to alienate the newly emerging European power.

THE 2001-2002 PERIOD

On the Cyprus question, five rounds of proximity talks were held between 3 December 1999 and 10 November 2000 "with a view to preparing the ground for meaningful negotiations which would lead to a comprehensive settlement". The opening statement made by the UN Secretary-General Annan at the fourth round on 12 September 2000 reaffirmed that the two peoples on the Island are politically equal parties who do not represent each other and underlined the need for the two parties to reach a comprehensive settlement through talks in which they would participate as equals. The Greek Cypriot side rejected it in a decision of its "House of Representatives" on 11 October 2000. On the other hand, as a response to a paper entitled "Oral Remarks", which was presented by the UN Secretary-General to the two sides on 8 November 2000, Turkey and the Turkish Republic of Northern Cyprus stressed that it was not possible to take the views expressed in this paper, which, let alone "confederation", fell behind even "federation", seriously. The Turkish side considered it not useful to continue with the proximity talks due to the negative way in which the talks

---

[87] Ishtiaq Ahmad, "Prospects of Cyprus Settlement After the Helsinki Summit", *Marmara Journal of European Studies*, c. 8, No. 1-2, 2000, p. 60.
[88] Theophanous, "Cyprus, the European Union...", p. 224.

progressed and until the reasonable and realistic parameters put forward by the Turkish Cypriot side were accepted.

One important recent development on the Cyprus question was the abolishment of the office of President's Special Envoy for Cyprus by the Americans. This development might be interpreted as that the new American administration was not willing to put pressures on the parties to the Cyprus problem. Since the Turkish side felt more outside pressures, they could be pleased with this incident. But the eruption of heavy economic crises in Turkey and the Turkish Republic of Northern Cyprus underlined the possibility that the Turkish side might be subjected to more pressures on Cyprus because of its for foreign economic help. Moreover, one possibility was that Cyprus would become a serious problem in Turkish-American relations. According to one scenario, Turkey would try to obtain the American opposition to the completion of the Greek Cypriot membership negotiations with the EU. Since they would know certainly that their efforts would not be successful, the Americans would only watch the Greek Cypriot side's becoming a full member of the EU. When the Turkish side, which was alienated totally, chose to integrate the TRNC with Turkey, their relations with the USA and the EU countries would deteriorate seriously and they would be isolated in the international arena. It can be derived from this scenario that the USA would not feel any necessity to pressurise the sides of the Cyprus problem.

After unsuccessful attempts of the UN representative to bring sides together again, on 4 December 2001 the leaders of the two Cypriot communities, Clerides and Denktash held an unexpected face-to-face meeting in the buffer zone in Cyprus. UN representative De Soto was also present for the purpose of note taking. De Soto read a statement after the meeting, announcing that the two leaders agreed to enter into direct talks in mid-January 2002. According to the statement, the negotiations would start without preconditions, as all issues on the table and continue under the auspices of the UN until a comprehensive settlement was achieved and nothing would be agreed until everything was agreed.[89]

The new development can be seen as the result of different factors. The EU will decide on the accession of Cyprus at the end of 2003 and it is possible that Cyprus can be among the first line countries whose accession process will be completed in 2004. For the Turkish Cypriots, it is important to launch one more initiative to find a political solution to the Cyprus problem with the Greek Cypriots before this process is completed. If their initiative bring success, they can join the EU with the Greek Cypriots in conjunction with the high possibility that Turkey will be granted a prospect of becoming member of the EU in a near future after this development. If Cyprus becomes full member of the EU before a political solution is found to the Cyprus problem, the Turkish Cypriots might have to take radical steps as a reaction. In this case, they will not want to be accused of not holding serious negotiations with the Greek Cypriot side before the process is completed. By initiating the new round of negotiations, they will be able to defend their radical acts in the future.

On the other hand, the Greek Cypriot side definitely expects that Cyprus will be a full member of the EU in a near future, a likelihood which will force the Turkish Cypriot side to recognise the authority of the Cypriot government and which will rob them of every kind of opportunity to take steps harming the Greek Cypriot interests. Holding inter-communal negotiations with the Turkish side for the time being will not bring any problem for them, and on the contrary, it will increase their prestige in the eyes of the international community. They

---

[89] http://www.mfa.gov.tr/grupb/bf/developmentsCyprus.htm.

have nothing to lose from the failure of the negotiations. Besides, the present negotiations will decrease the likelihood that the world powers such as the United States will oppose Cyprus's becoming member of the EU for strategic reasons.

In the new development, outside intervention is also possible. The Western world under the leadership of the USA now faces a new international situation after the terrorist attacks in the USA on 11 September 2001. In the new period, it is very important for the United States to maintain the unity of the Western world and to solve the problems constituting source of trouble for the West in order to struggle against new threats more powerfully. The Cyprus problem has always the potential to cause a major conflict within the West and to harm the US interests in critical regions such as the eastern Mediterranean, the Middle East and the Central Asia. Turkey and Greece are important partners of the USA, which have vital place in American policies directed to these regions. The American authorities believe that it is now high time to remove the Cyprus issue from the agenda of Turkey, Greece, the USA and the EU as an irritating point. It is possible that the Americans might have persuaded the Greek and Turkish authorities in bringing their respective allies in Cyprus to negotiating table again.

Chapter 9

CONCLUSION

THE ASSESSMENT OF THE 1960-1975 PERIOD

The only shadow over close relations between Turkey and the United States in the 1950s had been the US unwillingness to supply a stabilisation fund to Turkey to help its balance of payments problems. After a four-year debate, the Turkish government had to accept strict US conditions in 1958 to be able to obtain the fund.[1] After the withdrawal of Iraq from the Baghdad Pact as a result of a military coup, the United States assured Turkish rulers of the US commitment to Turkish security by signing a bilateral agreement in 1959. In the eyes of opposition Republican People's Party's members this American act was aimed at saving the rightist Democrat Party government. While RPP leaders warmly welcomed the overthrow of the DP regime by the military coup of 27 May 1960, which could be seen by them as an anti-American act in those circumstances, DP supporters believed that the Americans abandoned them and cite as proof growing US displeasure with their government toward the end of the 1950s.

Hence both the US attitude toward the coup and the military junta's actions in Turkey's alliance relations with the United States and NATO became particularly sensitive matters. In fact, in their first public announcement, Turkish military officers expressed their loyalty to their existing alliances and NATO, showing their intention not to make any changes in the traditional direction of Turkish foreign policy. The quick recognition of the new regime and the promise of economic and military aid to it by the United States proved that there would be no changes in US-Turkish relations. In fact, the Turkish military junta soon became more dependent on the USA because of its need for US financial assistance to achieve economic development and to improve the welfare of Turkish military officers. Therefore, it did not hesitate to sign bilateral agreements with the United States, to station the US-supplied Jupiter missiles on Turkish territory and even to facilitate the legislation of bilateral agreements with the United States by introducing a new constitutional procedure. Military rulers wanted to make some changes in rules applied to US personnel in Turkey but when the Americans seemed unwilling to give up their existing privileges, they did not pursue the matter.

---

[1] George S. Harris, *Troubled Alliance: Turkish-American Problems in Historical Perspective 1945-1971,* (Washington: American Enterprise Institute, 1972), pp. 74-75, Theodore A. Couloumbis, *the United States, Greece and Turkey: The Troubled Triangle,* (New York: Praeger, 1983), p. 19.

When the Cuban missile crisis broke in October 1962, the Turks still had warm feelings toward the United States. Turkish rulers and MPs proudly supported the US stance to expel the Soviet missiles from the Caribbean. There was no criticism in the Turkish press directed toward the firm US stance against the Soviet Union, which could cause a global nuclear war. When the possibility of trading Soviet missiles in Cuba with the Jupiters in Turkey was discussed in Western states and when it was proposed by Soviet Premier Khrushchev, the Turks did not make any comment about it and sincerely believed that their close ally America would not bargain the interests of a NATO member with the enemy camp.

Meanwhile, the pluralist 1960 constitution began to have its effects in Turkish politics. Using means provided by the constitution, marginal groups were able to voice their opinions and criticise basic tenets of the regime, including the traditional foreign policy line which was considered a taboo. Newspaper columns became the main platform of such discussions and criticism. As a start, the withdrawal of the Jupiter missiles were criticised on the ground that it decreased Turkey's strategic importance for the West and created a security gap for Turkish defence. During parliamentary discussions in 1963 the inadequacy of US military aid was subjected to criticism.

The most important thing which triggered the widespread anti-Americanism in Turkey was the Turkish belief that the United States did not work enough to stop atrocities against Turkish Cypriots, which began at the end of December 1963, but continuously prevented the Turkish government from intervening in Cyprus to protect lives and rights of Turkish people on the island. President Johnson's letter to Turkish Prime Minister İsmet İnönü in June 1964 further fuelled the anti-Americanism among Turkish people and brought radical changes in the thinking of Turkish rulers. Johnson had threatened that NATO might not come to Turkey's help if the Soviet Union attacked Turkey because of her intervention in Cyprus and he had reminded the Turks that they could not use US-supplied weapons in their actions in Cyprus. While mainly leftist groups and university students arranged mass demonstrations against the United States and attacked American buildings in major Turkish cities, Turkish authorities showed their disappointment over the US attitude with their statements. In one point Turkish Prime Minister İnönü hinted that Turkey could leave the Western camp. Nevertheless, frictions between the USA and Turkey on the official level did not last long. To change the unpleasant image of the United States among Turkish people, US leaders reiterated their commitment to Turkish security, offered more financial assistance and voted against the UN decision on Cyprus in December 1965, which supported the Greek cause. Turkish rulers announced that it was not their intention to change their foreign policy line and leave the Western camp.

After the rightist Justice Party came to power at the end of 1965, Turkish leftist groups increased their attacks against the United States and Turkey's alliance with this state and NATO. Columnists of Turkish newspapers except rightist ones joined leftists in criticising all aspects of Turkish-American relations, especially the Cyprus question and military contacts. Under public pressure and to prove their independence Turkish rulers took the following major actions which could be interpreted as anti-American: the withdrawal from the Multilateral Force, banning U-2 flights using Turkish territory, changing the duty status formula applied to US personnel, not allowing the use of the İncirlik base for non-NATO purposes, reviewing all bilateral military agreements with the USA and forcing this state to sign a new general military agreement. Turkish leaders also tried to improve relations with Eastern bloc countries through intensive state visits and economic agreements and to gain the sympathy of Third World and Arab countries by supporting their causes in the United Nations.

The Americans were not happy about the Turkish actions but they did not show resentment because these actions did not harm their fundamental interests which were fulfilled by the strong Turkish commitment to NATO and the US use of military facilities and bases on Turkish territory. The apparent pro-Turkish attitude of the United States during the November 1967 Cyprus crisis also ensured the closeness of US-Turkish relations on the official level until 1969. After 1969 Turkish rulers were subjected to US pressure on their opium production. The Americans had believed that Turkish opium provided 80 percent of heroin at US streets and thus made great contribution to the harrowing drug addiction problem among the American youth. Turkish authorities did not fulfil the US demand to prohibit opium cultivation because they did not want to lose the votes of poppy growers. Meanwhile, increasing terrorist actions against US personnel by Turkish leftists, who lost representation in the parliament to voice their opinion, posed another problem for the Americans.

The removal of the Turkish government from power by the military on 12 March 1971 and the subsequent rule by non-party, technocrat governments served mostly US interests. Under the martial law, extreme leftist groups were suppressed and thus anti-American criticism in newspaper columns and terrorist acts against US personnel stopped. More importantly, opium cultivation in Turkey was completely prohibited. However, the return of normal party politics at the end of 1973 brought problems for US-Turkish relations again. After an election period in which heavy criticism was directed against the opium ban, the coalition government of leftist Republicans and Islamist Salvationists decided to resume poppy production in June 1974 as an act of independence in spite of American protests. While the US Congress was busy with trying to cut off economic and military assistance to Turkey because of the new Turkish decision, the military coup in Cyprus and the subsequent Turkish intervention in Cyprus forestalled them.

The Turkish government was not unhappy with the US attitude toward its military intervention in Cyprus, which resulted in capturing 36 percent of the island, because the United States had not taken direct action to prevent or later to reverse the Turkish initiative. In fact, Turkish rulers were of the opinion that they had proved that their government was not under the US influence and was able to pursue Turkey's national interests effectively. However, the US Congress's action to impose an arms embargo on Turkey because of its intervention in Cyprus, starting from 5 February 1975, caused a new wave of anti-Americanism in Turkey. Turkish authorities were angry because they believed that the Congress action unilaterally violated principles of the US-Turkish alliance and undermined its basis. As a response, in July 1975 the coalition government of rightist parties, "the nationalist front", announced invalidity of US-Turkish bilateral agreements and closed down US facilities and bases in Turkey. Thus, relations between Turkey and the United States hit their lowest level though the alliance of the two states continued within the NATO framework.

In the 1960s and the 1970s, the goals and expectations of Turkey and the United States from their alliance were not so similar as they had been during the 1950s. Turkey wanted the alliance help its Cyprus cause whereas the United States expected that the close alliance relationship would induce the Turks to do a favour for America by prohibiting opium cultivation and by acting moderately on the Cyprus question. This situation caused problems in the two states' relations. In the 1960-1975 period, the US-Turkish alliance was considerably affected by developments in the international arena. The decrease of tension and conflict between the Eastern and Western blocs (détente) allowed both states to act more independently from restrictions of their alliance. The apparent decrease in the Soviet threat particularly let Turkish rulers improve their relations with Eastern bloc and Third World countries and give more emphasis to their national causes, especially the Cyprus problem. The Americans became less anxious about providing military and economic assistance to Turkey and went so far as to threaten Turkey with not protecting her against the Soviet camp.

In 1964, heavy US pressures on Turkish rulers prevented them from taking a major action in Cyprus, including military intervention. The Johnson letter in June 1964 in particular resembled an ultimatum sent by a colonial power to its vassal. However, the severe reaction of Turkish rulers and people induced the Americans to be more careful in their dealings with the Turks and avoid alienating them because they certainly did not want to lose benefits of their alliance with Turkey. Turkish actions after 1964 implied more independence from US influence. Turkey improved relations with states outside the Western camp, took some actions in military relations with the USA and supported causes of Arab and Third World countries in UN votings. However, she also remained strictly loyal to her commitment toward NATO, allowed the use of military bases on her territory by the United States and followed the US lead in UN votings on cold-war matters. Before 1971 Turkish rulers complied with most of the US demands on the opium question and showed sincere efforts to help the United States in this issue. However, in order not to lose electoral support and not to be seen as acting under the US influence, they did not fulfil the main American demand, prohibiting opium cultivation completely. The military-backed governments after March 1971 proved to be more receptive to US influences. They banned opium cultivation to prevent deterioration of relations with the United States.

The Ecevit government of 1974 was seen by many as the most independent of Turkish governments, pursuing Turkish interests without staying under US influence. In fact, it resumed poppy production and intervened in Cyprus militarily in spite of the US opposition. But at the same time it was anxious not to destroy the alliance with the USA nor to allow a serious deterioration of US-Turkish relations. Therefore, the Ecevit government was very careful in taking these decisions not to alienate the Americans. Moreover, the US administration was not altogether determined to prevent the Turkish intervention in Cyprus and on the opium question the Congress was doing enough to punish Turkey. The US arms embargo in February 1975 and the closure of bases by Turkey in July 1975 clearly showed that the Turkish-American alliance was not a patron-client relationship. However, Turkey's economic and military dependence on the USA was always a continuing fact in relations.

It has become clear from the study that a superpower inevitably gets involved in a matter which mainly concerns its small ally if this issue seems to have the potential to affect the alliance established by the superpower and the balance of power in a strategic region. As the leader of the Western camp, which had global interests, the United States got involved in the Cyprus question, which mainly concerned Turkey and Greece, and tried to influence its development to prevent any possible damage to NATO and her interests in the eastern Mediterranean. Superpowers certainly have the potential to influence decisions and actions of their small allies and even to force them to act in a certain way through threats of punishment. But they are restricted by certain factors such as their own interests while acting in this way. While they tried to prevent a proposed Turkish intervention in Cyprus, the Americans did not want to alienate the Turks totally and lose their alliance which brought considerable benefits for US interests. Moreover, Turkey was an independent state which could resist American demands especially on her vital national causes. Turkey's membership of NATO also diminished the possibility of any US armed action against Turkey such as had been applied to many Central American countries.

Open threats generally fail to force a small state to act in a certain way because they arouse public emotions. Public consensus on a matter which touches national feelings plays a great role in the determination of the small state's government in not yielding to pressures of its big ally. Turkey's adamant position on the Cyprus question and its military intervention in Cyprus could be explained by the tremendous support given by all segments of the Turkish population including the military.

Pressures from a superpower may lead its small ally to seek alternative sources of support for her security and national interests but the decision of this small ally to change sides or to opt for neutrality depends on her military and economic capabilities and the character of the international system. The small state may improve her relations with members of other blocs with the help of détente but she does not enter into defence contacts with these states if she does not want to lose her existing alliance. Turkish authorities had economic and cultural contacts with the Eastern bloc and the Third World and supported some of their causes in international forms but they did not buy a single weapon from these states in order not to loosen their defence co-operation with the West. In their eyes, the Western alliance provided the vital guarantee for Turkey's security.

Having alliance relations with a superpower may always bring difficulties for a small state. It may attract the threat of another superpower and may cause the involvement of the small state in superpower conflicts. The big ally's interference in internal affairs and its influence on domestic and foreign policy decisions are also possibilities. If the small power's elites are not careful in their dealings with the superpower and follow its lead with full trust, dangers for the small state increase. The Cuban crisis demonstrated all these dangers for Turkey. Turkish rulers were scolded by the American president severely on their intention to intervene in Cyprus. Turkey had to stop its opium production because of its alliance relationship with the USA. This incident also proved that military regimes which are militarily dependent on a superpower are more responsive to demands of the superpower.

One important fact is that internal conditions and public opinion on both sides play an important role in relations between two countries. Turkish policies on the opium and Cyprus questions and the US attitude on the opium and arms embargo issues were strongly influenced by internal public opinion. The sensitiveness of Turkish rulers to foreign influence and intervention, their long-pursued aim of integrating Turkey into the Western world, their evaluation of Turkey's strategic importance, their seeing the Cyprus issue as a vital national cause and the continuity of Turkey's traditional foreign policy line, too, had effects on US-Turkish relations. On the American side, anti-communism, the world leadership concept, realism during the Nixon administration, the Vietnam issue, the president's wide powers in formulating foreign policy, and the Congress's actions to curb the presidential power and to have a voice in foreign policy decisions were general elements of US foreign policy which also had repercussions on the US-Turkish alliance and the Cyprus question.

Some other conclusions on the Cyprus question may be summarised as follows: The Cyprus question was a test of the US-Turkish alliance in a matter which did not concern common security interests that constituted the basis of the alliance. The problem mainly concerned Turkish national interests and foreign policy. The United States interested in the development of the matter because of its global and strategic interests and policies, stemmed from being a superpower. Turkey would not advise or try to influence the United States in its policy toward Vietnam. The Johnson letter in 1964 had claimed that Turkish rulers had the commitment to consult with the US administration before taking any action in Cyprus. In fact, Turkish authorities always complied with this advice by informing the Americans on their action on Cyprus before initiating them. This situation gives the impression that the US-Turkish alliance bore some characteristics of the patron-client relationship. But it is also related to the Turkish perception that close allies should consult with each other in every matter concerning each state. Another reason for this attitude might be Turkish rulers' intention to use US opposition to appease agitated public opinion.

It is not true, as some Turks had claimed, that the United States was particularly opposed to the Turkish cause on Cyprus and supported the Greek side. She was mainly concerned with her own interests while reacting to developments in the Cyprus question. When she thought that pressuring Turkey was necessary she did not hesitate to act in this way. US pressures on Turkey before 1965 were really heavy and forced the Turks to abandon their proposed intervention in Cyprus. However, the Americans also had to consider the possibility of losing Turkey's alliance. Therefore, they did not take direct forceful actions such as the active involvement of the US Sixth Fleet in stopping Turkish ships. They also acted more cautiously after 1964 not to alienate the Turks, seeing the severe official Turkish response and the anti-Americanism among Turkish people. Turkey could threaten to leave NATO in the face of US pressures, but had to consider the consequences of her action. She certainly did not wish to be left alone against the Soviet threat; she needed US and NATO support for her security, and she did not want to weaken her position on Cyprus by losing all Western sympathy and understanding.

The US attitude toward the Cyprus problem before 1965 led Turkish rulers to be more cautious in their relations with the United States, suspecting that their interests could be adversely affected by US actions. It also inspired the Turks to have a more independent and flexible foreign policy by improving relations with the Eastern bloc, the Third World and neighbouring countries. So both the US-Turkish alliance and Turkish foreign policy were affected by developments in the Cyprus question.

The Americans managed to prevent Turkish intervention in Cyprus in November 1967. However, this time they took great care not to antagonise the Turks. Their influence was not too heavy at that time. But at the end the Americans achieved their objective of preventing Turkish intervention. In 1974 the United States failed to prevent the Turkish intervention in Cyprus. Its influence apparently did not work this time. But the Americans were not too determined in this direction. Turkey's strategic importance for US interests played a role in this attitude. The weakness of the US government because of the Watergate scandal was another factor. The Turks were not entirely free in their actions in Cyprus because of US pressures and opposition. They stopped their first intervention before achieving their original aims. And after capturing 36 percent of Cyprus they faced the punishment of the US Congress (the embargo and later conditioning of US assistance) whose effects have continued up to now. The embargo did not succeed in forcing the Turks to change their Cyprus policies radically but affected their future defence policies and increased their isolation in the international arena. The suspension of US activities in Turkish bases was Turkey's proof that she was not a satellite of the United States.

To summarise it, the following things could be said: The United States reluctantly became involved in the Cyprus question and reluctantly supported the scheme to station NATO soldiers in Cyprus. US officials believed that unification of Cyprus with Greece (Enosis) or Enosis with some concessions to Turkey would be the best solution of the Cyprus problem and worked for such schemes. While threatening to intervene in Cyprus militarily, Turkish rulers, especially Prime Minister İnönü, were not altogether determined to initiate such an action because of unpreparedness of the Turkish army. In any case, in 1964 American authorities were determined to stop a Turkish intervention in Cyprus. In the same period, Turkish authorities' hints on making changes in Turkey's traditional Western-oriented foreign policy were not genuine but were aimed at showing their disappointment over the Western attitude toward the Cyprus question.

During the Cyprus crisis of November 1967, US rulers did not show the same harsh attitude toward Turkish intervention threats but seemed to give more support to the Turkish position by working for the acceptance of Turkish demands. US officials ignored assassination and coup attempts against Greek Cypriot President Makarios between 1967 and 1974 but failed to predict the Cyprus coup on 15 July 1974. The US attitude after the coup showed that it was willing to accept the new situation and this forced and also gave a green light to Turks to intervene in Cyprus. US efforts to stop the Turkish action were not adequate and effective but also the Turks were unstoppable at that stage. The US attitude after the Turkish intervention tended to accept the new situation. The US arms embargo against Turkey in 1975 was mainly as a result of power competition between the Congress and the administration. But efforts of Greek-American lobbies and Congress dislike for the Turkish decision to resume poppy production also played a role in the embargo.

THE ASSESSMENT OF THE PRESENT SITUATION

Turkey's Point of View

Turkey supported the inter-communal talks on Cyprus, which were held in the context of the UN Secretary-General's good will, beginning in December 1999. However, determining the real character of these talks was very important for the Turkish authorities. In their opinion, since no suitable basis had been created yet to bring the sides together, the main purpose of those talks was to lay the groundwork for negotiations directed to finding a comprehensive solution. Turkish rulers considered the proximity talks as an important step which was taken in this direction and therefore they supported the continuation of the talks. However, as the two sides passed from one round to another, it became clear that the common ground could not be established and the Greek Cypriots did not give consent to recognising the equal status of the Turkish side. In that point, the Turkish authorities declared that the decision of moving to the phase of face-to-face negotiations would be taken by the president of the TRNC and the Turkish Cypriot government. They also asserted that the proposal of the Turkish Cypriots, projecting the establishment of a confederation and taking into consideration the EU aspect, was the most realist and viable alternative. Now it was up to the Greek Cypriots to take advantage of the talks to prepare the convenient ground. The Turkish government supported the views of the Turkish Cypriots completely and appreciated the leadership of Denktash.[2]

In his various statements, Turkish Foreign Minister İsmail Cem emphasised that it was the Turkish side, which was more active, more consistent in its opinions and which maintained the control over the development of the Cyprus issue. In his opinion, only the Turkish side brought proposals to the negotiating table, established dialogue with the USA, Britain and the EU on its own project, the confederation, and answered various opinions of these states in the matter. As a result, only the projects of the Turkish side were discussed and the other side did nothing other than rejecting the suggestions. Cem himself talked to the officials of the Western countries by feeling the comfort of being on the side which put the proposal of confederation and asked their opinion on the deficiencies of this project, but they could not find any deficiency. The only objection was raised against the term 'confederation'. According to Cem, the Turkish side was going on the right direction, its project was the strongest project and it should continue to follow this road. In this way, the insincerity of the Greek Cypriots would become apparent and the other powers would take more conciliatory attitude toward the Turkish side's position by understanding it more clearly.[3]

One position of the Turkish side, which was insistently proclaimed by Cem, was that Turkey would not raise the Cyprus issue with the Greek authorities in bilateral relations in the détente period between the two sides. Cem's statement in this matter was very clear: "Cyprus is not a matter of our bilateral relations... The Cyprus issue concerns only the two communities in Cyprus. Therefore we will not discuss this question in the context of the Greek-Turkish relations."[4] However, this attitude contradicted with the opinion of the Americans that the issue should be solved with the joint efforts of Turkey and Greece. Turkish authorities frequently complain about the actions of the Greek Cypriots, carrying bad intention. When the Greek Cypriots tried to prevent the international activities of the Turkish Cypriot universities, Turkish Foreign Ministry Spokesman Sermet Atacanlı considered it as an intervention in the right of education, demonstrating the hostile intentions of the Greek Cypriots toward the Turkish side.[5] The Turkish authorities also accuse the Greek Cypriot side of using the EU membership prospect as a tool to steal the rights of the Turkish Cypriots, granted by international agreements, and to tilt the balance between Turkey and Greece on Cyprus in favour of Greece. Therefore, the Turkish side strongly opposes to the intervention of the EU in the Cyprus question and to the establishment a connection between the Cyprus issue and Turkey's future membership in the EU. Turkish authorities also are not pleased with

---

[2] The statements of Vice Spokesman of Turkish Foreign Ministry Sermet Atacanlı on 17 February and 23 February 2000, *Dışişleri Güncesi: February 2000*, pp. 62, 123, the statement of the Turkish Foreign Ministry on 3 August 2000, *Dışişleri Güncesi: August 2000*, Ankara: TC Dışişleri Bakanlığı, p. 18, the statement of Turkish Prime Minister Ecevit on 8 September 2000, *Dışişleri Güncesi: September 2000*, Ankara: TC Dışişleri Bakanlığı, p. 43, the interview with Foreign Minister İsmail Cem on the Turkish television channel NTV, *Dışişleri Güncesi: May 2000*, Ankara: TC Dışişleri Bakanlığı, p. 17, the statement of the Turkish Foreign Ministry on 31 January 2000, *Dışişleri Güncesi: January 2000*, p. 144.

[3] The interview with Foreign Minister Cem on 2 April 2000 on the Turkish television Star *Dışişleri Güncesi: April 2000*, p. 32, the interview with Foreign Minister Cem on 28 May 2000 on the Turkish television TRT1, *Dışişleri Güncesi: May 2000*, p. 144, the press conference of Foreign Minister İsmail Cem on 1 September 2000, *Dışişleri Güncesi: September 2000*, p. 20, the interview with Foreign Minister İsmail Cem on 13 April 2000 on the Turkish television NTV, *Dışişleri Güncesi: April 2000*, pp. 135-136.

[4] The press conference of Foreign Minister İsmail Cem on 1 September 2000, *Dışişleri Güncesi: September 2000*, p. 19.

[5] The briefing of the Turkish Foreign Ministry on 27 March 2000, *Dışişleri Güncesi: March 2000*, p. 123.

the intervention of other third sides in the matter to force the Turkish side to a compromise by leaving aside its rights and interests. In their opinion, only the Cypriot communities can solve the problem.

Sporadic statements of the UN and US representatives to the effect that the Turkish and Greek Cypriot communities are equal peoples having separate and independent entities are considered by Turkish authorities as positive steps taken in the right direction. But they also face great difficulties in their foreign relations because of the restrictions imposed by the other powers on the basis of the Cyprus question. The American tendency of tying economic and military aid and sales to Turkey to the Cyprus issue is one matter displeasing Turkish rulers. The possibility of the Americans' pressurising the Turkish administration in finding a solution to the Cyprus problem by complying with EU demands is also a source of worry for Turkish officials. It might be speculated that Turkey would resist the American and EU pressures on Cyprus in order to prove that it is an important regional power having a say on international issues as well. In spite of experiencing serious economic and political problems, Turkish rulers' holding an adamant attitude on Cyprus is one possibility. Apart from openly protesting against the EU, some Turkish statesmen such as Foreign Minister Cem and Defence Minister openly state that they do not share and approve the views of the Americans on the Cyprus issue. They frequently declare that no power can put pressures on the Turkish side to accept a solution harming their interests.[6]

Cyprus has such an importance for Turkey that Turkish rulers feel compelled to continue their stance on the issue in spite of all outside pressures and negative developments. According to Turkish diplomatic circles, the gains, which were obtained in the Cyprus issue over the years, constitute the most important diplomatic victories of the Turkish Republic since its establishment.[7] Giving in the pressures on this matter will mean a total failure of the Republic's diplomacy. There are internal dynamics in Turkey, which should be taken into consideration by outside power trying to push Turkish authorities for a solution. The Turkish Cypriots are considered as an integral part of the Turkish people and their struggle is seen as the struggle of the Turkish people. Therefore, Turkey is ready to make every sacrifice to maintain the sovereignty of the Turkish Cypriots.[8] No Turkish government can put aside the interests of the Turkish Cypriots without risking a serious, hostile and even calamity-bringing reaction at home. On the other hand, Turkey's close relations with the USA and the generally West and its need for the Western economic, political and military assistance restrict its capability of action and make the Cyprus issue an important problem of Turkish foreign policy.

One claim on Turkey's internal dynamics related to Cyprus is that Turkish authorities have the tendency to use the Cyprus issue as a tool in Turkey's accession to the EU.[9] Two possibilities are mentioned in this regard. One possibility is that if the Turkish elite do not want to join the EU for the time being, it will take an adamant stance on the Cyprus issue to please the Turkish people and to provoke the EU authorities in not accepting Turkey to their organisation. Turning the Turkish people completely against the EU in this way will provide

---

[6] The joint press conference of Çakmakoğlu and Cohen on 15 July 1999.

[7] Ecmel Barutçu, *Hariciye Koridoru*, Ankara: 21. Yüzyıl Yay., 1999, p. 266.

[8] The speech of Turkish President Ahmet Necdet Sezer in Cyprus on 22 June 2000, *Dışişleri Güncesi: June 2000*, Ankara: TC Dışişleri Bakanlığı, p. 110.

[9] Mehmet Hasgüler, *Kıbrıs'ta Enosis ve Taksim Politikalarının Sonu*, İstanbul: İletişim, 2000, p. 274.

them the opportunity to pursue policies of their choice without any public hostility. The second possibility is that if Turkish authorities decide definitely to join the EU, they will change their Cyprus policies to please the Europeans and they will make Turkey's EU membership a condition of the solution of the Cyprus problem. Even if there are such tendencies among Turkish rulers, it is clear that reaching a vital objective of foreign policy by trusting in only one tool is not a rational act. Moreover, the special characteristics of the Cyprus question, mentioned above, do not allow its use for a flexible tool. Nevertheless, the claim that Turkey might use the Cyprus issue as a tool against Greece seems to have some validity. According to this claim, the presence of Turkish military forces in Cyprus leads to be cautious in the Aegean. "The Greeks are cognisant of the fact that in the event that they escalate the crisis in the Aegean to a hot conflict, this will force Turkey to take military measures in Cyprus."[10]

Given the fact that the Greek Cypriots are recognised as the only official representative of Cyprus, the Turkish side insists on the recognition of their administration as an independent and equal entity existing on the island before progressing on substantial talks.[11] In the opinion of the Turkish side, the basic parameter of the Cyprus question is the protection of balance between the Turkish and Greek communities, which is based on the principle of equality, as well as the balance between the positions of Turkey and Greece in the Aegean and Cyprus.[12] In this context, only a con-federal solution, which will be based on the equality and sovereignty of the Turkish and Greek Cypriot communities, will be a viable solution protecting the security of the two sides.[13] Some Turkish circles hope that the requirements and pressures of globalism as well as the recognition of the TRNC by some Central Asian or Muslim countries will end the isolation of the Turkish Cypriot administration in the international arena.[14]

The USA's Point of View

The United States established positions such as the special co-ordinator for Cyprus to facilitate negotiations between the Greek and Turkish Cypriots, to promote a comprehensive peace settlement on Cyprus and to ensure policy-level co-ordination of efforts related to Cyprus. American special envoys and co-ordinators work closely with the Cypriot parties as well as the interested governments, maintain an active dialogue with the Congress and have regular contacts with the Secretary General of the UN and his representatives.[15] The

---

[10] Barutçu, *Hariciye Koridoru*, p. 253, Fotios Moustakis and Micheal Sheehan, "Greek Security Policy After the Cold-War", *Contemporary Security Politics*, vol. 21, No. 3, December 2000, pp. 96-97.

[11] The press conference of Vice Spokesman of the Foreign Ministry Sermet Atacanlı on 19 January 2000, *Dışişleri Güncesi: January 2000*, p. 100, the statement of Vice Spokesman of the Foreign Ministry Sermet Atacanlı on 17 February 2000, *Dışişleri Güncesi: February 2000*, Ankara: TC Dışişleri Bakanlığı, p. 62, The press conference of Vice Spokesman of the Foreign Ministry Sermet Atacanlı on 23 February 2000, *Dışişleri Güncesi: February 2000*, p. 124.

[12] The speech of Turkish President Ahmet Necdet Sezer in Cyprus on 22 June 2000, *Dışişleri Güncesi: June 2000*, p. 109.

[13] The statement of the Turkish Foreign Ministry on 3 August 2000, *Dışişleri Güncesi: August 2000*, Ankara: TC Dışişleri Bakanlığı, p. 18.

[14] Ishtiaq Ahmad, "Prospects of Cyprus Settlement After the Helsinki Summit", *Marmara Journal of European Studies*, c. 8, No. 1-2, 2000, p. 68.

[15] The statement of the press secretary of the White House on 3 September 1999.

American authorities consider the Cyprus issue as the most important problem, on which the approaches of Turkey and the USA clashed with each other.[16] The Americans state that the status quo in Cyprus, which is based on the partition, cannot be acceptable and insist that inter-communal negotiations should be continued without any precondition.[17] American rulers also are firm in that a bizonal and bicommunal federation is the only way of solving the Cyprus problem.[18] Moreover, Washington criticises the Turkish Cypriots because of their insistence on the recognition of their state and the interruption of the EU membership process of the Greek Cypriots before reaching a comprehensive solution. The American pressures on the Turkish side aimed at leading them to resume substantial negotiations, to take positive steps for a rapid solution and to make considerable concessions cause tensions between the Americans and the Turkish side.[19]

The American rulers emphasise that the status of the Turkish Cypriots cannot be a precondition of starting substantial negotiations for a solution, but they suggest that it will be better if this issue is left to other phases to be solved as a part of the final solution.[20] As they recognise the leader of the Greek Cypriots as the president of Cyprus, the Americans avoid making any comment on the status of the leaders participating in the negotiations. In their opinion, the leaders represent their communities in some way. The authority in the north speaks on behalf of the Turkish Cypriots and the government in the south is the one the Americans recognise.[21] The American view that the Turkish side should cede some amount of territory for making it possible to reach a final solution displease the Turks. In fact, the American intervention in the matter on its own is considered by the Turks as a factor supporting the Greek Cypriots because the Greek Cypriot side are able to obtain the American support in many incidents thanks to the might Greek lobbies in the USA and they act in the comfort of the belief that the Americans will prevent a radical change which will harm their interests. The American authorities seek ways to prevent the eruption of crises because of the Cyprus problem since they know that they will have to intervene in such an event which will bring about more dangerous situations. Their main effort concentrates on pushing the Turkish side for a rapid solution. The American failure to fulfil Turkish demands in other areas weakens their ability to affect the Turkish side on Cyprus. On the other hand, President Clinton's statement in Athens on 20 November 1999 ("Turkey cannot be fully integrated successfully into Europe without solving its difficulties with Greece") gives the signal of cornering Turkey in its weakest point. In other words, Turkey's need to have partnership relations with the USA and the EU weakens its hand on Cyprus. President Clinton's statements cited in the White House report on 27 October 2000 demonstrates the American seriousness in this matter. "To see entrenched and unmoveable positions in Cyprus in what really ought to be a fairly straight-forward problem to solve, keep them apart and keep Turkey more at arm's length from Europe, I think it's price not worth paying... It just makes no sense

[16] Alan Makovsky, "Special Policy Forum Report: Ecevit's Turkey", Alan Makovsky, "Good Vibes, Little Cash in Store for Ecevit".

[17] The joint press conference of Çakmakoğlu and Cohen on 15 July 1999, the speech of American Secretary of State Madeleine K. Albright on 12 May 2000, the speech of President Clinton in Athens on 20 November 1999.

[18] The joint press conference of Çakmakoğlu and Cohen on 15 July 1999.

[19] Makovsky, "New Activism in Turkish Foreign Policy".

[20] The press conference of Moses in Larnaca Airport on 9 January 2001.

[21] Ibid.

in the larger context of the future of Greece..., Turkey... and the Cypriots themselves, to maintain this present impasse with all the bad feelings and conflicts and estrangements that it has brought us."

It is also possible to hear from the Americans statements which please the Turkish side. American Defence Secretary Cohen stated on 14 July 1999 that they preferred to live up to the Greek and Turkish governments to resolve their differences including the Cyprus issue and he emphasised that the US did not seek in any way to become an arbiter or any way to pressure either government.[22] According to the Americans, the structure and terms of a settlement are matters for Cypriots to decide and a negotiated settlement has to obtain the positive support of Greece and Turkey.[23] In the past, when rumours erupted that the US applied pressure tactics against the sides on a solution, the American authorities denied it. American Defence Secretary Cohen stated in his press conference in Ankara on 15 July 1999 that they did not seek to bring pressure on either Greece or Turkey on the Cyprus question and that they did not intend to try and impose their own view. He also emphasised their belief that the solution must be brought about through direct dialogue between the parties concerned.[24] American Special Co-ordinator for Cyprus Thomas Weston exhibited the same attitude with his statement on 8 September 1999: "I very firmly believe that addressing the issues on the island must come from the people and from the leaders on the island. It is not for the US or anyone else to seek to impose a plan from the outside."

Other views and attitudes of the Americans on the Cyprus issue can be summarised as follows: If the problem can be solved there will be no embargo imposed on the Turkish side and it will be possible move towards the two sides being more equal in their economic well-being. The Americans, who do not want to make any comment on the legality or illegality of the settlers in Cyprus,[25] would like to see a united Cyprus enters the EU, to be followed closely by the accession of Turkey to the EU. They do not come with ideas and suggest the sides accept their thoughts. On the contrary, American officials prefer to work in the framework of a dialogue out of which emerged certain ideas that are being considered.[26] They spend efforts for the continuation of negotiations, but they are not involved in the substance of the negotiations, which are held under the auspices of the UN, not the USA. If one of the sides do not want to continue with the process, their response to that side will be the same regardless of their ethnic origin: 'try to find a basis'.[27] American officials, who believe that a Turkey rejected by the EU would be a strategic loss for the West, warned the Europeans in the past that if Turkey were denied the EU candidacy, one of the negative consequences would be the end of the Cyprus diplomacy.[28] Clinton's speech in Athens on 20 November 1999 is important in pointing that Turkey will be persuaded to solve the Cyprus issue if it is accepted to the EU: "It is very much in your [Greek] interest to see Turkey become a candidate for membership in the EU, for that will enforce Turkish secular, democratic, modernising path, showing Turkey how much it has to gain by making progress on issues like

---

[22] The statement of Cohen on 14 July 1999.

[23] "US-Cyprus Relations" (From the web site of the American embassy in Cyprus).

[24] The joint press conference of Çakmakoğlu and Cohen on 15 July 1999.

[25] The statement of Moses in Nicosia on 10 March 2000.

[26] The press conference of Moses in the American embassy in Ankara on 11 January 2001.

[27] The press conference of Moses in Larnaca Airport on 9 January 2001.

[28] Makovsky, "Turkey and the European Union: One More Try".

Cyprus and the Aegean matters... For many of these same reasons, we...have also strongly supported the EU's decision to start accession talk with Cyprus."

The Last Word

The position of Turkey and the Turkish Cypriots are particularly sensitive. Although Turkey has definitely chosen the West as the only direction, to which its march will continue, there are some fears and doubts felt by the Turkish people, politicians and rulers including the military ones about the American and European attitude toward the issues of Turkey. The statement of one high-level military official that Turkey should consider co-operating with Iran and Russia in case it has problems with the Western countries and the suggestion of some leading politicians and statesmen that Turkey should not consider the EU membership as the only alternative can be sited as examples in this regard. The Cyprus issue is the most important matter on which Turkish rulers and people might challenge the West at all costs and which might be turned to a tool of anti-Western stance. It is at least clear that Turkish people will not sacrifice Cyprus, which is one of their most important causes, for short-term gains. Such an action will harm the Turkish perception that their state is an important regional country, which has the potential to affect world policies. On the other hand, Turkish authorities are aware that they cannot stay outside the EU and the Western world. Co-operation with the EU and the USA is a necessity for Turkish interests. Finding a political solution to the Cyprus problem will be a great help in this regard.

One possibility in this point is the initiation of a new bargaining in the context of the EU while maintaining the status quo on the island. In 1995, Turkey did not protest strongly against the EU decision of starting the accession negotiations with the Greek Cypriots in return for the removal of the Greek veto for the Customs Union Agreement. In 1999, Turkish authorities did not strongly criticise the EU decision that it would decide on the accession of Cyprus without seeing the solution of the Cyprus problem as a condition in return for the EU's granting candidate status to Turkey. Now, it is speculated that Turkish authorities will not raise objections to the completion of the accession process of the Greek Cypriot side in return for the EU decision to start accession negotiations with Turkey. This possibility gains weight especially in the light of the claim that Turkey will not able to launch radical actions such as the integration of the northern Cyprus to the mainland in the face of strong reactions of the USA and the EU. On the other hand, it is a fact that the EU and the USA want to see Turkey as their partners in protecting their interests in critical regions and in facing new threats. Therefore, they will not easily choose to alienate Turkey by imposing their own solution in the Cyprus issue. It is expected that they will try to encourage the sides to find a solution which will be acceptable to all concerning parties.

The Cyprus issue is not a simple ethnic problem, which can be solved with outside interventions. Since it concerns relations and interests of important regional and world powers, it has to be dealt with in this context. The important thing is the sincerity of the sides in finding a solution. If one of the sides distances itself from taking such an attitude by trusting in some international factors, processes and outside powers, the problem will continue to poison important relations and interests. The USA and the EU seem to give the impression that they do not support any particular side or viewpoint, but they expect serious steps from the parties for the sake of the Western alliance. Turkish Foreign Minister Cem points to some important criteria and draws a road map in finding a solution. In his opinion, the three things are important. Firstly, the recent tendency in international politics is that even communities having some common characteristics decide to establish separate states by abolishing their common state mechanism. In Cyprus, there are two communities, which have definite different characteristics and which had sour relations between themselves in the past; therefore it is almost impossible task to bring together absolutely different communities. Secondly, the Cypriot leaders should try to establish a common vision and agree on the final shape of their future joint state before dealing with other main aspects of the sought solution. Thirdly, the sides should respect the main viewpoint of each other without asking the other side to change its preconditions. Cem goes on stating the possible roadmap in this context. Firstly, the sides will reconcile their main positions and will establish a partnership state which will represent both communities with an agreement on which they will agree. Secondly, they will agree on authorities and functions which will be transferred to this state. Finally, they will agree on all the matters which they consider as vital.[29] Objections might be raised against these proposals, but it is important to state that the two communities might resolve their basic disagreements by making some concessions for the sake of a better future for themselves and all the other states involved.

---

[29] İsmail Cem, "Kıbrıs için Henüz Geç Değil", *Radikal,* 15 March 2002.

Appendix

THE TURKISH SIDE'S POSITION ON THE CYPRUS QUESTION AND THE EUROPEAN UNION CONNECTION

INTRODUCTION

The Cyprus question is one of the issues of world politics, which has not been solved in spite of intensive efforts conducted by different actors in different occasions and in various ways because of its complexity concerning clashing viewpoints of the two communities on the island as well as vital interests of important regional and global actors.[1] The most important development on the issue in the recent history is the involvement of the EU in the solution process with the application of the Greek Cypriots for the EU membership of the whole island. This was the most serious negative development from the Turkish point of view because the EU largely sided with the Greeks and Greek Cypriots while announcing its viewpoint or taking an action concerning the Cyprus question and because separate issues such as the membership of Turkey and Cyprus in the EU and the solution of the Cyprus problem were linked with each other.

In the latest stage of the Cyprus question, the representatives of the two communities on the island had conducted intensive negotiations to find a solution to the problem before the EU summit meeting, which would be held in December 2002 and which would decide about the finalisation of the membership process of Cyprus. The Americans, Europeans and UN officials, too, wanted a quick solution of the problem in the context of the EU membership process, which was considered as the last serious chance to be benefited. However, some facts were forgotten in the emerging suitable atmosphere, which had created serious hopes for solution. The Greek Cypriots were in an advantageous position because of the certainty of their EU membership, but they did not feel urgency for the solution of the problem and their negative actions in this direction did not attract the criticism of the EU circles. On the other hand, the Turkish Cypriots were not comfortable in protecting their interests since they were pressurised for a quick solution with heavy threats concerning their and Turkey's future

---

[1] On the Cyprus question, see Nasuh Uslu, *Türk-Amerikan İlişkilerinde Kıbrıs,* Ankara: 21. Yüzyıl Yayınları, 2000, Nasuh Uslu, "Kıbrıs Sorunu" in Bal, İdris (ed.), *21. Yüzyılın Eşiğinde Türk Dış Politikası,* İstanbul: Alfa, 2001, 262-301, Nasuh Uslu, "Kıbrıs Sorunu ve ABD" in Ülger, İrfan K. and Efegil, Ertan, (ed.) *Avrupa Birliği Kıskacında Kıbrıs Meselesi,* Ankara: HD Yayıncılık, 2001, 147-184.

interests. If the involved powers desire to solve the Cyprus problem permanently, they have to take the opinions and doubts of the Turkish side into consideration. This article tries to enlighten the position of the Turkish side in the latest stage of the Cyprus question.

The Attitude of the Greek and Greek Cypriot Side

There are important reasons for the Greek Cypriots not to be sincere in inter-communal talks on the Cyprus question. They have been recognised as the official representative of the island in the international arena since March 1964. They can join and express their opinions and cast their votes in international organisations on behalf of the Cypriots. For example, they were able to apply and to become eligible for the EU membership and they have succeeded in obtaining the unconditional support of the EU members for their cause on the Cyprus question at the disadvantage of the Turkish side. The Greek Cypriots also have the privileges of opening diplomatic offices throughout the world and being a member of effective groupings such as the Commonwealth and the non-aligned movement. As a result, they can propagate their causes in international forums easily. By denying the same opportunities to the Turkish Cypriots, the Greek Cypriot side wants to have upper hand, but this attitude cause difficulties in reaching a solution by creating an imbalance between the positions of the sides. The other side naturally tries to protect its interests by adopting seemingly a harsher stance.

It seems that the Greek Cypriots are not in a hurry for a solution because they have already obtained the recognition of the international community. On this sound base, they can test the patience of the other side, having the comfort that international pressures will increasingly culminate in their favour. They are aware that the Turkish side (the Turkish Cypriot state and Turkey) will have to give serious concessions in order to save themselves from Cyprus-related pressures for the sake of their national interests. It seems unreasonable for the Greek Cypriot side to share their internationally-recognised sovereignty over the island with the Turkish Cypriots unless they obtain considerable gains such as the dramatic reduction in the size of the Turkish territory and the comprehensive return of the Greek Cypriots to the north to own large amount of property. Given their long-held enosis desire, which shaped their past actions and policies, it seems that they have never given up the hope to gain the control of the whole Cyprus.

It is clear that the Greek Cypriots have tried to use the issue of EU membership since the beginning as a tool to promote their causes on the Cyprus question. This justifies the actions of the other side, which have been launched to prevent a total failure under the pressures of the European Union. For the Greek Cypriots, EU membership is a useful tool to impose political, economic and military pressure on the Turkish side and to obtain a settlement on their own terms.[2] They do not need an urgent solution because they have the international recognition, they are sure about obtaining the EU membership and support and they are able to keep the Turkish Cypriots isolated politically and pressurised economically. Naturally, the Greek Cypriot attitude of being insistent on owning Cyprus and continuing the Republic of Cyprus is seen by the Turkish side as the proof their reluctance for a quick solution.[3]

---

[2] Hüner Tuncer, "The Cyprus Issue: Recent Developments", *Perceptions,* September-November 2002, vol. 7, no. 3, http://www.mfa.gov.tr/grupa/percept/VII-3/HunerTuncer.htm.
[3] http://www.msnbc.com/news/198778.asp, 24 January 2003 (the statement of the President of the Turkish Republic of Cyprus, Rauf Denktaş).

The Greek government, too, encourages the adamant Greek Cypriot attitude by threatening to block the EU enlargement process if the European Union denies accession to the Greek Cypriots. As Greek Prime Minister Kostas Simitis stated clearly, the Greek government uses its position within the EU to force Turkey into yielding pressures on the Cyprus question by accepting the proposed plans. Greek rulers give the message that if Turkey does not work for a quick solution, its EU membership prospect will face great difficulties and its European vocation will not come to a successful end.[4] They insistently tell Turkish rulers that if a solution cannot be found in a near future, there will no point in continuing negotiations.[5] This attitude stems from the fact that the Greek and Greek Cypriot side does not see any urgency in finding a solution because they will not lose anything serious.

Carrying their problems with Turkey, including the Cyprus question, to Europe was one of the main foreign policy aims of the Greeks and the Greek Cypriots and, indeed, they have become successful in that. They were sure that they would gain the upper hand by obtaining the support of the Europeans. In fact, their real intention can be detected in their statements stressing a great victory in the history of Helenism. Greek Cypriot leader Glafcos Clerides demonstrated their excitement by stating that the Greek Cypriot membership in the EU was the greatest victory they had achieved since 1960.[6] Greek Prime Minister Simitis, too, was jubilant on the result and he said that the admission of the Greek Cypriot regime to the EU opened a new page in the history of Helenism and that Cyprus was now with them with a single sovereignty and administration.[7] In his opinion, Cyprus was admitted to the EU without any condition thanks to the Greek government's efforts and this was a great success, from which important lessons should be derived.[8]

The Greek and Greek Cypriot side demonstrate their reluctance in reaching a solution by giving negative responses to proposals put forward on the question. Greek Cypriot leader Clerides declared that they would reject the Annan plan if changes were made to meet some demands of the Turkish side. He was sure that a solution would be found to the Cyprus question before the end of 2003.[9] The election of Papadopoulos as the president of the Greek Cypriot administrations also implies that the Greek Cypriots want to gain more concessions by holding a more adamant attitude. In fact, Papadopoulos is known as a person having a harsher stance toward the Turks with his background as an ex-member of the terrorist organisation EOKA. He had announced that he would demand important changes in key issues when he became president. Although Papadopoulos stated after the election that he would negotiate issues with the Turkish side with a good spirit, his demands were unacceptable from the Turkish point of view. They included the return of more Greek Cypriot refugees to the Turkish territory, the withdrawal of Turkish soldiers from the island, the repatriation of Turkish refugees to their homeland and the creation of a strong central sovereignty.

The Greek Cypriots also give the impression that they do not want to grant any concession to the Turkish side because of historical hostilities. It seems that their utmost

---

[4] http://www.msnbc.com/news/195710.asp, 5 January 2003.
[5] http://www.msnbc.com/news/193175, 18 December 2002 (the statement of Greek Prime Minister Simitis).
[6] http://www.msnbc.com/news/195169.asp, 1 January 2003.
[7] http://www.msnbc.com/news/193069.asp, 18 December 2002.
[8] http://www.msnbc.com/news/192569.asp, 12 December 2002.
[9] http://www.msnbc.com.tr/news/201080.asp?cp=1, 12 December 2002.

priority is to prevent the Turks from obtaining any benefits in the course of solving the Cyprus question. The spokesman of the Greek Cypriot administration, Mihalis Papapetru, once expressed his concern that the Turkish Republic of Northern Cyprus might be recognised in the international arena if the international community believed that the Cyprus question could not be solved.[10] The Greek Cypriots believe that they can prevent the success of the Turkish side by creating disagreements among the Turks and the Turkish Cypriots and by cornering them in the international arena. As an example of this attitude, the foreign minister of the Greek Cypriot administration, Cosoulides, claimed that the most important obstacles in front of the admission of Cyprus to the EU as a whole were the Turkish army and Turkish Cypriot President Rauf Denktash.[11] The Greek Cypriot initiative of providing economic opportunities to the Turkish Cypriot people by bypassing the Turkish Cypriot administration seems to amount to nothing more than creating problems within the Turkish side. If they were sincere in helping the Turkish Cypriots, they could have abolished the inhuman embargo against them in the past.

THE EUROPEAN UNION'S ATTITUDE ON THE CYPRUS QUESTION

There are numerous reasons for the Turkish side not to be happy on the attitude of the European Union regarding the Cyprus question. First of all, the EU takes the recognition of the Greek Cypriot administration in the international arena as granted and does not want to discuss the legality of the present situation under the international law and international agreements. The Europeans do not see any necessity to debate the Turkish Cypriot argument that the Greek Cypriots have no legal or moral right to represent the whole island.[12] On the other hand, the Turkish Cypriots have difficulty in understanding the European attitude of completely disregarding the legal positions as far as the Turkish Republic of Northern Cyprus was concerned. They resent the Europeans' effectively announcing that they do not recognise the rights of the Turkish Cypriot side as stated in the Zurich and London agreements of 1959.[13] Facing this kind of attitude, Turkish Cypriot leader Rauf Denktaş sees himself right in criticising the Europeans on not considering him as an equal counterpart in official affairs. For example, when he was criticised because of not attending the Copenhagen summit in December 2002, Denktaş stated that he was not invited by the European Union because he was not taken into consideration by the Europeans.[14]

Some European actions also lead the Turkish Cypriots to think that the EU holds a biased negative attitude toward the Turkish side. For example, the decisions of the European Court of Justice have always found the Turkish side guilty and proposed measures against it. It has prevented the import of fruit and vegetables from the Turkish Cypriot territory and has established an effective embargo on the Turkish Cypriot economy. This embargo has had a devastating effect on the economy of the Northern Cyprus and has made the Turkish Cypriot

---

[10] http://www.msnbc.com/news/197830.asp, 18 January 2003.
[11] http://www.msnbc.com/news/198078.asp, 21 January 2003.
[12] Tuncer, "The Cyprus Issue: Recent Developments".
[13] Erol Manisalı, "What Happens if Cyprus Joins the EU without Turkey" in İrfan Kaya Ülger and Ertan Efegil (eds.), *Avrupa Birliği Kıskacında Kıbrıs Meselesi*, Ankara: HD Yayıncılık, 2001, p. 64.
[14] http://www.msnbc.com/news/197807.asp, 18 January 2003.

administration heavily dependent on the good will of outside powers,[15] leaving no room for it to adopt its own policies and to launch its own actions. The verdicts of the European Court of Justice on other issues, too, have consistently carried anti-Turkish sentiments. While it concludes that rights and interests of Greek Cypriot refugees are violated by the Turkish side, it does not take the past and present sufferings of the Turkish Cypriots into consideration. The European pressures on Turkey on complying with the verdicts of the European Court of Justice,[16] therefore, tie down the hands of the Turkish and Turkish Cypriot statesmen in negotiating a solution for the Cyprus question.

The attitude of the European Union on finding a solution to the Cyprus question, too, is not satisfactory for the Turkish side and has an anti-Turkish tone. At the beginning, the EU was of the opinion that the Cyprus question should be solved before the island became an EU member. The European Commission recommended in July 1993 that the accession process should follow the resolution of the problem.[17] However, the EU reversed its position soon and it saw no connection between the two factors. It also established a strong link among Turkey's accession process, improvements in negotiations held on the Cyprus issue and the EU membership of Cyprus. Turkey was required to constructively encourage the UN's attempts at finding a solution to the Cyprus dispute. The EU's new Cyprus policy included three aspects. Firstly, it would not regard the resolution of the Cyprus question as a precondition of EU membership of the island. Secondly, the EU would take all relevant factors into account when deciding on Cyprus' accession process. Finally, it would not create problems during the implementation process of the EU's internal regulations in each and every part of the island. It could be read easily that these three points were designed to please the Greek Cypriots, Turkey and the Turkish Cypriots respectively.[18] But the EU concentrated on the first approach while it ignored the other two, thus preferring to alienate the Turkish side.

The ambiguity of the EU's Cyprus policy is another factor disliked by the Turkish side. Since the details of this policy are not known by both sides and since both communities do not have any idea on the model, which will come about with the EU membership, they prefer to cling to their well-established positions. This process eventually bring benefits for the Greek Cypriots rather than the Turkish side because they are happy with their present situation, being the side which has obtained international recognition and support. If the EU announces that "the EU membership of a loosely centralised, single-sovereign, bi-zonal and bi-commmunal federal Cyprus is the only feasible and legitimate solution",[19] all the sides of the Cyprus question would feel heavy pressures on them to produce efforts in this direction. They would not dare to insist on their own choice of solution because they would not want to lose the support of the EU and the prospect of EU membership. The present opposite EU attitude makes the sides of the problem reluctant in engaging themselves in serious negotiation process aimed at an everlasting settlement. Particularly, the Greek Cypriot side

---

[15] Ishtiaq Ahmad, "Resolving the Cyprus Conflict Through EU Enlargement Process" in Ülger and Efegil (eds.), *Avrupa Birliği Kıskacında Kıbrıs Meselesi*, s. 56.

[16] The statement of the Secretary General of the European Council, http://www.msnbc.com/news/196436.asp, 9 January 2003.

[17] H. Tarık Oğuzoğlu, "Prennial Conflict or Everlasting Peace: the European Union's Involvement in Cyprus", *Perceptions*, July-August 2002, vol. 7, no. 2, http://www.mfa.gov.tr/grupa/percept/VII-2/tarik.oguzoglu.htm.

[18] Ibid.

[19] Ibid.

does not want to give up further concessions because it is aware that the EU casts its decisions and actions consistently in their favour.

The Turkish side also does not understand the EU insistence on the admission of Cyprus into the EU as the whole island. In their opinion, the existent two states on the island can be members of the EU separately if a solution cannot be found for the time being. In this sense, they point to the fact that the European countries encouraged Croatia, Slovenia and Macedonia to leave Yugoslavia and that they granted the Czech Republic and Slovakia the status of associate member to admit them to their organisation eventually as separate states.[20] In other words, the Turkish side believes that the EU's pressures for a quick solution are not based on realities, but they serve basically Greek Cypriot interests because they do not feel any urgency with their guaranteed membership status and are ready to wait for a long time to compel the Turkish Cypriots to come to their terms with the help of the Europeans.

The Turkish side also detects the EU's biased attitude in the military field. They point out that while the EU is constantly demanding the withdrawal of Turkish troops from the island and the disarmament of Cyprus, it turns a blind eye to the extraordinary arms build-up in the southern part of the island. The explicit EU support for Greece's military integration with the Greek Cypriot administration is one of the facts, which the Turkish side cannot comprehend easily. It is further speculated that this European attitude has something to do with the prospect that the European Security and Defence Initiative will use the military facilities, bases and other military potential in the Greek Cypriot part of the island in co-operation with Greece.[21] In other words, it is claimed that the Europeans favour the Greek side in their dealings with the island because they do not expect any benefit from the Turkish side and they believe that the Greek Cypriots can help them in numerous issues including the military field.

The EU's stance on the final solution of the Cyprus question and the eventual membership of Cyprus in the EU particularly irritate the Turkish side and lead it to launch desperate efforts to protects its vital interests. The European leaders give the impression that they always find the Turkish side responsible for any failure of inter-communal negotiations though the Greek Cypriot side, too, put forward important objections to proposed plans. This European attitude can be detected in the latest developments regarding the Annan plan prepared by the UN Secretary-General. There was no evidence whatsoever on that the Greek Cypriot side accepted the Annan plan's content altogether. In contrast, the Greek Cypriots elected a person, who raised important objections to the plan, as their president. Nevertheless, the chairman of the European Parliament, Pat Cox, held Turkey and the Turkish Cypriot administration responsible for the failure in reaching a final solution. Cox further caused a deep resentment in the Turkish side by stating that Cyprus would be represented in the EU organs as a whole after the accession agreement was signed.[22] The UN Secretary-General summoned the leaders of the Cypriot communities on 10 March 2003 to receive their final response. Neither side declared that it accepted the plan as a whole, but since that time the EU has put pressures mainly on the Turkish side by declaring that Turkey will never be a member of the EU unless the Cyprus question has been solved completely. On the other hand, the EU

---

[20] Ahmad, "Resolving the Cyprus Conflict Through EU Enlargement Process", p. 55.
[21] Manisalı, "What Happens if Cyprus Joins the EU without Turkey", pp. 66-67.
[22] http://www.msnbc.com/news/193342.asp, 19 December 2002.

officials do not put forward any criticism toward the Greek side and they declare that the accession process of Cyprus will be finalised smoothly.

In short, the EU has sharpened the division in Cyprus and has decreased the likelihood of finding a permanent solution to the Cyprus question by accommodating only the Greek Cypriot aspirations on becoming a EU member and other issues and altogether ignoring the interests, difficulties and concerns of the Turkish side.[23] Turkey and the Turkish Cypriot administration believe that the EU's approach is biased in favour of the Greeks and therefore, they feel the need to be cautious in accepting proposals coming from or being supported by the EU. If the Turkish side is convinced that their vital interests including their security will be damaged unless the EU develops a more balanced attitude, it will be impossible to persuade them with some future economic benefits to support the EU-sponsored plans and solutions.[24]

The most threatening possibility from the Turkish point of view is that the EU will determine its policies toward Cyprus in the context of its emerging as a new global player in world politics and that it will choose to benefit from the island for its global policies by co-operating with the Greek Cypriots. It seems that a new world order comes to existence gradually and the EU wants to be a major global player in this new system. Therefore, it is natural from the EU point of view to try to dominate the Mediterranean and Aegean seas as a part of its strategy of expanding its influence and increasing its power. The intensive EU efforts on finalising the accession process of Cyprus can be evaluated in the context of the strategic importance of Cyprus in the eastern Mediterranean. Therefore, it is not surprising that the Chairman's office of the EU declared in February 1995 that Cyprus was in the EU's area of interest.[25] As one of the main players in the new world order, the EU had decided that Cyprus would be within the EU's future borders and it would try to impose its own conditions in the Cyprus question. The Turkish side feels suspicions in this point that the EU wants to absorb the island more easily by bringing the entire island first under the sovereignty of the Greek Cypriots.[26] This logic continues in such a line that since the Greek side is closer to the European identity and since the Turks are traditional enemies of Europe for centuries, Cyprus will be included in the EU territory by bringing the island under the Greek sovereignty. Meanwhile, giving an imaginary EU perspective to Turkey will serve this purpose because Turkey will feel compelled to solve the problem to the liking of the Europeans not to be left alone outside the European institutions.[27]

THE TURKISH SIDE'S POSITION

Although a considerable number of Turkish Cypriots are in favour of being EU member, most of them do not support the Greek Cypriot side's unilateral application to the EU. Again, the majority of the Turkish Cypriot people prefer separate application of both communities to

---

[23] Ahmad, "Resolving the Cyprus Conflict Through EU Enlargement Process", p. 52.

[24] Oğuzoğlu, "Prennial Conflict or Everlasting Peace: the European Union's Involvement in Cyprus".

[25] Manisalı, "What Happens if Cyprus Joins the EU without Turkey", p. 64.

[26] Ibid., pp. 63, 66.

[27] Ibid., pp. 67, 74.

the EU.[28] It is true that the Turkish Cypriot public opinion turned to pro-Annan plan to a great extent in order to able to be citizens of the EU when it became clear that the administrations on the island would not accept it as it stand. However, this does not change the fact that the Turkish Cypriots have been alienated by the EU's unjust attitude toward the application of the Greek Cypriots.

The Turkish Cypriots argue that the Greek Cypriot application to the EU is illegal because the international agreements prohibit the Republic of Cyprus from joining any organisation which does not include the guarantor powers, namely Greece, the United Kingdom and Turkey, without obtaining their consent. Apart from this legal objection, the Turkish side also practically considers that accession terms cannot be concluded until a settlement has first been agreed on the Cyprus question because this will decrease the likelihood of finding a solution between the sides. It seems that the EU insists on a quick solution because of the time problem emanating from the EU's enlargement calendar. But the Cyprus question and the EU's enlargement are separate issues and creating artificial pressures to comply with the EU's timetable might bring about extra difficulties for the solution of the problem. If a quick solution is desired, in that case, the Greek Cypriot side, too, should be made aware of the time problem with the warning that its accession process might not progress smoothly.

Some guarantees are proposed to the Turkish Cypriot side and Turkey to ensure them against the possible damages of the completion of the Cyprus's accession process. However, these guarantees might not be turned to international agreements and even if it is done so there is no guarantee for the implementation of these agreements given the demise of the 1960 treaties. The Turkish side naturally suspects that once Cyprus becomes an EU member, the EU might treat the issues involving Cyprus as internal matters and might not allow Turkey to intervene in those matters. Given the fact that there is no guarantee that Turkey will become a full member of the EU, the Turkish side understandably fears that it might lose everything concerning its vital interests regarding the Cyprus question. Indeed, it will not be difficult for the mighty European Union to assimilate and neutralise the small Cypriot Turkish community within its body. It is clear that Turkey will not see any urgency in pressurising the Turkish Cypriots for a quick solution if it cannot obtain any guarantees on the completion of its EU membership in the foreseeable future.

It seems that the EU will finalise the accession process of the Greek Cypriot administration without any delay. But it is highly likely that such an occurrence will bring about serious risks and dangers for all the sides involved.[29] The accession of Cyprus to the EU as a divided state with the exclusion of the Turkish Cypriots from the process might cause deep crises between the Cypriot communities as well as between Greece and Turkey by eventually threatening peace and security in the eastern Mediterranean. In such likelihood, Turkey might lose the prospect of becoming an EU member forever and another serious crisis might erupt between the EU and Turkey. But the losers will not only be the Turkish Cypriots and Turkey. The Greek Cypriots would be deprived of living in a unified Cyprus, where they could enjoy the three fundamental rights. The anti-EU forces in Turkey would increase their

---

[28] Ertan Efegil and Özgen Görgünler, "A Survey on the Public Opion's Concerns About the Proposals of the TRNC, South Cyprus, the UN and the EU" in Ülger and Efegil (eds.), *Avrupa Birliği Kıskacında Kıbrıs Meselesi*, ss. 129, 131.

[29] Tuncer, "The Cyprus Issue: Recent Developments", Oğuzoğlu, "Prennial Conflict or Everlasting Peace: the European Union's Involvement in Cyprus".

political powers and the emergence of radical changes in traditional Turkish policies would be a high possibility. Of course, the European states including Greece would be affected by such a development seriously. Greece would not be comfortable about its security since it would have to live next to a Turkey, which was estranged from the EU. Finally, Turkey might pursue anti-EU policies in the eastern Mediterranean, the Balkans and the Middle East and thus it might harm vital EU interests in these regions.

In contrast to the great relief on the Greek and Greek Cypriot side, stemmed from being sure on the Greek Cypriot membership of the EU, Turkish and Turkish Cypriot people have mixed feelings and opinions on the EU membership and the solution of the Cyprus question because they are not sure about the possible future benefits and losses. Different public opinion polls, conducted among the Turkish Cypriots, point to different results. While an opinion poll gave the supporters of the Annan plan a great lead, the results of another poll were absolutely vice versa.[30] In the opinion of the minister of environment and tourism in the Turkish side, Serdar Denktaş, the supporters of President Denktaş's initiatives traditionally constituted 65-70 % percent of the Turkish Cypriot people and this did not change while the Annan plan was negotiated. However, as Serdar Denktaş admits, the great majority of the Turkish Cypriots (about 80%) desires the end of the uncertainty and longs for the opening of a new era.[31] Particularly the young Turkish Cypriots are not interested in the historical background of the Cyprus question, but they want the solution of the problem as soon as possible. They believe that the non-solution of the problem is the main reason behind economic, social and political difficulties facing the Turkish Cypriot people.[32] The widespread participation in demonstrations held in the Turkish Cypriot part of the island in favour of the solution of the Cyprus problem and the Annan plan and the slogans chanted in these protests give the impression that the Turkish Cypriots are not happy on their rulers' response to the Annan plan and they are in favour of the EU membership at all costs.

However, it should not be forgotten that the desperate situation of the Turkish Cypriots is, to a great extent, a result of the international embargo imposed on them with the efforts of the Greek Cypriots. Besides, the Turkish Cypriot opposition expects that the Greek Cypriots will support their pro-EU stance by demonstrating their desire for solution in various ways, but their expectations are not met. The Greek Cypriot people do not seem helpful in finding a solution to the Cyprus problem and the accession of Cyprus to the EU as an undivided island. Their main concern is to obtain concessions from the Turkish side as many as possible before the EU membership process has been completed. Therefore, it is natural for them not to co-operate with the Turkish Cypriot opposition on the EU accession process. In addition, the Greek Cypriot attitude of granting Cyprus passports to the Turkish Cypriots can be considered as benefiting from their desperate situation.

The Turkish Cypriot rulers naturally fear that the other side aim to empty their state in order to be able to control it eventually. They express their support for a solution after some improvements are made in the Annan plan, but they are not happy on the EU and Greek Cypriot attitude of trying to deceive the Turkish Cypriot people with some baits such as granting them EU citizenship. When these people arrange demonstrations in favour of the EU membership and the Annan plan, the Turkish Cypriot rulers feel that their position are

---

[30] http://www.msnbc.com/news/195847.asp, 6 January 2003.
[31] http://www.msnbc.com/news/198648.asp, 24 January 2003.
[32] Efegil and Görgünler, "A Survey on the Public Opion's Concerns About the Proposals of the TRNC, South Cyprus, the UN and the EU", pp. 142-143.

weakened in protecting vital national interests.[33] In this way, they are subjected to more outside pressures and the other side is able to gain the upper hand. Under such pressures, Turkish and Turkish Cypriot statesmen sometimes give excessive responses as it could be seen in the following statements: "We will not give up even one inch territory... Failing in giving support to Denktaş amounts to treachery."[34] "If the Turkish Cypriot Parliament decides to accept the Annan plan, I will tell them to find another person to sign the plan. It is a document, which will annihilate a people within 5 to 10 years."[35]

As for the solution of the Cyprus question, the Turkish side believes that the establishment of a federation with a strong government and two weak political entities is not a viable settlement because a deep hostility and mistrust have emerged between the two communities on the island in a long history.[36] Since they were recognised as equal political partners at the beginning and since one of them gained the international recognition in the latter stage, both of them should use its free self-determination right if a true federation will be established. It is a fact that no single Cypriot nation has been created. If a superior authority with comprehensive powers is imposed on the two communities, it will violate their separate, distinctive national characteristics.[37] The use of free self-determination right to create a partnership state will be more appropriate because it will respect sovereignty and independent political personality of the two sides. In fact, the UN's last proposal of solution is conformity with these criteria. It includes a new partnership state with a single international legal personality based on the political equality of the sides, which will have their own laws.

Nevertheless, the Turkish side has the feeling that their expectations on co-founding partnership and political equality are not met fully in the context of the Annan plan and that the central government is strengthened with the transfer of authority of taking critical decisions in such fields as foreign policy, finance and security to it.[38] The Turkish Cypriot rulers insist that the new partnership state should not be the continuity of the present state because it was established illegally with the exclusion of the Turkish Cypriots from the administration by force. The new state should also not be the mere extension of either state that presently exists on the island because it will not be possible in this way to end the old hatreds, disagreements and debates. If the two existing political entities on the island are transformed into co-founder, equal and sovereign partners of the new partnership state, this formulation will create a more viable solution.[39] In the new state, each partner state should represent only its own people and should not claim sovereignty or jurisdiction over the other. The co-founding partners should have exclusive control over their own affairs except the matters which are explicitly assigned to the partnership state. However, the Turkish side considers the proposed structure of the Presidential Council as contrary to these criteria.[40]

---

[33] http://www.msnbc.com/news/196733.asp, 12 January 2003 (the statement of the prime minister of the Turkish Republic of Northern Cyprus, Derviş Eroğlu).

[34] http://www.msnbc.com/news/197545.asp, 16 January 2003 (the statement of the chairman of the Turkish Grand National Assembly, Bülent Arınç).

[35] http://www.msnbc.com/news/197807.asp, 18 January 2003 (the statement of Turkish Cypriot leader Rauf Denktaş).

[36] Ahmad, "Resolving the Cyprus Conflict Through EU Enlargement Process", p. 53.

[37] Efegil and Görgünler, "A Survey on the Public Opion's Concerns About the Proposals of the TRNC, South Cyprus, the UN and the EU", p. 125.

[38] Armağan Kuloğlu, "Birleşmiş Milletler Kıbrıs Çözüm Planı Çözümün Neresinde?", http.//www.avsam.org, 17 February 2003.

[39] Tuncer, "The Cyprus Issue: Recent Developments".

[40] Kuloğlu, "Birleşmiş Milletler Kıbrıs Çözüm Planı Çözümün Neresinde?"

Since the Turkish Cypriot vice president has no veto power and since the vote of one Turkish Cypriot member is sufficient for the enactment of any legal arrangement, the Turkish Cypriots feel that their affairs are hijacked in a tricky and indirect way.

The bi-zonality of the new partnership state and having a secure territorial basis are among the most important concerns of the Turkish Cypriots because they have a smaller population and they faced great sufferings, difficulties and massacres in the past because of the actions of the other community on the island. They agree to give up some part of their territory as a part of the future solution. For example, there is almost a consensus among them that the Maraş area could be given as a good will demonstration. However, the Turkish Cypriots insist on that territorial arrangements should not cause great disturbances with large scale of new dislocations.[41] In this sense, if distinct territories or cantons are created within the territory of either side, new confrontations should be expected in the future. The Turkish side also raises objections against the inclusion of Karpaz peninsula in the Greek Cypriot side and the extension of the Greek Cypriot territory to the north of the Lefkosa-Magusa motorway on the ground that the security depth is lost for the northern part.[42] The Turkish Cypriots also concern that with the new arrangement, the fertile part of the Turkish Cypriot territory, which also include most of the water resources of the north, (Güzelyurt) will be delivered to the Greek Cypriots. On the property question, the Turkish side prefers a global exchange of properties together with compensations to meet losses. The possible return of more than 60 thousand Greek Cypriots to the north under the new arrangement is particularly irritating for the Turkish Cypriots. In this way, the population rate of the Turkish Cypriots in the north will decrease continuously, a considerable number of the Turkish Cypriots will become refugees and the size of the Turkish territory will be reduced greatly. Some Turkish statesmen point out that these changes might create serious clashes and conflicts among the Turks by provoking the Turks, whose interests will be violated, against the others.[43]

The Turkish Cypriots are also worried about the economic consequences of the integration of the island within itself and with the EU. It is speculated that the unification of an under-developed region with a more economically advanced region may exacerbate the economic inequality between them.[44] The Turkish Cypriots naturally want the compensation of their losses, which they have suffered since the end of 1963 because of the actions of the Greek Cypriots. The concentration of the talks only on the return of the Greek Cypriots to their former properties is seen as a practice of double standard by them. The Turkish Cypriot side also feels the danger that it will lose the ability to act independently and to protect its interests efficiently once it has been admitted to the EU together with the Greek Cypriot side. It is expected that the Turkish Republic of Northern Cyprus will not be able to vote independently and will not have the right to veto within the EU.[45] On these lines, Turkish Cypriot leader Rauf Denktaş claims that the Turkish Cypriot people will perish in the near future and will become a rootless and ineffective community.[46]

---

[41] Efegil and Görgünler, "A Survey on the Public Opion's Concerns About the Proposals of the TRNC, South Cyprus, the UN and the EU", p. 126.

[42] Kuloğlu, "Birleşmiş Milletler Kıbrıs Çözüm Planı Çözümün Neresinde?"

[43] http://www.msnbc.com/news/196454.asp, 10 January 2003 (the statement of the prime minister of the Turkish Republic of Northern Cyprus, Derviş Eroğlu).

[44] Ahmad, "Resolving the Cyprus Conflict Through EU Enlargement Process", p. 57.

[45] Manisalı, "What Happens if Cyprus Joins the EU without Turkey", pp. 74-75.

[46] http://www.msnbc.com/news/198180.asp, 21 January 2003.

As it is the case for other states, the security concern is a paramount interest for the Turkish side, too. A permanent solution for the Cyprus question has to meet security interests of all the sides. It is clear that the Turkish Cypriots have been able to survive with their separate cultural and political identity because of the intervention of Turkey as one of the guarantor powers when the Cyprus agreements were violated. Therefore, the Turkish Cypriot rulers seem reluctant in accepting the withdrawal of the Turkish troops from the island and the termination of the guarantor position of Turkey. They feel that the Annan plan is not clear on ensuring the security of the Turkish Cypriots and that the proposal of entrusting security to a multi-national force under the UN mandate is not a realist alternative given the failure of the UN forces in preventing armed conflicts.

The younger generation of the Turkish Cypriots, who did not live through armed conflicts and who did not live under a strict embargo in the cantons at the mercy of the Greek Cypriots, consider a European force or an international force as sufficient to provide stability and peace in Cyprus.[47] However, the Turkish Cypriot rulers, who lived through great difficulties in the past, are not comfortable on the fact that Turkey's effective and actual guarantee in the Annan plan.[48] Rauf Denktaş states clearly that they will not accept any agreement, which will abolish the basic rights of Turkey, granted by the 1960 treaties on Cyprus.[49] The Turkish Cypriots, who fear that they will be made dependent on the mercy of the Greek Cypriots, need to be assured that Turkey's legitimate and legal rights will be incorporated in the new treaty. In fact, the Turkish side is particularly sensitive to the balance the 1960 treaties established between Turkey and Greece concerning Cyprus. If the Cyprus question is solved with no reference to the 1960 treaties or if Cyprus becomes a member of the EU against the wishes of the Turkish side, the balance between Greece and Turkey will collapse and Turkey has to take measures to compensate it. Turkish rulers are aware that their interests on the island are well established and independent of the dynamics of their relations with the EU and that Turkey's presence in Cyprus guarantees Turkey's prominent role in the realisation of security and stability in the eastern Mediterranean.[50]

CONCLUSION

Turkish officials and the Turkish Cypriots are not happy with the present situation in Cyprus and have no interests at all in the continuation of the problem because they are the ones, who suffer from the non-solution because of the pressures and embargoes they face. Nevertheless, they are not in the position to sacrifice their vital interests concerning the issue by giving consent to a quick solution, which will be imposed on them with the threats of isolating them in the international arena and blocking their future membership in the EU. They rightly point to the unjust attitude and opinions of the Greeks, the Greek Cypriots and the Europeans on the issue. The Turkish side is aware that the Greek Cypriots act with the comfort that they will be accepted to the EU with a future prospect that finding a solution

---

[47] Efegil and Görgünler, "A Survey on the Public Opion's Concerns About the Proposals of the TRNC, South Cyprus, the UN and the EU", p. 143.

[48] http://www.msnbc.com.tr/news/203962.asp?cp1=1, 1 March 2003 (the statement of Turkish Cypriot leader Rauf Denktaş).

[49] http://www.msnbc.com.tr/news/204197.asp?cp=1, 3 March 2003.

[50] Oğuzoğlu, "Prennial Conflict or Everlasting Peace: the European Union's Involvement in Cyprus".

favouring their terms will be possible with the support of the EU countries. It is difficult from the Turkish point of view to comprehend the fact that the Greek Cypriots, who stole the Cypriot administration with their illegal acts, are not protested because of their non-conciliatory attitude in finding a solution to the problem, but their accession procession progresses smoothly. Facing the Greek Cypriot attitude of using the EU as a tool for their causes and declaring a victory for Helenism and enosis as a result of securing their membership in the EU, the Turkish side becomes more determined in protecting their interests against constant heavy pressures coming from the Western institutions. Of course, they do not want to stay outside the Western structures and to give up their aim of becoming an integral part of the West, but they are not ready to sacrifice their vital interests for this sake and they expect understanding from the West for their position.

In the minds of Turkish Cypriots and Turkish rulers, the negative stance of the EU on the Cyprus question is quite clear. The EU does not question the legitimacy of the Greek Cypriot administration and does not take the claims on the legality of the Turkish Cypriot regime into consideration. The decisions of the EU institutions have always carried an anti-Turkish tone disregarding the viewpoint of the Turkish side and harmed Turkish interests while they have taken care of the Greek Cypriot concerns. The EU attitude of insisting on the membership of Cyprus before the problem has been solved and considering the solution of the problem as a precondition for Turkey's EU membership is also regarded by the Turkish side as an unfair approach. Of course, the Turkish Cypriots believe that the EU might contribute to the solution of the Cyprus problem if it gives supports for a loosely centralised, single-sovereign, bi-zonal and bi-commmunal federal Cyprus. However, the present EU stance and the adamant Greek Cypriot attitude encouraged by it constitute irritating headaches for the Turkish side and discourage them in pushing for a permanent solution by working together with the Greek Cypriots and the Europeans.

BIBLIOGRAPHY

PRIMARY SOURCES

The Documents

Arar, İsmail (ed.), *Hükümet Programları 1920-1965*, İstanbul: Burçak Yayınevi, 1968.

Bilge, Suat et al., (eds.), *Cyprus: Past, Present, Future*, Ankara, 1964.

Bozbeyli, Ferruh (ed.), *Parti Programları: Türkiye'de Siyasi Partilerin Ekonomik ve Sosyal Görüşleri, Belgeler*, İstanbul: Ak Yayınları, 1970.

"Correspondence Between President Johnson and P. M. İnönü, June 1964, as Released by the White House, January 15, 1966", *Middle East Journal*, vol. 20, Summer 1966, pp. 386-393.

Cumhuriyet Senatosu Tutanak Dergisi, 1960-75, Ankara: Türkiye Büyük Millet Meclisi.

Demirel, Süleyman, *Başbakan Süleyman Demirel'in Onuncu Basın Toplantısı*, Ankara, 1968.

Demirel, Süleyman, "Başbakan Süleyman Demirel'in Onyedinci Basın Toplantısı, 7 February 1970", *Dışişleri Bakanlığı Belleteni,* February 1970, pp. 98-140.

Dışişleri Bakanlığı Belleteni, 1960-1975, Ankara: T. C. Dışişleri Bakanlığı.

Documents on American Foreign Relations, New York: Harper Brothers, 1957.

Documents on International Affairs 1951, 1956, 1957, 1958, 1959, the Royal Institute of International Affairs, Oxford University Press.

Faulds, Andrew (ed.), *Excerpta Cypria for Today: a Source Book on the Cyprus Problem*, Lefkosha, İstanbul, London: K. Rüstem and Brother, 1988.

Foreign Relations of the United States 1952-1954, Washington: the US Government Printing Office, 1986.

The Historical Background of Cyprus and the Turkish Republic of Northern Cyprus, Ankara: The Cyprus Turkish Cultural Association.

Keesing's Contemporary Archives 1960-1975, Keesing's Publications Limited of Bristol.

Magnus, R. P., *Documents on the Middle East*, Washington: American Enterprise Institute, 1969.

Millet Meclisi Tutanak Dergisi 1960-1975, Ankara: Türkiye Büyük Millet Meclisi.

US Congress, Committee on Foreign Affairs, Committee on Foreign Relations, *Legislation on Foreign Relations Through 1979, Current Legislation and Related Executive Orders*, vol. 1, Washington: US Government Printing Office, 1980.

US Congress, House of Representatives, *Turkish Opium Ban Negotiations*, Hearing Before the Committee on Foreign Affairs, 93rd Congress, 2nd Session, July 16, 1974, Washington: US Government Printing Office, 1974.

US Congress, House of Representatives, *International Aspects of the Narcotics Problem*, Hearings Before the Subcommittee on Europe of the Committee on Foreign Affairs, 92nd Congress, 1st Session, July 7,8,9, and 30, 1971, Washington: US Government Printing Office, 1971.

US Congress, Senate, *the Military Aspects of Banning Arms Aid to Turkey*, Hearing Before the Committee on Armed Services, 95th Congress, 2nd Session, June 28, 1978, Washington: US Government Printing Office, 1978.

US Congress, Senate, *United States Security Agreements and Commitments Abroad, Greece and Turkey*, Hearings Before the Subcommittee on United States Security Agreements Abroad of the Committee on Foreign Relations, 91st Congress, 2nd Session, Part 7, June 9 and 11, 1970, Washington: US Government Printing Office, 1970.

Other Primary Materials

ABD Dışişleri Bakanı William Rogers'ın Kongre'ye Sunduğu Rapordan Bölümler, Ankara: Amerikan Basın ve Kültür Merkezi, 1972.

Amerika'da Onbir Gün, Ankara: Yarın Yayınları, 1967. (The Account of the visit of Turkish President Cevdet Sunay to the United States.)

Aybar, Mehmet Ali, *Bağımsızlık, Demokrasi, Sosyalizm: Seçmeler 1947-1967*, İstanbul: Gerçek Yayınevi, 1968.

Ball, George, *The Past Has Another Pattern: Memoirs*, New York, London: W. W. Norton, 1982.

Binnendijk, Hans and Friendly, Alfred, *Turkey, Greece and NATO: The Strained Alliance*, A Staff Report to the Committee on Foreign Relations, United States Senate, March 1980, Washington D. C.: US Government Printing Office, 1980.

Bitsios, Dimitri S., *Cyprus: the Vulnerable Republic*, Thessaloniki, Greece: Institute for Balkan Studies, 1975.

Boran, Behice, *Türkiye ve Sosyalizm Sorunları*, İstanbul: Tekin Yayınevi, 1970.

Collins, John M., *Greece and Turkey: Some Military Implications Related to NATO and the Middle East*, A Report for Special Committee on Investigations of Committee on Foreign Affairs, 94th Congress, 1st Session, February 28, 1975, Washington: US Government Printing Office, 1975.

"Cypriot Complaint of Turkish Aggression and Interference in Its Internal Affairs", *International Organization*, vol. 18, 1964, pp. 478-485.

"Cypriot Complaint of Turkish Aggression and Interference in its Internal Affairs", *International Organization*, vol. 19, 1965, pp. 84-88, 331-335, 981-988.

Çağlayangil, İhsan Sabri, *Anılarım*, İstanbul: Yılmaz Yayınları, August 1990.

Demirel, Süleyman, *Büyük Türkiye*, İstanbul: Dergah Yayınları, 1975.

Demirel, Süleyman, *1971 Buhranı ve Aydınlığa Doğru*, Ankara: Adalet Partisi, 1973.

Ecevit, Bülent, *Ortanın Solu*, İstanbul: Tekin Yayınevi, 1973.

Erim, Nihat, *Bildiğim ve Gördüğüm Ölçüler İçinde Kıbrıs*, Ankara: Ajans-Türk, 1975.

Grimmett, Richard F., *Turkish-US Defense Relationship: the Arms Embargo Issue*, the Library of Congress, Congressional Research Service, Washington: US Government Printing Office, 1978.

Grimmett, Richard F. and Laipson, Ellen B., *Turkey's Problems and Prospects: Implications for US Interests*, Report Prepared for the Subcommittee on Foreign Affairs, US House of Representatives by the Foreign Affairs and National Defense Division, Congressional Research Service, Library of Congress, March 3, 1980, Washington: US Government Printing Office, 1980.

Grimmett, Richard F., *United States Military Installations and Objectives in the Mediterranean*, Report Prepared for Subcommittee on Europe and the Middle East of the Committee on International Relations by Foreign Affairs and National Defense Division, Congressional Research Service, Library of Congress, Washington: US Government Printing Office, 1977.

Kissinger, Henry, *Years of Upheaval*, London: Weidenfield and Nicolson and Michael Joseph, 1982.

Laipson, Ellen B., *Congressional-Executive Relations and the Turkish Arms Embargo*, Washington: US Government Printing Office, June 1981.

Papandreou, Andreas, *Democracy at Gunpoint: the Greek Front*, London: Andre Deutsch, 1970.

"Question of Cyprus", *International Organization*, vol. 20, 1966, pp. 306-313.

"Question of Cyprus", *International Organization*, vol. 22, 1968, pp. 974-977.

Resmi Temaslar, Sayın Başbakan ve Bn. Erim'in Birleşik Amerika'yı Ziyareti, 18-23 March 1972. No place, publisher and date.

Spain, James W., *American Diplomacy in Turkey: Memoirs of an Ambassador-Extraordinary and Plenipotentiary*, New York: Praeger, 1984.

Türkeş, Alparslan, *Temel Görüşler*, İstanbul: Dergah Yayınları, 1975.

Türkeş, Alparslan, *Yeni Ufuklara Doğru*, İstanbul: Kutluğ Yayınları, 1974.

SECONDARY SOURCES

Turkish Newspapers and Magazines

Akis, weekly.
Cumhuriyet, daily.
Dış Politika - Foreign Policy, magazine.
Forum, weekly.
Hürriyet, daily.
Milliyet, daily.
Tercüman, daily.
The Turkish Yearbook of International Relations, Ankara: Ankara University, magazine.
Yön, weekly.

Books and Articles

Adams, Thomas W., "The First Republic of Cyprus: A Review of an Unworkable Constitution", *Western Political Quarterly*, September 1966, No. 19, pp. 475-490.

Adams, Thomas W. and Cottrell, Alvin J., "American Foreign Policy and the UN Peace-Keeping Force in Cyprus", *ORBIS*, vol. 12, No. 2., Summer 1968, pp. 490-503.

Adams, Thomas W. and Cottrell, Alvin J., *Cyprus Between East and West*, Baltimore: The John Hopkins Press, 1968.

Ahmad, Feros, *The Turkish Experiment in Democracy 1950-1975*, London: The Royal Institute of International Affairs, C. Hurst and Company, 1977.

Ahmad, Ishtiaq, "Resolving the Cyprus Conflict Through EU Enlargement Process" in Ülger, İrfan Kaya and Efegil, Ertan (eds.), *Avrupa Birliği Kıskacında Kıbrıs Meselesi*, Ankara: HD Yayıncılık, 2001.

Alford, Jonathan (ed.), *Greece and Turkey: Adversity in Alliance*, Aldershot: Gower, International Institute for Strategic Studies, 1984.

Altan, Çetin, *Ben Milletvekili İken*, Ankara: Bilgi Yayınevi, 1971.

Altan, Çetin, *Sömürücülerle Savaş*, İstanbul: Dönem Yayınevi.

Arcayürek, Cüneyt, *Çankaya'ya Giden Yol 1971-1973*, Ankara: Bilgi Yayınevi, 1985.

Arcayürek, Cüneyt, *Yeni Demokrasi, Yeni Arayışlar*, Ankara: Bilgi Yayınevi, 1984.

Armaoğlu, Fahir H., "Recent Developments in Turkish Foreign Policy", *Foreign Policy (Dış Politika)*, March 1971, vol. 1, No. 1, pp. 85-94.

Armaoğlu, Fahir H., "Türk-Amerikan Münasebetleri", *Son Çağ Dergisi*, No. 24, June 1967.

Armaoğlu, Fahir H., "Turkey and the United States: A New Alliance", *The Turkish Yearbook of International Relations*, vol. 6, 1965, pp. 1-15.

Armaoğlu, Fahir, "1974 Cyprus Crisis and the Soviets", *Foreign Policy (Dış Politika)*, vol. 4, Nos. 2-3, 1974, pp. 177-183.

Aron, Raymond, "the Quest for a Philosophy of Foreign Affairs" in Hoffmann, Stanley (ed.), *Contemporary Theory in International Relations*, Englewood Cliffs, New Jersey: Prentice-Hall Inc., 1960.

Ataöv, Türkkaya, *Amerika, NATO ve Türkiye*, Ankara: Aydınlık Yayınevi, 1969.

Attalides, Michael A., *Cyprus: Nationalism and International Politics*, Edinburgh: Q Press Ltd., 1979.

Attalides, Michael A. (ed.), *Cyprus Reviewed: A Seminar on the Cyprus Problem*, Nicosia: Jus Cypri Association, 1977.

Ausland, John C. and Richardson, Colonel Hugh F., "Crisis Management: Berlin, Cyprus, Laos", *Foreign Affairs*, vol. 44, No. 2, January 1966, pp. 291-303.

Aydın, Mustafa, "Cacophony in the Aegean : Contemporary Turkish-Greek Relations", *The Turkish Yearbook of International Relations*, No. 27, 1997.

Ayres, Ron, "Turkish Foreign Relations", *Khamsin* (Journal of Revolutionary Socialists of the Middle East), Special Issue, *Modern Turkey: Development and Crisis*, London: Ithaca Press, No. 11, pp. 117-127.

Bağcı, Hüseyin, "Cyprus: Accession to the European Union- A Turkish View" in Axt, Heinz-Jürgen and Brey, Hansjörg (eds.) *Cyprus and the European Union: New Chances for Solving an Old Conflict?* Münih: Südosterapa-Gesellschaft, 1997.

Bahçeli, Tözün S., *Communal Discord and the Stake of Interested Governments in Cyprus 1955-1970*, Ph.D. Thesis, The University of London, the London School of Economics and Political Science, 1972.

Bahçeli, Tözün, "Cyprus in the Post-Cold War Environment: Moving Toward a Settlement" in Calotychos, Vangelis (ed.), *Cyprus and Its People: Nation, Identity and Experience in an Unimaginable Community 1955-1997*, Boulder: Westview Press, 1998.

Barnet, Richard J., *Intervention and Revolution: The United States in the Third World*, London: Paladin, 1972.

Barutçu, Ecmel, *Hariciye Koridoru*, Ankara: 21. Yüzyıl Yay., 1999.

Batu, Hamit, "New Developments in Turkish Foreign Policy", *Foreign Policy (Dış Politika)*, vol. 5, No. 4, 1976, pp. 5-17.

Bayülken, Ümit Haluk, "The Cyprus Question and the United Nations", *Foreign Policy (Dış Politika)*, vol. 4, Nos. 2-3, February 1975, pp. 71-142.

Bayülken, Ümit Haluk, "Turkey's Foreign Policy", *Foreign Policy (Dış Politika)*, vol. 3, No. 1, March 1973, pp. 67-82.

Bell, Coral, *the Diplomacy of Détente: the Kissinger Era*, London: Martin Robertson, 1977.

Bilge, Suat, "The Cyprus Conflict and Turkey" in Karpat, Kemal H.(ed.), *Turkey's Foreign Policy in Transition 1950-1974*, Leiden, Netherlands: E. J. Brill, 1975.

Bilge, Suat, *Büyük Düş: Türk-Yunan İlişkileri*, Ankara: 21. Yüzyıl Yay., October 2000.

Birand, Mehmet Ali, *Diyet: Türkiye ve Kıbrıs Üzerine Uluslararası Pazarlıklar,* İstanbul: Ağaoğlu Yayınevi, 1979.

Birand, Mehmet Ali, *30 Sıcak Gün,* 4th Edition, İstanbul: Milliyet Yayınları, 1976.

Birand, Mehmet Ali; Dündar, Can and Çaplı, Bülent, *12 Mart: İhtilalin Pençesinde Demokrasi*, Ankara: İmge Kitabevi, 1994.

Black, Joseph E. and Thompson, Kenneth W. (eds.), *Foreign Policies in a World of Change*, New York: Harper and Row, 1963.

Boll, Michael M., "Turkey's New National Security Concept: What It Means for NATO", *ORBIS*, vol. 23, Fall 1979, pp. 609-631.

Botsas, Eleftherios N., "The US-Cyprus-Turkey-Greece Tetragon: the Economics of an Alliance", *Journal of Political and Military Sociology*, vol. 16, No. 2, Fall 1988, pp. 247-262.

Boyd, James M., "Cyprus: Episode in Peacekeeping", *International Organization*, vol. 20, 1966, pp. 1-17.

Bölükbaşı, Suha, *Superpowers and the Third World: Turkish-American Relations and Cyprus*, New York: University Press of America, 1988.

Bölükbaşı, Süha, "The Turco-Greek Dispute: Issues, Policies and Prospects" in Dodd, Clement H. (ed.), *Turkish Foreign Policy: New Prospects*, Huntingdon: The Eothen Press, 1992.

Brandon, Henry, *the Retreat of American Power*, London: the Bodley Head, 1973.

Brands, H. W., Jr., "America Enters the Cyprus Tangle 1964", *Middle Eastern Studies*, vol. 23, No. 3, July 1987, pp. 348-362.

Bruce, Leigh H., "Cyprus: A Last Chance", *Foreign Policy*, No. 58, Spring 1985, pp. 115-133.

Burt, Richard, "Turkey and Administration" in Harris, George S.(ed.), *The Middle East in Turkish-American Relations*, Washington: the Heritage Foundation, 1985.

Camp, Glen D., "Cyprus Between the Powers 1980-1989", *Cyprus Review*, vol. 1, No. 2, Fall 1989, pp. 65-90.

Camp, Glen D., "Greek-Turkish Conflict Over Cyprus", *Political Science Quarterly*, vol. 95, No. 1, Spring 1980, pp. 43-70.

Camp, Glen D., "Island Impasse: Peacemaking on Cyprus 1980-1994" in Calotychos, Vangelis (ed.), *Cyprus and Its People: Nation, Identity and Experience in an Unimaginable Community 1955-1997*, Boulder: Westview Press, 1998.

Campany, Richard C., *Turkey and the United States: the Arms Embargo Period*, New York: Praeger, 1986.

Campbell, John C., "the Mediterranean Crisis", *Foreign Affairs*, July 1975, pp. 605-624.

Campbell, John C., "the United States and the Cyprus Question, 1974-1975" in Coufoudakis, Van (ed.), *Essays on the Cyprus Conflict*, New York: Pella Publishing Company, 1976.

Caporaso, James A., "Dependence, Dependency, and Power in the Global System: A Structural and Behavioral Analysis", *International Organization*, vol. 32, No. 1, Winter 1978, pp. 13-44.

Castleberry, H. Paul, "Summary of Proceedings of the Pacific Northwest Political Science Association, Conflict Resolution and the Cyprus Problem", *the Western Political Quarterly*, vol. 17, No. 3, September 1964, pp. 118-130.

Cem, İsmail, *Tarih Açısından 12 Mart*, İstanbul: Cem Yayınevi, 1980.

Clogg, Richard and Yannopoulos, George (eds.), *Greece Under Military Rule*, London: Secker and Warburg, 1972.

Coufoudakis, Van (ed.), *Essays on the Cyprus Conflict*, New York: Pella Publishing Company, 1976.

Coufoudakis, Van, "the Dynamics of Political Partition and Division in Multiethnic and Multireligious Societies: the Cyprus Case" in Coufoudakis, Van (ed.), *Essays on the Cyprus Conflict*, New York: Pella Publishing Company, 1976.

Coufoudakis, Van, "United States Foreign Policy and the Cyprus Question" in Attalides, Michael A. (ed.), *Cyprus Reviewed: A Seminar on the Cyprus Problem*, Nicosia: Jus Cypri Association, 1977.

Coufoudakis, Van, "Turkey and the United States: the Problems and Prospects of a Post-War Alliance", *Journal of Political and Military Sociology*, vol. 9, No. 2, Fall 1981, pp. 179-196.

Coufoudakis, Van, "United Nations Peacekeeping and Peacemaking and the Cyprus Question", *The Western Political Quarterly*, vol. 29, No. 3, September 1976, pp. 457-473.

Coufoudakis, Van, "US Foreign Policy and the Cyprus Question: An Interpretation", *Millennium*, vol. 5, No. 3, Winter 1976-77, pp. 245-268.

Coufoudakis, Van, "Domestic Politics and the Search for a Solution of the Cyprus Problem" in Salem, Norma (ed.), *Cyprus: A Regional Conflict and its Resolution,* New York: St. Martin's Press, 1992.

Couloumbis, Theodore A. *the United States, Greece and Turkey: the Troubled Triangle*, New York: Praeger, 1983.

Couloumbis, Theodore A. and Hicks, Sallie M. (eds.), *US Foreign Policy Toward Greece and Cyprus: the Clash of Principle and Pragmatism*, Washington D. C.: Center for Mediterranean and the American Hellenic Institute Studies, 1975.

Couloumbis, Theodore A. and Hicks, Sallie M., "The Impact of Greek Americans Upon United States Foreign Policy: Illusion or Reality?" in Attalides, Michael A. (ed.), *Cyprus Reviewed: A Seminar on the Cyprus Problem*, Nicosia: Jus Cypri Association, 1977.

Crabb, Cecil V. and Holt, Pat M., *Invitation to Struggle: Congress, the President and Foreign Policy*, Washington D. C.: Congressional Quarterly Inc., 1980.

Crawshaw, Nancy, "the Republic of Cyprus: From the Zurich Agreement to Independence", *The World Today*, vol. 16, No. 12, December 1960, pp. 526-540.

Crawshaw, Nancy, "Cyprus: Collapse of the Zurich Agreement", *The World Today*, vol. 20, January-December 1964, pp. 338-347.

Crawshaw, Nancy, "Cyprus After Kophinou", *The World Today*, October 1968.

Crawshaw, Nancy, *The Cyprus Revolt: An Account of the Struggle for Union With Greece*, London, Boston: G. Allen and Unwin, 1978.

Crawshaw, Nancy, "Subversion in Cyprus", *The World Today*, vol. 27, January-December 1971, pp. 25-32.

Crawshaw, Nancy, "Uncertainties in Cyprus", *The World Today*, vol. 28, August 1972, pp. 330-333.

CSIA European Security Group, "Instability and Change on NATO's Southern Flank", *International Security*, vol. 3, Winter 1978, pp. 150-177.

Çelik, Edip, *Türkiye'nin Dış Politika Tarihi*, İstanbul, 1969.

Çelik, Vedat A., "Speech by Vedat A. Çelik, Representative of Turkish Cypriot Community Before UN Special Committee on October 29, 1974", *Foreign Policy (Dış Politika)*, vol. 4, Nos. 2-3, February 1975.

Deliceırmak, Orbay (ed.), *Haklılık ve Kararlılık*, Lefkoşa, February 1993.

Demirer, Mehmet Arif, *Türkün Onur Sorunu: Kuzey Kıbrıs Türk Cumhuriyeti*, Ankara: Turhan Kitabevi, 1993.

Denktash, Rauf R., *The Cyprus Triangle*, London: K. Rüstem and Brother, 1988.

Denktash, Rauf R., "The Cyprus Problem, 23rd Year", *Turkish Review Quarterly Digest*, vol. 1, No. 4, Summer 1986, pp. 5-48.

Dışişleri Güncesi: January-December 2000, Ankara: TC Dışişleri Bakanlığı.

Divine, Robert A., *Since 1945 Politics and Diplomacy in Recent American History*, New York, London: John Wiley and Sons Inc., 1975.

Dobell, W. M., "Division Over Cyprus", *International Journal*, vol. 22, No. 2, Spring 1967, pp. 278-292.

Dodd, Clement H., *The Cyprus Issue: A Current Perspective*, Huntingdon: the Eothen Press, 1994.

Dodd, Clement H., *The Cyprus Imbroglio*, Huntingdon: The Eothen Press, 1998.

Dodd, Clement H., "Confederation, Federation and Sovereignty", *Perceptions*, vol. 4, No. 3, September-November 1999.

Domhoff, G. William, "Who Made American Foreign Policy 1945-1963?" in Fox, Douglas M. (ed.), *The Politics of US Foreign Policy Making*, Pacific Palisades, California: Goodyear Publishing Company Inc., 1971.

Dull, James, *The Politics of American Foreign Policy*, Englewood Cliffs, New Jersey: Prentice-Hall Inc., 1985.

Ecevit, Bülent, "Dış Politika", *Özgür İnsan*, September 1972.

Ecevit, Bülent, *Dış Politika*, Ankara: Yarın Yayınları, 1967.

Ecevit, Bülent, "Turkey's Security Policies" in Alford, Jonathan (ed.), *Greece and Turkey: Adversity in Alliance*, Aldershot: Gower, International Institute for Strategic Studies, 1984.

Efegil, Ertan and Görgünler, Özgen, "A Survey on the Public Opion's Concerns About the Proposals of the TRNC, South Cyprus, the UN and the EU" in Ülger, İrfan Kaya and Efegil, Ertan (eds.), *Avrupa Birliği Kıskacında Kıbrıs Meselesi*, Ankara: HD Yayıncılık, 2001.

Ehrlich, Thomas, *Cyprus: 1958-1967*, London: Oxford University Press, 1974.

Eichinger, Franz, "Cyprus and the EU from the German Point of View" in Axt, Heinz-Jürgen and Brey, Hansjörg (eds.) *Cyprus and the European Union: New Chances for Solving an Old Conflict?* Münih: Südosterapa-Gesellschaft, 1997.

Emiliou, Nicholas, "Knocking on the Door of the European Union: Cyprus' Strategy of Accession" in Axt, Heinz-Jürgen and Brey, Hansjörg (eds.) *Cyprus and the European Union: New Chances for Solving an Old Conflict?* Münih: Südosterapa-Gesellschaft, 1997.

Eren, Nuri, *Turkey, NATO, and Europe: a Deteriorating Relationship*, Paris: Atlantic Institute for International Affairs, 1977.

Erim, Nihat, "Reminiscences on Cyprus", *Foreign Policy (Dış Politika)*, vol. 4, Nos. 2-3, 1974, pp. 156-163.

Ertegün, Necati M., *The Cyprus Dispute and the Birth of the Turkish Republic of Northern Cyprus*, London: K. Rüstem and Brother, 1984.

Ertegün, Necati M., *Inter-Communal Talks and the Cyprus Problem*, Nicosia: Turkish Federated State of Cyprus, 1977.

Ertegün, Necati M., *The Status of the Two Peoples in Cyprus*, Lefkosha: The Public Information Office of the Turkish Republic of Northern Cyprus, 1990.

Evans, Peter, *Dependent Development: the Alliance of Multinational, State and Local Capital in Brazil*, Princeton: Princeton University Press, 1979.

Evran, Mustafa, "Türkiye-Avrupa Birliği İlişkileri Çerçevesinde Kıbrıs'ın Avrupa Birliği Üyeliğine Başvurusu" in Eminer, Çiler and İlkman, Gülden (ed.), *Avrupa Birliği ve Kıbrıs*, Lefkoşa: KKTC Dışişleri ve Savunma Bakanlığı.

Fatouros, A. A., "How to Resolve Problems by Refusing to Acknowledge They Exist: Some Legal Parameters of Recent US Policy Toward Greece and Cyprus" in Couloumbis, Theodore A. and Hicks, Sallie M. (eds.), *US Foreign Policy Toward Greece and Cyprus: the Clash of Principle and Pragmatism*, Washington D. C.: Center for Mediterranean and the American Hellenic Institute Studies, 1975.

Ferguson, Yale H. and Weiker, Walter F. (eds.), *Continuing Issues in International Politics*, Pacific Palisades, California: Goodyear Publishing Co., 1973.

Fisher, Ronald J., "Conclusion: Path Towards a Peaceful Cyprus" in Salem, Norma (ed.), *Cyprus: A Regional Conflict and its Resolution,* New York: St. Martin's Press, 1992.

Foley, Charles, *Island in Revolt*, London: Longmans, 1972.

Franck, Thomas M. and Weisband, Edward, *Foreign Policy by Congress*, New York, Oxford: Oxford University Press, 1979.

Fulbright, J. William, *The Arrogance of Power*, New York: Random House, 1966.

Galen, Justin, "Turkey As a Self-Inflicted Wound: the Narrowing Options for US Defence Policy", *Armed Forces Journal International*, June 1980, pp. 62-73.

Gazioğlu, Ahmet C. (ed.), *Cyprus, EU and Turkey: Selected Extracts from the World Press*, Nicosia: CYREP, 1998

Geyikdağı, Mehmet Yaşar, *Political Parties in Turkey: the Role of Islam*, New York: Praeger Publishers, 1984.

Goldbloom, M., "United States Policy in Post-War Greece" in Clogg, Richard and Yannopoulos, George (eds.), *Greece Under Military Rule*, London: Secker and Warburg, 1972.

Gönlübol, Mehmet, "NATO and Turkey: An Overall Appraisal", *The Turkish Yearbook of International Relations*, vol. 11, 1971, pp. 1-38.

Gönlübol, Mehmet, "NATO, USA and Turkey" in Karpat, Kemal H.(ed.), *Turkey's Foreign Policy in Transition 1950-1974*, Leiden, Netherlands: E. J. Brill, 1975.

Gönlübol, Mehmet, "Türk-Amerikan İlişkilerinde Genel Bir Değerlendirme", *Foreign Policy (Dış Politika)*, vol. 1, No. 4, December 1971, pp. 5-18.

Gönlübol, Mehmet et al., *Olaylarla Türk Dış Politikası 1919-1973*, Ankara: A.Ü., S.B.F. Yayınları, No. 407, 1977.

Gönlübol, Mehmet and Ulman, Haluk, "Türk Dış Politikasının Yirmi Yılı 1945-1965", *SBF Dergisi*, vol. 21, No. 1, March 1966.

Grantham, Dewey W., *The United States Since 1945: the Ordeal of Power*, New York, London: McGraw-Hill Inc., 1976.

Greek Cypriot Economic Blockade and Embargo Against the Turkish Cypriot Community, Lefkosha: Turkish Cypriot Human Rights Committee, June 1983.

Gruen, George E., "Ambivalence in the Alliance: US Interests in the Middle East and the Evolution of Turkish Foreign Policy", *ORBIS*, vol. 24, No. 2, Summer 1980, pp. 363-378.

Gürkan, İhsan, *NATO, Turkey and the Southern Flank: A Mideastern Perspective*, New York: National Strategy Information Center, 1980.

Haas, Richard N., "Managing NATO's Weakest Flank: the United States, Greece and Turkey", *ORBIS*, vol. 30, No. 3, Fall 1986, pp. 457-473.

Hackett, C., "Ethnic Politics in Congress: the Turkish Embargo Experience" in Said, Abdul A.(ed.), *Ethnicity in US Foreign Policy*, New York: Praeger, 1977.

Hale, William, "Turkey, NATO and the Middle East" in Lawless, Richard (ed.), *Foreign Policy Issues in the Middle East*, Occasional Papers, No. 28, Durham: University of Durham, 1985.

Hale, William M. and Norton, John D., "Turkey and the Cyprus Crisis", *The World Today*, vol. 30, September 1974, pp. 368-371.

Hammond, Paul Y., *Cold War and Détente: the American Foreign Policy Process Since 1945*, New York: Harcourt Brace Jovanovich Inc., 1975.

Handel, Michael, *Weak States in the International System*, London: Frank Cass, 1981.

Harris, George S., *Troubled Alliance: Turkish-American Problems in Historical Perspective 1945-1971*, Washington: American Enterprise Institute, 1972.

Harris, George S., "Cross-Alliance Politics: Turkey and the Soviet Union", *The Turkish Yearbook of International Relations*, vol. 12, 1972, p. 1-32.

Harris, George S.(ed.), *The Middle East in Turkish-American Relations*, Washington: the Heritage Foundation, 1985.

Harris, George S., "Turkey Between Alliance and Alienation", *Foreign Policy (Dış Politika)*, vol. 8, Nos. 3-4, 1980, pp. 117-125.

Harris, George S., *Turkey: Coping with Crisis*, Boulder: Westview, 1985.

Harris, George S., "Turkey and the United States" in Karpat, Kemal H.(ed.), *Turkey's Foreign Policy in Transition 1950-1974*, Leiden, Netherlands: E. J. Brill, 1975.

Hasgüler, Mehmet, *Kıbrıs'ta Enosis ve Taksim Politikalarının Sonu*, İstanbul: İletişim, 2000.

Heinze, Christian, *Cyprus Conflict 1964-1985*, London, Nicosia, İstanbul: K. Rüstem and Brother, 1986.

Henze, Paul B., "Out of Kilter: Greeks, Turks and US Policy", *National Interest*, vol. 8, Summer 1987, pp. 71-82.

Higgins, Rosalyn, "Basic Facts on the UN Force in Cyprus", *The World Today*, vol. 20, January-December 1964, pp. 347-350.

Hitchens, Christopher, *Cyprus,*, London: Quartet Books, 1984.

Holsti, Ole R.; Hopmann, P. Terrence and Sullivan, John D. (eds.), *Unity and Disintegration in International Alliances: Comparative Studies*, New York: John Wiley and Sons, 1973.

Howard, Harry N., "The Bicentennial in American-Turkish Relations", *Middle East Journal*, Summer 1976, pp. 291-310.

İnan, Kamran, "Cyprus, 1974 Crisis", *Foreign Policy (Dış Politika)*, vol. 4, Nos. 2-3, 1974, pp. 66-70.

İsmail, Sabahattin, *Self-Determinasyon ve Kıbrıs Türk Halkı*, İstanbul: Kastaş Yay., June 1990.

İsmail, Sabahattin, *Egemenlik, Konfederasyon ve Kıbrıs Türk Halkı*, November 1993.

İsmail, Sabahattin, *Kıbrıs Üzerine Bildiriler*, Lefkoşa: CYREP, 1998.

İsmail, Sabahattin, *150 Soruda Kıbrıs Sorunu*, İstanbul: Kaştaş Yay., August 1998.

Jacovides, A. J., "the Cyprus Problem and the United Nations" in Attalides, Michael A. (ed.), *Cyprus Reviewed: A Seminar on the Cyprus Problem*, Nicosia: Jus Cypri Association, 1977.

Joseph, Joseph S., *Cyprus: Ethnic Conflict and International Concern*, New York: Peter Lang, 1985.

Karaosmanoğlu, Ali L., "Cyprus: What Kind of a Federal Solution?", *Journal of South Asian and Middle Eastern Studies*, vol. 3, No. 3, Spring 1980, pp. 33-46.

Karpat, Kemal H.(ed.), *Turkey's Foreign Policy in Transition 1950-1974*, Leiden, Netherlands: E. J. Brill, 1975.

Karpat, Kemal H., "War on Cyprus: the Tragedy of Enosis" in Karpat, Kemal H.(ed.), *Turkey's Foreign Policy in Transition 1950-1974*, Leiden, Netherlands: E. J. Brill, 1975.

Keashly, Loraleigh and Fisher, Ronald J., "Toward a Contingency Approach to Third Party Intervention in Regional Conflict: a Cyprus Illustration", *International Journal*, vol. 45, No. 2, Spring 1990, pp. 424-453.

Keohane, Robert O., "the Study of Political Influence in the General Assembly", *International Organization*, vol. 21, 1967, pp. 221-237.

Kitromilides, P. M., "From Coexistence to Confrontation: the Dynamics of Ethnic Conflict in Cyprus" in Attalides, Michael A. (ed.), *Cyprus Reviewed: A Seminar on the Cyprus Problem*, Nicosia: Jus Cypri Association, 1977.

Koumoulides, John T. A.(ed.), *Cyprus in Transition 1960-1985*, London: Trigraph, 1986.

Krahenbuhl, Margaret, *Turkish-American Relations: An Affair to Remember*, Santa Monica, California: Rand Corporation, December 1974.

Kuniholm, Bruce R., "Turkey and NATO: Past, Present and Future", *ORBIS*, Summer 1983, pp. 421-445.

Kuniholm, Bruce R., "Turkey and the West", *Foreign Affairs*, vol. 70, No. 2, Spring 1991, pp. 34-48.

Kurat, Yuluğ Tekin, *Elli Yıllık Cumhuriyetin Dış Politikası 1923-1973*, Ankara: Türk Tarih Kurumu, 1975.

Laipson, Ellen B., "US-Turkey: Friendly Friction", *Journal of Defence and Diplomacy*, vol. 3, No. 9, September 1985, pp. 21-37.

Laipson, Ellen B., "Cyprus: A Quarter Century of US Diplomacy" in Koumoulides, John T. A. (ed.), *Cyprus in Transition 1960-1985*, London: Trigraph, 1986.

Laipson, Ellen, "The United States and Cyprus: Past Policies, Current Concerns" in Salem, Norma (ed.), *Cyprus: A Regional Conflict and its Resolution,* New York: St. Martin's Press, 1992.

Landau, David, *Kissinger: the Uses of Power*, London: Robson Books Ltd., 1974.

Landau, Jacob M., *Radical Politics in Modern Turkey*, Leiden, Netherlands: E. J. Brill, 1974.

Landau, Jacob M., *Johnson's 1964 Letter to İnönü and Greek Lobbying of the White House*, Jerusalem: The Hebrew University, 1979.

Landau, Jacob M., "Johnson's 1964 Letter to İnönü and the Greek Lobbying at the White House", *Turkish Yearbook of International Relations*, vol. 14, 1974, pp. 45-58.

Larrabee, F. Stephen, "Yunanistan ve Balkanlar: Politika Önerileri" in Allison, Graham T. and Nikolaydis, Kalipso (eds.), *Yunan Paradoksu*, (translated to Turkish by Bülent Tanatar), İstanbul: Doğan Kitap, October 1999.

Lawless, Richard (ed.), *Foreign Policy Issues in the Middle East*, Occasional Papers, No. 28, Durham: University of Durham, 1985.

Legg, K. R., "Congress as Trojan Horse, the Turkish Embargo Problem 1974-1978" in Spanier, John and Nogee, Joseph(eds.), *Congress, the Presidency and American Foreign Policy*, New York: Pergamon Press, 1981.

Leigh, M., "the Legal Status in International Law of the Turkish Cypriot and the Greek Cypriot Communities" in Ertegün, Necati Minür (ed.), *the Status of the Two Peoples in Cyprus*, Lefkoşa: The Public Information Office of the Turkish Republic of Northern Cyprus, 1990.

Lesser, Ian O., "Bridge or Barrier? Turkey and the West After the Cold War" in Fuller, Graham et al., *Turkey's New Geopolitics: From the Balkans to Western China*, Boulder, 1993.

Lewis, Geoffrey, *Modern Turkey*, New York: Praeger, 1974.

Liska, George, *Nations in Alliance*, Baltimore: John Hopkins University Press, 1968.

Liska, George, *Alliances and the Third World*, Baltimore: The Johns Hopkins Press, 1968.

Mackenzie, Kenneth, *Turkey in Transition: the West's Neglected Ally*, London: Institute for European Defence and Strategic Studies, 1984.

Mackenzie, Kenneth, *Turkey: After the Storm*, London: the Institute for the Study of Conflict, 1974.

Makovsky, Alan, "New Activism in Turkish Foreign Policy", *SAIS Review*, Winter-Spring 1999.

Mandell, Brian, "The Cyprus Conflict: Explaining Resistance to Resolution" in Salem, Norma (ed.), *Cyprus: A Regional Conflict and its Resolution,* New York: St. Martin's Press, 1992.

Mango, Andrew, *Turkey: A Delicately Poised Ally*, Beverley Hills, California: Sage, 1976.

Manisalı, Erol, "What Happens if Cyprus Joins the EU without Turkey" in Ülger, İrfan Kaya and Efegil, Ertan (eds.), *Avrupa Birliği Kıskacında Kıbrıs Meselesi*, Ankara: HD Yayıncılık, 2001.

Markides, Kryriacos C., *The Rise and Fall of the Cyprus Republic*, New Haven, Conn., London: Yale University Press, 1977.

McGhee, George, *The US- Turkish- NATO- Middle East Connection: How the Truman Doctrine and Turkey's NATO Entry Contained the Soviets*, London: Macmillan Press Ltd., 1990.

Miller, Linda B., *Cyprus: the Law and Politics of Civil Conflict*, Cambridge, Mass.: Harvard University Center for International Affairs, 1968.

Miroff, Bruce, *Pragmatic Illusions: the Presidential Politics of John F. Kennedy*, New York: David McKay Company Inc., 1976.

Moon, Bruce E., "Consensus or Compliance? Foreign Policy Change and External Dependence", *International Organization*, vol. 39, No. 2, Spring 1985, pp. 297-329.

Moritz, Charles (ed.), *Current Biography 1975*, New York: H. W. Wilson, 1976.

Morris, Roger, *Uncertain Greatness: Henry Kissinger and American Foreign Policy*, London: Quartet Books, 1977.

Moustakis, Fotios and Sheehan, Micheal, "Greek Security Policy After the Cold-War", *Contemporary Security Politics*, vol. 21, No. 3, December 2000.

Mütercimler, Erol, *Kıbrıs Barış Harekatının Bilinmeyen Yönleri,* İstanbul: Yaprak Yayınevi, 1990.

Nelson, H. D. and Kaplan, I., "National Security" in Nyrop, Richard F., *Turkey, A Country Study*, Washington: The American University, 1980.

Nye, Roger Paul, *The Military in Turkish Politics 1960-1973*, Ph.D. Thesis, Graduate School of Arts and Sciences, Washington University, 1974.

Nyrop, Richard F., *Handbook for the Republic of Turkey*, Washington: the American University, 1973.

Nyrop, Richard F., *Turkey, A Country Study*, Washington: The American University, 1980.

Oberling, Pierre, *The Road to Bellapais: the Turkish Cypriot Exodus to Northern Cyprus*, New York: Columbia University Press, 1982.

Oğuzoğlu, H. Tarık, "Prennial Conflict or Everlasting Peace: the European Union's Involvement in Cyprus", *Perceptions,* July-August 2002, vol. 7, no. 2, http://www.mfa.gov.tr/grupa/percept/VII-2/tarik.oguzoglu.htm.

Olson, William C.; McLellon, David S. and Sondermann, Fred A., *The Theory and Practice of International Relations*, Englewood Cliffs, New Jersey: Prentice-Hall Inc., 1983.

Orkunt, Sezai, *Türkiye-ABD Askeri İlişkileri*, İstanbul: Milliyet Yayınları, 1978.

Özbudun, Ergun, *The Role of the Military in Recent Turkish Politics*, Occasional Papers, No. 14, Center for International Affairs, Harvard University, November 1966.

Özdemir, Hikmet *1960'lar Türkiye'sinde Sol Kemalizm: Yön Hareketi*, İstanbul: İz Yayıncılık, 1993.

Polat, Yılmaz, *Washington Entrikaları*, İstanbul: Milliyet, 1999

Polyviou, Polyvious G., *Cyprus: Conflict and Negotiation 1960-1980*, London: Duckworth, 1980.

Polyviou, Polyvious G., *Cyprus: The Tragedy and the Challenge*, Washington: American Hellenic Institute, 1975.

Psomiades, H. J., "the United States and the Mediterranean Triangle: Greece, Turkey and Cyprus: A New Phase" in Attalides, Michael A. (ed.), *Cyprus Reviewed: A Seminar on the Cyprus Problem*, Nicosia: Jus Cypri Association, 1977.

Purvis, Hoyt, "Tracing the Congressional Role: US Foreign Policy and Turkey" in Purvis, Hoyt and Baker, Steven J.(eds.), *Legislating Foreign Policy*, London: Westview Press, 1984.

Ramady, M. A., "The Role of Turkey in Greek-Turkish Cypriot Communal Relations" in Coufoudakis, Van (ed.), *Essays on the Cyprus Conflict*, New York: Pella Publishing Company, 1976.

Reddaway, John, *Burdened with Cyprus: the British Connection*, London, Nicosia, İstanbul: K. Rüstem and Brother and Weidenfield and Nicolson Ltd., 1986.

"Republic of Turkey: Special Report", *Journal of Defense and Diplomacy*, vol. 3, No. 9, September 1985, pp. 28-37.

Robinson, Richard D., *the First Turkish Republic: A Case Study in National Development*, Cambridge, Mass.: Harvard University Press, 1963.

Rodan, Steve, "Russia Asks Israel to Keep Out of S-300 Deal", *Defense News*, 23 February- 1 March 1998.

Roper, John, "The West and Turkey: Varying Roles, Common Interests", *The International Spectator*, vol. 34, No. 1, January-March 1999, pp. 89-102.

Rothstein, Robert L., *Alliances and Small Powers*, New York: Columbia University Press, 1968.

Rothstein, R. L., "On the Problems of Being Small and Poor" in Olson, William C.; McLellon, David S. and Sondermann, Fred A., *The Theory and Practice of International Relations*, Englewood Cliffs, New Jersey: Prentice-Hall Inc., 1983.

Rubin, Barry, "Middle East Policy in the Turkish Context" in Harris, George S. (ed.), *The Middle East in Turkish-American Relations*, Washington: the Heritage Foundation, 1985.

Rustow, Dankwart A., *Turkey: America's Forgotten Ally*, New York: Council on Foreign Relations, 1987.

Said, Abdul A.(ed.), *Ethnicity in US Foreign Policy*, New York: Praeger, 1977.

Salih, Halil İbrahim, *Cyprus: The Impact of Diverse Nationalism on a State*, Alabama: University of Alabama Press, 1978.

Sander, Oral, "Turkey: the Staunchest Ally of the United States? Forces of Continuity and Change in the Strategic Relationship", *The Turkish Yearbook of International Relations*, vol. 15, 1977, pp. 10-24.

Sarıca, Murat; Teziç, Erdoğan and Eskiyurt, Özer, *Kıbrıs Sorunu*, İstanbul: İstanbul Üniversitesi Yayınları, No. 2071, 1975.

Schlesinger, Arthur M., Jr., *The Cycles of American History*, Boston: Houghton Mifflin Company, 1986.

Schlesinger, Arthur M., Jr., *The Imperial Presidency*, London: Andre Deutsch, 1973.

Sezer, Duygu, *Kamuoyu ve Dış Politika*, Ankara: SBF Yayını, No. 339, 1972.

Sezer, Duygu, "Turkey's Security Policies" in Alford, Jonathan (ed.), *Greece and Turkey: Adversity in Alliance*, Aldershot: Gower, International Institute for Strategic Studies, 1984.

Shaw, Stanford J. and Shaw, Ezel Kural, *History of the Ottoman Empire and Modern Turkey, Reform, Revolution and Republic: the Rise of Modern Turkey, 1808-1975*, vol. 2, Cambridge: Cambridge University Press, 1977.

Shoemaker, Christopher C. and Spanier, John, *Patron-Client State Relationships: Multilateral Crises in the Nuclear Age*, New York: Praeger, 1984.

SİSAV Dış İlişkiler ve Savunma Araştırma Grubu, *Kıbrıs Sorunu: Gelişmeler ve Görüşmeler*, İstanbul: SİSAV, September 1990.

SİSAV Dış Politika ve Savunma Grubu, *1997 Yılı Sonu İtibariyle Kıbrıs Sorunu*, İstanbul: SİSAV, March 1998.

Sowerwine, James Edward, *Dynamics of Decision Making in Turkish Foreign Policy 1961-1980*, Ph.D. Thesis, University of Wisconsin, Madison, 1987.

Soysal, Mümtaz, *Aklını Kıbrıs'la Bozmak*, Ankara: Bilgi Yay., August 1995.

Spanier, John and Nogee, Joseph (eds.), *Congress, the Presidency and American Foreign Policy*, New York: Pergamon Press, 1981.

Stavrinides, Zenon, *The Cyprus Conflict: National Identity and Statehood*, Loris Stavrinides Press, 1976.

Stavrou, Nikolas A., "Kissinger's Tilt on Cyprus, the New Style of Crisis Diplomacy" in Couloumbis, Theodore A. and Hicks, Sallie M. (eds.), *US Foreign Policy Toward Greece and Cyprus: the Clash of Principle and Pragmatism*, Washington D. C.: Center for Mediterranean and the American Hellenic Institute Studies, 1975.

Stearns, Monteagle, *Entangled Allies: US Policy Toward Greece, Turkey and Cyprus*, New York: Council on Foreign Relations Press, 1992.

Stearns, Monteagle, "Yunan Güvenlik Meseleleri" in Allison, Graham T. and Nikolaydis, Kalipso (eds.), *Yunan Paradoksu*, (translated to Turkish by Bülent Tanatar), İstanbul: Doğan Kitap, October 1999.

Stephens, Robert, *Cyprus: a Place of Arms*, London: Pall Mall Press, 1966.

Stern, Laurance, "Bitter Lessons: How We Failed in Cyprus", *Foreign Policy*, vol. 19, Summer 1975, pp. 34-78.

Stern, Laurance, *The Wrong Horse: the Politics of Intervention and the Failure of American Diplomacy*, New York: Times Books, 1977.

Stoessinger, John G., *Crusaders and Pragmatists: Movers of Modern American Foreign Policy*, New York, London: W. W. Norton and Company, 1979.

Strong, Robert J., *Bureaucracy and Statesmanship: Henry Kissinger and the Making of American Foreign Policy*, New York, London: University Press of America, 1986.

Şahin, Haluk, *Gece Gelen Mektup: Türk-Amerikan İlişkilerinde Bir Dönüm Noktası*, İstanbul: Cep Kitapları, 1987.

Tamkoç, Metin, *The Turkish Cypriot State: The Embodiment of the Right of Self-Determination*, London: K. Rüstem and Brother, 1988.

Tamkoç, Metin, *The Warrior Diplomats: Guardians of National Security and Modernization of Turkey*, Salt Lake City: University of Utah Press, 1976.

Taşhan, Seyfi, "Turkey's Relations with the USA. and Possible Future Developments", *Foreign Policy (Dış Politika)*, vol. 8, Nos. 1-2, 1979, pp. 11-32.

Taşhan, Seyfi, "Turkish-US Relations and Cyprus", *Foreign Policy (Dış Politika)*, vol. 4, Nos. 2-3, 1974, pp. 164-176.

Theophanous, Andreas, "Cyprus, the European Union and the Search for a New Constitution", *Journal of Southern Europe and the Balkans*, vol. 2, No. 2, 2000

Toker, Metin, *İsmet Paşayla 10 Yıl 1954-1964*, vol. 1, 2, 3, and 4, Ankara, 1965, 1966, 1967, İstanbul, 1969.

Toker, Metin, "İsmet Paşa ile 4 Buhranlı Yıl", *Milliyet*, 4-11 February 1969.

Tuncer, Hüner "The Cyprus Issue: Recent Developments", *Perceptions,* September-November 2002, vol. 7, no. 3, http://www.mfa.gov.tr/grupa/percept/VII-3/HunerTuncer.htm.

Ulman, A. Haluk, "Geneva Conferences, July-August 1974", *Foreign Policy (Dış Politika),* vol. 4, Nos. 2-3, 1974, pp. 46-65.

Ulman, A. Haluk, "NATO ve Türkiye", *SBF Dergisi,* vol. 22, December 1967.

Ulman, A. Haluk and Dekmeijian, R. H., "Changing Partners in Turkey's Foreign Policy, 1959-1967", *ORBIS,* vol. 11, Fall 1967, pp. 772-785.

Uslu, Nasuh, "Körfez Savaşı ve Amerika'nın Politikaları", *Ankara Üniversitesi SBF Dergisi,* vol. 54, No. 3, July-September 1999, pp. 165-199.

Uslu, Nasuh, *Türk-Amerikan İlişkilerinde Kıbrıs,* Ankara: 21. Yüzyıl Yayınları, 2000.

Uslu, Nasuh, "Kıbrıs Sorunu" in Bal, İdris (ed.), *21. Yüzyılın Eşiğinde Türk Dış Politikası,* İstanbul: Alfa, 2001, 262-301.

Uslu, Nasuh, "Kıbrıs Sorunu ve ABD" in Ülger, İrfan K. and Efegil, Ertan, (ed.) *Avrupa Birliği Kıskacında Kıbrıs Meselesi,* Ankara: HD Yayıncılık, 2001, 147-184.

"US Foreign Policy Toward Greece: Panel Discussions" in Couloumbis, Theodore A. and Hicks, Sallie M. (eds.), *US Foreign Policy Toward Greece and Cyprus: the Clash of Principle and Pragmatism,* Washington D. C.: Center for Mediterranean and the American Hellenic Institute Studies, 1975.

Vali, Ferenc A., *Bridge Across the Bosporus: the Foreign Policy of Turkey,* London, Baltimore: John Hopkins Press, 1971.

Vanezis, P. N., *Cyprus: the Unfinished Agony,* London: Abelard-Schuman, 1977.

Vanezis, P. N., *Makarios: Pragmatism v. Idealism,* London: Abelard-Schuman, 1974.

Watanabe, Paul Y., *Ethnic Groups, Congress and American Foreign Policy: the Politics of the Turkish Arms Embargo,* London: Greenwood Press, 1984.

Weintall, Edward and Bartlett, Charles, *Facing the Brink: A Study of Crisis Diplomacy,* London: Hutchinson and Co. Ltd., 1967.

Wildawsky, Agron, "The Two Presidencies" in Fox, Douglas M. (ed.), *The Politics of US Foreign Policy Making,* Pacific Palisades, California: Goodyear Publishing Company Inc., 1971.

Winsdor, Philip, *NATO and the Cyprus Crisis,* Adelphi Papers No. 14, London: the Institute for Strategic Studies, November 1964.

Wolfe, James H. "United States and the Cyprus Conflict" in Skjelsbaek, Kjell (ed.), *The Cyprus Conflict and the Role of the United Nations,* Norwegian Institute of International Affairs, November 1988.

Xydis, Stephen G., *Cyprus: Reluctant Republic,* The Hague: Mouton and Co., 1973.

Xydis, Stephen G., "Cyprus: What Kind of Problem" in Attalides, Michael A. (ed.), *Cyprus Reviewed: A Seminar on the Cyprus Problem,* Nicosia: Jus Cypri Association, 1977.

Zervakis, Peter, "The Accession of Cyprus to the EU: The Greek Viewpoint" in Axt, Heinz-Jürgen and Brey, Hansjörg (eds.) *Cyprus and the European Union: New Chances for Solving an Old Conflict?* Münih: Südosterapa-Gesellschaft, 1997.

INDEX